Baroque Personae

D1570053

BAROQUE
PERSONAE

EDITED BY
ROSARIO VILLARI

TRANSLATED BY
LYDIA G. COCHRANE

THE UNIVERSITY OF CHICAGO PRESS
CHICAGO & LONDON

ROSARIO VILLARI teaches at La Sapienza University in Rome and is affiliated with the Institute for Advanced Study, the Newberry Library, and the University of Oxford.

Originally published in Italian as *L'uomo barocco* by Editori Laterza in 1991, © 1991, Gius, Laterza & Figli. The chapters by Henry Kamen, Geoffrey Parker, Brian P. Levack, and James S. Amelang are published from the authors' original English-language versions, revised. The chapter by Daniel Dessert has been translated from the author's original French-language version, revised.

The University of Chicago Press, Chicago 60637
The University of Chicago Press, Ltd., London
©1995 by the University of Chicago
All rights reserved. Published 1995
Printed in the United States of America
04 03 02 01 00 99 98 97 96 95   1 2 3 4 5

ISBN: 0-226-85636-4 (cloth)
0-226-85637-2 (paper)

Library of Congress Cataloging-in-Publication Data

Uomo barocco. English
    Baroque personae / edited by Rosario Villari ; translated by Lydia
G. Cochrane.
        p. cm.
    "Originally published in Italian as L'uomo barocco by Editori Laterza,
1991"—CIP info.
    Includes bibliographical references and index.
    1. Civilization, Baroque.   I. Villari, Rosario.   II. Title.
CB401.U6613   1995
940.2'52—dc20   94-47217
                                                                      CIP

CONTENTS

INTRODUCTION

Rosario Villari

"Baroque personae" is an unwonted expression, if not downright startling and novel. In other, not too distant times, the use of the term "Baroque" would have been grudgingly admitted in connection with works of art or literary tendencies, but not as a way to qualify the more general cultural, religious, or political experiences and conditions during the period in European history from roughly the late sixteenth century to the late seventeenth century, the period considered in the present volume. In the first issue of Roberto Longhi's review *Paragone* (January 1950), Giuliano Briganti even rejected use of the term in the history of art on the grounds that it was an abstract and generic definition of style applied to different and historically unspecified phases of development and circumstances. "Baroque," Briganti wrote, is a "strange word, so pleasurable to pronounce, so mysteriously allusive, so apparently defining. . . . When we read the term 'Baroque' in a work on the history of art we do not know precisely what [the author] is alluding to, and confusion generates ambiguities." True, Benedetto Croce had already spoken of the "Baroque age." He restored the term to its traditional pejorative meaning, however, and he broadened its use beyond stylistic definition to apply it to the underlying characteristics of a culture that was an expression of decline and moral crisis in a particular place and time.

This is hardly the occasion to repeat the history of a term whose more recent development spans nearly a century, interesting and significant as the question is, not only from the viewpoint of the histories of art and literature. Nor can we trace the reasons that have led various historians to use the term in its more general sense—José Antonio Maravall's introduction to his *Culture of the Baroque* (*La cultura del barocco*) seems to me a telling example—or review the problems and misinterpretations deriving from its use. It seems to me sufficient, for the purposes of this volume, to note that since the 1960s, the term "Baroque," in spite of its originally negative cast and its ambiguity, has become widely used and accepted, has in part been detached from its original meaning—so closely

1

connected to the fields of art and literature—and has been extended to apply to sectors outside the Mediterranean area and the world of the Counter-Reformation.

Today no one raises an eyebrow if a work on "The Baroque State" contains studies referring specifically to the France of Louis XIII and touching, by analogy, on problems that all Western European countries to some extent shared (though with important differences) in a particular phase of the ancien régime. In the case of this particular work, *L'Etat baroque,* its editor, Henry Méchoulan, subscribed to the definition of the term "Baroque" given in the *Dictionnaire de l'Académie française* (1740): "irregular, bizarre, uneven." Méchoulan asks:

> What other concept could describe the political strangeness of France in the early seventeenth century, which saw the rise of a new form of power that no dictionary could yet account for? The magician-king reigned with a cardinal [Richelieu] guided by the reason of a state that he was forging in the midst of contradictions, convulsions, and revolts. . . . From those multiple antagonisms there would arise the State that astonished and dazzled by its imposing and dominating grandeur, like a work by Bernini.

Strangeness and novelty, contradiction, revolt, astonishment, bizarreness, grandeur: these are the notions that lie somewhere between an approximate concept of style and an attempt at a general description of a historical epoch, the state, politics, and all the collective and individual reality of a particular period in European history.

Albeit with the necessary precautions and with no pretense to discover in the overall world of the seventeenth century any compact spiritual and intellectual unity, historians today tend to attribute unique characteristics and a particular way of thinking, feeling, and acting to the period in question. Perhaps it is precisely for its ambiguity and for the multiple meanings it has acquired along the way that the label "Baroque" now seems particularly appropriate for that period.

Scholars have agreed in viewing the seventeenth century as "a tangled knot of differing tendencies" (Alberto Tenenti), a century of crisis (Roland Mousnier), an era of widespread disorder (Pierre Chaunu) in which society was dominated by a sense of threat and instability that gave rise, in reaction, to a conservative and repressive culture (José Antonio Maravall). Like many others, Américo Castro drew a drastic conclusion from this vision: "It does not seem to me," he once wrote in a discussion of the question with Maravall, "that Baroque is an agent or a promotor of history." This view of the Baroque as a phenomenon that emerged and spread tumultuously for nearly a century stands opposed to an emphasis on the tendencies, which eventually triumphed, toward absolutism on the political plane and classicism on the plane of thought, art, and the spiritual life.

Europeans of the seventeenth century themselves had a particularly dramatic idea of the period in which they were living. The impression they transmitted to posterity was that theirs was an iron century, a *mundus furiosus,* an age of tumults and agitations, oppression and intrigues in which "men, become wolves, devour one another." It was an age of disorder, of subversion, of overturning the social hierarchy and dreaming impossible dreams. It was an epoch of great tensions that often were viewed in a purely negative light rather than as necessary stages for reaching a higher social and political equilibrium and deeper and broader creative capacities.

The "Baroque" penchant for conflict impressed historians for its intensity, its wide diffusion, and the influence that it had on ways of thinking and acting. The clash of political and religious ideals, continuous and widespread warfare, growing social unrest, revolution, punctilious questions of precedence that permeated the everyday ritual of both administrations and the church, frequent duels—all of these have been seen as characteristic of the period. The idea of a bellicose age is widely accepted, even though no rigorous and systematic comparison with other turbulent and disturbed periods in European history has ever been made. Some years ago John Elliott suggested that even for the period of the Wars of Religion in the sixteenth century one might speak of a generalized revolutionary crisis; his interpretation met with some doubts, but they did not defeat the idea, now widely accepted, that the first half of the seventeenth century was singular in this respect.

There is another level, however, on which we need to consider the question of the Baroque penchant for conflict. What was unique in Baroque conflictuality lay less in tension between one historical subject and another than in the presence of apparently incompatible or obviously contradictory attitudes existing within one and the same historical subject. There are innumerable examples in the culture and the everyday reality of the Baroque world of the coexistence of traditionalism and a search for novelty, conservatism and rebellion, love of truth and the cult of dissimulation, wisdom and folly, sensuality and mysticism, superstition and rationality, austerity and "consumerism," and the affirmation of natural law and praise of absolute power.

For a long time, scholars—faced with the task of penetrating the mystery of this internal and structural contradiction and influenced by the powerfully negative image that has been passed on of the Baroque age, its tensions, and its ills—have unquestioningly accepted the idea that Baroque society was unable to work collectively to further the progress of civilization. Contradictions and conflictuality were long considered the sign of a blockage and a stasis of propulsive forces. One typical idea that was widely accepted, for example, was that of a state progressing by the will of the sovereign alone in face of a society protesting and struggling against constraints and unable either to adapt to the centralizing dynamism of the monarchy or to shake off the yoke of oppression. In this view, outstanding figures such as Giordano Bruno, Galileo Galilei, Jean Bodin, Francis Bacon, René Descartes, William Harvey, Paolo Sarpi, and Baruch Spinoza were seen more as anticipations of later developments than as authentic expressions of their own times.

As well as offering a particularly dramatic and conflictual vision of social reality, the seventeenth century was particularly active in creating rigid models of social types, formulas, fixed criteria of interpretation, and "exemplary" judgments on events and persons and in imposing them on the culture of the time and on people's minds. This grandiose undertaking, which was realized through a genuine "boom" in chronicles and other works on contemporary events, through widespread popular religious preaching, and through a nascent apparatus for mass political propaganda in journalism, pamphlets, broadsides, and manifestos, was linked, on the one hand, to the need to give political, moral, and ideal legitimacy to the exercise of a power that was becoming ramified in society and tending (within certain limits) to overpower particularisms and traditional structures; on the other hand, it was born of a need to justify resistance and opposition. This undertaking undeniably exerted a great influence on contemporaries, but at the same time it strongly conditioned the culture and the historiography of later ages by passing along images and stereotypes that often only partially corresponded to reality.

Admittedly, we cannot easily deny the validity of an overall vision of a world torn by social and political conflicts and tormented by war and its aftermath. Nor can one ignore the fact that during some phases of the seventeenth century revolutions and wars took on dimensions unknown in the immediately preceding centuries. But that does not mean that endemic protest and conflict on the elementary level, not to mention disorder, rebellion, and anarchy, mastered and kept under control by state action only with greatest difficulty, were primary and universal characteristics unique to the seventeenth century.

Baroque society was a body, a social organism whose every element had its own special place and function and that was itself internally structured and organized according to recognized and accepted hierarchies. The swath of disorder and confusion undeniably broadened during the Baroque age: we need only think of the expansion of urban areas, which often outstripped the cities' ability to incorporate the waves of newcomers within traditional organizational structures. The excess population grew; the "marginalized" proved worrisome and prompted reactions and legislation of various kinds (not always restrictive or repressive). All in all, however, such phenomena seem to have remained under control; in no absolute sense could they be said to have dominated the general climate or overturned the principle of far-flung organization that governed urban and, to some extent, rural society in the Baroque age.

As a general rule, the formation of the new monarchical power did not conflict with that widespread particularistic and particular structuring of society; rather than trampling local structures in its advance, monarchical power typically made use of them for purposes of taxation, military organization, and public order. The strength of the Baroque state was based on an alliance among the central power, the community, corporative institutions, autonomous local powers, and so forth. The state repressed particular powers when they proved a hindrance or antithetical to the "service of the king" but above all it sought to make use of them, insert them into the overall design, and coordinate them with the action of the monarchy. Hence in certain aspects it consolidated them.

Military billeting was a frequent reason for dissent and for friction between the central power and the local communities that had to provide lodgings for the troops. But in an age before barracks and modern army organization, how could the sovereign have administered his army without some degree of agreement and consent on the part of the local communities? It is undoubtedly true that at times billeting was imposed violently and abusive practices existed, hence there were protests and rebellions. Aside from certain literary works (Calderón de la Barca's *El alcalde de Zalamea* is the most obvious example), there are innumerable historical documents and clamorous events that bear witness to this, but there was also collaboration between the central power and the local community regarding laws, statutes, and customary norms, and the sovereign intervened when the laws were not respected.

Something similar might be said regarding the fiscal system. Anti-tax sentiment was endemic in the seventeenth century, and anti-tax revolts sprang up throughout Europe. On this point there seems to have been a profound and irremediable break between the various populations and the rulers, even when those who opposed the monarch's policies and rose in protest had no political motivations: even in the worst moments of anti-fiscal violence the cry "Long live the king!" rang out. Was this a simple and ingenuous attempt at an alibi? A cover-up or a primitive sort of dissimulation? It undoubtedly was in many cases, and there were times when, on higher social levels, such protests became more sophisticated and took on a wealth of political and cultural overtones. But it is also true that precisely in the Baroque age an attachment to the sovereign—to the idea or the myth of the king—was widespread and strong on the lower levels of society. Even in a land as mistreated and squeezed dry as the Kingdom of Naples it took a lot to make village folk, who yearned to come under the royal demesne rather than remain in the fief of a baron, break with that attitude and allow their ancient affection for the king to turn into hatred. Emmanuel Le Roy Ladurie has rightly spoken, in this regard, of "a love-hate relationship . . . between the monarchical state and the community." Obviously, this was not a one-way relationship in which the sovereign took and gave nothing in return. At base there was a balance, albeit one that was often hard to maintain, particularly in times of war.

Thus there was a difference—at times a striking one and one perhaps greater and more acute than in other phases of European history—between historical reality and the images that the century gave of itself, imposed on contemporaries, and transmitted to later ages. The inner logic of specific instances of this difference would be an interesting topic for investigation. This would involve looking at the mechanisms employed at the time for seeking consensus and social cohesion, but also at those used to neutralize persons and groups who threatened to disturb that consensus; it would involve the ways people thought and the relationship between ideologies and the interests of the various groups in society. Historians have been working for some time now to throw light on this question and on the question of the conflictuality and contradiction (in the sense outlined above) that have been recognized as special traits of the Baroque. The studies collected in the present volume are both testimony to the rethinking that is in process and an attempt to correct a number of elements in the traditional typology of Baroque figures in general and certain socio-professional figures in particular.

It is true that the present volume stresses institutions, ideologies, thought patterns, and social structures over literature and art. To put it differently, the "types" that are delineated here offer a picture of those elements rather than presenting the sensibility, particular or general, of people of the Baroque age. Even within these constraints, however, the picture is far from complete. Our aim was not to reconstitute the whole historical panorama of the century but to describe certain of its aspects and unique types. Furthermore, we need to keep in mind that even though the seventeenth century was a markedly creative age teeming with novelties, not all of which were negative, it inherited many things from the preceding century and from the late Middle Ages. Certain figures repeat earlier models with variations that, significant and important as they are, do not justify autonomous treatment. I am thinking here of the condition of women, of the figures of the peasant and the craftsman as economic operators, and of the mentality of the great lords. This volume can profitably be read, both as a way to fill in eventual gaps and to grasp better what is new in the seventeenth century, in conjunction with the volumes on the Middle Ages and the Renaissance originally published in Italy by Laterza and published in America in English translation by the University of Chicago Press. Our goal in this volume was to integrate a vision of the state, the church, science, and culture with a vision of society as a whole and of the tendencies and currents that ran through it. A second goal was to consider the Baroque period as a phase of history in which problems, situations, and even human types were changing, rather than as a collection of static characteristics. Scenarios changed surprisingly much from the founding phase of the Baroque period to the second half of the seventeenth century, and the age as a whole might well be seen as one of accelerating transformation. Even with great and obvious differences of content and intensity, the seventeenth century was to some extent similar to our own in that respect.

What lends homogeneity to this volume is that all the essays presented here reflect profound changes in historical judgment of the seventeenth century. The reader will find here an image of the statesman that seems almost the exact opposite of the conventional and widespread image. A profound vocation for the general interest and an attention, at times to the point of obsession, to the good of the state and of the monarchy were dominant in the thought and action of the more typical statesmen of the Baroque age, Mazarin for one. Even the client-patron system that flourished with particular intensity in the seventeenth century appears here in a new light—that is, as a system that, in one of its phases, served to focus dispersed and disorganized forces on the task of constructing and reinforcing the state.

War was tightly tied to the Baroque. We see this in the age's sense of devastation and disaster, in an increase in the soldiers' destructiveness and blind violence, and in the impact of all the ills of war on society, the peasantry, women, and the defenseless inhabitants of the cities. Geoffrey Parker's essay reminds us of all that, but he also shows continuity and the development of a military revolution that began during the Renaissance—a process, that is, that consisted not only in the armies' heightened offensive and defensive capabilities and in higher levels of destruction but that also led to a rationalization of the relationship between armies and civil society. The military apparatus remained an onerous and even a growing burden, but toward the end of the Baroque age its relationship to civil society became less savage and less left up to chance from the point of view of provisioning, the billeting of troops, the remuneration of soldiers, the connection between the army and the nation, and more.

A change is even clearer and more explicit in the case of the financier. Daniel Dessert shows that the "model" constructed and universally imposed within the culture and the mentality of the seventeenth century (and in notable measure accepted by historians of later centuries) corresponds only partially to historical reality. Dessert refers almost exclusively to France, but the problems he discusses, including the distorted representation of the figure and the activities of the financier, were shared by the rest of Europe.

The figure of the bourgeois traced by James Amelang differs notably from the portrait put forth by a long tradition that culminated in Fernand Braudel. Amelang sees the bourgeois of the Baroque age, not as a "traitor" to a historical task, but as a champion of rationality and prudence and the standard-bearer of a capacity for enjoying life that contrasts with the forced austerity of preindustrial society. What he has to say regarding this discrepancy is applicable to many other aspects of the Baroque age involving the organization of power, the relationship between government and subjects, the expression of religious values, the church, the conception of social values, political culture, the connection between artistic production and the commission system, and the relationship between the development of science and public institutions.

These are only a few of the ways in which this volume presents new angles of vision and trends in interpretation. Now that I have given what seems to me a key to reading this volume, the time has come to entrust it to the reader and to his or her curiosity and judgment.

I

THE STATESMAN

Henry Kamen

"IF THESE THE TIMES, then this must be the man," wrote the poet Andrew Marvell in celebrating the first anniversary of the protectorate of Oliver Cromwell in England, and it has become customary to present the great men of state as either called forth by the age or, even more decisively, reshaping the age, as though they had a role beyond that of common men. Such a view distorts the past, for it turns a blind eye to the ways in which political power was really exercised, and it exaggerates the options available to men in politics. A statesman was, after all, produced by his own social system and could only operate within the confines of that system. This was particularly true when, as in the seventeenth century, traditional mechanisms of power—provincial loyalties, status groups—worked hard to assert themselves against the growing authority of the central monarchy.

Though the notion of government as an art was a product of the Renaissance and highly influential in that period, that notion continued to be the dominant idea about the state until the mid-seventeenth century. Statecraft was deemed to be a science to which princes should be educated and ministers trained. Manuals, of which one of the earliest and most notorious was Machiavelli's *The Prince* and one of the last was possibly Louis XIV's *Memoirs* written for his son, were written on a premise that was possibly valid for the former but no longer for the latter: that men of state had the means to determine the destinies of those living within their territories. This presupposed that the decisions of the statesman could be enforced within a relatively small political and geographical area, and that deficiencies would be his fault. Already, however, the worldwide monarchy of Philip II had demonstrated that barriers of space and of time could frustrate every government decision. The ideals of conduct laid down by statesmen consequently need to be set within their context: they laid out not the practice but the ideal of the exercise of power and they set out moral ideals that may have been sincerely held but that cannot normally be taken as reflections of the real world, a point made forcefully by Machiavelli.

It follows that the principles by which they allegedly operated their craft were often an academic exercise rather than a reflection of what they really did. Historians have assured us solemnly that "reason" was dutifully cited by both Richelieu and Olivares as a basic principle of action, and that Richelieu insisted on "doing everything by reason." Like most of the other high truths uttered by politicians, the wonder is that we have bothered to catalogue them, since statesmen would have been unlikely to claim they were acting in despite of reason. In practice, the statesmen of the Baroque period continued to work within essentially medieval parameters. The area of their political capacity was so strictly delimited that it is not surprising they came to see their role as that of artisans, professionals who worked with a few basic raw materials and produced a recognizable end product. To this extent it is legitimate to refer to the "craft" of government. The imagery of the time supported this by, for example, presenting the subject matter of government either in medical terms as a "body" to be secured from ill or in nautical terms as a "ship" to be steered away from harm. On either account the statesman was a professional who had to learn and put into practice certain basic precepts that, properly carried out, became an art.

The writers of the Baroque age are full of these concepts. Manuals of statecraft had in the sixteenth century been written for princes; by the seventeenth century perspectives on power had broadened, and advice was tendered not simply to the nominal but also to the effective wielder of power, so that statesmen began to be written to and, more important, even write about their own craft. As a result key works such as Richelieu's *Memoirs* and *Political Testament* and de Witt's program, as presented through the prose of Pieter de la Court's *Interest of Holland,* give us important clues about how statesmen perceived the process of government. Interwoven with perceptive comments, however, there were always ritual invocations, whether in the realm of theory with affirmations of the need for "justice," or in that of foreign affairs with denunciations of the enemies of the crown. Like any other artisan, a statesman needed some rough guide to practice in a period when party political programs did not exist, and it is significant that in lieu of expounding their own ideas they were always happy to extend their patronage to writers willing to evolve ideas for them. Olivares, who was by no means lacking in ideas of statecraft, also ruled himself by maxims, most of which he had culled from ancient authors and that he brought into use in every crisis, sometimes inaptly. It is not clear to what extent he took these sayings seriously, for he was also attuned to realities and felt that "the art of government does not consist in being acute but in being moral and practical." Olivares's Castile was exceptional in that it was the only European state in which a large number of writers, the famous *arbitristas,* were encouraged to offer advice to the government of the day.

Unfortunately, as with all politicians who write their "memoirs," the historian cannot trust the evidence without looking deeper. The more we burrow into the undergrowth of European politics in the seventeenth century, the more it appears obvious that the effective importance of the "great man" is minimal and that, as Fernand Braudel pointed out long ago about the person of Philip II, we "see him imprisoned within a destiny in which he himself has little hand, fixed in a landscape in which the infinite perspectives of the *longue durée* stretch into the distance both behind him and before."

The role of statesman presupposes a nation-state, but the modern state scarcely existed in Baroque Europe. Machiavelli's context was the city-state, and he envisaged the practice of politics within an Italy populated by principalities where the will of the prince was easily enforced. "State-craft," fundamentally, was the practice of politics in a city-state. It followed that there was no known science in respect of the government of larger entities that did not yet exist. Though England had a recognizable unity that followed from its nature as part of an island, no other nation had attained the identity suggested by its name: France, Spain, Italy, and Germany were concepts and not realities, defined by a vague geographical boundary but very little else. The last three of these countries were clearly no more than a conglomeration of autonomous states, but even in France there was a striking lack of unity in laws, government, jurisdictions, taxes, and language. Parisians traveling south needed an interpreter if they required the simplest necessity. Inevitably, much of the theoretical writing of the early seventeenth century was concerned with trying to establish the lineaments of an identity. But how could this be done? How could the nation-state be an object of concern if it did not exist? And though the word "nation" existed, what did it mean? Ronsard had written:

> L'espagnol L'Espagne chantera,
> L'italien les Italies fertiles,
> Mais moy, Françoys, la France aux belles villes
>
> *(The Spaniard will sing of Spain, the Italian of fertile Italian lands, but I [will sing] of France with its fair cities)*

from which we perceive the nation as being little more than an object of patriotic sentiment, which perhaps was the most that the age could achieve, in default of any concrete political structure. Nor did the sentiment always mean loyalty, a lack which provoked Richelieu in his *Testament* to complain that "there is never a war against France without Frenchmen on the enemy's side." For the Baroque statesman such patriotic sentiment was of less practical value than a firm loyalty to the monarchy, and Olivares asserted that "I am not *nacional,* that is something for children," in the sense that unity came from the crown, not from mere sentiment. Yet sentiment too had its place: in 1635, at a time when patriotism became necessity as a rallying cry against France, which had just declared war, Olivares confessed that "I place my trust in the nation."

The "nation," of course, represented a feeling for one's own country over and against other countries and did not fit easily into normal political theory. Statesmen found it more congenial to work with the idea of the state as representing an entity called "the people," though they never permitted the notion to get out of hand. Olivares claimed that "it is always important to pay attention to the voice of the people," but the statement remained in the realm of theory and the count-duke was notoriously hostile to representative assemblies. Richelieu's views were firmer: "All students of politics agree that when the common people are too well off it is impossible to keep them peaceable." Cromwell, the revolutionary, was perhaps the most conservative of all, an unwavering opponent of any voice for the people, least of all for those with no property, "men that have no interest but the interest of breathing." The practical men of politics accepted that they must serve the people, but they also agreed that the people must have no voice in politics.

The essential mark of all the major Baroque statesmen was that their interests were identical with those of "the prince," who for them was the state. The basis of the state was seen as the prince, on the principle that he was the only focus of power. It followed that the statesman was above all merely the servant of the prince. The statesman, in the earlier concept that prevailed in the Renaissance, was no demiurge but merely a servant of the body politic; for Machiavelli "a man entrusted with government must never think of himself, and should never concern himself with anything but the prince's affairs." Even as late as the Baroque age, the word "state" had for many no meaning if used apart from the prince: the word does not occur in Olivares's vocabulary in the sense of a government, and even Richelieu used it in the sense of "domination, or a fixed order in commanding and obeying." At the dawn of the modern period all the functions of state were vested in the prince: his personal finances (called in late medieval England "household" government) were those of the state, his declarations of war involved the state. Power was fully invested in him, par excellence the man of state, and those who helped him to rule ("ministers") were his servants, dependent on his will alone. This wholly personal concept of power continued to predominate throughout the seventeenth century, when indeed it was inflated to new heights by the doctrine of absolutism. The concept of personal princely power carried, it is true, certain implicit restrictions, but even these tended in the last resort to fortify his total authority.

The prince was the primary loyalty of every chief minister of a monarchy. The clearest example of all was Mazarin. Though the completer of the work of Richelieu and dedicated thoroughly to his own survival and betterment, throughout his career his only objective was the strengthening of the monarchy, and ironically his culminating advice to his pupil Louis XIV was that the prince must be his own statesman and do without the services of a chief minister. It was the supreme achievement of a statesman to declare that statesmen were redundant if the state were to achieve its objectives.

If there was a statecraft, a science of government, it had to be learned by the prince. It followed that the statesman was the tutor. Both Richelieu and Olivares felt that part of their duty was to advise and educate the king, and Olivares was particularly gratified that under his tutelage Philip IV grew into an excellent horseman and a fair linguist (in French). It was a task fulfilled most successfully of all by Mazarin with his political education of the young Louis XIV between 1653 and 1661. Mazarin went further: he bequeathed to the future Sun King the entire team of central government, namely Le Tellier, Fouquet, Lionne, and Colbert, who laid the basis for the evolution of his state.

The relationship between servant and master was a personal one, unrecognized by tradition and therefore in France the object of the intense hostility of pamphlet literature during the Fronde. In Spain during the course of the seventeenth century the office of chief minister became regularized through the system of *validos:* both Olivares and Lerma were *validos,* their influence directly depending on the will of the king. Ministers were absolutely dedicated to the person of the king and put that loyalty before any policy interests, but logically they held that any desirable policy interest was essentially the interest of the king. It was Olivares's view that "when the prince makes up his mind, the minister has to forget entirely the opinion that he held and accept that his views were mistaken." Richelieu stated that "the public interest must be the sole end of the prince and his councilors," but the interests of all three were in practice made identical. The dedication of these ministers to promoting the personal role of the king may be seen at its finest in Olivares's encouragement of the construction of Philip's luxurious palace and gardens in the Buen Retiro, a project criticized by contemporaries as "a fancy of the count-duke." Richelieu's outstanding contribution to the beauty of his king's Paris was his own sumptuous Palais-Cardinal: "L'univers entier ne peut rien avoir d'égal / Aux superbes dehors du Palais-Cardinal [The whole universe can have nothing to equal the superb aspect of the cardinal's palace]," wrote Corneille.

The affirmations of dedication to the service of the state do not amount to a statement of policy, for by definition the statesmen could have no policy that was not already that of the state. The famous claim by Richelieu in his *Testament* that he had before him the threefold need to elevate the king, crush the nobles, and tame the Protestants was a retrospective musing rather than a statement of intentions. It is now recognized that virtually no aspect of the policies of the statesmen was, or was intended to be, original. Every aspect of Richelieu's internal and external policy was inherited from his predecessors: the alliance with Lutherans abroad, for example, had been initiated already by Francis I. Olivares likewise was little more than the heir of the *arbitristas* and of a long tradition of reformism in Castile.

Given the personal basis of political service, it followed that ministers did not in principle come to power with reform programs in mind; yet in practice they always had a clear set of priorities in their heads, even if their formal intentions were to preserve the existing political system. Generally known as "first" ministers, servants of state did not in practice hold any title corresponding to their functions. Richelieu was called "principal minister" from 1629, but the title was known before; Olivares always called himself the king's "faithful minister," John de Witt was held to be merely Pensionary of Holland, a sort of secretary to the Estates of Holland, but in practice he controlled the political affairs of both Holland and the United Provinces and moreover had a leading part in foreign affairs. Each of these statesmen was fulfilling a role which did not formally exist in the country's constitution. Not surprisingly, they felt that theirs was an extraordinary role, involving duty and obligation to the whole state, and that any hostility they invited was because of their role. Richelieu in 1630 affirmed that "I have no personal enemies, and I have never offended anyone save in the service of the state."

The devotion to the crown had an exceptional case in Mazarin, whose fidelity to the king was always paramount, but who in his early years as minister (and, despite his cardinalate, given for services to Rome, still a layman) showed too close a dedication to the Queen Mother, at forty-three on Louis XIII's death still a charming and attractive Spanish lady. Already in 1644 when Mazarin fell ill it was commented that "la reine allait visiter tous les jours le cardinal plusieurs fois avec tant de soin que chacun prenait occasion d'en mal parler [the queen went to see the cardinal several times a day, so assiduously that everyone was talking about it]," and the relationship, which appears never to have become intimate, provoked some of the most daring of the Mazarinade pamphlets.

It is fair to ask whether the statesmen were equipped to have ideas.

All had a good education, even a commoner like Cromwell, who went to his village school and then spent a year at Cambridge, where he was bored with the humanities and preferred mathematics. Olivares was unusual in having gone for two years to a university, at Salamanca, where there is no proof of his doing any work, and in any case he left when called by his father to fill the role left vacant by the death of his elder brother. Others had an advantage greater than mere education, for they gained the experience of travel. Foremost perhaps was de Witt, who accompanied his father to Scandinavia in 1645 and then together with his brother Cornelis did the Grand Tour to France and England during the momentous year 1648, and he had the curious privilege of meeting Charles I when the king was in the custody of Parliament. Richelieu belittled the importance of education, and he dismissed maxims (the stock-in-trade of Olivares) as fitting only for "a pedantic mind." For him the requirements of a statesman were "firmness of mind, stable judgment, a reasonable acquaintance with literature, a general knowledge of history and of the organization of states around the world, especially the home country."

The theoretical model to which Baroque statesmen adhered was that of absolutism, a doctrine that in one form or another triumphed throughout Europe and influenced both ideas and institutions. Essentially, absolutism required that the sovereign should have no earthly superior—a notion that became necessary owing to the political instability and social crisis of the late sixteenth century. The problem was that there were different types of sovereignty to which the doctrine was applied and there were always debates over sovereignty itself. For example, some Catholic thinkers argued that though princes were absolute their power derived only from the consent of the people, thereby creating a conflict between the rights of the governed and the duties of the governors. Even in France, where absolutism as a theory achieved most success, theorists insisted that the absolute prince was restricted by rights of religion and property and by fundamental laws.

Absolutism was originally a theory of princely power and therefore not apparently relevant to ministers of state, but it was the ministers who supported it in practice. Despite the crises in the state during the previous half-century, in the course of the early seventeenth century confidence in monarchical power was restored and the power of kings extended: the entire ministerial achievement of Richelieu consisted in winning for the crown an authority and initiative that it had never before possessed. The steady rise of French absolutism provoked a strong reaction among many in both England and the United Provinces, but essentially there was no difference of approach over the nature of government. When the English Parliament overthrew what it considered to be an absolute system of Stuart rule, it set up in its place a form of rule that was far more absolute, claiming (in the Rump Parliament's declaration of 1649) unlimited powers and the right to make laws even without the consent of the people.

Republican statesmen were not immune to monarchical sympathies. Cromwell felt in the 1650s that a settlement with "somewhat of monarchical power in it" would be best for England, and when the debate over the headship of state reached an impasse in 1652 he mused to Whitelocke, "What if a man should take it upon him to be king?" Even in what we think of as the republican United Provinces the notion of kingship was alive, and it nurtured the cause of the princes of Orange. The great enemy of the House of Orange, John de Witt, was not alien to the idea either. He was a "republican" only in the sense that he was loyal to the Republic and strongly opposed to the Orangist party, but in practice if he had been born under a monarchy he would have served it just as faithfully, and he rebuked an English friend who decried the monarchy in England. Moreover, de Witt was frankly oligarchic, and if he shared the opinions of Pieter de la Court, whose famous tract *The Interest of Holland* (1662) he sponsored, clearly antidemocratic. Court's work excluded from participation in politics all women and servants, all crippled and poor, "together with all others who had exercised any trade or worked for a daily wage in anyone's service," categories that restricted the franchise and political activity to a tiny minority of independent men.

Within the chaos of concepts, statesmen were determined to ensure simply that the authority of the state remain unshaken, and they were often indifferent to the forms that any theory might take. Cromwell in particular professed to have no preference among the different systems available, and was firm only in his hostility to democracy; for the rest, to him all forms of government were "dross and dung in comparison with Christ." Yet in practice he inclined to the absolutism of one-man rule, and it is no coincidence that Thomas Hobbes's concept of the *Leviathan* (1651) arose out of his experience of mid-century England.

Does this drift towards absolutism in the Baroque mean that there was a decline of constitutionalism and a loss of freedom? The evidence would suggest that this was certainly the case. Viewed superficially, state initiatives were made at the expense of the interests that had hitherto shared power with the state. In England one may point to periodic conflicts that may have been of minor importance when first raised in Parliament but that gathered force and during the Eleven Years Tyranny prepared the ground for the sharp differences, especially religious, that precipitated civil war. In Spain the outbreak of constitutionalism in Castile between 1600 and 1610 was followed by the more authoritarian rule of the count-duke, and that in turn was followed by the attempts to interfere with provincial privileges. In France there were no Estates General after 1614. It is plausible to argue that despite all these facts there was no conscious intention to reject representative bodies: Richelieu, after all, took pains to consult the Assembly of Notables, and Olivares had himself elected to the Castilian Cortes in order to deal with opposition directly. It may be that such statesmen had liberal intentions, but the general trend of the age was certainly against parliaments. Perhaps the most typical rejection came in Cromwell's outburst at the dissolution of the Long Parliament in 1653: "You are no Parliament, I say you are no Parliament; I will put an end to your sitting!" It was a decade that all over Europe marked the end of an epoch: the Diet of Brandenburg lost its power after 1653, the last Zemsky Sobor of Russia met in that year, the last Danish parliament met in 1660 before surrendering its powers, the Parlement de Paris was silenced in the 1660s, and Habsburg Castile had no Cortes after 1665.

Fundamentally, of course, the restriction of its political role was no threat to the political elite, which was confirmed in its social privileges. Cromwell reminded one of his Parliaments that they, the elite, were the backbone of stability: "A nobleman, a gentleman, a yeoman: that is a good interest of the nation." His oath as Protector said that his primary duty was to "secure property." Ironically, he was the only one of our major European statesmen to be strictly a "commoner"; all others were from the gentry, even de Witt. De Witt came from the "regent" class, who were not nobles but certainly not commoners, and he asserted his elite standing further in 1660 by taking on the legal status of *heer* (lord) through his possession of seigneurial land. It is important to bear in mind that for all leaders the strengthening of the state also involved the strengthening of the social order, so that in real terms there was no contradiction between absolutism and the interests of the ruling elite. Indeed, absolutism reinforced the elite. Due care had of course to be taken: in the Swedish Royal Council in 1636 Oxenstierna affirmed that "we need to stand as mediators between king and subjects, and speak not only for the rights of the crown but for the law of the land and the due liberties of the country." The "liberties" so warmly defended by Sweden's elder statesman were soon to be permanently protected by the adoption of absolute government in 1680, a step that the Danes had already taken in 1660.

In short, as conservatives all our statesmen had a very restricted vision of rights and of freedom, and they were decidedly no friends to what is now considered to be political liberty. Cromwell probably spoke the most about liberty, but he was also the one who most complained about "abuses" of liberty. Whenever he used the word it carried a special meaning: in Ireland he proclaimed that "we come to maintain the glory of English liberty," and he invited the Irish "to use liberty and fortune equally with Englishmen." As always in politics, the same word meant different things to different people, and possibly nowhere more than in the Catalonia of the 1630s, where the Catalans distrusted the new freedoms offered by the count-duke. Was it a freedom to have their traditional rights modified? They did not think so. For the statesmen, therefore, one of the most profound problems was to find public consent for their policies, but none of them succeeded in obtaining it, not even Richelieu, whose policies were vilified by the pamphleteers of the Fronde. The greatest of them all, Cromwell, was the one who failed most miserably in trying to rally either elite or people to his side: stumbling from one political experiment to another, he was unable to find any basis for an agreement, and, as Christopher Hill says, he ended up "sitting on bayonets and nothing else."

The illusion projected by works such as Richelieu's *Political Testament* is the idea that the man of state is created only by the king. Richelieu was in theory addressing the king, and therefore he flattered him with the image of a state in which everything depended on the royal will. In sober reality, there were crucial mechanisms of power and interest that helped both to create the statesman and to keep him in the position he had acquired.

The first and most important of these was the use of patronage, which involved the free use of the advantages of office. In the age before the existence of parties, patronage was the only available way of harnessing political forces, and every statesman was obliged to make use of it in order to stay in power. Ministers such as Richelieu or Olivares did not rely on the goodwill of the king alone; they relied equally on the goodwill of the political elite, and if they had lacked this then their careers would have been short indeed. Unfortunately, there is no study of the political connections of Olivares. By contrast, we know that Richelieu, and after him Mazarin, constructed a powerful system of clientage.

The bonds of political loyalty were always the basis of power, but such bonds were easier to construct in a small state like England than in a diverse structure such as France. It was recognized, however, as a Provençal noble of the seventeenth century put it, that "it is necessary to cultivate the acquaintance of the great and the powerful without whose support you cannot maintain a party." Efforts were therefore made in France to build up bonds of interest that tied the center to the provinces, a system that suited the provincial elites, who in this way could also help to influence the center. The basis of all clientage was necessarily kinship, with marriages as the principal cement, but clientage was also based on influence and on money, all of which served to build up networks that at one and the same time served the needs of the local elite and those of the central state. The use of money (that is, bribery) in politics was commonplace and not normally deemed immoral. Resort to clientage did not mean that existing institutions were bypassed; on the contrary, they were part of the system. The French intendants, for example, were a crucial link in the chain, and in 1656 we find the intendant of Burgundy, Bouchu, reporting to Mazarin that "I am using with all imaginable care my credit and that of my friends and relatives in this assembly [the Estates] in order to make the king's intentions succeed."

The patronage network of Richelieu and Mazarin belonged both to the state and to themselves personally. This confusion of private and public interest was strictly speaking "corruption," but in the Baroque age no contradiction between the two was perceived, since the statesman obviously served the state. Only when the private interest seemed to compete with that of the state, as with Fouquet's sumptuous estate at Vaux-le-Vicomte, did the public interest (that is, the crown) demur.

The uses and forms of patronage were many. We may summarize them within the framework of three themes: wealth, family, and clientage.

The accumulation of wealth was condemned by critics as proof of personal avarice, and there is every reason to accept their view. The unremitting accumulation of wealth by Richelieu and Mazarin can only be explained by a personal obsession, a hunger for goods that exceeded all bounds. Each cardinal was by the time of his death easily the richest man in France after the king. Joseph Bergin writes that "Richelieu's central conviction seems to have been that power required magnificence." From the beginning of his career he deliberately confounded private with public interest. As chief adviser to the Queen Mother and director of her political and private administration from about 1620, he used her officials to promote his interests, and he placed his so-called "creatures" within her power structure, so that after the Day of Dupes in 1630 he effortlessly took over the influence she had formerly enjoyed. In the same way, when he assumed a position of power in the king's employ, he used government officials to promote his private interests. This, together with his access to all the sources of profit in the state, made it possible for him to accumulate an incredible fortune.

A large part of it was in cash income, and an equally great part in land. The land was rapidly and systematically acquired during his term of office, including scattered estates around the country, purchased largely for investment, and high-quality land in the key areas of Paris, Fontainebleau, and St Germain, all of it adding up to a value of over five million livres and representing the biggest concentration of land amassed by any individual in the entire history of ancien régime France. The truly outstanding achievement was that where all other land accumulated by the higher aristocracy was used to produce income for pressing debts, in Richelieu's case the lands were wholly free of debt and produced nothing but pure income. As a churchman, the cardinal could also exploit the church: in an age when the Counter-Reformation was theoretically trying to reform and abolish plurality, Richelieu ended up with possession (apart from his titular see of Luçon, which he gave to a client in 1623) of fifteen abbeys (including the famous one of Cluny) and four priories. At his death his estate, one-quarter of which was in land, was worth some twenty million livres, not counting the magnificent asset of the Palais-Cardinal in Paris, and in addition he had an annual income of about one million livres.

A cardinal since December 1641 and a member of the Royal Council, Mazarin succeeded Richelieu at his death as head of the Council and also of the Queen's household, with the patronage that both posts brought. The posts he subsequently accumulated were astonishing: governor of Fontainebleau, of La Rochelle, of Le Havre, of Auvergne, of Breisach, of Alsace, abbot of seventeen abbeys including that of Cluny, duke of Nevers and Mayenne, and many others; their revenues and those drawn from a range of official as well as secret sources gave him an immense fortune and enabled him to collect a range of properties in Paris and Rome, and notably the Palais Mazarin (now the Bibliothèque Nationale), all of which he bequeathed at his death to the king, thus conforming even more than Richelieu with the attitude that what was his belonged to the state, just as what belonged to the state belonged to him. Like Richelieu, he devoted much of the wealth to patronizing the arts; for example, he founded the Academy of Painting (1648) and brought the musician Lully from Italy.

It was also possible for a statesman to become rich in republican Holland. After his election as Pensionary of Holland in 1653, de Witt's fortune expanded appreciably, the bulk of it forming investments in bonds and in land. His post helped him also to obtain a rich wife (he was only thirty when he married). Marriage and influence together gave him a solid fortune, which however was not spent on outward display. Sir William Temple, writing a few years later of the United Provinces, recalled "the simplicity and modesty of their Magistrates in their way of living," and he commented of de Witt that "the whole train and expence of his Domestique went very equal with other common Ministers of the State; his Habit grave and plain and popular; His Table what only serv'd turn for his Family or a Friend"; in public "he was seen usually in the streets on foot and alone, like the commonest Burger of the Town." This is comparable to Cromwell, who rose from being a modest landowner to the recipient (voted to him as Protector in 1654) of seventy thousand pounds a year for his family and expenses, an income he enjoyed quite apart from his normal huge landed revenue (in 1651 Parliament had voted him lands worth four thousand pounds a year). Yet the Venetian ambassador commended the Protector's "unpretending manner of life, remote from all display and pomp, so different from the former fashion of this kingdom." In later years luxury crept in (in 1658 it was reported that "Cromwell has introduced the Spanish habit"), a reminder that Cromwell was a liberal man with no dogmatic Puritan cast of mind.

Olivares started on the road to riches with the built-in advantage of coming from a leading noble clan of Andalusia, the Guzmáns. His rapid accumulation of honors was typical of all rising statesmen: in the royal household he obtained key posts such as that of Master of the Horse and Grand Chamberlain, but he also took in a large number of other nominal posts such as that of cavalry general. The honors did not in themselves enrich; for that it was necessary to accumulate land, which he did doggedly, buying up estates and towns in order to create for himself, in the vicinity of Seville, the dukedom of San Lúcar, based on the town of that name. With this status Olivares made his family the equal of the greatest lords of Castile.

The placing of family followed automatically on attaining power. Unless they were singularly unfortunate—or, like Cromwell, caught up in an unstable situation—the statesmen of the Baroque came to establish dynasties on an almost royal scale. On first entering office, they took care to gratify and place all the relevant members of their family. The first task of de Witt in office was to place his "wide network of family relations" as well as his friends: it was the least he could do with the patronage available to him. Some of the posts he controlled as Pensionary; others he controlled as one of Holland's representatives in the States General. The highly oligarchic nature of politics in the northern Protestant countries meant that marriage and family placement was seldom a useful way of controlling power. By contrast, in France and southern Europe it was accepted that relatives would be placed in key positions, and once again Richelieu is the outstanding case. Richelieu's brother Alphonse became archbishop of Lyons, his cousin Charles de la Porte commander of the artillery and marshal, and other relatives from the various branches of the family filled posts in the army, navy, administration, and finances. One niece married into the royal family and became duchess of Enghien, others through marriage became duchesses and countesses. The family network constructed through nepotism not only created a dynasty, it also became central to the system of government operated by the cardinal and continued after him by Mazarin. The latter, as a foreigner and a bachelor, had less of a family to gratify, but he did quite as well as his predecessor. His relatives benefited enormously and rose with him into the highest ranks of the kingdom: his seven nieces, the "Mazarinettes," became respectively countess of Soissons, duchess of Mercoeur, princess of Conti, duchess of Modena, duchess of Mazarin, duchess of Bouillon, and princess of Colonna (this last was Marie, whose idyllic love affair with the young Louis XIV in 1658 was brusquely broken by the cardinal "for the good of the realm").

Olivares likewise relied heavily on his family, the distinguished line of Guzmán, for support, and he rewarded them correspondingly. Given the close marriage links between members of the Castilian aristocracy, the rewarding of the clan—the *parentela*—meant that jobs went to a whole grouping of aristocrats, in his case the interrelated kin of the houses of Zúñiga, Guzmán, and Haro. Among those who did well out of the count-duke's regime were his brother-in-law the count of Monterrey, who was created successively grandee, ambassador to Rome, and viceroy of Naples, and his nephew, Don Luis de Haro, who later succeeded him as chief minister of the king. The placing of family, in all these systems of nepotism, guaranteed a network of loyalty based on the closest tie of all—blood—and one that extended not only into the palace but through key areas of the countryside. Unfortunately in the case of Olivares, family was not always dependable, and key figures in the clan subsequently played a part in bringing about the fall of the chief minister.

The most interesting but possibly least reliable way for the statesman to secure power was through clientage. Properly speaking, clientage did not exist until it was superimposed on and fed into existing patterns of political loyalty, so that the client did not betray prior loyalties when he attached himself to a new loyalty. In modern times this might be perceived as a "power base." Clientage could, of course, be based simply on friendship, but such friendship could also be political, as when based on co-operation in local administration. The obvious basis of clientage was self-interest: men would be drawn into a network only if it benefited them in money or in status, and the patron therefore had to have at his disposal a substantial fund of gifts and honors, what the Castilians called *mercedes*.

The need for clientage arose out of the deficiencies of the state in the Baroque age. No government in Europe possessed any bureaucracy capable of binding the interest of the provinces to the center, and statesmen therefore had to create this link out of the existing social system, without putting too much strain on local privileges. Few statesmen succeeded in the task. The social systems of northern Europe—in England, Sweden, and the United Provinces—were not amenable to this form of control. In Spain Olivares failed signally to recruit clients where he might most have needed them, in the crown of Aragon or in Portugal, and he remained restricted to a fairly narrow power base in Andalusia. It is only in France that historians have been able to find statesmen with a solid clientage.

Though Richelieu is usually thought of as a man wielding power from the center, it should be emphasized that his position necessarily depended on a secure position in the provinces, as shown by his control over select governorships. Bergin has shown that "every important governorship in the maritime provinces of France from lower Normandy to the proximity of the Gironde was in his hands," including cities such as Le Havre, Nantes, and La Rochelle, and that the remaining seats of power in the area were in the hands of relatives, for example, a cousin holding Brest. But the network of clientage was not restricted simply to this corner of the country. Sharon Kettering has shown vividly how in Provence the minister managed to extend the influence of the central government by creating a network interconnected by ties of kinship, marriage, friendship, clientage, and office holding that stretched outside the province to Versailles and Paris. The members of this network were not grandees but lesser nobles, whose collaboration allowed France to operate as a political unity. It was a Provençal nobleman who in 1633 declared to Richelieu, "I have no greater ambition in the world than to be your creature."

In considering the way in which the provinces might collaborate with the center, we should not lose from sight the fact that virtually all our men of state were defeated by the provinces. Though Europeans may have felt a sentiment for their nation, they were even more attached to their own province, and local elites were reluctant to follow the politics of the capital city. De Witt's failure to make the elites pursue a common interest precipitated his fall. Cromwell's inability to find an agreement was perhaps the most notable: from the beginning he had no chance of support on the English periphery, in Scotland and Ireland. His most abject failure, however, was with the English provincial elite, and in the end the only persuasion he could offer was brute force. Olivares antagonized the non-Castilian elites, and it is not surprising that in the end the Castilian elites also deserted him with the treason of Medina Sidonia in his own home country, Andalusia, a bitter pill for a man whose aspirations were never confined to a mere province.

By the same token even Richelieu—despite his clientage—and Mazarin failed. The Fronde was a fitting commentary on the inability of the statesmen to elevate the interests of the state above those of the province. By the middle years of the seventeenth century the autonomous province—Holland, Provence, Catalonia—was still the basic political unit of modern Europe. The nation was shaping itself but was still not yet in sight. As late as 1660 Louis XIV with his army had to besiege a rebellious Marseilles, which appealed in vain to Spain for help.

There was one field of activity that kings and ministers alike felt was their supreme specialty: that of foreign policy. All statesmen were conscious imperialists. Politics involved the exercise of power, but foreign policy was the ultimate exercise of power: had not Machiavelli declared that "the art of war is all that is expected of a ruler"? In the Baroque period over three-fourths of a state's income was normally spent on war or the preparation for war, and foreign policy inevitably attracted the statesman's primary attention.

Politicians expressed their aggressive intentions in terms of upholding the dignity of the king. Olivares in 1625 claimed that "I have always desired to see Your Majesty enjoying a reputation in the world equal to your greatness and qualities," and Richelieu informed his king that one of his principal concerns was "to restore your reputation among foreign nations to the station it ought to occupy." Richelieu also observed in 1629 that "it is difficult for a prince to have great reputation and great repose, since frequently the esteem of the world is gained only by great actions." By this period of history, royal reputations were ceasing to be won in person, though Louis XIII in the campaigns of the 1620s against his mother and then against the Huguenots was certainly an active participant. By contrast, Philip IV's appearance with his troops was a mere formality. The most outstanding exception to the diminishing role of kings was the great Protestant "Lion of the North," Gustavus Adolphus of Sweden.

Like their masters, the men of state felt they should win honor on the field. De Witt was trained to arts of peace and must be seen as the exception, but it is astonishing that a Spanish nobleman such as Olivares should have been completely lacking in practical experience of warfare. Sweden's chancellor Axel Oxenstierna was an administrator rather than a soldier, but he accompanied his king and directed many decisions affecting the military, so that in practical terms he had direct and extensive experience of the field. As a man of the church Richelieu was not supposed to be a soldier, but his famous personal direction of the siege at La Rochelle in 1628 surely earns him recognition. Cromwell was, by any standards, the leading soldier of his age.

Domestic policies in the seventeenth century were largely restricted to maintaining law and order, so that the greater part of the energy of statesmen went into foreign affairs. It is no coincidence that standard biographies of de Witt, Olivares, and Richelieu give most attention to their role in the international arena. By definition such a role was aggressive. The part played by de Witt may not appear so, since the Republic under him was trying to avoid war in order to survive, but his diplomacy was frankly aggressive and consequently fits into the common mold. Despite his own peaceful temperament and cautious policies, his ministry coincided with the greatest number of accumulated threats to the Republic, and it was arguably foreign policy—the threat from France—that determined his fall.

Because statesmen hazarded their reputation in foreign policy, later historians have judged them by it. Few emerge with their reputations untarnished. The most disastrously affected of all was Olivares, whose search to salvage Spain's reputation was wrecked with the loss of his own reputation through the war over Mantua in 1628. Olivares's failure was in a sense that of the entire Spanish imperial experience: torn between overwhelming commitments and inadequate resources, the monarchy did not "decline," it simply failed to meet the challenge. Moreover, the growing rediscovery within the different parts of the monarchy of their own identities, by Catalonia, for example, in 1640 or by Naples in 1647, threatened to undermine the premise on which Olivares had worked, namely that all the realms would cooperate more closely with Castile. It took a failure in the foreign field to precipitate failure at home. A parallel may perhaps be made with Sweden, which in the same years was attempting to pursue abroad an imperial dream that could not possibly be justified by the limited resources available to the home government. When Oxenstierna affirmed in 1632 that the only settlement he envisaged in Germany was one "with our foot on their neck and a knife at their throat," he was using the language that subsequent statesmen of Sweden continued to adopt but which ended with the crumbling of the empire by the end of the century.

By contrast, the failure of Cromwell on the world scene was more apparent than real, and of all the aspects of his regime the only one remembered with approval was his foreign policy. Samuel Pepys noted in 1667 that contemporaries did "commend him, what brave things he did and made all the neighbour princes fear him." The Dutch ambassador in 1672 told Charles II that "Cromwell was a great man, who made himself feared by land and sea." The English were given a sense of pride at the newly discovered power both of their armies (against the Scots at Dunbar, against the Spaniards at Dunkirk) and of their navy (the defeat of the Dutch, the taking of Jamaica by the otherwise disastrous expedition to the West Indies, the seizure of the plate fleet by Blake in 1657). Cromwell offered the English a world strategy that defied both their trade competitors, the Dutch, and their ideological enemy, Spain: it was a perspective that laid the foundations of the future British Empire. Cromwell's imperial achievement seems all the more brilliant because it was so brief and was followed by the inept foreign policy of his successors.

Of all the statesmen of the age Richelieu alone is fortunate to receive the favorable judgment both of contemporaries and of historians, and almost exclusively for his aggression—that is, for his contribution to the greatness of France. The evidence is not in doubt. As Victor Lucien Tapié concluded in his *France in the Age of Louis XIII and Richelieu,*

The France of 1643 is far larger than the France of 1610, extending well beyond the valley of the Somme to the plateaux of Artois. . . . She dominates Lorraine and Alsace, Metz, Nancy, Colmar and the bridges over the

upper Rhine. She has a foothold in Italy, she occupies Roussillon, and pro-
tects Catalonia. By her alliance with Portugal she has driven a wedge into
the Iberian peninsula. The revival of her seapower enables her to trade in
the Mediterranean, the Atlantic, and northern seas. She has colonies in
Canada and the West Indies. . . . There are French trading posts on the Sen-
egalese coast and on Madagascar. In less than twenty years France has become a country of greater importance in the world than ever before. (Lockie
translation, 430–31)

The success story was only beginning, for the gains were small in comparison with what France was to achieve within another half-century. For
those then and now who see all this as the conscious achievement of one
man, Richelieu's position as the outstanding statesman of his age seems
unassailable.

There was a price that had to be paid for imperial adventure, and
statesmen were assuredly responsible for the growing burden of taxation
and debt. Under Richelieu state taxation probably quadrupled; under Olivares in Castile it doubled; Sweden's war expenditure bankrupted the
treasury. The effective result of the triumphs of foreign policy was accelerating misery, shown nowhere more clearly than in the regular popular
revolts that plagued the French countryside during the war years of the
two cardinals. Popular misery, however, was not a concept that troubled
the vocabulary of statesmen, and war was revered as a contribution to
the honor of the state regardless of its impact on those who paid with
their taxes and with their lives. At a later date Louis XIV claimed that
"nothing touched my heart and soul more deeply than my realization of
the complete exhaustion of my peoples due to the immense burden of
taxation"; the triumphs of Richelieu had led to this, but Louis XIV himself was to increase yet further the burden on the French taxpayer.

Because they did not form, like modern politicians, part of a structure
that reflected opinion or that consulted with supporters, Baroque statesmen were wholly isolated from the day-to-day workings of the body politic, and relied on a tiny circle of advisers only. They did not feel they had
to justify themselves to any constituency other than History, and as a
result did not resort to one of the most powerful weapons of the modern
state, propaganda, which was allotted no recognized role in politics. Instruments of social control such as the pulpit were recognized as such
and given their due role, but the printing press was not yet an instrument
of state.

Strangely, however, propaganda began to be used to justify warfare,
and it reached its apogee in the voluminous pamphlet literature of the
Thirty Years War. Various European states ventured into organizing a

propaganda press for precisely the same motive of war. The famous *Gazette de France* of Richelieu (1631) was directed at European and not at domestic opinion. Its field of reference was foreign policy, and the fact that its editor, Théophraste Renaudot, was a Protestant influenced the cardinal's many Lutheran allies. In Cromwellian England the press was largely controlled by Secretary Thurloe, whose sphere of authority was significantly foreign affairs; by the 1650s only two newspapers survived, each a mouthpiece of the government. This restricted role for propaganda was subject to one major exception: in the revolutionary disorders of the mid-century in London, Paris, and Barcelona, opposition groups for the first time in European history used the press to attack the policies of the state, giving us thereby some of the richest collections of opinion available to historians. By the later seventeenth century the importance of propaganda was beginning to be recognized. In Holland, de Witt was compelled to use the printed word against the powerful opposition, and de la Court's *Interest* was "concerned to make the excellence of the government of the States clear against the objectionable nature of that of the *stadhouders*"—that is, the House of Orange.

The people, then, were beginning to penetrate the sacred mysteries of power, but it was a predemocratic age and in reality statesmen in time of distress and failure looked not to the people but only to God, to whom alone they justified themselves. The affinity of the Catholic statesmen with God was genuine but seems somehow distant when compared with the intimacy professed by their Protestant counterparts. None, perhaps, was on closer terms with God than Oliver Cromwell. A Leveler critic said of him in 1649, "You shall scarce speak to Cromwell about anything, but he will lay his hand on his breast, elevate his eyes and call God to record; he will weep, howl and repent even while he doth smite you under the fifth rib." God and Providence appear in all his discourses and writings, a common feature of the Puritan tradition in England but of particular significance with the Lord Protector, who molded all his policies on God, who saw all his victories as "mercies" of God, and who could open a meeting of the Council of State in 1654 with the words, "God has not brought us hither but to consider the work that we may do in the world."

What then did the great men of this age achieve? All struggled against fearful opposition, and only Richelieu and Oxenstierna may be considered to have completed their programs. Opposition was not only bitter and unrelenting (de Witt suffered attempted assassination, Richelieu exposed at least eight major plots against his life), it was also personal, despite Richelieu's claim that his only enemies were those of the state. It would be naive to imagine that their personal weaknesses of character were not crucial in provoking opposition. Many who felt they shared common ground with Cromwell were later to denounce him as treacherous; a Scotsman called him "an egregious dissembler and a great liar." Much of the campaign against Mazarin arose from dislike of him as a person, and the Mazarinades were frequently and bruisingly personal:

> Un vent de fronde
> a soufflé ce matin;
> Je crois qu'il gronde
> contre le Mazarin.
>
> *(A Fronde wind blew*
> *this morning; I think it*
> *blows against Mazarin.)*

The vast mass of the Mazarinades (well over five thousand survive) represent a valuable source of opinion on the evils of men of state, especially since in attacking Mazarin many also consciously intended to attack Richelieu. Why did they denounce Mazarin? He was a foreigner, an Italian; he spoke French with an atrocious accent; he had introduced Italian tastes (opera) and Italian vices (the obscene pamphlets unanimously accuse him of sodomy); he was a tyrant, like Richelieu; he had misused finances for his own profit; he had enriched himself, like Richelieu.

Men in politics needed broad backs to suffer criticism, and for the same reason might be of a tolerant disposition. In France the state itself was committed to toleration of Huguenots, and Richelieu's reflection in the *Testament* that "prudence does not permit anything so hazardous as to risk uprooting the grain while pulling up the tares" was nothing more than a polite repetition of what many famous Frenchmen had stated before him. Foreign alliances with Protestant states obviously added further reason for practicing toleration, but the cardinal went further than passive tolerance by his close association with Huguenot intellectuals such as Valentin Conrart, to whom he entrusted the formation of the Académie Française. Surprisingly, Olivares must also be placed among those of tolerant inclination: tolerating Protestants could not arise as an issue, since there were none to tolerate, but the count-duke was sensible to the injustices suffered by those of Jewish origin, and on many occasions he made clear his opposition to cultural discrimination of any sort. In England and Holland traditions of bigotry vied with those of freedom, and both Cromwell and de Witt were on the side of freedom. The Lord Protector, despite his terrible repression of the Catholic Irish, time and again expressed his hostility to any sort of religious coercion. "I meddle not with any man's conscience," he said, "but if by liberty of conscience you mean liberty to exercise the mass . . . ": the statement defined both the principle and the limits on it. He saw no reason for narrow-mindedness among Protestants, and in a famous appeal to the Scots Calvinists in 1650 he urged them to "think it possible you may be mistaken." In 1654 he lamented the difficulty of attaining religious liberty: "Everyone desires to have liberty, but none will give it."

De Witt, according to a biographer, "wanted no zeal, and could not understand why theories should so agitate men." While not in favor of diversity of opinion, he displayed a practical tolerance towards Catholics, Mennonites, and Jews, the minorities that he most encountered in his political life. The Dutch Republic had imposed the Calvinist creed of a minority on a majority Catholic population, but de Witt took no steps to enforce the intolerant anti-Catholic laws while supporting them in theory. For this he was regarded by Calvinist zealots as a hypocrite. It was of de Witt's period as Pensionary that the English diplomat Sir William Temple made the immortal observation, "Religion may possibly do more good in other places, but it does less hurt here," and to the general tolerance of the Dutch he attributed "the vast growth of their Trade and Riches, and consequently the strength and greatness of their State."

Anyone attempting to evaluate the statesmen of this time is inescapably impressed by their industry. Without any reliable bureaucracy to help them, they were obliged to attend personally to even the most minute affairs of government, and therefore were apt to suffer from overwork and depression. Christopher Hill does not hesitate to call Cromwell a "manic depressive," and Gregorio Marañón likewise calls Olivares a "manic depressive." Did the cares of state induce depression and madness? Contemporaries remarked Cromwell's alternating bouts of melancholy and hysteria: the Puritan Richard Baxter said of him that he was capable of states of hilarity, "as another man is when he hath drunken a cup too much." By contrast, when unnerved by bad political news Cromwell took ill and retired to bed. Many of Olivares's statements, both public and private and even from as early as the 1620s (when his daughter's death drove him to bouts of depression), suggest an extreme mental tension that eventually, on his deathbed, turned into madness. An indefatigable energy, reflecting an internal despair but turned outward into an almost fanatical service to the king: this seemed to be the nature of Olivares. Is it all that different from Temple's judgment on de Witt: "A man of unwearied Industry, inflexible Constance, sound, clear and deep Understanding, and untainted Integrity; so that whenever he was blinded it was by the passion he had for that which he esteemed the good and interest of the State"?

On this note of anxiety, should we dismiss the Baroque statesmen as failures? Olivares's plans ended in disaster, Cromwell's regime disappeared, the rule of the regents in Holland ended with the bloody murder of the de Witt brothers, Oxenstierna's attempts to stabilize Sweden ended with the abdication of Queen Christina, Mazarin's ministry precipitated a civil war. The frankly negative hues of the picture are in some measure unjust. Only Olivares can truly be written off as a failure, since the policies he adopted were unworkable and provoked further problems in their turn. In greater or lesser degree, all the others made positive and lasting contributions to their people. The stability that John de Witt introduced into the public life of the United Provinces was the factor that most facilitated the assumption of power by William III of Orange. Without Oxenstierna's careful guidance of the Swedish constitution through the royal minority after Gustavus Adolphus's death in 1632, both monarchy and empire may have collapsed. The place of Cromwell and Richelieu in the forefront of history is a measure of the profound contribution each made to their nation's eventual rise to world status. Even Mazarin, vilified and neglected, must be remembered as the tutor and architect of the absolute kingship of the Sun King.

"In truth," said Olivares in 1634, "there are many things we are neglecting, and not the least of them is history." In order to salvage his reputation for posterity, he accordingly imported an Italian to be his official historian. Rightly concerned about his own fate in history, Richelieu assembled a vast number of papers, notes, and opinions that he certainly expected posterity to read but that he was unable to prepare for publication and his admirers edited after his death. Even absolute power, however, stops short at the grave, and the reputation of men of state has fluctuated from generation to generation, dependent on the mercy of public opinion and the diligence of historians. Oliver Cromwell's body was dug up after the Restoration in 1660 and hanged on the public gibbet at Tyburn. No fate could have been more humiliating and vulgar, yet within six years he was being discussed as a great man, and the novelist Henry Fielding observed that "Cromwell carried the reputation of England higher than it ever was at any time," and by the nineteenth century he was seen by one prominent historian as "the greatest Englishman of all time."

Kings were notoriously ungrateful masters, as Olivares and Fouquet and many others found to their cost. It is pleasant then to give the last word to a king who found words to express his gratitude to one of the great statesmen of the time. In December 1630, at the beginning of his brief but brilliant campaign in Germany, Gustavus Adolphus wrote to Chancellor Oxenstierna:

> Assuming that we survive, your plans seem to have a good chance of success, and you may expect to gain the applause of posterity, particularly if you reinforce good counsel with your habitual zeal and energy in executing

it. I wish there were others who could deal with our affairs with the same discretion, fidelity, and knowledge: if there were, I am sure that the country's service and the welfare of us all would be safer than it is. I urge and entreat you, for Christ's sake, not to lose heart if the issue be otherwise than we would have it. . . . If anything should happen to me, my family will become objects of compassion. Natural affection forces these lines from my pen in order to prepare you—as an instrument sent to me from God to light me through many a dark place—for what may happen.

Were there any other princes who thought of their ministers of state as a light shining in the darkness?

BIBLIOGRAPHY

Bergin, Joseph. *Cardinal Richelieu: Power and the Pursuit of Wealth.* New Haven: Yale University Press, 1985.

Elliott, John H. *The Count-Duke of Olivares: The Statesman in an Age of Decline.* New Haven: Yale University Press, 1988.

———. *Richelieu and Olivares.* Cambridge and New York: Cambridge University Press, 1984.

Hill, Christopher. *God's Englishman: Oliver Cromwell and the English Revolution.* London: Weidenfeld & Nicolson, 1970; New York: Dial, 1970; Harper & Row, 1972.

Kettering, Sharon. *Patrons, Brokers and Clients in Seventeenth-Century France.* New York: Oxford University Press, 1986.

Méthivier, Hubert. *La Fronde.* Paris: Presses Universitaires de France, 1984.

Roberts, Michael. *Gustavus Adolphus: A History of Sweden, 1611–1632.* 2 vols. London and New York: Longmans, Green, 1953–58.

Rowen, Herbert H. *John de Witt: Statesman of the "True Freedom."* New Haven: Yale University Press, 1988.

2

The Soldier

Geoffrey Parker

“ **T**his, ” Fulvio Testi, Italian poet and military commander, wrote in 1641, “is the century of the soldier.”[1] He was right. On the one hand, there were more hostilities in Europe than ever before; on the other, they involved unprecedented numbers of troops. Thus in the course of the entire seventeenth century there were only four years of complete peace; the Ottoman, Austrian, and Swedish states were at war for two years in every three, the Spanish monarchy for three years in every four, and Poland and Russia for four years in every five. In 1600, when Spain was fighting England and the Dutch Republic and France was fighting Savoy, the total size of all the armies on foot in Europe probably numbered less than 250,000. By 1645 this total had certainly doubled, for more than 200,000 soldiers fought in Germany and the Netherlands to achieve victory in the Thirty Years War (1618–48), a further 100,000 were involved in the Civil Wars in the British Isles, and yet more were engaged in conflicts between France and Spain, between Denmark and Sweden, and between the Ottoman Empire and the Venetian Republic. By 1706, however, with both the War of Spanish Succession and the Great Northern Wars in full swing, perhaps 1.3 million troops were mobilized—almost 400,000 of them in France alone. In the course of the seventeenth century, it would seem that an unprecedented total of between ten and twelve million Europeans became soldiers. But who, precisely, were those warriors? Where did they come from? How were they supplied? And what was their fate?

Raising an Army

Almost all the soldiers of the Baroque age, like those of the Renaissance, began as volunteers who enlisted of their own free will. The process was remarkably similar all over Europe. The principal recruiting officer was normally the captain and the principal unit was the company. Each captain chosen by the government received a commission to raise a company in a specific area, and he would first name his junior officers and order a standard to be made. Then with colors, a drummer, and his officers, he would visit the various towns and villages specified in his commission. In each place the local magistrates would be expected to provide the captain with an inn or an empty house to serve as a headquarters where the company colors were unfurled and the drummer beat a tattoo to attract volunteers. From those who came to offer their services the captain chose men who were healthy and sane, who were aged over sixteen and under forty, and who, so far as possible, were "neither married nor only sons who would cause loss to their parents or their villages." The names of the recruits were then entered on the company's list (they "enlisted"), and they received a cash payment and perhaps a suit of clothes, plus free shelter and food while they waited for the levy to be completed. At that point (usually two to three weeks later) the Articles of War were read out to the troops, stating the penalties that would attend any future misconduct. The men were required to raise their right hand and swear to accept these ordinances, the most important of which concerned the soldier's duty, on pain of death, to carry out without question every order he received and to remain in service until he was officially dismissed. By this act the soldiers formally entered the service of the state that had recruited them, and in token thereof they received their first month's pay (albeit the money was actually paid to the captain, who deducted any advances already made in the form of food, pocket money, or clothes before giving each man his due). After that, the company marched off either directly to the theater of operations or to a port of embarkation.

The normal geography of recruiting also proved to be remarkably similar all across Europe. Upland pastoral villages had traditionally been the nurseries of armies—especially the sub-Alpine lands of South Germany, Austria, and Switzerland—and the seventeenth century was not an exception. Most soldiers in most armies during the Baroque age apparently came from two other areas, however—the towns and the war zone itself. Thus a study of French soldiers recruited in the mid-seventeenth century shows that 52 percent came from the towns whereas less than 15 percent of the French population as a whole lived in towns. The reasons for this were simple: in the first place, the towns normally possessed a considerable floating population that, especially in periods of economic depression, might find employment in an army a welcome alternative to starvation at home; in the second, most country people would come to the town's market at regular intervals and would thus take news back to their villages about the presence of any recruiting officer in the vicinity. So on both scores it made good sense for the captain to concentrate his efforts in the urban centers. It also made good sense to recruit as close to the war zone as possible, both because of the increased dislocation there and because of the reduced distance to be traveled to "the front." Although few armies kept systematic records of their troops in the seventeenth century, the fragmentary available evidence suggests that the average age of the soldiers at enlistment was about twenty-four, and that almost one-quarter of them joined up in their teens.

These raw facts provide a clue to the principal motive of those who volunteered for military service: hardship. Most of them would have echoed the refrain of the soldier in Cervantes's *Don Quixote* (Part II, book xxxiv): "Necessity takes me to the war; if I had money, truly I would never go." Some were "social failures," men who had already left their villages and tried unsuccessfully to make a living in the towns, who could not (or would not) follow the trade or calling of their fathers, or who, in the unsympathetic words of the Irish government in 1641, "are men for the most part unskillful in agriculture or manufacture and have been so much bred in sloth and idleness as they are inept, and indeed indisposed, to labor on useful industry, which is one of the causes of their want and poverty, whence they are now induced to seek their fortune abroad."[2] But to these were often added men thrown out of work by economic recession or whose crops had been devastated by natural or human agency. All recruiting officers noted that it was far easier to find men when prices were high or when work was scarce, and the amount of money paid as "enlistment bounty" varied accordingly. In France the bounty paid in the winter of 1706–7 stood at around 50 livres because prices were relatively low; in 1707–8, as prices rose, it dropped to 30 livres, and in 1708–9 to only 20. In 1709–10, after the worst winter in a century, men enlisted without asking for a bounty at all, for the price of bread was so high that enlistment offered the starving poor one of their few chances of survival.

But not all volunteers were driven by economic hardship. A second and somewhat smaller group comprised those who desired a "change of scenery." Some were indeed impelled by a temporary crisis at home such as the threats of an irate father (or putative father-in-law) or the risk of appearing in court for some criminal or moral offense. Others simply desired to see the world or to add some military experience to their general education. It was common, for example, for English gentlemen engaged in the "Grand Tour" in the 1620s and 1630s to spend a few weeks under canvas amid the siege works of an army in the Netherlands. Others still were attracted by the excitement and danger of military endeavor with the chance of winning glory and the thrill of belonging to an exclusive "in-group" (which in Germany even created a vocabulary of its own, *Rotwelsch*).[3] Sir James Turner, a Scot who fought for both Denmark and Sweden during the 1630s, confessed that he went to the wars because "a restless desire [had] entered my mind to be, if not an actor, at least a spectator of these wars which at that time made so much noise over all the world."[4] Finally, Robert Monro—another Scotsman in Swedish service, who wrote the first regimental history in the English language, *Monro his Expedition with the Worthy Scots Regiment call'd Mackays*— although admitting to a desire for travel and adventure and for military experience under an illustrious leader, placed above these motives for fighting on the continent the desire to defend the Protestant faith and the claims and the honor of Elizabeth Stuart, his king's sister and the widow of the defeated "Winter King" of Bohemia.

But Monro was an officer and was therefore free to choose the cause for which he would fight; most of his men had another motive—they were commanded to do so by their clan chief, for almost all of the soldiers in Mackay's regiment were named Mackay! Likewise many of the Scots troops brought by James, marquis of Hamilton, to serve Gustavus Adolphus in 1631 bore the same name as their colonel. It was the same in France. Even when the armies of Louis XIV rose to four hundred thousand men, recruiting by officers of their relatives and personal "lieges" still played an important part in securing volunteers. Clearly, adding a family or a feudal bond to normal military obligations could only strengthen the cohesion of units, and so colonels employed either kindred or neighbors as their officers whenever possible and recruited as many of their vassals as they could.

Finally, as the century advanced yet another motive for enlistment became prominent: an increasing number of volunteers now chose the army as their career because they were literally born to it. The marriage registers kept by garrison churches reveal that both brides and grooms were often *huius castri filia* (or *filius*: a "child of this army"), while the muster rolls of many units involved in the latter stages of the Thirty Years War included an increasing number of soldiers who, like the children of "Mother Courage," had done nothing but serve in armies. Clearly, when one war ended these men who knew no other trade would be likely to seek another conflict in which to exercise their profession. Small wonder that after the Thirty Years War ended in 1648 Germany became a prime recruiting ground for other states.

There was nothing new in this, however, for most early modern armies regularly included a substantial foreign component. Thus the Spanish Army of Flanders, the first large standing army in Europe, comprised Spanish, Italian, Burgundian, and Netherlands troops—all of them subjects of the king of Spain—but perhaps one-third of the army came from England, Ireland, and (above all) Germany. There were good reasons for this multinationalism. In the first place, it was simply not possible in the seventeenth century for a state suddenly to raise a major army entirely from its own subjects. In the words of a perceptive French military writer, Blaise de Vigenère, "As for the Spaniards, one cannot deny that they are the best soldiers in the world; but there are so few of them that scarcely five or six thousand can be raised at a time." The same was true of the French army: Cardinal Richelieu noted in his *Political Testament* (1642), "It is almost impossible to undertake major wars successfully with French troops alone."[5] At least one-fifth of the armies of both Louis XIII and Louis XIV were recruited abroad: twenty-five thousand Irish soldiers are believed to have fought for France between 1635 and 1664, alongside numerous German and Swiss regiments raised in both Catholic and Protestant states.

A second good reason for raising foreign as opposed to local troops was to minimize the risk of desertion. As a commander of the Spanish Army of Flanders observed in 1630: "If there should be war in Italy, it would be better to send Netherlanders there and bring Italians here [to the Netherlands], because the troops native to the country where the war is being fought disband very rapidly and there is no surer strength than that of foreign soldiers." Shortly afterwards he added: "At the moment no war can be fought . . . except with the foreign troops, because the local units disintegrate at once."[6] The Spanish monarchy therefore operated what amounted to a military expatriation system in which troops were deliberately sent abroad to serve. Although no other state went to such lengths, the Dutch, Polish, Russian, Imperial, and Swedish armies all relied heavily on foreign formations throughout the seventeenth century.

These "foreign troops," however, although they too were largely volunteers, could not be recruited directly by commission because they were the subjects of other states. Instead they were raised by independent military contractors or entrepreneurs. The terms were simple to arrange: a contract was signed that bound the government to advance a certain sum of money to the contractor, together with the promise of regular fixed wages thereafter, and the right to name all his own officers; in return the contractor undertook to present a given number of men within a certain time at an agreed place. Most contractors could work fast because they were professionals; they normally kept a skeleton force of officers and NCOs permanently on call, ready to raise the rest within a matter of days.

The system reached its apogee during the Thirty Years War, during which some fifteen hundred individuals were raising troops under contract all over Europe from Scotland to Russia for one or more warlords. Perhaps four hundred military enterprisers operated between 1630 and 1635, raising and maintaining fully equipped companies, regiments, and brigades. There were also several successful attempts to raise entire armies in this way, with a "general contractor" undertaking to recruit a corps of many regiments for a state. Although Albert of Wallenstein, who raised a whole Imperial army on two occasions (in 1625 and 1631–32) is the most famous example of this extreme form of military devolution, there were others: Count Ernest of Mansfeld for the Dutch in the 1620s; the marquis of Hamilton for Sweden, and Duke Bernard of Saxe-Weimar for France in the 1630s.

The basic qualification for a military entrepreneur was management skills. Victory in action was, somewhat surprisingly, not a prerequisite, for some leaders (such as Mansfeld and Dodo von Knyphausen in the 1620s) seem to have led their army from one defeat to another while nonetheless managing to hold their troops together through the skillful and ingenious organization of limited resources. But wealth proved essential for success. Wallenstein advanced over six million thalers to the emperor between 1621 and 1628, with which he funded the army that defeated the Protestant coalition ranged against him and overran both North Germany and the Jutland peninsula. Bernard of Saxe-Weimar, whose inheritance as a younger son was tiny, in 1637 estimated his personal fortune at 450,000 thalers (roughly one-third of it in cash, one-third in letters of exchange, and one-third in a Paris bank), which enabled him to hold together the forces that took Breisach, France's precious bridgehead across the Rhine, the following year.

On the whole, the prestige of these commanders usually proved sufficient to attract volunteers; but when it was not they sometimes received assistance from the local authorities, anxious to get rid of "undesirable elements" such as criminals or the "idle poor." Thus in 1626 the clansmen who joined Mackay's regiment to serve in Denmark were augmented by some prisoners from the local jails who were taken to the docks under heavy guard and made to swear before embarkation "that they shall never return again within this kingdom under pain of death." In the following year another Scots colonel was empowered to impress into his regiment for service in Germany all "strong and sturdy beggars and vagabonds, masterless men and idle loiterers who lack trades and competent means to live upon." The government justified this somewhat cavalier attitude towards the unemployed because (it claimed) they "spend their time in alehouses, and so are unprofitable burdens to the country; whereas they might be very well spared to serve in the wars, and were better so to be employed than to lie so unprofitably loitering at home."[7]

This practice therefore amounted to a form of conscription, and it was sometimes used even for "national levies." Thus in 1646 the Spanish war ministry arranged a swoop on the brothels and taverns of Madrid: all eligible males found within were manacled, bundled into carts, and taken to fight for the king in Catalonia. The following year the ministry informed its officers that if troops could not be raised in any other way, "if there are any men in the prisons of the kingdom of a suitable age for service, provided they are not there for heinous offenses [*delictos atroces*] they may be set free, commuting their sentences to service in these companies for a limited period."[8] But such desperate measures remained confined, in almost all countries, to times of extreme military pressure and to social groups commonly regarded as "expendable." The sole permanent form of compulsory military service to be found in early modern Europe was the *indelningsverk* (or "allocation system") introduced into Finland and metropolitan Sweden during the first quarter of the seventeenth century. The government attempted a first scheme of universal impressment in the 1600s, compiling registers that listed all men over the age of fifteen. Then, after 1620, a fixed ratio was established whereby one soldier had to be provided, equipped, and fed by each parish for every ten eligible male parishioners. However, some social groups remained more likely than others to be drafted: those absent from the meeting held to select the soldiers were—predictably—among the first to be conscripted, while noblemen, clerics, miners, armaments workers, or the only sons of widows were normally exempt. Inevitably in this predominantly rural society, most Swedish soldiers were therefore peasants: in the voluminous (but as yet little analyzed) records of the national forces that created Sweden's continental empire in the seventeenth century, *bonde* (peasant farmer) is by far the commonest entry in the enrollment lists. Each year the government specified the overall number of recruits required and allocated a quota to each province and parish. The totals may seem small— eleven thousand in 1628, eight thousand in 1629, nine thousand in 1630, and so on—but it must be recalled that Sweden was a small country with a total adult male population of less than five hundred thousand.

Paradoxically, one reason why so many men had to be raised— whether by commission, contract, or conscription—was that a considerable number of the new recruits soon began to regret their decision to enlist. Particularly during the first half of the century, even though it bore the death penalty desertion represented a major problem for all armies, especially during the long sieges that constituted the most common military action of the Baroque age. Thus at the siege of Bergen-op-Zoom by the Spanish Army of Flanders in 1622 almost 40 percent of the 20,600 soldiers encamped around the town were lost, many of them by desertion. From the walls of Bergen the guards regularly saw their adversaries slyly leave their posts, pretending to forage for wood or for vegetables to dig up, gradually moving farther and farther away from the trenches until they finally made their break for freedom. Others, at least twenty-five hundred men (one-third of the total wastage), adopted the desperate remedy of deserting to the very town they were besieging! "From dawn until dusk one could see the soldiers jumping like rabbits from their holes, leaving the trenches, hedges, thickets, and ditches where they had hidden, in order to run breathless to the town." On one occasion, a group of attackers threw down their arms during an assault and defected to the other side in order to escape. Some of the deserters were Italians, newly arrived in the Netherlands; all they asked for in Bergen was "a little bread and a little money" with, if possible, a safe-conduct to go home. One of them gave a particularly expressive account of conditions among the besiegers: "Where have you come from?" asked the guards. "D'infierno"—from hell—he replied.[9]

The French government during the first half of the century acted on the assumption that in order to bring twelve hundred men to the front it was necessary to recruit two thousand, since desertion and sickness would normally account for 40 percent of the levies in the first few months. Thus in 1635, the first year of open war with Spain, commissions were issued to raise 145,000 men in order to produce an effective strength at the front of just 69,000. Executing a handful of those caught deserting seemed to bring no improvement, for the problem arose not from fear but from desperation. As the commander-in-chief of the Spanish Army of Flanders put it in 1635:

> The majority of the soldiers who serve in these provinces do so with much discontent and affliction. Of the four or five thousand applications for a discharge that are pending, the majority say that they will be happy with just a permit to leave in payment for all their services. This arises from the fact that the fighting here is very fierce, of long duration, and great hardship, whereas the lack of wages causes great misery; so that those who come here think about this, and about the state in which they see their compatriots, and they soon regret that they ever came.[10]

Desertion rates therefore only fell when conditions of service improved—when regular pay, a constant supply of food, and some system of leave were introduced. The feat was first achieved in France, where Louis XIV's powerful minister of war, the marquis of Louvois, did much to improve the lot of the French soldier. Thanks to this, and to draconian penalties not only against deserters but also against those who assisted and sheltered them, desertion began to come under control. Nevertheless between 1684 and 1714 some 16,500 illegal fugitives from the army went in chains to Marseilles as convicts to serve on the galleys.

SUPPLYING WAR

However, the majority of the troops raised in Europe throughout the Baroque age, whether recruited by commission, contract, or conscription, did not desert. They accepted military discipline and the conditions set out in the Articles of War in the expectation of receiving pay, sustenance, and (in certain circumstances) plunder in return for their services. But to promise was one thing, to perform was quite another. Throughout the first half of the century, and in some countries long afterwards, no government actually commanded financial resources sufficient to maintain all its armed forces. Although taxes were raised, loans taken out, and assets alienated, the cost of waging war regularly exceeded the funds available. So instead of paying each man his due in cash, most armies were supported by a complicated scheme of "alternative finance." The system of devolution was bitterly satirized in a contemporary novel about the Thirty Years War, *Der abenteuerliche Simplicissimus Teutsch* (*The Adventures of Simplicissimus the German*). Its author, Hans Jakob Christoffel von Grimmelshausen, treated the subject with an elaborate simile that compared the army hierarchy on paydays to a flock of birds in a tree. Those on the topmost branches, he claimed, "were at their best and happiest when a commissary-bird flew overhead and shook a whole panfull of gold over the tree . . . for they caught as much of that as they could and let little or nothing at all fall to the lowest branches, so that, of those who sat there, more died of hunger than of the enemy's attacks." [11]

In fact Grimmelshausen's vision was somewhat distorted because the birds on the lowest branches—the army's rank and file—actually received considerable sustenance by other means. First came plunder. Every soldier's dream was to participate in the successful assault on a town that refused to surrender, because then, according to the contemporary Law of War, it could be sacked and its inhabitants legitimately deprived of their liberty, their property, and even their lives. The ransoms and goods acquired at the sack of a rich town could turn every victorious soldier into a prince. Thus the Imperial troops who sacked Mantua in 1630 or the French army that ravaged the Palatinate in 1688–89 returned home with tons of booty, while the plunder accumulated by Cromwell's Ironsides during their successful Scottish campaign from the battle of Dunbar in 1650 to the sack of Dundee one year later filled sixty ships. But lesser targets might also provide considerable enrichment. Merchant convoys could be ambushed and either looted or ransomed; unfortified villages or isolated farmhouses could be sacked and burned with impunity. Nor was violence directed only at property: men, women, and children were tortured if the troops suspected they knew of further hidden supplies; women were routinely raped, often repeatedly. A saying during the Thirty Years War ran, "Every soldier needs three peasants: one to give up his lodgings, one to provide his wife, and one to take his place in Hell."

Such conduct was not only cruel, however, it also proved to be "inefficient," both because supplies and workers that might be valuable to other units in the army were alienated, destroyed, or removed and because it risked provoking civilian counterattack. Thus when the army commanded by Gustavus Adolphus entered Bavaria in the summer of 1632, according to one of its colonels, Robert Monro, "The peasants on the march cruelly used our soldiers (that went aside to plunder) in cutting off their noses and ears, hands and feet, pulling out their eyes, with sundry other cruelties which they used; being justly repaid by the soldiers, in burning of many villages on the march, leaving also the peasants dead, where they were found." [12] In order to avoid such wanton destruction, the army severely punished soldiers who oppressed civilians. At least five men in Monro's regiment were executed by firing squad, and several others were condemned to death by the military provost for the maltreatment of the civilian population.

As wars continued it became essential to establish a more rational means of exploiting local resources, beginning with the provision of free accommodations. This had already become standard practice in states with a standing army such as Spanish Milan, and the archives of garrison towns like Alessandria bristle with documents (letters, orders, bills, statements) concerning the cost of lodging the garrison in private houses and supplying them with beds, bed linens, candles, firewood, dishes, room service, and even whores. [13] Even when the soldiers slept four or five to a bed, it was reckoned that troops survived better when billeted in private houses than when quartered in barracks, despite the inevitable loss of discipline. As Michel Le Tellier, then an inspector of the French army in Italy, wrote in 1642: "Two months' pay and lodgings with the peasants in [France] is worth a lot more [to the troops] than three months' pay and a barracks in Turin." [14]

These cozy (and, to the state, economical) arrangements were only viable for a garrison of modest proportions. Few towns in seventeenth-century Europe could boast over ten thousand inhabitants: they (and still less the rural areas) simply could not feed and lodge for very long twenty, thirty, even (toward the end of the century) one hundred thousand soldiers. The growth in the size and permanence of armies therefore gave rise to the development of alternatives to "free quartering." Increasingly, the soldiers were expected to live when not on active service in multi-bed, purposely built barracks and, when on the march, in tents. For other essentials—above all for food, clothes, and transport—resort was made to "contributions" in the form of tax assessments levied directly from each community in the army's vicinity, paid either in cash or in items needed by the troops. At the crudest level, the "contributions" were extracted against a simple threat: the village would be burned to the ground unless the troops' needs were met. But this technique was inappropriate if an army anticipated a prolonged stay in an area, for one could only put a place to the torch once. A new system therefore grew up, beginning in the Low Countries in the early years of the century under the direction of the

Genoese military entrepreneur Ambrogio Spinola, who commanded the Army of Flanders between 1603 and 1628. It was pointed out to him that "if he would master and overcome his enemies . . . he should set his affections more upon the people than upon his soldiers. For . . . whilst their pay is a-digging in Peru, your soldiers may starve in Flanders; but if you make much of the people they will give you bread together with their blessings." [15]

Over time, the regimental and company clerks on the one hand and the local magistrates on the other worked out a schedule of contributions. A receipt was signed for all items issued to the troops, and the total was then deducted both from their future wages and from the taxes due to the government from the community. In addition, local commanders issued letters of protection that (in theory at least) guaranteed that the village would not have to pay contributions to any other military units in the area. When an army went on campaign the scheme marched with it: an "early warning system" sprang up among communities along an army's projected line of march so that the necessary provisions for the troops could be made ready in advance. Once again, the cost of all items provided was set against taxes due.

The state still needed to provide a certain amount of money, but it represented only a fraction of what the army actually cost. In a letter of January 1626, written at the beginning of his first generalship, Wallenstein informed the Imperial finance minister that he needed "a couple of million thalers every year to keep this long-running war going." But this was written at a time when Wallenstein's army included 110,000 men and cost at least ten million thalers! Moreover none of the emperor's money went directly to the troops: instead Wallenstein used it to maintain his personal credit and to provide his officers and soldiers with the goods and services essential to their survival as an effective fighting force. Thanks to this and to the contributions, wages could wait until the war's end.

By the 1640s most military administrators reckoned to supply between one-half and two-thirds of their troops' wages in kind. This worked to the advantage of the soldiers as well as of the government, for, as Miguel de Cervantes wrote, war makes the miser generous and the generous man profligate, and the soldiers tended to spend their money the moment they got it. Michel Le Tellier, the French minister of war, agreed: "Far from husbanding their resources," he wrote somewhat later, "troops often spend in one day what they are given to last for ten, so they never have anything with which to buy clothes and shoes." [16] Providing these essential items directly therefore made good economic sense for the soldiers as well as for their paymasters. But it is doubtful whether many civilians saw benefits in the alternative system. Admittedly the exact "cost" of contributions will never be known because not all the relevant records have survived; still they certainly constituted a severe and at times damaging burden on the civilian population involved, particularly during the Thirty Years War. It has been estimated, for example, that the Swedish armies between 1631 and 1648 raised ten to twelve times as much through contributions as arrived from the treasury in Stockholm. Village, towns, and even cities could be totally ruined by the arrival of troops in their vicinity.

In the second part of the century, however, contributions ceased to be the mainstay of military finance. In the case of France, for example, by the 1690s they probably accounted for no more than 20 percent of the army's receipts—and their collection had become far more orderly. Now towns and villages were notified of the contributions demanded of them on printed forms, with the blanks individually filled, mailed in advance by post. But extorting even one-fifth of the cost of Louis XIV's armies directly from communities still weighed heavily upon them and could often only be exacted against the threat of putting recalcitrant villages to the torch. In 1691 the king himself observed, "Although it is terrible to be obliged to burn down villages in order to force people to pay the contributions, since one cannot make them pay by either menace or mildness, it is necessary to continue to use extreme means."[17]

One reason for the declining reliance on contributions in supplying war was the desire for equipment of better quality and, above all, of greater uniformity. In the first few decades of the century, to judge from the art of the period and from the military costumes preserved in various museums, it would seem that soldiers normally wore what they wished. But some efforts were made to standardize dress and to create "uniforms." Thus when the duke of Neuburg in southern Germany created a militia in 1605, he wished all its men to be equipped in "similar military livery." Likewise the city of Nuremberg ordered its guards, raised in 1619, all to dress alike, and the duke of Brunswick-Wolfenbüttel's two new regiments of the same year were all to be clothed in blue. But these were the exception. Although Gustavus Adolphus of Sweden also commanded regiments that were known by colors ("the red," "the blue," and so forth), this seems to have referred only to the regimental standards under which they fought.

In his "Handbook of War" (Kriegsbüchlein), published in 1651, Hans Conrad Lavater of Zurich included some pages on military attire, but he confined his remarks to garment design and quality without mentioning color. Above all, he advised the prospective soldier, clothing should be "sensible": strong shoes, stout breeches, and thick stockings; two heavy shirts; a buff coat of leather shielded from the rain by a cloak; a wide felt hat to keep off both sun and showers. The garments should be generously cut for added warmth, he continued, but should have no fur and few seams in order to deny breeding grounds to vermin. Clearly no sort of "uniform" was envisaged, and it is easy to see why. To begin with, not all the troops in the armies of the earlier seventeenth century belonged to the same warlord. Among the Imperialists during the 1640s were Saxon, Bavarian, Westphalian, and Spanish units as well as Austrian regiments. Furthermore, even a single formation would include men raised at a wide variety of times and places. In 1644 a Bavarian regiment for which detailed records have survived could boast men from no fewer than sixteen national groups, the largest of which were Germans (534 soldiers) and Italians (217), with smaller numbers of Poles, Slovenes, Croats, Hungarians, Greeks, Dalmatians, Lorrainers, Burgundians, French, Czechs, Spaniards, Scots, and Irish. There were also fourteen Turks. Even if all these men had been issued with the same uniform upon joining the regiment, their clothes would soon wear out and require replacement by items either plundered from the civilian population, stripped from the dead, or purchased during rare moments of leisured affluence. So although clothing of one particular hue may have predominated for a period in a given regimental wardrobe, before long the men would have either become threadbare and dust-covered veterans or else the harlequin figures in rainbow attire portrayed by the military artists of the period.

For much of the seventeenth century, troops on the same side, lacking a uniform, were obliged to adopt distinguishing marks, usually a sash, a ribbon, or a plume of a particular color. Thus the soldiers of the Habsburgs, whether Austrian or Spanish, always wore a red token; those of Sweden wore yellow (or yellow and blue); those of France wore blue; and those of the Dutch wore orange. If two separate armies joined forces a further token was required: when, for example, the various units fighting for William III, many of them wearing distinctive regimental uniforms, combined in northeast Ireland just before the battle of the Boyne in 1690, all the troops placed a green token (often a leafy branch or a fern plucked on their line of march) in their hats.

By that time such a precaution was unusual. In the 1640s the French war ministry was still ordering clothes to be made for the army in one of three fittings—one-half "normal," one-quarter "large," and one-quarter "small"—but saying nothing about the quality or the color. However, when Count Gallas, the Imperial commander-in-chief, placed an order with Austrian clothiers to supply six hundred uniforms for his regiment in 1645, he enclosed a sample of the precise material and the color (pearl gray) to be copied. He also sent samples of the powder horns and cartridge belts to be manufactured en masse by local suppliers. By the end of the century, thanks to a host of similar measures, the same degree of uniformity had been achieved on a national scale, with all troops in a given army wearing coats and breeches of the same color and armed with equipment of the same basic design.

The difficulties inherent in this achievement should not be underestimated. First came the weapons. At the beginning of the seventeenth century, roughly one-half of the infantry required thirteen-foot pikes and body armor; the rest needed five-foot matchlock muskets with their forked rests (or else the shorter and lighter arquebus), plus powder flasks, shot, and slow matches; the cavalry troopers required half-armor and pistols or lances; and all troops needed swords and helmets. As the century advanced, the proportion of firearms, and therefore the number of troops requiring ammunition and accoutrements, increased to about two-thirds. Although these weapons did not have to be absolutely identical (even in the 1690s every soldier was expected to mold bullets from his own lump of lead), a considerable degree of standardization was nevertheless required. That such artifacts could indeed be mass-produced may be seen from the collection of seventeenth-century arms and armor in the Arsenal at Graz in Austria, where thousands of weapons and their accoutrements, all standardized to a high degree though made in various workshops, lie ready for immediate use. Eight thousand men could be equipped, upon demand, within a single day.

Less easily accumulated were horses. In the first decades of the century, it is true, cavalry made up less than 10 percent of most armies in Western Europe: when France went to war against Spain in 1635, orders were issued to raise 132,000 infantry but only 12,400 cavalry. Yet even this relatively small total continued to pose supply problems, since each cavalry trooper would need at least three mounts in the course of a campaign (and sometimes more: at the battle of Breitenfeld in 1631 the Tuscan officer Ottavio Piccolomini had seven horses shot from under him in the course of the day), to say nothing of the horses required by the general staff, the officers, the artillery, and the baggage train. As the size of European armies grew and as the size of their cavalry component increased to around 20 percent later in the century, the horse breeders of Europe found a buoyant market. Naturally there were occasional bottlenecks—after a bloody battle or after an unexpected decision to mobilize—but by and large, simply because military demand proved so constant in the Baroque age, after 1650 most armies could usually find enough horses to supply all their needs.

Food, however, was a different matter. To begin with, no early modern army consisted only of combatants. Many soldiers were accompanied by wives or mistresses; more still had servants or lackeys. When the Spanish Army of Flanders marched to the siege of Bergen-op-Zoom in 1622, three Calvinist pastors in the beleaguered town recorded virtuously that "such a long tail on such a small body never was seen . . . such a small army with so many carts, baggage horses, nags, sutlers, lackeys, women, children, and a rabble that numbered far more than the army itself." [18] It may have been true, although the archives of the Army of Flanders suggest that camp followers during the Low Countries' Wars rarely exceeded 50 percent of the total troops during the seventeenth century. However, in 1646 two Bavarian regiments fighting in Germany consisted of 480 infantrymen accompanied by 74 servants, 314 women and children, 3 sutlers and 160 horses, and of 481 cavalry troopers with 236 servants, 9 sutlers, 102 women and children, and 912 horses.

They all required food and drink. The daily allowance of 0.75 kilograms (a little more than a pound and a half) of bread, 0.5 kilograms (something more than a pound) of meat or cheese, and 2 liters (almost two quarts) of beer (which was the notional ration due to every soldier) sounds reasonable enough, but multiplied by the total number of mouths to feed in an army it created problems that only large cities with long-established alimentary infrastructures normally had to face. An army of thirty thousand soldiers would perhaps have forty-five thousand mouths to feed. To produce the standard bread ration for everyone required 80,000 kilograms of flour to be ground and baked every day; to provide the necessary 22,500 kilograms of meat required the daily slaughter and preparation of 2,500 sheep or 250 bullocks (a surprisingly high figure, owing to the relatively small size of livestock in early modern times); while the beer ration required the brewing and distribution of 90,000 liters of beer every day. Furthermore, ovens (each requiring five hundred bricks) were needed to bake the bread, plus wood to fire the ovens, carts to transport the flour, the ovens, and the wood, and so forth. Finally, the horses needed for this, as well as for the cavalry, the artillery, the officers, and the baggage wagons—a total of perhaps twenty thousand beasts with a major field army—would consume some ninety quintals of fodder, or four hundred acres of grazing, each and every day.

In the second half of the seventeenth century, as army sizes grew, the challenge of organizing such concentrations of military equipment for sustained operations led one state after another to resume the tasks previously delegated to military enterprisers. Perhaps appropriately the pioneer was the only nation in Baroque Europe to be ruled by a professional soldier: the British Republic. No sooner had Charles I been executed in January 1649 than the new Republican government in London decided to invade and conquer Ireland. It was recognized from the outset that because of Ireland's poverty and backwardness the expeditionary force could not "live off the land" but would have to take all its provisions with it. Since England had been at war since 1642, however, the key industries were already on a war footing and could respond rapidly to new orders. Accordingly, between June 1649 and February 1650, some 6 million kilograms of wheat and rye, 250,000 kilograms of cheese, 150,000 kilograms of biscuit, 500,000 liters of beer (plus lesser quantities of salt, salmon, bacon, rice, and raisins) were shipped to Dublin. It would seem that the Republic provided its sixteen thousand soldiers in Ireland with 90 percent of their daily bread, 50 percent of their daily cheese, and 40 percent of their daily beer (the cost being deducted from their pay): a remarkable achievement. But there was more. The army commanded by Oliver Cromwell also brought with it a considerable store of ready money, partly for the soldiers' wages but also for the purchase of additional supplies. A proclamation was issued guaranteeing that "it shall be free and lawful for all manner of persons to . . . bring any provisions unto the army . . . and receive ready money for goods and commodities they shall so bring and sell." All soldiers caught plundering were hanged.[19] Furthermore, over the winter of 1649–50, when Cromwell's army was in winter quarters, the London government organized the dispatch of 17,950 sets of clothes (shoes, stocking, shirts, and breeches) together with 17,000 meters of woven cloth with which to make topcoats and 19,000 meters of canvas to make tents ready for the new campaign. This logistical achievement helped to secure the English conquest of Ireland within a remarkably short time, and it was repeated for the successful 1650–51 campaign in Scotland.

Within three years Cromwell's army thus managed to unify the entire British Isles for the first time: the orders of the government in London were now received and obeyed in every corner of the archipelago without exception. To be sure, the combat effectiveness of Cromwell's army, forged in the civil wars in England, was crucial to this achievement, but his troops were only able to campaign successfully, often in remote areas where no army had ever campaigned before, thanks to their superb supply system. As one of those involved later recalled, "Nothing is more certain than this: that in the late wars both Scotland and Ireland were conquered by timely provisions of Cheshire cheese and biscuit."[20]

The British example was keenly studied abroad, particularly by France (with whom Cromwell formed a brief alliance, so that their armies fought together on the continent for some years). The young French king, Louis XIV, quickly saw the value of a standing army and became convinced that a network of regular suppliers and of military magazines was needed for its support. With a peacetime army of 150,000 men, a steady and predictable demand existed that soon created—as it had in Republican Britain—a permanent, specialized infrastructure capable of responding to sudden military emergencies with food, clothes, and equipment for the new troops. With such centralization it was but a short step to uniformity, and by the 1680s the French army was already all dressed in the "national blue" and was equipped with weapons of standard design. Of course the cost was outrageous—Louis XIV spent 75 percent of the state's revenues on war in the 1690s (Cromwell had spent 90 percent in the 1650s!)—but the rewards seemed impressive: the borders of France were advanced in all directions and the power of the state over its subjects increased. The new model armies had proved their worth; the methods pioneered by Cromwell and Louis XIV were swiftly copied all over Europe.

THE FATE OF THE SOLDIER

In 1601 Lord Mountjoy (Queen Elizabeth of England's successful commander in Ireland) allowed his defeated enemies to enlist in foreign armies because (he claimed) "it has ever been seen that more than three parts of the four of these countrymen do never return, being once engaged in any such voyage." [21] Recent research has confirmed this grim arithmetic. The parish of Bygdeå in northern Sweden, for example, provided 230 young men for service in Poland and Germany between 1621 and 1639 and saw 215 of them die there, while five others returned home crippled. Although the remainder—a mere ten men—were still in service in 1639, it is unlikely that any of them survived to see the war's end nine years later, for of the 29 Bygdeå conscripts of the year 1638 all but one were dead within a year of their departure for Germany. Enlistment, in effect, had become a sentence of death. Not surprisingly, the number of adult males in Bygdeå decreased by 40 percent, from 468 in 1621 to 288 in 1639, and the age of the conscripts gradually fell as more and more teenagers were drafted, never to return. Of the soldiers sent abroad in 1639, one-half were only fifteen years old and all but two were under eighteen. By 1640 the number of houses in the parish headed by women had increased sevenfold. Total losses in the Swedish army between 1621 and 1632 have been estimated at fifty to fifty-five thousand; losses between 1633 and the war's end in 1648 were probably at least twice as high.

Nor was this high military mortality unique to Sweden. It has been estimated that overall probably one out of every four or five soldiers who enlisted in the armies of Baroque Europe died each year on active service, with the ratio increasing as the century advanced. Thus perhaps six hundred thousand soldiers died during the Thirty Years War (1618–48; an average of twenty thousand per year) and seven hundred thousand during the Spanish Succession War (1702–13; an average of sixty-four thousand per year).

How can these high figures be explained? One critical tactical innovation of the seventeenth century that increased the threat of death in action was the relentless rise of more effective gunpowder weapons. Of course the field gun, the musket, and the pistol had all been used before, but they had seldom been used to such deadly effect. After 1600, improvements in iron casting made it possible to reduce the weight of most firearms, making them easier to transport and more accurate to shoot; better firing methods—above all the flintlock mechanism from the 1630s—made them more reliable; the invention of the socket bayonet in the 1670s allowed the musket to be used to cut and thrust as well as to fire.

But the most important improvement in the use of firearms lay in the realm of tactics, starting with the military reformation wrought by Maurice of Nassau upon the Dutch army. Inspired by the methods of Imperial Rome and Byzantium described by Aelian and Leo VI, in the 1590s Maurice devised new ways of deploying his troops in action. In place of the phalanxes of pikemen, forty and fifty deep, that had fought the battles of the sixteenth century, he drew up his men only ten deep. His formations were smaller, and they achieved their impact more by firepower than by pike charges. No less than one-half the soldiers in Maurice's army fought with muskets. These changes sound simple, but they made necessary profound adjustments in military organization. On the one hand, reducing the depth of the line inevitably meant extending it, thus exposing more men to the test of hand-to-hand combat and to the incoming fire of the enemy; on the other, because the line was thinner, more discipline and more coordination were required from each man. Above all, the Dutch army perfected the technique of volley firing, which involved the men in each rank discharging their musket simultaneously at the enemy and then retiring to reload while the other nine ranks followed suit, creating a continuous hail of fire. But to perform this maneuver in the face of the enemy required considerable fortitude, perfect coordination, and great familiarity with all the actions involved. Therefore Maurice reintroduced the drill used in the Roman army.

Maurice's insistence on precision and harmony in war mirrored the general preoccupation of the Baroque age with geometrical forms—whether in building, riding, dancing, gardening, painting, fencing, or fighting—and his ideas were widely admired and imitated. As early as 1603 a French military work devoted an entire chapter to "The Exercises Used in the Dutch Army," and in 1608 the first pictorial drill manual of Western Europe, composed by Maurice's cousin, John of Nassau, was published at Amsterdam as *The Exercise of Arms* under the name of Jacob de Gheyne, a well-known engraver. Many other works imitated de Gheyne's technique of a numbered sequence of pictures to illustrate the precise maneuvers required to handle military weapons and to organize troops for war. Then in 1616 Count John opened a military academy (the first in Europe) at his capital, Siegen, expressly to produce a professional officer corps. The first director of the *Schola militaris*, Johann Jacob von Wallhausen, published several manuals of warfare modeled on the Dutch example, which formed the basis of all teaching at Siegen (where training took six months, with arms, armor, maps, and models for instruction provided by the school).

The diffusion of the new tactics did not occur merely in print or in school, however: Maurice also supplied military instructors to foreign states. Brandenburg requested and received two instructors in 1610, and in the course of the next ten years others went to the Palatinate, Baden, Württemberg, Hesse, Brunswick, Saxony, and Holstein. Even the tradition-minded Swiss, who had first demonstrated the potential of the pike in their struggle against fifteenth-century Burgundy, were forced to take note: in 1628 the Berne militia was reorganized on unashamedly Dutch lines, with smaller companies and greater firepower. However, Maurice's most influential disciple was unquestionably Gustavus Adolphus of Sweden. On a tour of Germany in 1620 Gustavus saw many different forms of military organization and fortification, and he read all the major books on the subject. On his return he took Maurice's reforms slightly further by reducing the depth of the musketry line in the Swedish army from ten to six ranks and by increasing its firepower through the addition of four light field pieces per regiment. Every man was given rigorous training in his work by the numerous officers and NCOs. An effort was made to keep the troops busy all the time, digging ramparts, scouting, or drilling. The king sometimes gave his troops personal instruction in the new discipline: he would himself show new recruits how to fire a musket standing up, kneeling, and lying down. Units recruited abroad were made to watch demonstrations of the "Swedish order of discipline" by the veterans, including the double volley with the musketeers standing but three deep, one rank on their knees, the second crouching, the third standing in order to "pour as much lead into your enemies' bosom at one time [as possible] . . . and thereby you do them more mischief . . . for one long and continuous crack of thunder is more terrible and dreadful to mortals than ten interrupted and several ones" (according to Sir James Turner, who saw the deadly tactic in operation).[22]

The most important difference between the Swedish and Dutch "military revolutions" lay not in technique but in application and in scale. Maurice of Nassau rarely fought a battle (and when he did so his field army numbered scarcely ten thousand men) because the terrain on which he operated was dominated by a network of fortified cities that made battles largely irrelevant, since the towns still had to be besieged. Gustavus, however, operated in areas that had been spared from war, and even the threat of war, for seventy years or more. There were therefore far fewer well-defended towns—although where they existed they had to be besieged—and the control of large areas could therefore be decided by the outcome of a battle. The most favorable publicity that the new military system could have found was Gustavus's victory at Breitenfeld in 1631. It was the classic confrontation between the traditional battle order used since the Italian wars of the Renaissance and the new: the Imperialists, standing predominantly in pike squares thirty deep and fifty wide, faced a Swedish army six deep for musketeers and five for pikes, with twice as many field guns. The superiority of firepower was overwhelming. The Swedish artillery could throw a nine-kilogram iron shot about seventeen hundred meters every six minutes; Gustavus's musketeers—who made up slightly more than one-half the total—could fire repeated salvos of lead shot, each one about twenty millimeters in diameter, with considerable accuracy up to fifty meters (and with about 50 percent accuracy up to one hundred meters).

These various developments spelled death for large numbers of soldiers, but although the medical practitioners of early modern Europe could cure many "clean" wounds caused by swords and pikes, they were powerless to heal the bones shattered by musket and cannon ball. Seven thousand six hundred men—over one-fifth of the defeated Imperialists—were killed at Breitenfeld, and as the century advanced and the percentage of musketeers and the number of field guns increased, the number of battle casualties increased accordingly. Thus at the battle of Malplaquet in 1709 both sides lost roughly 25 percent of their strength, in all amounting to perhaps fifty thousand dead in a single day. Losses in battle usually seem to have been heavy, however long the engagement itself lasted. If the two sides were evenly matched, as at Malplaquet, the slaughter on the field was terrible. If, on the other hand, the odds were uneven, the defeat of the small force might be followed by hot pursuit and yet greater slaughter, since many fugitive soldiers, and sometimes entire units, could be killed in cold blood by their adversaries (sometimes assisted by the local peasantry). Even an orderly retreat could have a high cost in human life. Thus after its defeat at the battle of Tuttlingen (in Bavaria) in November 1643, the French army under Turenne was compelled to abandon its baggage and fall back to the Rhine in the depths of winter: of the sixteen thousand men who survived the battle, barely one-third survived the retreat. The following year, an Imperial army that had invaded Holstein was adroitly forced by its enemies to return through areas so devastated that most of the troops died of starvation. According to a contemporary chronicler, of the eighteen thousand men who began the retreat barely one thousand reached their homes, so that "it would be hard to find a similar example of an army brought to ruin in such a short time without any major battle." As Cardinal Richelieu noted in his *Testament politique* at precisely this time, "One finds in the history books that many more armies perished through lack of food and lack of order than through enemy action."[23]

Sieges, far more common than battles in most wars, were equally destructive of men. Thus in 1628, of the 7,833 English soldiers embarked at Portsmouth for the relief of La Rochelle in France, 409 were lost almost at once in the landing on the Île de Ré, 100 in the trenches, and 120 by dysentery; 3,895 more died either in ill-fated assaults on the French redoubts or in the final retreat; a further 320 went missing. Only 2,989 survived the campaign to return home to Portsmouth in October: a loss of 62 percent in three months. During the blockade of Stralsund in the same year Mackay's Scots regiment of nine hundred men served among the defenders for six weeks continuously. According to their colonel even their food was brought to them at battle stations, and "we were not suffered to come off our posts for our ordinary recreation, nor yet to sleepe . . . [while] our clothes never came off, except it had been to change a suit or linings." Not surprisingly, during these forty days of intense active service no less than five hundred men of the regiment were killed and a further three hundred (including the colonel) injured. Yet the Scots considered themselves lucky, for had Stralsund been taken by assault they might all have been killed, like the garrison of Frankfurt-on-Oder in 1631, who were slaughtered in defeat where they stood. It took six days to bury the three thousand Imperialist defenders, together with the eight hundred soldiers who died making the assault, so that "in the end they were cast by heapes in great ditches, above a hundred in every grave."[24]

Needless to say, many soldiers died of other causes than wounds. For, as Sir James Turner observed, even without the hazard of combat military life was hard, especially for new recruits "who knew not before what it was like not to have two or three meals a day and go to bed at a seasonable hour at night," for now they had to "lie constantly in the fields with little or no shelter, to march always on foot and drink water." In 1620 an army of Italians marching from Lombardy to the wars in the Low Countries was dismissed by an observer as "not men to be reckoned with: those in the first two ranks were good enough, with a martial spirit about them, but the rest were poor boys between sixteen and twenty years old, sickly and ill-clothed, the majority without hats or shoes. Their carts are already full of sick men, although they have only been on the march five days, and I firmly believe that . . . half of them will fall by the wayside."[25] The journey from Milan to Brussels meant a march of a thousand kilometers, and it included crossing the Alps (usually by the Mont Cenis Pass), but at least this was a journey through friendly territory. Other armies were less fortunate. Between 1630 and 1633 the Swedish army marched five thousand kilometers through Germany—from Peenemünde in the Baltic, via Mainz on the Rhine and Munich in Bavaria, back to Brandenburg, fighting most of the way. In 1654, in a three-months campaign through the inhospitable glens and passes of the Scottish Highlands, the conquering

English army covered some sixteen hundred kilometers. Not surprisingly, more men died of exhaustion than of enemy action.

Finally, besides wounds, exhaustion, and starvation, many soldiers died through disease. In the Scots brigade serving in Germany between 1626 and 1633 some 10 percent of the regiments appear to have been sick at any one moment, with epidemics increasing the rate dramatically from time to time. The Imperialists who entered Italy in 1630–31 to participate in the War of Mantua brought with them bubonic plague, which not only decimated their own forces but also cut a wide swath through the population of Lombardy (and furnished Alessandro Manzoni with the unforgettable background for *The Betrothed*).

But what of the soldiers who did not die in service? Some were spared, at least temporarily, by capture. During the first half of the century, common soldiers were normally either freed after swearing not to bear arms against the victor for a certain period, or else they were encouraged to join the army to which they had surrendered. In 1631 even the Italians captured by Gustavus Adolphus in his Rhineland campaign were welcomed into the Swedish army (though they deserted as soon as they reached the foothills of the Alps the following summer). In 1645 in England, after the great Parliamentary victory of Naseby, many Royalist soldiers (either captured in the battle or at the subsequent surrender of garrisons) joined Cromwell's army. But clearly this practice of turning yesterday's enemies into tomorrow's bodyguards was potentially dangerous, and so as the century advanced a series of alternatives became the norm. Thus the ransoming of prisoners of war became standard. After the battle of Jankow (1645), for example, the entire general staff of the defeated Imperialists was offered for ransom by the victors at 120,000 thalers. But this was exceptional: normally a tariff of ransoms was agreed and published in advance—so much for a general, so much for a colonel, and so on down the scale—and prisoners were exchanged after a campaign according to their "value." In the meantime full wages were earned by the troops while they were prisoners of war and free bread rations were issued to their wives.

Better care was also taken of the wounded and the sick, with special military hospitals established by most governments in the course of the seventeenth century. Here the Spanish Army of Flanders led the way, with a hospital at Mechelen (founded in 1585 and eventually equipped with 330 beds and served by a staff of 49) where soldiers were treated, with remarkable success, of everything from diseases like syphilis and malaria through combat injuries to psychological stress and battle trauma (termed *mal de corazón* in the documents). The troops themselves helped to finance this service through a deduction of one real per month from every man's monthly wage and the yield of fines imposed on officers and men for blasphemy. The Army of Flanders also established a special home for its crippled veterans (the "Garrison of Our Lady of Hal"), which in 1640 numbered 346 men. In return for nominal guard duties these soldiers received free board, pay, and lodging. Until the 1650s, however, these humane arrangements in the South Netherlands apparently remained unique. Most commanders seem to have had little time for their wounded except on special occasions: at the height of a Swedish attack on the Alte Veste near Nuremberg in 1632, Wallenstein went around his defenders throwing handfuls of coins into the laps of the wounded in order to encourage the rest. But sooner or later other states followed Spain's lead: France with the Hôtel des Invalides (for both injured and old soldiers) from 1670, Britain with the military hospitals of Kilmainham (Dublin) from 1681 and Chelsea (London) from 1684, and so on.

However not all the soldiers of the Baroque age died, grew old, or were injured in service. A considerable number got rich and retired with their winnings. Thus the Imperialist commander Henrik Holck, once a poor man, returned to his native Denmark in 1627 rich enough to pay 50,000 thalers in cash for an estate on Funen; the Swedish general Hans Christoph Königsmarck, who began his military career as a common soldier, died in 1663 with assets worth almost 2 million thalers (183,000 in cash, 1.14 million in letters of credit, 406,000 in lands); and John Churchill, perhaps England's most successful general, retired with the title of duke of Marlborough and a substantial "gratuity" from the nation that enabled him to build a sumptuous residence (Blenheim palace just outside Oxford). Titles and lands were perhaps the commonest reward for military commanders—especially those who had served as contractors for one or more regiments—in the seventeenth century. They may not always have received their full arrears of pay, but they certainly collected ample alternative compensation. Thus in the region around Stralsund in Pomerania, annexed by Sweden at the Peace of Westphalia in 1648, 40 percent of all farms passed into the hands of former army officers (the average domain consisting of fourteen farms), and in Ireland following the Cromwellian conquest in 1649–50 the arrears of both officers and men were settled in lands confiscated from the vanquished (with an average of around fifteen acres). Company officers could also become rich by profiting from the purchase of houses in occupied towns that they would sell later for a profit; by accepting bribes from selected households in return for exemption from billeting; and by inflating artificially the size of their unit in order to claim more food rations and more wages than their due. They, like their men, could also derive some benefit from plunder.

The real problem, however, was not getting rich but staying rich. Sydnam Poyntz, an English officer of humble origins serving in the Thirty

Years War, was not the only man who made his fortune several times over only to lose it again through misfortune or carelessness. As a French moralist noted in 1623, for every soldier who grows rich by war "you will find fifty who gain nothing but injuries and incurable diseases." But perhaps this statement, which of course cannot be verified, was a little too cynical, for injuries and incurable diseases were by no means confined to soldiers. As Thomas Hobbes wrote, the life of all men and women in the seventeenth century was "uncertain, nasty, brutish, and short."[26] In a Baroque Europe where death, disease, and destitution were the common companions of war, it was often safer to be inside an army than outside. Those who, like the soldier in *Don Quixote,* were driven to the wars by necessity may not always have made the wrong career choice. It was after all, as Fulvio Testi said, "the century of the soldier."

NOTES

1. I am most grateful to John A. Lynn, Jane H. Ohlmeyer, and J. Scott Wheeler for generously providing me with some important unpublished material for this chapter.

2. British Library, *Egerton MS* 2533, fol. 121, Lords Justices in Dublin to Secretary Vane, August 3, 1641.

3. A nine-page "Sprachbüchlein" of current soldiers' slang was included in Hans Michel (Johann Michael) Moscherosch, *Wunderliche und warhafftige Gesichte Philanders von Sittewald,* 2 vols. (Strasbourg, 1640–42), "sechster Gesichte: Soldaten Leben."

4. Sir James Turner, *Memoirs of His Own Life and Times,* ed. Thomas Thomson (Edinburgh: n. p., 1829), 3.

5. Blaise de Vigenère, *L'art militaire d'Onosander, autheur grec,* fol. 170v (Paris, 1605); Armand-Jean du Plessis, Cardinal-Duke of Richelieu, *Testament politique,* ed. Louis André, 7th ed. (Paris: Laffont, 1947), 394–95, available in English as *The Political Testament of Cardinal Richelieu,* trans. Henry Bertram Hill (Madison: University of Wisconsin Press, 1961).

6. Bibliothèque Royale, Brussels, MS 16149, fols. 41v–45 and 53v–54v, marquis of Aytona to Philip IV of Spain, December 19, 1630 and April 2, 1631.

7. David Masson, ed., *The Register of the Privy Council of Scotland* (Edinburgh: H. M. General Register House, 1877–), 1625–27 (1899), 385, 542–43.

8. Archivo General de Simancas, *Guerra Antigua,* 1616, unfoliated, consulta of the Council of War, October 2, 1647.

9. *Bergues sur le Soom assiégée* ... (Middelburg, 1623; reprint, Charles Louis Campan, ed., Brussels: Société de l'histoire de Belgique, 1867), 132–33, 255, 321–22, and 407.

10. Archives Générales du Royaume, Brussels, *Secrétairerie d'Etat et de Guerre* 213, fols. 157–58, Cardinal Infante Don Fernando to King Philip IV, October 11, 1635.

11. Hans Jakob Christoffel von Grimmelshausen, *Der abenteuerliche Simplicissimus Teutsch*, bk. 1, chap. 16 (Montbéliard, 1669).

12. Robert Monro, *Monro his Expedition with the Worthy Scots Regiment call'd Mackays*. 2 vols. (Edinburgh, 1637). Vol. 2, pg. 122.

13. See, for example, in Archivio di Stato, Alessandria, the multivolume series *Alloggiamenti*. Volume 4, fol. 133, contains an order for the magistrates to provide eight whores for each company of the garrison.

14. Quoted by Louis André, *Michel Le Tellier et l'organisation de l'armée monarchique* (Paris: F. Alcan, 1906; reprint Geneva: Slatkine, 1980), 73.

15. Cambridge University Library, *Additional Manuscript* 4352, fol. 7, "Discourse concearning ye affaires of Ireland" (ca. 1645), referring to a conversation between Spinola and Jean Richardot.

16. Quoted in André, *Michel Le Tellier*, 341.

17. Archives de Guerre, Paris, A[1] 1041, fol. 303, Louis XIV to Marshal Catinat, July 21, 1691 (draft).

18. Campan, *Bergues sur le Soom*, 247.

19. Wilbur Cortez Abbot with Catherine D. Crone, *The Writings and Speeches of Oliver Cromwell*, 4 vols. (Cambridge, Mass.: Harvard University Press, 1937–47). Vol. 2 (1940), pp. 111–13.

20. Quoted by C. H. Firth, *Cromwell's Army: A History of the English Soldier during the Civil Wars, the Commonwealth and the Protectorate*, 4th ed. (London: Methuen; New York: Barnes & Noble, 1962), 223.

21. Mountjoy to the English Privy Council, May 1, 1601, quoted in R. D. Fitzsimon, "Irish Swordsmen in the Imperial Service in the Thirty Years' War," *The Irish Sword* 9 (1969–70): 22.

22. Sir James Turner, *Pallas Armata: Military Essays of the Ancient Grecian, Roman and Modern Art of War* (London: by M. W. for Richard Chiswell, 1683), 237.

23. Bogislaus Philipp von Chemnitz, *Königlichen schwedischen in Teutschland geführten Kriegs* (ca. 1650), ed. J. J. Nordström and P. F. A. Dahlgren, 4 vols. (Stockholm: P. A. Nordstedt, 1855–59), vol. 4, pg. 168; Richelieu, *Testament politique*, 480.

24. Monro, *Expedition*. Vol. 1, pp. 62, 67, 79–80; vol. 2, pg. 35.

25. Turner, *Memoirs*, 4, 6; Archives de l'Etat, Geneva, *Portefeuille Historique* 2651, Dr. Isaac Wake to the council of Geneva, Turin, July 4, 1620.

26. Eméric Crucé, *Le nouveau Cynée* (Paris, 1623), 13; Thomas Hobbes, *Leviathan* (London, 1651).

3

THE FINANCIER

Daniel Dessert

T HE BAROQUE AGE was not only the "century of the saints." Indeed,
if the effects of the triumphant Counter-Reformation were felt
throughout the continent, it was because that movement brought
with it a number of concerted attempts, by Catholics, to use pastoral care,
reform, and missions to reconquer terrain momentarily abandoned to the
various forms of Protestantism. The enormous and spreading revival of
militant Catholicism was not confined to the religious domain: it
prompted various but always fundamental repercussions in other domains as well, in which financial problems had just as important a place
as missionary zeal or disputes over grace. The "Catholic crusade" was
expressed in a direct and armed confrontation with the Protestant forces.
To some extent religious wars prefigured or engendered conflicts between
nations. Political rivalries and imperialism—Habsburg imperialism in
particular and its corollary in national reactions in France, England, and
the Low Countries—prompted or reinforced the emergence of monarchies of national unity. Thus the weight of the state increased in a European
universe that was emerging little by little from its medieval matrix. The
(relative) triumph of monarchic power over feudal society in France, England, and Spain fostered the rise of a centralized judiciary and fiscal administration that allowed European monarchies to extend control over all
their territories. At the same time it became necessary to keep up increasingly large permanent armies. Because the religious wars shifted imper-
ceptibly to becoming national wars, Europe was soon divided into a Protestant Europe allied with the (Catholic) "most Christian" king, vic-
toriously withstanding the "most Catholic" king and the Empire. Thus
the sixteenth century—the Age of Gold—came to an end, a century that
had seen Spain enjoying all the treasures of the "Indies," which, by widespread redistribution, had benefited all of Europe.

Thanks to these nearly ceaseless hostilities, the seventeenth century was the century of Mars. War swept through the entire continent—civil and religious war in France and England, national war with the rebellion of the United Provinces. The formation of regular armies of as many as a hundred thousand men permanently in arms soon posed serious financial problems unknown in medieval times, when armies of only several thousand men were banded together for a particular occasion. The same was true of the naval forces that played an increasing role in the destiny of nations, as demonstrated by the fate of the "invincible" Spanish Armada and the rise, then the consolidation, of the United Provinces, which, without a navy, could hardly have imposed their independence on their powerful neighbors and their former tutor. In short, as military techniques advanced, soldiers and sailors required ever more arms, equipment, and supplies. As for their pay, its punctual distribution conditioned strategy: no money, no troops. Montecuccoli summarized the problem in a famous aphorism: "Three things are needed for war: first, money; second, money; third, money." This need for cash came on top of the normal requirements of a centralized state for its administration and its diplomacy. Thus it is hardly surprising that the financial question was not only particularly acute in the Baroque age but an obsession for all governments.

The nature of monetary instruments further complicated the problem. In Europe of that day the only known universal means of payment was metallic coin: gold, obviously, but also, and above all, silver, plus the rough copper coins used in everyday life. After the late fifteenth century, Europe profited from the influx of metals from the New World, which created an unexpected increase in the money supply that incontestably facilitated the expansion of states and the success of their political aims. In this sense, war took advantage of a special situation, but in the long run it demanded more than the governments could provide. It was not long before the amount of metal in circulation no longer sufficed for both the needs of the ordinary economy and the insatiable needs of war. This gap between supply and demand represented the chief challenge to all European states, and the fortune (or the misfortune) of the great nations of the old Continent depended upon their success in accumulating the precious gold and silver metals. The various rulers' habitual resources were insufficient to cover their expenses, their war expenses in particular. As martial ventures multiplied, every state faced a deepening debt that threatened to engulf its ambitions. Thus the inevitable struggle between Spain and France translated into a merciless war of money for both peoples and political programs, and in such a situation any individual capable of offering any help, any relief, even modest, to governments in financial difficulty quite logically occupied an important place on the national scene.

This is the background of the financier, a central personage in the society of the Baroque age. After all, he possessed the exceptional, mysterious, and almost miraculous privilege of having resources available when everyone else, beginning with the state itself, was penniless. This gift—which he owed either to his own purse or to credit with third parties—made the money manager a special individual, much courted for that reason but also envied, hence decried by all who were fascinated, irritated, or disturbed by that bizarre aptitude. His brilliant exterior and his obvious wealth endowed him with a dubious aura in which his contemporaries saw both polemical stereotypes and prosaic realities. What is more, the term "financier" has varied in its connotations according to national experience and the humor of historians. It covers a variety of actual situations. Some have used the term for bankers who lent money to the sovereign and guaranteed troop payments effectuated through a network of correspondents throughout Europe. Others have applied it to individuals who held liquid assets of uncertain origin that they advanced to rulers in difficulty at substantial rates of interest. Following the first view, capitalism in the form of commercial and banking interests was the chief response to the monetary crises that shook European powers during the seventeenth century, and the world of commerce and its initiatives for generating profits explain the preponderance of Italian and German bankers in the early modern state. Behind such men lurks the world economy dear to Fernand Braudel, which they dominated in their capacity as specialists in commercial and manufacturing exchanges. The second view requires a more rigorous definition of the money manager, one that takes into account his specific task, his sociological function, and his underlying motivation. Here the financier, not a transparent personage like the banker or the merchant, hid a surprise or two. In a sense banal and basically anonymous, he needs to be unmasked to reveal the discreet circuits that he animated but took great pains to hide from profane eyes.

The usual definition of the financier is as the person who handled the prince's money—an extremely vague definition because any subject of a state who used metal currency for ordinary transactions merited the name of "financier" in a world in which royal privilege gave the monarchy a monopoly over the emission of money. The term should really be reserved for persons who provided the sovereign with the funds that enabled him to meet his obligations. In a word, the financier was a sort of gold broker. This means that despite common opinion, not all those who passed for financiers—bankers and munitions sellers of various sorts—were true financiers. The bankers lent money against state revenues; the credit they offered the king was a false advance, a simple delay in payment, rather than financing in the strict sense. Because the financier provided his own funds he was an essential cog in the machinery of state, and when financial problems were acute he became a social archetype. As a species, financiers have never flourished better than they did under the Bourbon monarchy.

France, with its eighteen to twenty million inhabitants, its extremely varied terrain and fertile soil, its high population and diversified production, came to be the wealthiest monarchy in the West. It was also the country in which power was most continuous, since it was concentrated in the hands of the king (although in this period we are still far from what is usually understood as absolutism). The rapid growth of authority in France was accompanied by the development of an entire judiciary and administrative infrastructure that, despite local opposition, extended over the entire kingdom. This meant that the royal administrators played an important role in society, a role that was enhanced when the sale of offices made the exercise of those posts hereditary. Contrary to what some have suggested, administrative officials did not threaten the power of the aristocracy, whose control over landed income guaranteed that it would remain the prime economic and social force in France, while its oldest houses remained attached to their warrior hegemony. This enabled the king, who ruled over both men and goods, to pursue an aggressive political agenda aimed at imposing his primacy over all of Europe. The struggle with the House of Habsburg was simply one step on the road to hegemony. The Bourbon monarchy, following a centuries-long tradition, saw itself as heading a military state. And indeed, France alone was capable of bringing up its troop strength, within less than fifty years, from a few tens of thousands of men to nearly four hundred thousand, an extraordinary figure for the age. Nor did that effort prevent France, first under Richelieu and then under Colbert, from creating a navy and an entire maritime infrastructure that enabled it to defeat Spain and compete, at least temporarily, with the United Provinces and England.

In view of these militaristic policies, hostilities became the norm rather than the exception. Between 1610 and 1715 France was at war one year out of two, and when it was not actually fighting it was preparing the next combat. This is why financial needs were so very pressing. The king of France was chronically at wit's end and his coffers chronically empty. At every crisis he escaped disaster thanks to the unfailing backing of money interests that came to his aid in spite of the risks involved. French financiers made up a special social category, and, more than anywhere else, the state was dependent upon them. In his social characteristics, his importance in the economy as a whole, and the role that he played vis-à-vis the nation's leaders, the French financier was a figure emblematic of all the problems posed by money managers in the Baroque age. He will be the center of our analysis, not out of chauvinism, but because he was the prototype of the species.

"To put oneself into finance," as contemporaries said, was more than a simple career choice. Such a decision launched a budding financier on a road riddled with dangers, for society and its prejudices made him a marginal figure and a target for all sorts of hostility. In a sense, it was a decision comparable to the religious vocation. In both cases a person voluntarily broke with the world, either for the universally respected service of God or for a scorned adoration of the Golden Calf. Handling money, along with its inevitable consequence and primary aim, profit, placed our candidate in the way of the many negative attitudes concerning money. In a profoundly Christian universe energized by the passions of the Counter-Reformation; in a society whose elites felt or affected scorn for everything to do with the "mechanical arts," commerce, and, even more, financial activities, which they considered beneath them; in a society in great part made up of peasants hard-pressed by the tax collector, it was easy to declare the financier the common enemy and see him as of a breed to be denounced and pursued unremittingly. The obvious social and material success that the profession seemed to offer only reinforced a hatred fed by spite and secret envy. Thus a first definition of the financier that relies on outward appearances might see him as a person who stood up to society and challenged its laws, moral, sacred, and even political. A truly uncomfortable position. If we fail to look closer we will have an image of the financier that is almost entirely negative and riddled with contradictions.

By definition the financier flouted the teachings of the church, which, in all ages, prohibited lending at interest and, in practice, equated money-lending with usury. The Counter-Reformation did little to attenuate the biblical message. The Blessed Alain de Solminihac, bishop of Cahors and a perfect example of the reform-minded prelate in France, set the tone. His terrible judgment, beyond appeal, was that "usury, one of the sins most pernicious for the salvation of souls," was evil because contrary to natural law, divine law, and canon law. Alain's colleague and friend Nicolas Pavillon, the ultra-Jansenist and most austere bishop of Alet, defended Alain's intransigence in his *Rituel*. The financier must necessarily be ejected from Christian society for being what he was; his function destined him for the flames of Hell. It is hard to see why, in a world as religious as that of the seventeenth century, any individual (though there were many who did so) should want to expose himself to this sort of blanket condemnation. This is a first contradiction inherent in the financier: it seems strikingly paradoxical that a society imbued with the sacred should produce so many people who contravened its most rigorous and most explicit prohibitions. From the outset, the financier was something of a pariah, and his difficult relations with his fellow citizens did little to improve a position in all regards painful.

All subjects of the king heaped scorn on the financier. He was the person responsible for managing and collecting state revenues, and the people felt his presence through a series of intermediaries, all of whom they perceived as persecutors. When the state was at war the peasantry bore an increasingly harsh tax burden, paying not only the direct tax—the taille—but also indirect taxes on the circulation and consumption of agricultural products, including wine, beer, and salt, and manufactured goods. Indirect taxation tripled in the one decade from 1630 to 1640. Richelieu's attempt to defeat the House of Habsburg meant that France waged a war of money opposing the wealthiest nation in Christendom and the crown that controlled the wealth of the New World. Each side threw its full resources into this test of strength. On both sides, the ruler's subjects would be bled dry, crushed if necessary, in that attempt to carry off the final victory.

Carrying out this program required careful manipulation of the body social: in spite of the monarch's absolutist claims, the notion of the citizen's free consent to taxation was yet to be discovered. Both the taille, a tax collected by assessment, and long-standing indirect taxes such as the unpopular gabelle on salt were collected by a large administrative corps that was in part royal (for the taille), in part private and "farmed out" to individual collectors in the form of the *fermes générales*. Because relations between the population at large and the financiers always took place in a situation of coercion, they readily turned into open conflict. Clashes between the populace and the financiers' agents often took a dramatic turn, and as war dragged on, the people grew increasingly impatient with the many fiscal levies. When poor harvests made life in rural areas even more precarious, the peasants' sense of being picked clean by the payment of forced taxes inevitably turned into anger.

Throughout France, the financier came to be seen as greedy, a man deaf to the suffering of the poor who exercised his malevolent skills through his factotums. In short, an intolerable oppressor. The furor with which *les gabelous*—the collectors of the gabelle—were met was a clear indication of what would await their master. A number of attacks on tax agents took place in the villages: how many more were assaulted, even assassinated? The more or less open complicity of the country gentry (on occasion, of great lords as well) encouraged sedition. The nobility made use of this endemic agitation to defend its position in the provinces, increase its popularity, and, above all, counter the king's efforts to centralize power and found his own preeminence on the ruins of the aristocracy's past splendor.

Constraints such as these, all of which had a connection with war, explain the outbreak of *émotions* throughout France between 1635 and 1675—insurrections that were based largely in anti-tax sentiment. Among these were the rebellions of the Croquants in the Angoumois and Poitou (1636) and of the Nu-Pieds in Normandy in 1639 and the revolt over tax-stamped paper in Auvergne in the summer of 1675. The cry "Vive le Roi sans Gabelles!" that rang from one province to another was a clear expression of both resentment over taxes and rejection of the financier. The people's anger was directed at a remote personage, unreachable and known only through his agents. As a figure detested all the more for being evanescent, he could be burdened with the full weight of the people's resentment. This sweeping condemnation of the financier was not restricted to the lower classes: it was also typical of the power elites, whose ostracism was all the more formidable for coming from the country's leaders and role models.

When war went on and ordinary revenues dried up, the monarchy needed to invent expedients (fertile imaginations were usually up to the task) that were labeled *affaires extraordinaires*. These were a package of financial operations ranging from the emission of government bonds to loans against security, the alienation of demesnial lands, and the sale of offices. The latter technique increased dramatically during the seventeenth century, since all judiciary and administrative positions bore a price. Every well-off subject of the king of France was a potential officeholder. Necessity being the mother of invention, the monarchy found "extraordinary" ways to raise revenue, and government bonds, loans, the sale of offices, and the concession of special rights created a market under the control of the state, which drew up agreements with persons charged with the resale of such instruments to the public. These contracts were called *traités* or *partis,* and those who dealt in them, soon known as *traitants* and *partisans,* joined the lower echelons of the world of finance. The terms *traitant* and *partisan* came to symbolize everything that made finance odious, and these money-handlers, urged on by the monarchy's pressing financial needs, dragged the crown into an endless downward spiral by the use of methods whose facility hid their pernicious effects. Such men continually proposed new ways to assuage the government's hunger for gold and silver and to garner juicy profits for themselves. For once their prime—and willing—victims were not the common people but the wealthiest levels of society.

In seventeenth-century France, office holding was by far the best means of social promotion for the better-off members of rural society and the merchant bourgeoisie. The exercise of a small parcel of administrative or judiciary power reflected on the person who held that power, all the more so when the reward for a successful career might be membership in the elite. Men whose supreme ambition was to be nobles could satisfy that ambition through posts that granted access to the nobility—in the second degree (nonhereditary) for positions with the royal courts; even better, in the first (hereditary) for such posts as king's secretary. Moreover, the sale of offices meant that the most highly prized positions commanded higher prices; consequently, those who held them realized higher gains and had better access to the wealth that noble groups yearned for. This means that everything concerning offices and their administration was close to the hearts of the bourgeoisie and nobles "of the robe."

The same was true for state bonds—*rentes sur l'Etat*. This was a convenient way to raise money for the state and was often camouflaged behind the fiction of the Hôtel de Ville of Paris as guarantor. Along with income from landholdings, state bonds contributed greatly to the founding and consolidation of the estates of wealthy Frenchmen. Everything regarding their wealth (notably, punctual interest payments) was a sensitive matter, not subject to banter. The wealthy followed the management of the *affaires extraordinaires* with avid attention. The least moves of the financiers, who were always ready to speculate, aroused anxiety: the social and political effects of market fluctuations, far from being restricted to the private sphere, were immediately felt in public life. The ups and downs of such *affaires,* as manipulated by the money managers, could lead to sharp dips in the economy, each one of which created increased tension in the money markets.

The requirements of war forced the state to procure cash by issuing more bonds, creating more offices, and speculating on the alienation of demesnial lands, acquiring them at a favorable price by exercise of state authority before a new alienation occurred. The proliferation of such "extraordinary measures" was aimed primarily at the wealthier members of the bourgeoisie and the nobility, who soon worried that these expedients were being overused. When too many posts were created, their price fell. Similarly, an increase in the state debt meant higher interest payments and made payment problematic. Hence officeholders cognizant of the gravity of the situation, which the money managers' diabolical spirit of invention only made worse, declared themselves enemies of the entire world of tax finance. The movement, which began among highly influential members of the Parlement, soon spread to all categories of society. The magistrates in that body feared a threat to their own wealth but they also saw the financier as a symbol of the absolutist state, hence their economic quarrel with the crown was an expression of political opposition.

Faced with the reinforcement of the king's power and his efforts to have the Parlement's function reduced to registering royal decrees, the magistrates chose the comforting role of fathers of the oppressed people. The pretext was excellent: they protected their own corporative association by attacking a component of public power that was attempting to limit their claims and aspirations.

Little wonder, in such an atmosphere, that the financier was depicted as the emanation of a state that had become a Moloch cruelly devouring its own children. The financier, referred to pejoratively as a *maltôtier* or a *traitant,* became the target of bitter attack from a social microcosm whose economic, political, and social interests were suddenly threatened. Philippics and calls for revenge rang out all over France. In this sense, the Fronde in Parlement drew its strength from a popular sentiment that was as much anti-financier as it was anti-fiscal. The old aristocracy was not far behind. For much the same reasons as the officeholders, the aristocrats joined the chorus of lamentations. They took the occasion to proclaim an ethical question—the defense of their social and moral integrity against invasion of their ranks by rich parvenus who, backed by their new money, sullied the virtue of a group also under threat from the growth and the ambitions of the monarchy. In short, everyone agreed that the financier was public enemy number one.

Paradoxically enough, it was Richelieu, the incarnation of the state and its will to be absolute and a man who was himself the object of suspicion, who best summarized the problem: "The financiers are an evil, but they are a necessary evil." Although financiers had become indispensable to the state, which could not act or even exist without their ministrations, their growing importance was a matter of concern. Richelieu was well aware of how dependent his decisions and his moves were upon businessmen, and he found that subordination unbearable. He energetically attacked financiers for the excessive (eventually, the prohibitive) price that he paid for their services. The monarchy, obligated to pay in the least painful manner possible for a war whose end was never in sight, knew that it was trapped in an aberrant structure of existent loans that it was unable to pay off. As ready cash became scarcer, the financiers had to pay a higher price for it and, in turn, their ministrations became more costly. The rates of interest that they charged the state grew ever higher, reaching first 25 percent, then 30 percent, and, in certain cases, as much as 50 percent. Little wonder that they were seen as predators feeding on the ruins of the state! The monarchy's resentment of the species it had created was not far behind the anti-financier sentiment of the French in general.

The monarchy had little choice, however, as the sheer size of its debt pushed it toward bankruptcy. The idea of wiping out its debts, to the detriment of the financiers, its principal creditors, was one that arose quite naturally. Such a move would also enable the crown to restore its diminished popularity and reinforce a somewhat shaky authority. Thus we see the monarchy first denouncing, then attacking, the least-loved group in France: in sessions of the Chambres de Justice that punctuated the seventeenth century (the first was held in 1601, others came in 1605, 1607, 1624, 1648, and 1662), the courts served the state's twin objectives of eliminating the debt and winning back the hearts of the French. It was an excellent tactic for disarming the opposition, a coalition of bourgeois, officeholders, and nobles. As a result, the seventeenth-century financier was from all points of view a social outcast, which explains his contemporaries' dim view of him.

The image of the financier in seventeenth-century sources varies little, whether it comes from literature or more directly from genealogical documents and memoirs. We find an unvarying portrait—or caricature—of the financier repeated ad infinitum (to the point of becoming a stereotype) in pamphlets like the "Bréviaire des Financiers" or in the *Historiettes* of Tallemant des Réaux and the *Caractères* of La Bruyère. Even if the portrait was false, this overwhelming agreement shows that the French of the Baroque age believed it to be true. Authors take pains to stress the characteristics of the financier that best harmonized with contemporary prejudices. Some rail at the obscure, lowly origins of all financiers. To hear them talk, all financiers were the offspring of stable boys and serving women, men who had used *la maltôte* to rise from the dregs of society and who had wormed their way into the aristocracy by their money, either indirectly, through positions that ennobled their holders such as secretary to the king—*la savonnette à vilain,* "commoners' soap"—or more directly, by means of "scandalous" marriages between their offspring and the children of nobles of the robe or of the sword. The lackey turned financier was a universally accepted credence and a prime verity that no one dreamed of contesting.

If ancien régime society found the financier's shameless rise unacceptable, his personality came in for criticism as well. He was judged worthy of scorn because morally and physically deformed. La Bruyère speaks of his soul as being shaped out of "rubbish and mud" (*d'ordure et de boue*). His ruthlessness, his cowardice, his excesses, and his tenor of life were stigmatized, but also his fatuity and his naivete, qualities that led him to make a flagrant display of insolent luxury, sumptuous and multiple houses and lands, and a fabulous lifestyle at a time when "honest people" were living in miserable poverty. He aped the high aristocracy, whose nobility he sullied by claiming noble ancestors. Some of the Mazarinades indulged in the lowest, most calumnious insinuations: all means to degrade him were fair. These virulent and defamatory writings are striking proof of the hatred and envy that the financier's glittering success inspired.

This black picture, which stressed the inverse of all the values of honor, loyalty, disinterestedness, and birth that the aristocracy revered, reinforced the social myth of the lackey turned financier. Moreover, the archetype implied a complete political philosophy: the whole nation was being fleeced by the worst sort of rascals, since the elites as well as the people fell victim to this social outcast, this excrescence of the most despicable levels of society. This singular view justified all manner of moves in which the elites posed as advocates for humble folk as an efficacious way to defend their own interests. This was accompanied by barely veiled criticism of the centralizing monarchical power for permitting social promotion of a sort that undermined the very foundations of ancien régime society. Criticism was often political: some financiers (Fouquet, the superintendent of finances, for one) were presented as henchmen of a corrupt minister; other targets of abuse (Concini, Mazarin) were foreigners, which added a spice of xenophobia to the polemics.

Thus the financier, as viewed by his contemporaries, was a strange figure. In a social hierarchy as rigid as that of the seventeenth century, it was unthinkable for an individual who had started from nothing to rise so high, and equally unthinkable that the metamorphosis be repeated hundreds of times. The discrepancy between the distorted image of the financier in the minds of his contemporaries and his profile as drawn by sociological investigation in fact reveals something that needed to be hidden in order to preserve the basic stability of the kingdom. In reality, the contradiction sprang from an ambiguity.

A biographic study of from one thousand to twelve hundred major French financiers of the seventeenth century based on notarial documents, the records of the Conseil royal des Finances, and court documents issued by the various Chambres de Justice provides a very different portrait of the financier from the one that emerges from literary sources.

Financiers were not born in the gutter. One false notion gone. Another is that they were foreigners. Hardly. Despite the fame of some businessmen, Italians such as Sébastien Zamet, the Lumagues, and the Mascranys, or Germans such as Hervart, the overwhelming majority of French financiers—over 75 percent—were native-born Frenchmen from the northern half of the kingdom. Their families came, for the most part, from Paris and the Île de France, from the provinces on the eastern borders of France (Champagne and Burgundy), or from the Loire Valley (Touraine, Anjou, and the Orléanais). Lyons and the Lyonnais and Languedoc were the leading places of origin among the 25 percent minority from the south of France. This uneven geographic distribution is quite understandable, and it reflects the close connections between power and money. Paris was the traditional capital of the monarchy; the Île de France, its cradle; the lands of the Loire, its center of gravity from the late fifteenth to the late sixteenth century: families who were physically closer to the seat of the monarchy had a better opportunity to aid the crown in the exploitation of its finances. Champagne and Burgundy served as bases for military operations, which explains the presence of financiers from those two provinces. Armies on the move required provisions and equipment for the troops, and they created commercial and banking opportunities to fulfill those needs. The more audacious financiers soon took the short step from providing munitions for war to financing it. Lyons, the banking center of the kingdom and a city that had long had Italian banking families among its residents, generated a number of financiers for the same reason.

A second basic characteristic of the financier is that he was Catholic. Protestants represented only an extremely small portion (5 percent) of financiers, a proportion that was exaggerated by the image of a few famous figures—Rambouillet, Tallemant, Hervart, Samuel Bernard— whose names were always cited to support the polemical view of Huguenot control of finance. This point, incidentally, reopens the question raised by Max Weber of the connection between capitalism and Protestantism. It is clear that in seventeenth-century France there was a well-defined break between the world of finance, which was exclusively Catholic (most of the Huguenot families soon abjured), and banking, which remained more cosmopolitan but was dominated by Protestants, as Herbert Lüthy has demonstrated. This dichotomy, which in part arose out of the different but complementary activities of the two sectors, can also be explained by a third characteristic of the financier: he was generally an officeholder.

In about 80 percent of cases, French financiers held an office, even several exercised conjointly. Logically enough, the offices they held usually involved accounting, since such posts concerned the monarchy's resources. Some of these were that of *receveur général des finances* in the various *généralités* (the largest geographical financial unit) or *trésorier général* of the largest government bureaus: the *garde du Trésor royal*, the *trésorier des Parties casuelles*, the *trésorier du Marc d'or*, the *trésorier de l'Ordinaire* or *de l'Extraordinaire des guerres*, the *trésorier de la Marine*, or the *trésoriers* of the provincial Estates of Provence, Languedoc, or Brittany. Posts in the central administration, in particular in the Chancery, came a close second to those in finance. In particular, posts in the financial branches of the central administration (*intendants des finances* and secretaries of the Conseil des Finances) were often taken by financiers, as was that of clerk (*greffier*) of the Conseil privé. On closer inspection of the milieus in which financiers were born and in which they operated, it is clear that holding an office was neither new nor a sign of success; office holding and success both came out of the management of public funds.

A study of the social status of the fathers and paternal grandfathers of the financiers shows that they came from a homogeneous milieu: 75 percent of the fathers of financiers and 65 percent of their grandfathers were also officeholders. These men often held posts in finance, accounting, or administration; when their posts were in the law courts they ranged from the lowest echelons of court clerks to judges in the royal courts. The social milieu of the financiers' fathers-in-law resembled their fathers' world of administrators, accountants, and jurists, with officeholders accounting for 74 percent of them. This shows that business people, like other seventeenth-century social and professional categories, practiced a strict endogamy that helped to keep them in the places where decisions were made and was of great assistance to them professionally. A large majority of those listed as simple private citizens came from backgrounds in the law or the major branches of financial administration, public or private. They were clerks for prominent accountants or employees in the administrative offices of the *fermes générales* or the *affaires extraordinaires*. These statistics demonstrate that very few financiers— around 10 percent—came from backgrounds in banking or commerce, though this proportion may have been higher early in the century.

This reinforces a point fundamental to the social and economic history of France: contrary to broadly accepted notions, finance was not based on commerce in the larger sense. There was a profound gulf between the world of trade and the world of finance, although certain bankers (and some of the most famous bankers, men such as Zamet, Hervart, and Particelli d'Hémery) went into finance. Their cases were untypical. It is true that at times activities that both bankers and financiers pursued— purveying munitions and weapons, manufacturing, colonization—make it hard to tell them apart, but joint pursuits did not erase the distinction between them. Finance did not operate within commercial economic circuits. That was why the money manager had to operate in unique ways.

The last trait of the financier, and one that was fundamental to French society of the seventeenth century, was that he was in fact noble. Obviously, his nobility did not date from time immemorial, given that one financier out of two had been ennobled, either by the post he held or by letters of nobility (among which are a small number of *lettres de relief* transferring feudal property that seem to indicate special favors). Few financiers, what is more, had privileges of nobility that were limited to their person alone, excluding the other members of their family. Even odder than the extension of noble status to the entire family, a considerable number of financiers, king's secretaries in particular, had been noble for two, three, and more generations. Some chancery posts (the famous *savonnettes à vilain*) were eagerly sought precisely because they conferred hereditary nobility after twenty years on the job or when the officeholder died in office. How can we explain, then, why some financiers sought such a post when their fathers had held it before them and had occupied it long enough to be ennobled? The hope of social promotion is not enough to explain why financiers were attracted to posts as king's secretary. Men whose wealth consisted partly in real estate may have found the post's fiscal advantages appealing, as royal secretaries were dispensed from payment of transmission taxes on land. They may have found the opportunity to join the small world that gravitated around the center of power even more important than such privileges. There great matters were discussed and planned. Holding an office was something like a passport into the exclusive domains of financial alchemy. Be that as it may, the financier of the Baroque age undeniably became part of the social elite. For a very limited minority of financiers this was not a recent phenomenon: the highest echelons of finance could boast of an old name if not one covered with military glory. Nobility is always difficult to ascertain, however, as the sources (the genealogical sources in particular) need to be used with great care. Forgeries and usurped family trees abounded, and the royal genealogists exposed them ferociously, even gleefully. Beyond the discussions among the experts in titles of nobility, the fact remains that some financiers' claims to nobility cannot be rejected out of hand, and there are examples of nobility acknowledged for a century or more that discourage sweeping generalizations. Names such as those of the Bauyn brothers, Mathé de Vitry-la-Ville, and the Lacroix went back to the early sixteenth century; that of the Duflos and the Rioult d'Ouilly families from the late fifteenth century; that of the Le Courtois d'Averly and the Lelay families from the late fourteenth century.

The portrait of the financier and of his relations with society as a whole would not be complete without an examination of the size and structure of his wealth. Probate inventories and the records of the Chambres de Justice are invaluable sources in this connection, although, by their very nature, they involve a margin of error. During the monarchy's periodic prosecutions of its financial factotums, certain financiers' goods were seized, thus providing us with an opportunity to gain some notion of their holdings at the time of their fall. What we see is the positive sides of their ledgers; we have much less information on their debts, which they tended to exaggerate when things turned against them. Their credits are very probably whittled down, thanks to precautions they may have taken when they felt the first whiff of the coming storm and made haste to put some of their holdings (liquid assets in particular) in a safe place.

These reservations aside, such documents enable us to estimate the average wealth of financiers and, even more significant than the size of their estate, its composition. We discover that nearly 60 percent of these men were not millionaires, a magnificent outward appearance or their own boastful declarations to the contrary. Ostentation served to reinforce their credit and had little relation to their real wealth. The fortunes that financiers acquired were comparable to those of the leading members of

Parlement, of the middle level of the nobility, or of the major wholesale merchants, traders, and bankers. Only exceptional individuals like Maynon, Boylesve, or Bernard could compete with the high nobility and the ministers, and no financiers reached the dizzying wealth of Richelieu, who left some twenty million livres at his death, or Mazarin, who left about twice that sum.

The totals are interesting, but their distribution is even more so. These fortunes typically showed a clear two-part split. First, there were traditional holdings (houses, lands, posts), the customary investments of the French elites and the ones that business people used as reserves and security for loans. Such investments accounted for under 40 percent of the holdings of most financiers, a proportion that declined as the century advanced. Second, they had a portfolio of financial holdings that represented over half their total wealth and that might, in extreme cases, be as much as 82 percent of total wealth (as with Jeannin de Castille, who held the post of *trésorier d'Epargne*), or even 95 percent (with Oursin, who was *receveur général des finances*). Such portfolios were a mass of papers: certificates for royal treasury bonds, payment orders, assignments, stock certificates, loan certificates, promissory notes, and rental contracts. Their volume reflected the rampant inflation in royal finances in crisis and sorely tried by unending war. Obviously, the better part of the holdings had little value: investments in the private sector were often backed by entities in bankruptcy; investments in the public sector were widely discredited for the state's chronic inability to pay interest. Frequently, particularly when one monarch succeeded another or when the Chambres de Justice came into session, it was evident that the fiscal world was constantly flirting with bankruptcy—a professional hazard encountered by from one-fifth to one-fourth of all financiers, who ended their days penniless. Little wonder that the prestige items—furniture, silver, art objects—usually associated with the "good" financier and lending him an appearance of opulence occupied such a small place in his inventory. These trappings much impressed and highly irritated his contemporaries, but they did not account for much of his total wealth, where they represented from 1 percent to 5 percent at the most.

Another singular phenomenon is the financiers' lack of liquid assets. These men, who were unique in their ability to advance cash sums to the king of France at all times, had practically no liquid assets when their goods were seized or when death approached. Furthermore, 40 percent of them left their heirs no cash whatsoever, and 29 percent less than five thousand livres. One immediate conclusion is that not all their funds were registered when their holdings were inventoried, their families spiriting away the cash. Another is that when threatened with prosecution they took precautions and placed their savings in a safe place. Both may have been true in many cases, but a large number of coins is never easy to hide for the simple fact of their weight and bulk. A tax farmer's share of the collected taxes could be close to 450,000 livres, which would amount to 150,000 silver écus or a weight of 4,050 kilograms! What is more, when in troubled times a financier was denounced for hoarding piles of coins, the search always proved fruitless. The informant had invented the story out of spite. The inescapable conclusion is that the financiers were much less wealthy that they declared themselves to be, than they seemed, and than the public believed. There is an ambiguity here or, more precisely, a contradiction with all that was written and said about them. The paradox disappears when we judge the financier by the standards of the society in which he lived.

Given the seventeenth-century mind, the lackey turned financier could not have existed. In spite of what his contemporaries had to say about him, the financier was never a parvenu; rather, he was the product of a milieu and the result of a process that required several generations. Objectively, there were too many obstacles standing in the way of that metamorphosis. Money management could not be improvised.

The profession required subtlety and thorough training. How could a servant or a poor peasant whose intellectual environment had always been meager or totally deficient have possibly gained the knowledge and mastered the techniques of one of the most challenging professions? A few might conceivably have realized that prodigious achievement, but, given the weight of social restrictions, they would have remained totally isolated. The secret rituals of royal finance and the mysteries of credit and exchange could not be learned in a day. Financiers also had to digest enough juridical knowledge to find their way in the thickets of legislation connected with financial affairs and to try to settle the many and inextricable lawsuits that finance engendered. The profession required a long and diversified preparation that included an acquaintance with commerce and its customs, a familiarity with the techniques of money changing, an apprenticeship in the administration of tax farms and the collection of extraordinary taxes, and a knowledge of the law. To accomplish all this, the budding financier needed the cultural support of people of his own kind; a lackey—even a very talented lackey—could not help being an isolated seedling planted in a terrain that was by its nature foreign to him if not hostile.

The financier-lackey would encounter social difficulties as well as cultural ones. Under the ancien régime the self-made man was an incongruity. All achievement at the highest levels was the product of incessant labor on the part of successive generations and was indistinguishable from the fortunes of the lineage. As we have seen, the financier who held an important office had been shaped by his family. He and all his kin belonged to the same social stratum, and his advancement in the world was more the emergence of his clan than it was the birth of a personality, even when that personality was remarkable. This has been demonstrated regarding Jean-Baptiste Colbert. Colbert was raised in the tradition of tax farming, and his successes were prepared and advanced by a far-reaching and powerful familial network. All seventeenth-century financiers were an integral part of families that offered them an inherited capital in the form of the influence of allied families and the experience of forebears. All the functions and posts that promised glittering success were transmitted by blood. The posts of *receveurs généraux des finances* and *fermiers généraux* passed from one titleholder to another by means of such networks. It was thanks to internal solidarity that, after 1632, a family conglomerate of the Bonneau, Pallu, and Milon families (and, as an adjunct, the La Porte family) remained in control of major tax-collecting functions for over a century. Such ties were created by the women of the family, through marriage alliances, which means that they are not always obvious and can be clarified only by genealogical research. Thus women indirectly guaranteed the continuity of important financial responsibilities within one family or one group of related families.

In this closed universe, the poor lackey who started out with no support network and no kin had no access to the game. He had no training, no connections. Consequently, he had no way to procure credit. Thus he would run right into the ultimate obstacle facing any would-be financier, the brick wall of money. He would have no hope of becoming a financier if he did not possess or was not able to procure substantial sums. In the natural order of things, a young man could tap such resources from within wealthy merchant and office-holding families. Furthermore, it was by frequenting the social circles of the aristocracy, the nobility of "the robe," or the upper echelons of the administration that he would find loans to supplement his own purse. But loans were made only to people one could be sure of—that is, to people who were solvent. Money managers could only be recruited from the social strata of officeholders—in the judiciary, finance, or the administration—the milieus out of which they arose and with which they formed a powerful microcosm close to royal power and to the councils in which the financial policies of the state were elaborated. A self-made man, by definition without guarantees or contacts, would have been turned away from such a universe from the start.

Contrary to his contemporary image, the financier challenged neither the body social, nor the political system, nor the moral values of the French. By his family, his career, and his status, he was part of the elite, set off from others in his class only by a highly risky profession with a poor reputation. In reality, the legend concerning his dubious or ignoble origin and his supposedly limitless wealth did more to protect than to harm him. The stock character and mythic figure of the "lackey-financier" provided popular resentment with a convenient scapegoat for its miseries. The cliché operated as a social lightning rod and masked the true identity of the men who worked within and gravitated around finance. Because of the myth, opinion misjudged the true role of the financier in seventeenth-century France. He seemed to be both an essential cog in the machinery of state and the chief cause of its malfunctioning and, by that token, of all the ills that afflicted the population. A noble and an officeholder, he seemed determined to fleece his peers by inventing new *affaires extraordinaires* aimed particularly at them. Here too we see ambiguity and a contradiction between his acts and his status. Is it true that the financier worked against the interests of his caste? The ambiguity disappears the minute we place the financier back within the fiscal and financial system of the monarchy. The contradiction is only apparent, and it dissolves when we grasp the financier's true nature, which involved an inherent ambivalence.

In his essence, the financier was no adversary of the state, nor of the elites. His role was indispensable to them. In the state, he animated the financial supply chain that was a precondition for the operation of the royal fiscal and financial system. It was the way in which the royal revenues were collected that made the money manager sacrosanct rather than the complexity and diversity of the sovereign's resources. All moneys—from the taille, the farmed indirect taxes, or the *affaires extraordinaires*—flowed into the various public coffers by a clever but gigantic system of advances on the part of the very persons who then managed them. The financier became a partner of the crown. His funds primed the financial pump that drained off capital.

The chief problem that faced the financier was obviously constant access to liquid assets. The financier did not himself have sufficient cash reserves, which meant that he had to search for funds among people who had money—wealthy and powerful lenders among the elite who were eager to see their capital earn a profit but just as eager to maintain an anonymity that safeguarded their good reputation. The financier's operations were conceivable only with the interested and discreet aid of such people. Thus the money manager gradually slipped into the role of intermediary between the monarchy and its potential lenders. At that point he no longer seemed a negative figure who offended society's notions of good taste, but rather a highly useful agent standing shoulder to shoulder with the monarchy and permitting the powerful to invest their money with impunity. On the practical level this was a singular reversal of the popular perception of the financier: rather than seeming to stand against the world, he was working for the good of the regime and society. A servant of power and of the wealthy, his ambivalence explains the ambiguity that surrounded him. The movement of public credit through obscure and highly complicated channels explains that phenomenon.

The financiers themselves admitted that the better part of their loans came from the funds of third parties. This was done in two ways. First, the lender could be given a part interest in a financial company in which, as a backer, he shared in all profits (or losses) in proportion to his investment, but had no active voice in the management of the company. Second, he could offer a simple loan at a rate of interest fixed in advance (the legal and most common rate was 5 percent), in which case he had no further rights or obligations. In the first system the financier's role was as a figurehead; in the second, as a credit instrument. In order to float his loan, he issued certificates, promissory notes for which the lender might take an assumed name if they were payable to the bearer, or ordinary interest-bearing obligations.

The security for such loans was not state revenues (the state's credit was weak) but rather the private holdings of the financier or financiers writing the contracts—their landholdings, real estate, and official posts. Creditors, who saw real estate and posts as safe investments, were reassured by guarantees of the sort. Moreover, these instruments offered the advantage of laying the lenders' moral and religious scruples to rest. Promissory notes and bearer bonds made no mention of interest and only bore the due date, and interests respected the canonical rates. Was this hypocrisy? Not completely. It is true that these certificates and notes included both capital and interest and that the sums paid by the lender were indeed less than the figure mentioned on them. In a society in which form was an integral part of substance and counted as much, this procedure resolved what seems to us a contradiction. The financier offered moral tranquility, diverting to his person and his function all the bad conscience that went along with money-making. He became a sort of go-between, a channel through which all public financial life passed. He permitted the satisfaction of a quest for profit that was never openly expressed and over which society threw a veil of modesty and virtue.

The money manager performed a basic function. He represented sizable financial interests, but also considerable social and political interests. In spite of the care that lenders took to remain anonymous in this obscure aspect of finance, we can throw some light on those who, discreetly but avidly, took part in the game of official finance. The financier is like Russian dolls in that he concealed a series of profiteers. Acquaintance with the lesser fry subjects the world of finance to the harsh light of day and explains the ambiguities of the profession. The *fermier général* Thomas Bonneau and his seconds, Pierre Aubert, Claude Chatelain, Germain Rolland, and Marc-Antoine Scarron provide a highly instructive example.

This small group of major money managers dominated the tax system of the *fermes générales* from 1632 to 1661. Bonneau financed their company by launching loans, following methods described above and that have left many traces in the archives, in particular among notarial documents. Analysis of a systematic sampling of such documents reveals that the sociological world of these wealthy businessmen supported the financier in all his ventures. These investors were themselves *maltôtiers* just as much as the financiers, but they had the advantage of not sharing in the most obvious risks involved.

A study of 185 such lenders can help to define the "other financiers" of France. Typically, the lender was a noble (75 percent) and an officeholder (65 percent). The range among officeholders is fairly broad, from accountants to judges and including king's secretaries and members of Parlement (40 percent). Although these officeholders include a sizable contingent of nobles, some were commoners, and 16 percent were members of old and powerful aristocratic families. Finally, 5 percent of lenders were women, most of them widows, and prudent widows to boot. They provide one more demonstration of the falsity of the usual notions concerning the alienation of women under the ancien régime. Thanks to scrupulous clauses in their marriage contracts, women became a vehicle for wealth and a means for its conservation among old French families. They were often expert businesswomen actively involved in financial activities.

A genealogical study of these families shows that they grouped, so to speak, in atoms, then in molecules. Nearly all were related in one way or another. The lenders' universe mirrored that of the financiers: as nobles, by their status as officeholders, and with their alliance networks, lenders and financiers reflected the same multifaceted capitalist world. Such documents also offer a picture of the number and extent of the investments involved. Very few people in this sample—some 5 percent—invested regularly in tax farms, but those who did so invested large sums amounting to several hundred thousand livres. The rest invested tens of thousands of livres when the economic situation seemed propitious. The documentation is fragmentary, however, and the sums invested in tax farms may have been merely one investment among others that these lenders placed with the financial companies. Be that as it may, it is clear that finance was the domain of the elite, in particular of the milieus of the robe and the sword. Thus it served the state at the highest levels—a further indication of the close connection between power and society.

The most illustrious names of "the robe," families that had given the monarchy great civil servants such as Phélypeaux or Mesmes, appear along with the names of old families like La Trémoille, La Rochefoucauld, and Laval. Despite the prejudices against tax farmers, neither sort of family thought their little excursions into the domain of *la maltôte* unworthy of them as long as appearances were safeguarded. What is more, tax farming was one financial activity among many, and it was advisable to diversify one's investments. I might note that such families entered into a game that, in the long run, tended to impoverish their peers and, in the case of officeholders, to turn against them. Were such people not thinking straight? Were they acting illogically? Not really. It is amusing to note that some of the biggest investors were members of Parlement—d'Aligre, Turquant, president Tambonneau, and president Violle. The latter even took part in the Fronde and was thus among the sworn enemies—in theory—of the financiers.

In reality, the lure of profit swept aside all conventions, all group interests, and all ideals. Particularly when earnings were sure and guaranteed. When the financial system jammed, disappointing the hopes of investors, they all changed course. When dangers increased, these indirect actors in the financial drama flew to join forces with the enemies of *la maltôte*, adding their voices to the chorus of vigorous complaints. At that point the wails of the victims of the system were mingled with those of its hidden artisans, who wept instead for their lost profits. As the fiscal and financial system evolved in contact with an unavoidable, costly, and permanent state of war, the full social and political implications of finance became more evident, putting the financier in his true place. He was merely a cog, and a rather secondary one, in an enormous machine that was breaking down.

In its desperation, the state allowed stopgap measures to proliferate to the point that they lost their efficacy because credit had run out. Money then went underground to wait for better days, and the monarchy was forced to avow its de facto bankruptcy. The financiers, who could foresee a purge on the horizon, sought to protect themselves. They knew that sooner or later they would pay the price for the government's predicament. They took the usual precautions: they put holdings in their wife's name; they hid securities and, probably, cash in religious institutions; they recruited front men for some ventures, and so forth.

The Chambre de Justice could then be called, more in order to declare the state's bankruptcy and put out propaganda than to effect any genuine reform of the system. The financier would be brought before a special court presided over by judges named by a commission (thus at the king's orders), who tried one case after another on criminal charges and with no appeal. The financier had to present his accounts and make restitution of sums that the judges pretended to believe had been appropriated improperly. Worse, the court investigated all the fraudulent activities with which the financier might have been involved during his time in office and treated such offenses as misappropriation of public funds. The charge of theft from the king was an extremely serious accusation and, if proven, was punishable by death. Furthermore, incriminating reports were likely to come flooding in, since the population at large was mobilized against the "infamous wretch" under accusation and informants were generously rewarded.

The financier did not remain inactive in adversity, however; he defended himself exploiting the full resources of the law. The age had perfected the art of pettifoggery, and to demonstrate the veracity of the state's debts to him the financier could avail himself of conditions freely consented to by the monarchy itself. This engendered a massive amount of court proceedings that slowed deliberation and limited the efficacy of the court's efforts. When a financier was judged guilty, the state, declaring itself a privileged creditor, could confiscate his goods and put them up for auction. Posts, lands, and houses (which were difficult to conceal) thus profited the king, whose turn it was to enrich himself at the expense of his ex-purveyor.

The investors who had lent their écus to the financier with such discretion were hardly indifferent bystanders to the state's recuperation of funds. Their reactions may have been discreet at first, but they became less so when no happy outcome to the financier's difficulties seemed forthcoming. At first the investors preferred to wait and see, but when they began to realize that the holdings that guaranteed their own loans to the financier were about to be confiscated they surfaced to claim their due. The monarchy, they complained, had harmed them by attacking their agent. It had committed a dreadful injustice and was guilty of unconscionable behavior. Since these investors represented the most prominent groups in French society and were the most staunch supporters of the regime, the state found it unwise to offend them at the risk of setting off political and social unrest. Every financial crisis of the ancien régime threatened to degenerate in this manner and to challenge the very foundations of the monarchy.

The state knew just how far to push its advantage. It was indeed anxious to wipe out its debts, but in doing so it did not want to set off a crisis whose outcome might get out of hand. Thus it chose compromise. The transaction, which took place after the opening of the Chambre de Justice, followed an unvarying procedure.

The king suspended the execution of sentences and offered an amnesty to those who had been judged guilty; in exchange, the financiers agreed to pay fines in amounts and in accordance with payment schedules set by the Ministry of Finance. More often than not, each loan that the financiers had made to the state was handled separately. In this manner, the state carried out its bankruptcy without having to say so, and it retained capital in the form of the lands, houses, and offices that had guaranteed the financiers' loans. This enabled those who had lent money to the financiers to recuperate a good part of their investment. They were not to be stripped of their all. At this point a new equilibrium was established and money that had disappeared from circulation began to surface, taking advantage of the reestablishment of peace and the bleeding of the financiers. The market was swept clean of all the paper that had encumbered it. What is more, although the monarchy encouraged the opposite impression, the financiers came out of their trials if not unscathed at least not too badly off. Lowering clouds still threatened them, however, particularly during the Fronde, when a number of them went to jail. Still, no one lost his head. A psychodrama produced for the benefit of the general population had come to an end. Dire things had been threatened and severe punishment of financiers promised, but when all the histrionics and sword rattling had ended, not much happened. Parlement softened its attitude when it came time for action, and its transactions masked the real bargaining imposed by the royal fiscal and financial system.

At this point the full dimensions of the financier begin to come into clearer focus. Socially a middleman and politically a vehicle for policy (with all the vicissitudes that role implies), he was also a member of a faction. To gain entry to the king's business, he needed to have recommendations to the Minister of Finance and his colleagues and to the other ministers. As for the wealthy and powerful investors who supplied him with funds, they too belonged to the upper echelons of "good society" that were the chief support of the state and that, in the last analysis, were the state. The financier's ambivalence showed clearly when it came time to pay taxes. In that crucial moment it was easy for one political and financial faction to eliminate an opposing lobby by increasing certain persons' tax burden. Events in 1665 give a spectacular illustration of this.

In his struggle against Fouquet, the superintendent of finance, Colbert claimed that Fouquet headed a band of financiers who, with Fouquet's complicity, had drained the public coffers with impunity. The young Louis XIV, who was intent on restoring the authority of the monarchy, accepted Colbert's version of the matter without a murmur. Colbert took advantage of the king's acquiescence to remodel the financial personnel of the kingdom to his own liking. Cardinal Mazarin's former employee used the Chambre de Justice of 1661 to wipe his own slate clean. Draped in his full dignity as a punctilious manager, Colbert brought down some of the late prime minister's former cronies, all of whom (as well as Colbert himself) had contributed to the construction of Mazarin's immense—and dubious—wealth. By juggling the amounts of their fines, Colbert crushed the financiers he wanted to crush under the pretext that they had collaborated with Fouquet. The fines were colossal: Boylesve, the *intendant des finances,* was sentenced by the Chambre de Justice to pay 1,576,000 livres, a sum that was transmuted into a tax of 6,000,000 livres; the *trésorier de l'Epargne,* Jeannin de Castille (a cousin of Fouquet's), who had been sentenced to pay 1,117,800 livres, had this amount "moderated" to 8,000,000 livres; the Monnerot brothers, sentenced to pay 6,350,000 livres, actually paid 10,000,000 livres. These men had to cash in their entire portfolios, but they also had to give up their landholdings and sell off their prestigious offices. They were totally ruined.

This maneuver gave Colbert an opportunity for a new deal of the cards. He set up a lobby of financiers loyal to him that included a good number of his friends and kin: Marin, Berryer, Berthelot, and Daliez monopolized posts in the central financial administration and handled enormous sums in direct and indirect revenues. Thus a new faction sprang out of the ashes of the old. With the minister's blessing, it took over the business of the state and, soon, the economy of the entire kingdom. The "Colbert system" was in place. The same men also ran the companies engaged in sea trade—the Compagnie du Nord, the Compagnie des Indes orientales, the Compagnie des Indes occidentales, and the Compagnie de la Méditerranée—backed manufacturing in Languedoc, and exploited industries that purveyed to the growing royal navy.

It is clear that the financier differed from his contemporaries' vision of him. Far from being a near outlaw who defied society, he was totally integrated into the political and social life of the Baroque age and was an essential part of the machinery of state and an active participant in all settlings of accounts. Behind his sumptuous appearance (one reason for his denigration) lay a quite different reality, in some ways more serious, more painful, and, at times, even bitter.

BIBLIOGRAPHY

Bayard, Françoise. "Les Chambres de Justice de la première moitié du XVIIIe siècle." *Cahiers d'Histoire* 19, no. 2 (1974): 121–40.

———. "Comment faire payer les riches? L'exemple du XVIIe siècle français." *Histoire économique et financière de la France: Etudes et documents* 1 (1989): 29–51.

———. *Le monde des financiers au XVIIe siècle.* Paris: Flammarion, 1988.

Bercé, Yves-Marie. *Histoire des croquants: Etude des soulèvements populaires au XVIIe siècle dans le sud-ouest de la France.* 2 vols. Geneva: Droz, 1974. Available in English as *History of Peasant Revolts: The Social Origins of Rebellion in Early Modern France.* Translated by Amanda Whitmore. Ithaca: Cornell University Press, 1990.

Bonney, Richard. *The King's Debts: Finance and Politics in France 1589–1661.* Oxford: Clarendon Press; New York: Oxford University Press, 1981.

———. *Political Change in France under Richelieu and Mazarin, 1624–1661.* Oxford and New York: Oxford University Press, 1978.

Bosher, J. F. "Chambres de Justice in French Monarchy." In *French Government and Society, 1500–1800: Essays in Memory of Alfred Cobban*. London: Athlone Press, 1973.

Collins, James B. *Fiscal Limits of Absolutism: Direct Taxation in Early Seventeenth-Century France*. Berkeley: University of California Press, 1988.

Dent, J. *Crisis in Finance, Crown, Financiers and Society in Seventeenth-Century France*. Newton Abbot: David & Charles, 1973.

Dessert, Daniel. *Argent, pouvoir et société au Grand Siècle*. Paris: Fayard, 1984.

———. *Fouquet*. Paris: Fayard, 1987.

———. "Le 'Laquais-financier' au Grand Siècle: Mythe ou réalité?" *Revue XVIII siècle* 122 (1979): 21–36.

Dessert, Daniel, and Jean-Louis Journet. "Le Lobby Colbert: Un royaume, ou une affaire de famille?" *Annales E.S.C.* 30, no. 6 (1975): 1303–36.

Lüthy, Herbert. *La Banque protestante en France de la révocation de l'Edit de Nantes à la Révolution*. 2 vols. Paris: SEVPEN, 1959–61.

Martin, Germain, and Marcel Besançon. *L'Histoire du crédit en France sous le règne de Louis XIV*. Paris: L. Larose et L. Tenin, 1913. Vol. 1, *Le crédit public*.

4

THE SECRETARY

Salvatore S. Nigro

THE PRINCE'S RIB

"GREAT PALACE" and even "a city in the form of a palace" in Urbino was the setting for the model of the perfect courtier ("without defect and heaped with all praise") described by Count Baldassare Castiglione in his *Il libro del cortegiano* of 1528. A printshop in Venice was the birthplace of the prototype for the new texts written by professional writers for the guidance of the perfect secretary, expert in the art of letter writing. Castiglione offered instruction in the ideal type of courtly virtues; this manual offered specialized professional instruction in all the skills of the ideal applicant for a post of "secretary." The name of the treatise was *Il principe;* it was written by the secretary to Duke Alfonso II d'Este, Giovan Battista Nicolucci, called Il Pigna (from the sign of a pine cone marking his father's grocery store), and was published in Venice in 1561.

Il Pigna's book had already been completed and the colophon printed when the printer-publisher Francesco Sansovino decided to add a "Table of Notable Things" consisting of a meticulous topical index, arranged in alphabetical order, of headwords of the questions treated in the book. This was undeniably a useful addition and one that helped the reader find his way in a large work that was densely printed and that, except for its division into three books, had no chapters or marginal headings. The index, its attendant synopses, and a map were added for the convenience of the printer, however, not for that of the reader. They made it easier for Sansovino to lift sections out of Il Pigna's text that he could then reprint, in a move close to plagiarism, as separate publications to be sold from his printshop. In fact, Sansovino used the "Tavola" to pick out of the work that Il Pigna had written for the edification of a "heroic" prince and a "loving" ruler ("the total opposite of a tyrant") a self-contained and typographically separate section on the person who filled the office of secretary. Entries in the section on secretaries of the "Tavola" read: "The office of the secretary is highly honorable"; "The secretary's participation in all other offices"; "Secretaries in England"; "Private secretaries compared to the angels closest to God"; "Secretary more highly esteemed by Princes than by Republics, and why"; "Secretaries' duty of true loyalty." The index defined each subject and described the various headings in a lively and promising manner, so that when they migrated elsewhere they readily became full sentences and logical sequences in a more specialized manual. This was the origin of *Il secretario,* a work that Sansovino—already a printer, a rewrite man, a writer, and a populizer—prepared and signed with his own name. The work appeared in four books in 1564; it was republished in seven books in 1579, and it went through fourteen editions between 1579 and 1608.

Il Pigna, who was himself a secretary, filled his work with autobiographical details and thinly disguised self-promotion, and he stressed the eminence of the secretary, a man proud of an aristocracy within the world of letters comparable to that of the nobility in society in general. Rather than a functionary, Il Pigna's secretary was a counselor to the prince; a "philosopher" capable of combining "the active life with the contemplative" and "honorable civic actions" with "worthy business transactions." The secretary was an ancillary intelligence who operated in a society in which a social order congruent with cosmic order functioned as a linear connection between the high and the low. At the top of this hierarchy stood a prince whose duty it was to rule the world "more to give it perfection than to receive perfection from it"; the prince contained "something of the divine in his loving diffusion of himself to his citizens"; he worked by "drawing them to him, thus resembling God, who penetrates [human hearts] by means of the angels." The secretary's collaboration with the master he served was to be measured by this standard. His counsel and instruction did not pertain to the "science" of government but only to the "fortuitous things" that required the skills that his position and his experience could provide. The secretary was one ray of the splendor of the Prince to whose service he brought his specialized competence:

> Such are usually the private secretaries whom the theologians compare to the angels closest to God because they are close to the Prince, not in the service of the body or of the faculties, but in that of the spirit, from which all things follow and which makes the office most honored, exercising as it does the most worthy part of discourse on human affairs, since matters of state are the most important in this world. Furthermore, he who is most familiar with and closest to the Prince possesses [such matters] best, and he

who possesses them best is most skilled in them, and he who is most skilled in them can most readily and best speak about them. And since this is an office that participates in all the others, whereas no other office has any part in it, [the secretary] has to be skilled in operations of all sorts.

Sansovino took over Il Pigna's pages. It was simple plagiarism. He even followed the arrangement of the section on the secretariat as it was outlined in the "Tavola" of *Il principe*. Still, when this material was copied and reproduced, the change of context produced a different sort of discourse. Sansovino's *Il secretario* was born of a rib taken out of Il Pigna's *Il principe*, but Sansovino transformed that discursive work on the training of a prince into a treatise on composition that instructed secretaries (directly or by example) on means and rules for epistolary correspondence. He promised that his book would "show and teach the way to write letters in proper fashion and with art on any subject whatsoever. Including titles given according to the standing and function of all persons, those of rank and the common sort. And with many letters of princes and written to princes in various times and on divers occasions."

The model of the orator drawn from Cicero and Quintilian and applied to the courtly modes of "speaking and writing well" was thus transferred to the training of the perfect secretary. This process had started in the *Institutioni al comporre in ogni sorte di rima della lingua volgare* of Mario Equicola (1541), a work cast in the form of rhymed rules of composition intended to "inform" a "secretary of the princes" on how to carry on his duties. A parallel development led to the fifteenth-century treatises on the perfect ambassador, among them Ermolao Barbaro's *De officio legati* and Tasso's dialogue, *Il messaggiero*. What matters here is that Sansovino's work was the first in a long series claiming to "form secretaries" and "teach letters"—works that were summarized by Giulio Cesare Capaccio in a treatise entitled *Il segretario* printed in Rome in 1589 (and later in Naples in 1594 and in Venice between 1597 and 1607) and updated by Gabriele Zinano in a homonymous treatise printed in Venice in 1625. These catalogues mention works by Tasso (1587), Battista Guarini and Angelo Ingegneri (1594), Bartolomeo Zucchi (1595), Tommaso Costo (*Discorso pratico fatto ad un suo nipote intorno ad alcune qualità che debbe aver un buon segretario*, 1602), Benedetto Pucci (1608), and Panfilo Persico and Vincenzo Gramigna (1620). Additions to this list might include Bernardino Baldoni (1628), Lorenzo Onesti (1652), Giovan Battista Da Ripa Ubaldini (1665), and Domenico Federici (1667). It might also mention a brief piece in praise of the secretary in the pages of the *Giornale de' letterati* of 1690 and, finally, Michele Benvenga's *Il proteo segretario di lettere* (1689 and 1706).

THE ANGEL'S HAND

Il Pigna's propaganda depicted a secretary who was a philosopher also versed in letters. He was a "true" and "secret" counselor who suited his "teachings" to the exercise of "heroic" power, in which he participated in his role as educator. As Il Pigna explains, "The hero who possesses all exterior qualities in combination with the perfection of all virtues, seeing himself having in hand the governance of the people, for which he is comparable to God himself, does not want his profession to be attending to the study of letters and philosophy but rather the rule of the city, administering justice and arms as a reward for the good and a punishment for the guilty." The secretary "formed" the prince: he was the angelic part of political power, the "form" of a power. He was of such high dignity that he might even legitimately aspire to succeeding the ruler, as had happened in the past to "Eumenes, the chief secretary to Alexander the Great" and "most eminent after him," who "succeeded him in the kingdom."

It is surprising that when he drew up his "Tavola" to Il Pigna's *Il principe* Sansovino failed to refer to Plutarch's anecdote concerning Eumenes. Alexander's secretary had an entry in the index, but it mentioned his name and his position with no gloss or heading to refer to the outcome of his adventures. This absence becomes downright astonishing when we note that Sansovino discussed Eumenes at some length in his own *Il segretario*. Although Sansovino's manual followed Il Pigna's treatise, using the same terminology and the same examples, in the process of borrowing words and plagiarizing the text Sansovino made radical changes in individual concepts and in the overall meaning of the work. Sansovino's work described a totally new sort of secretary: he was no longer merely a counselor and a cultivated scrivener with a limited function as an expert in rhetoric whose efforts were applied to the epistolary correspondence of the lord whom he served.

Il Pigna compared the secretary to an angel; Sansovino repeated the comparison and transmitted it, word for word, to the tract writers of the eighteenth century. Sansovino "trimmed" the original text, however, avoiding a strict copy:

> The secretary . . . must remember that he is the heart and the mind of the court: since he sees matters pertaining to the Prince's state arise from their first roots, he will put them in his own breast just as if in an impregnable fortress or, to put it better, as if in a most holy and secure sacristy, from which his name perhaps comes, out of respect for which his loyalty must be just as great as the transactions that are revealed and entrusted to him.

The secretary's functions depended upon secrecy and discretion. His acquaintance with the ruler's correspondence and his knowledge of the ciphered codes used by the chancery enjoined on him the duty of silence. His first task was to win his master's confidence, in his work and by means of his writing. This was slow work in which the indirect approach proved the best. Ingegneri counseled imitating the virtues of the snail: "Writing," he advised, punning on the two meanings of *lumaca* (a snail; spiral stairs) was "like a spiral staircase, by which [the secretary], behind the scenes and by the shortest route, rises to familiarity with his patron, into whose trust he cannot arrive as quickly by the grand staircase, that is, by the high steps of court service." Tasso emphasized the secretary's gift for silence: "It may happen that the secretary's entire service and his entire life are silent persuasion." "Explaining by letter" or "explaining concepts in the form of a letter" was the "soul" of the "profession." The secretary's mission was truly angelic in that he put into words and into "lines of ink" on paper the "first root" and the "pith" of "concepts" that were not his own but those of his divine employer. Capaccio put it this way:

> Therefore participation in royal thoughts seems to have something of the divine about it, from which it follows that, as minister to intellects, in the same way that all men express the treasures of the mind with language, so he [the secretary], with his pen, makes the formless raw material of others' concepts clear and distinct; and in the form of a letter he brings splendor to the shadowy idea that receives light and spirit from his expressions; he makes distant things seem present, he facilitates negotiations, he puts times in harmony, he establishes memory, and wherever his letter arrives he subjugates the world.

The phenomenology of the secretary's angelic powers went so far as to present him as the hermeneutic interpreter of things merely hinted at, or of what people neglected to say. Gramigna stated:

> It may happen that as soon as his patron begins to speak the clever secretary will have understood what he is driving at, and that he can also seek (as is often the case) to provide his patron with something that, because he may have forgotten it or not expected it, he might otherwise have let slip by, to the detriment of his reputation or with harm to the negotiation.

Certainly a "gentleman," thanks to his "loyalty" and his "knowledge," the secretary or "pen-speaker" (*dicitor di penna*) was ultimately the "executor of the will of others"; he was a "loyal sign" of the employer whose orders he followed. As Persico put it, he was *di ragione altrui* (a reflection of others' thoughts); in the execution of their orders, he must "garb himself in his patron's sentiments" (Tasso). The "angelic" secretary disappeared in the message that he transmitted in a letter: it was not his "I" that spoke in correspondence but the person of his patron. If not downright invisible, the secretary rarely appeared, and he worked "with silent industry" and "without making a show" (Persico). He should not seek fame or glory. Tasso stated that "the honors . . . of the secretary are often hidden, as are secrets. . . . Thus the aim of secretaries is not glory . . . but the good graces of their patrons." Persico added, "Therefore it is often prudent to dissimulate one's understanding and knowledge; to be miserly of oneself and concealed." The classical model for this paragon was Sallustius Crispus, secretary to Tiberius, whom Tacitus praised in his *Annales* for his strength of character, "underneath a vigorous mind fit for great affairs, all the keener for its indolent, sleepy mask" (III 30, Grant translation).

There were no portraits of the secretary, nor could there be one. His body, his gestures, his clothing, and his pronunciation must all be such that he remained in the background; he must be inconspicuous, conformist, anonymous. To become a secretary was to choose solitude. Angelo Ingegneri forbade him any regional or city accent. He must be healthy and of a robust constitution, but his body, Costo declared, must be contained in an armor of clothing of severe cut, black (as Castiglione had advised nearly a century earlier) or at most gray "if he were young." Giovanni della Casa's *Il galateo* added that he should not wear a sword or plume in his hat and criticized the "feathered" Neapolitan and Spanish secretaries. To avoid indiscreet and prying eyes, he was advised to seek "solitude and calm" in a room far from the center of activities. His retiring habits should preclude joining social conversation with dinner guests. Costo declared, "Gravity, honesty, and modesty in every act are fitting to the profession of the secretary. . . . For this reason the best course is to flee conversation as much as possible, and it would please me very much if you ate in your room alone, because at table the courtiers usually buzz like cicadas and rarely is their chatter honest." Costo advised his nephew, whose career as a secretary was just beginning, to keep a tight rein on his tongue and avoid involuntary use of words that might be misunderstood: "You must take care not to use words that are less than honest or that, even if they are in themselves honest and said with good intentions, have some semblance of obscenity, such as *un cotale, vostra natura, montare, materia e forma, fessura,* and the like, which can be taken in the wrong sense."

Since he was a physical part of the mind of his patron, who was the inspiration of all things, and since he had the function of putting his patron's thoughts into execution, the secretary was not represented as a whole body. He was, for instance, "*a hand* of the will of the prince and an instrument of his governance." This is how Diego de Saavedra Fajardo portrayed the secretary in his *Idea de un príncipe político-cristiano, representada en cien empresas* (1640), where an illustration shows a hand emerging from a cloud holding a pair of compasses "because not only must he write but also measure and regulate resolutions and encompass opportunities and times." A German work, *Der teutsche Secretarius,* written in 1655 by Georg Philipp Harsdörfer, also stressed the hand and the writing instruments of the secretary. This time the secretary's hand was as muscular as a laborer's hand—a nourishing hand, as Rubens said (with the help of the psalmist). It was notably different from the nerveless hand of the Petrarchan lyrical tradition, and a far cry from the hands with interlaced fingers that Raphael shows in his portrait of Castiglione. Here the secretary's hand resembled the one that Don Quixote offered the inn-keeper's daughter: "Take, I say, this hand. . . . I presented it to you, not that you may kiss it, but that you may admire the contexture of the sinews, the interlacement of the muscles, the width and spaciousness of the veins, whence you may infer the strength of the arm that owns such a hand" (I, 43, Robinson Smith translation). The *hidalgo*'s hand and the secretary's hand were related to the anatomical studies of hands and arms engraved by Jan Stephan van Calcar for Vesalius's *De humani corporis fabrica* (1543).

The secretary's hand was industrious, accustomed to hard work. The sections in the treatises that served as manuals of rhetoric and guides to secretarial skills offered practical advice on how to write letters of all sorts—persuasive, demonstrative, judgmental, complimentary; "familiar, official, and business" letters. The manuals gave advice on how to write a letter, on its unifying "thread," its "order" and "concepts"; on how to arrange ideas; on spelling and punctuation; on writing hands, titles, inscriptions, superscriptions, and subscriptions; on how to introduce quotations and maxims; on the choice of seals (large, small, made with rings); on writing paraphernalia such as "pocket knives, scissors, pens, inkwells, paper, ink, wax, string, [and] sand." The sender of the message determined what was written, but how it was written was up to the secretary. Guarini reinforced that notion: only the person who did the writing (the "instrument of politics") had knowledge of and skill in "rhetoric":

> There is a great difference between the areas proper to the rhetorician and political and moral principles. The latter treat the 'why' of things; the former are limited, so to speak, to the 'how.' Politicians base their actions in reason; rhetoricians, in opinion; politicians depend on the assent of the wise alone; rhetoricians depend on that of the common people.

The secretary was a "child of obedience" and a "friend of servitude": "Thus the secretary must obey; it is his portion, just as that of the patron is to command" (Zinano). The secretary must be acquainted with "history, ancient and modern" and be aware of "today's news," which was "history, present and alive." He might also be a poet, except that when he expressed his patron's thoughts he must write not as an adept of the

Muses but as a follower of Mercury, the god of commerce, and act "like a man who must keep negotiations alive with his words" (Capaccio).

For his manual work (*le manifatture*) the secretary had available copiers, couriers, and postriders who copied drafts, sealed correspondence, prepared letters for sending, and dispatched them. He also had assistants. Nonetheless, he had sole responsibility for keeping a record of his patron's correspondence, for its organization and safekeeping, and for knowledge of the "expedient of ciphers" or coded messages. He had to be on the lookout for forgers and counterfeiters. Pio Rossi, a Hieronymite monk, warned of these dangers in the first "course" of his "banquet"—the *Convito morale per gli etici, economici e politici* (1639): "The greatest dangers that a secretary runs are having his hand counterfeited and being taken in by forged writings." History had lessons to teach here. Celio Malespini boasted of a new and fabulous skill, the art of "counterfeiting the hands of others" and forging "all sorts of letters" and offered his skills to the highest bidder, for instance, in a letter dated August 19, 1579, addressed to the doge of Venice and to the Council of Ten of the Venetian Republic. It is no coincidence that the study of graphology arose in the seventeenth century with Camillo Baldi's *Trattato come da una lettera missiva si conoscano la natura e qualità dello scrittore* (1622), a work that promised a way to open a "Socratic window" into the writer's heart.

Writing letters required skill: "One must have regard not only to what one writes but also to whom one writes in order to govern one's pen and humble it or raise it according to each person's deserts" (Benvenga). The secretary had to be careful to be consistent in his use of the titles with which the correspondents—important correspondents in particular—were addressed. To avoid discourtesies and errors, the secretary might keep a private book in which he noted the exact title accorded each correspondent in the first letter sent to him or her. The secretary's work was subject to the patron's whims, and open to criticism from rival secretaries who kept an eye on official and even private correspondence and were ready to pick out the least fault or the slightest grammatical error and make much of it. Tommaso Costo discovered this when he was involved in a quarrel (epistolary, of course) with a man in the service of Don Cesare d'Avalos named Andrea Romanazzo, a man whom Costo declared was made "of the stuff of a corner barber rather than a secretary." Romanazzo reacted:

You go about criticizing me and saying that you have four of my letters in which there are a number of errors, and that you were resolved to bear them to signor don Giovanni [d'Avalos]. On my word as a gentleman, I swear that when I heard this I laughed so hard that the gentlemen of the court who were present were obliged to do the same; and this not because

I presume that my writings are in any way irreproachable, which would be a strange aberration, but rather because I am sure that they are not so full of defects as to be rightly subjected to criticism or censure by you.

Costo counterattacked using Romanazzo's own weapons. He procured several of his rival's letters and covered them with as many corrections as a schoolboy's homework. He then used the letters as a lesson on proper secretarial procedures:

You must know, then, that whoever chooses the profession of writing letters must, in my opinion, consider three things without which one can never write well: the first is for whom one writes, the second, about what, and the third, to whom. For whom first, because it is not the same thing to write for oneself and for others, and, when one writes for others, [it is not the same] to write for a man of low estate, or for a private knight to lords of high estate, or from equal to equal, or from great lords to inferior persons, and so forth because, according to the rank of the person for whom one writes and that of the one to whom [one writes] one must, using one's judgment, use terms and words that honestly show the greater estate of the one and the lesser of the other, according to the degree of difference between them.

Secretaries, in particular those of "middling and minor success," felt the need for edifying treatises, which were all the more efficacious when based on practical experience. Tasso recognized the value of Ingegneri's personal experience in a sonnet published to accompany the latter's *Buon secretario* (1594, 1595, and 1607) and his *Perfetto secretario* (1613):

E tu nel Vatican la nobil forma
del segretario a noi descrivi e mostri:
in lei pur te, co'l tuo Signore, espresso.

*(In the Vatican you describe to us and show us
the noble form of the secretary, and in [that
form] you express yourself and your Lord.)*

It was in fact true that nearly all secretaries—for laymen or for prelates—determined what was written. They were guiding angels whose "angelic knowledge" came to the aid of those who aspired to become "eminent ministers of hidden thoughts," as Angelo Grillo said in a line from a poem that served as an epigraph to Zucchi's *L'idea del segretario,* a highly successful work that went through five printings before 1614. The treatise writer's angelic hand thus urged on and guided the hand of the scribes of God, much like the hand of the angel in the first version of the *St. Matthew and the Angel* (1602) that Caravaggio painted for the altar of the Contarelli chapel in the church of San Luigi dei Francesi in Rome.

The angelic theme provided a theological, hence a mythological, genealogy for a bourgeois service in search of noble origins. Capaccio stated: "Those who speak of the secretary, comparing him to the angels in authority, and who move from writing letters to the grandeur of the heavens are simply trying to demonstrate the merit of that title and the supreme prerogatives of the office." When Capaccio wrote that both the secretary and the angels could boast of a "venerable antiquity," he was evidently unaware of the involuntary humor in his comparison, which echoed a gallant pleasantry in Castiglione's *Il cortegiano*: "Madam, your age is nothing but your resemblance to the angels, who are the first and eldest creatures that God ever made" (II, 64, Singleton translation). The secretary could also point to the historical precedent of Eumenes, the secretary who took his royal patron's place. The removal of that mythological ancestor of the Baroque secretary from the "Tavola" to Il Pigna's *Il principe* changed his significance from an exemplification of promotion to royalty (something that was impossible and anachronistic) to an expression of an honorable antiquity.

THE FINGER OF HARPOCRATES

The term "secretary" was derived from "secret"—more accurately, from the *secretum,* which referred both to the study and to the archive, to a place for writing secret things and a place for storing them. In either case, the secretary was compared to a "screen" or even a "stomach." He was a master of discretion and an expert in silence and secrecy, as Fulvio Testi boasted of himself. The "second course" (1657) of Pio Rossi's moral lexicon, the *Convito morale,* contained a suggestive and imaginative entry concerning secrecy: "This most precious liquor (of secrecy, that is) requires a capacious receptacle, dark, impenetrable, and flawless; otherwise, if it were small and narrow, [its content] would overflow its rim." What Rossi meant by "rim" was any sign of emotion: glances, blushes, sudden pallors, sighs. Emotions were to be hidden behind an inexpressive face and a hard exterior. What was most to be feared was a loose tongue. And the mouth, which mediated between internal thoughts and external expression, should be closed. It was best to place the index finger firmly over it. This was the way Harpocrates, the god of discreet silence, was pictured. The wise secretary would do well to imitate a statue of that Egyptian deity: "The protection of Harpocrates, whom the Egyptians adore with a finger over his mouth to denote silence, is fitting for a secretary," Rossi declared in the entry on "The Secretary" in *Convito morale.* Another writer-secretary, Torquato Accetto, also insisted on the virtues of silence. Between 1621 and 1626 he wrestled with the problem of reconciling the "sweet" silence in his own chambers that he found necessary to write poetry and the more difficult silence of the secretariat that was necessary in his professional service:

> Poiché del sole ogni gradito raggio
> poiché vuol parte de la notte ancora
> la servitù gentil, che sempre onora
> il silenzio, la penna e 'l pensier saggio,
>
> io, che la seguo (qual mi sia), non aggio
> libera per le Muse e lieta un'ora
> se non la scemi, o sonno, a la dimora
> che toglie agli occhi stanchi il grave oltraggio.
>
> Ben vorrei, grato oblìo d'ogni mio male,
> (per men sentir la sorte aspra e rubella)
> che ne' riposi miei fermassi l'ale.
>
> Ma, per furar mio nome a tua sorella,
> ti fuggo; e s'io non ho virtute eguale,
> piacciati almen ch'io tenti opra sì bella.

> *(Because this discreet service, which always honors si-lence, the pen, and wisdom, takes up all the day and part of the night, I, who do my utmost in it, have not one hour of happy liberty for poetry, unless you, O sleep, steal it from the nightly hours of rest that take the weight of weariness from my tired eyes. Well do I wish, O sleep, who make me forget all my woes, that your wings would enfold my rest so that I might feel less keenly the pain of my harsh and adverse fate. But I flee you to snatch my name from your sister [Death]. And if my talents prove unequal to the task, may you at least be pleased that I attempt such worthy undertakings.)*

Gramigna also used an image involving statuary, contrasting a little theater for wooden or metal marionettes and a large, prestigious, elegant stage for the performance of religious dramas in order to distinguish between puppet-like letter copiers working under the direction of charlatans and true, statue-like secretaries whose movements depended upon celestial influences:

> If I must speak my mind to you freely, I liken these secretaries to the statues of Memnon who moved little if at all by their own volition but were moved when set off by the Sun appearing in the east and striking them with its rays. By the same token, such men would not know what to do with their pens if there were no one to direct their intellect and hand by continually whispering in their ears.

There is a kinship between Harpocrates and the secretarial automaton that needs someone to whisper in his ears; between the statue of silence and the statue that stands ready to spring to life on command. We need only think of the implications that the theme of silence had for the imagery of medieval and early modern times, particularly in the fine arts. Silence was connected with obedience (for example, in the sculptures in the baptistery of the Cathedral of Bergamo); it was represented along with prudence and humility (as in the fourteenth-century frescoes of the Maestro delle Vele in the vaulting of the lower church of St. Francis in Assisi) or with wisdom and impregnable faith (in the sixteenth century in Celio Calcagnini's *Descriptio silentii*).

With Memnon we come to the automaton, Persico's servant-machine or *stromento animato,* and the neo-Platonic definition of the secretary-servant. The definition of the secretary as servant also appears in treatises of neo-Aristotelian inspiration in the context of discussions of politics as a practical science. Was the secretary's function an "active" *habitus*? Was its pertinence political or rhetorical? Did it include command on the part of someone who used his intellect to plan moves, or did it just involve the physical execution of someone else's commands? Where did it fit in the hierarchy of active pursuits, where "action" was considered superior to "labor"? The conclusion was obvious. In Guarini's words: "Rhetoric . . . is the . . . true philosophy, from which [the secretary] takes the principles and the strength of his pen, and he receives but does not initiate the political concepts that he manipulates by rhetoric alone; nor is he expected to support them with the same theoretical reasoning as the politician, but rather with the practical reasoning of the orator." Nonetheless, in political moves based on service, servants, and secrecy, it was inevitable that the "mind" of command and the "body" of its execution became mutually dependent. This dependency went beyond the strategic ties of friendship that Persico recommended to both patron and servant—a notion that he borrowed from Giovanni della Casa's treatment, in his *De officiis* (in Italian, *Degli uffici comuni tra gli amici superiori e inferiori*), of the mutual benefit derived from friendships between inferiors and superiors. Invoking a collaboration between doctrine and experience, Persico stated: "Thus, since the secretary's love for and loyalty to his lord are essential, the latter must, of necessity, unite their souls with the bond of friendship; conversely, when lords entrust such ministers with their most secret interests and thoughts, their conversation will draw them closer and bind them ever more tightly."

As a technician with special skills in rhetoric and persuasion, the learned secretary was an artisan of power and of its legitimation. He was an important element in the nascent society of mass communications; in fact, it could not do without him. Thus Matteo Pellegrini could reverse the terms of the situation to state, in his *La difesa del savio in corte* (1634), that at base it was the secretary who commanded "nobly" through the prince with whom he was obliged to "lead [his] life." As Pellegrini stated: "Thus may the learned man willingly serve the prince by showing him the path of good counsel, since his counsel is a sort of command" (II, 9). The image of Harpocrates, in a century in which Giovanni Bonifaccio's *Arte de' cenni* (1616) made a science of gesture, expressed a paradox—that of speaking of one's own statements in order to "speak" of one's own silence. Torquato Accetto sounded a similar note when he protested against his lack of liberty and his servitude in a short treatise entitled *Della dissimulazione onesta* (1641), which spoke of the "honest" art of dissimulating one's very dissimulation and letting the voice of protest filter through a silence imposed by declared necessity. Dissimulation was an honest defense, a white lie (Pio Rossi called it "a weak sort of prudence"). Gabriel Chappuys, the translator of Ulrich von Hutten's *Aula,* author of an adaptation of that work, *La Misaule,* and translator of Castiglione's *Il cortegiano,* spoke of "a praiseworthy dissimulation that can be converted into prudence." It differed from simulation, which was a dishonest and aggressive form of lying: "One simulates something that is not, the other dissimulates something that is." Dissimulation was "a veil made of honest shadows and violent respects which serves not to form falsehood but to give respite to the truth." Justus Lipsius and neo-Stoicism taught that *constantia* and tactics based on prudence diminished deceit and suffering and lessened the grip of the iron hand of power. "Being a favorite and being a secretary do not go well together: simply because he has trusted you, the prince will be chary of you; he will hate you as his tyrant because it will seem to him that you hold his liberty in your hand when he has placed his conscience in you." Thus Anton Giulio Brignole Sale, in the sixth discourse of his *Tacito abburattato* (1643), banished all notions of friendship that were not the formal amity of "appearances" and the "fallacious rise and fall" of a "perpetual ball game" in which the "smoke" of favors equaled the "smoke" of obsequy. Friendship was "commerce" (*mercatura*) and wariness between persons who entered into relations with one another.

Antonio Querenghi, a secretary to cardinals, figures in a dialogue in Gramigna's *Il segretario,* along with Cardinal Scipione Cobelluzzi (whose secretary Gramigna was) and Count Alfonso Fontanelli. Reality had become theater, but both fiction and the depiction of types had roots in the passions of real life. Querenghi was no statue, and even less a puppet. To judge from his papers for the years 1615–17, which he spent for the most part in the service of Cardinal Alessandro d'Este, Querenghi's responsibilities included supervision of his employer's household and retinue down to the least detail of the cardinal's affairs. Querenghi was well aware of the need for silence—this time, a silence that prevented him from playing a role worthy of his cultural achievements precisely because he was constrained to remain mute. He was no mouthless statue (*astomos*) like Calcagnini's Harpocrates, but he knew that his patron held absolute power over those in his service, and that the servant must withdraw into obedience: "I must resign myself to the wishes of his highness, obliterating my own thoughts, as I do in so many other things in his service." Costo would have said that the fault was Querenghi's: his philosophical culture made him "overqualified" for the post. Costo might also have repeated his advice to his nephew: "It does not seem to me important that you cultivate the speculative sciences. Their loftiness, which leads to disdain of every other profession as unworthy, would turn your mind from your office so that you would care less for it and be tempted to abandon it or serve your patron badly."

In his own way, Costo had a high consideration for the position of secretary. This was because the writing of letters put him in contact with "princely" people of valor and high rank rather than with the lowly. He had nothing but scorn for the majordomo who had charge of the lower echelons of the household staff—cooks and kitchen boys, pantry workers, stewards, grooms, wine stewards, and cellarmen. Still, he knew that the secretary's nobility was fragile, precarious, and easily undermined, and he criticized patrons for their lack of sensitivity when they used their "servants of the pen" as if they were cupbearers, food tasters, or wine tasters.

> I cannot refrain from blaming the madness of one titled lord and what I might call the ineptitude (if he did not seem to me worthy of pity) of the secretary who served him. When the latter entered into [the lord's] service, constrained by necessity, he bowed his shoulders to bear every burden that the unthinking patron put on him, among other things, demanding that [the secretary] pour his drink when he ate. And more than once he reproached him because the wine was not to his liking, saying that it was up to him to supervise the sideboard and not bring him wine if it was not good. See what a beast he was: that poor young man was virtuous and served him as a secretary, and he demanded that he be a wine-boy.

The statue could not resign, but the wine-boy could. "If you should ever be unlucky enough to find yourself in such a situation, ask for your release, and do whatever you can rather than stoop to doing things that do not suit your office."

THE BODY OF PROTEUS

He may have been expected to be a statue, a puppet, or a wine-boy, but the secretary enjoyed a world that was all his own, a "theater of marvels" in which he was an expert in scenic effects and illusions. His was the fluid, changing world of Baroque writing, a mobile and magical world. The "invisible" had a body that the secretary recognized as his own: the body of Proteus. And within that body he commanded and enjoyed the privileges and pleasures of an apocryphal perspective.

It all began with a dove's neck. Tasso declared in his *Il messaggiero:*

> Just as the feathers on a dove's neck, although always the same and of the same color, at times appear ruby-colored, at times like sapphires, and at times these colors seem to change, according to how they are turned to the sun's light, so the actions of men, which are always the same, can show different facets according to how they are presented to the consideration of others. Therefore any one action, placed differently in the light of reason, seems now good, now evil, now mixed; deserving of praise, excuses, or vituperation.

This, Tasso declared, was the ambassador's art. An ambassador must be able to "make things change face" according to how they were disposed. It was a short step from this advice in the realm of diplomacy to the art of sending letters—which Angelo Grillo called "messengers." Guarini said, speaking of the secretary's versatility, "He must be clever and have a very versatile and mannered style with a rich vocabulary and an abundant command of forms. He must know how to do with his pen and his person what Proteus did with his body, transmuting it into all possible forms and varying it to his need."

Michele Benvenga made use of this earlier literature in his *Proteo segretario di lettere.* Benvenga depicted a writer who sets language free by the use of inflated metaphors, an unbridled master of verbal distortions and tricky images that enable him to say and not say, to both show and conceal his intent, to feint a move in one direction but in fact take another. Given that the secretary must "transform himself in the multiple interests of his lord," vesting himself in those interests "without divesting his patron," this new Proteus must "vary his expression since he cannot vary the matter and, in imitation of cut crystal, multiply its appearance in various guises." Furthermore, "With his varying perspectives he flatters resemblances and puts spine back into the spineless. With his fecundity, he holds the negotiations to one consonant voice, and, inflating it without adding to it quantitatively, he makes of it a miracle without miracles." Proteus was a past master of mirror tricks and *trompe-l'oeil.* He was a magician of words. He threw vocabulary on the gaming table, calculating the risk: "A prodigious atomist . . . [he takes] a few notes, one might almost say alphabetical signs, and merely by putting them in a new order and in new places, he generates everyone's thoughts without reproducing them."

The letters that the secretary wrote were "meteors," "messengers," and "doves." Sheets of letter paper were doves' necks: "That mixture of violet and rose that, seen on the dove's neck from one side, adorns it and, from the other, disappears, symbolizes the reflections of friendship on the whiteness of the sheets." The secretary's reason for being was related to the colors on the dove's neck. But they weakened and disappeared when too much was made of them: "He becomes invisible for being too much seen."

With this striking paradox the secretary of the Baroque age takes his leave. We have reached the end of the dubious offspring of Il Pigna's counselor as they were fashioned for and consigned to print. To the greater glory of the secretary's changeable and fleeting semblances in all their acrobatic and elusive forms.

BIBLIOGRAPHY

Abel, Günter. *Stoizismus und Frühe Neuzeit zur Entstehungsgeschichte modernen Denkens im Felde von Ethik und Politik.* Berlin and New York: De Gruyter, 1978.

Aricò, Denise. "Anatomie della 'dissimulazione' barocca (in margine all' 'Elogio della dissimulazione' di R. Villari)." *Intersezioni* 8, no. 3 (1988): 565–76.

Baldi, Rita. *Giovan Battista Pigna: Uno scrittore politico nella Ferrara del Cinquecento.* Genoa: ECIG, 1983.

Basso, Jeannine. *Le genre épistolaire en langue italienne (1538–1622): Répertoire chronologique et analytique.* 2 vols. Rome: Bulzoni; Nancy: Presses universitaires de Nancy, 1990.

Bernini, Ferdinando. "Un segretario inedito del Seicento." *Rivista d'Italia* (July, 1909): 85–102.

Bolzoni, Lina. "Il segretario neoplatonico." In *La Corte e il "Cortegiano".* 2 vols. Rome: Bulzoni, 1980. Vol. 2, *Un modello europeo.* Edited by Adriano Prosperi. Pages 133–69.

Bossis, Mireille, and Charles A. Porter, eds. *L'épistolarité à travers les siècles: Geste de communication et/ou d'écriture.* Colloque, Centre culturel international de Cerisy La Salle. Stuttgart: F. Steiner-Verlag, 1990.

Calamandrei, Piero. Introduction to Francesco Sansovino, *L'avvocato, e Il segretario.* Pages 7–64. Florence: Le Monnier, 1942.

Calcagnini, Celio, Celio Malespini, Giuseppe Battista, and Pio Rossi. *Elogio della menzogna.* Edited by Salvatore S. Nigro. Palermo: Sellerio, 1990.

Chastel, André. "Signum harpocraticum." In *Studi in onore di Giulio Carlo Argan.* 3 vols. Rome: Multigrafica, 1984–85, Vol. 1, pp. 147–53.

Costo, Tomaso, and Michele Benvenga. *Il segretario di lettere.* Edited by Salvatore S. Nigro. Palermo: Sellerio, 1991.

Costanzo, Mario. *I segni del silenzio e altri studi sulle poetiche e l'iconografia letteraria del Manierismo e del Barocco.* Rome: Bulzoni, 1983.

Courtine, Jean-Jacques, and Claudine Haroche. *Histoire du visage: Exprimer et taire ses émotions XVIe-début XIXe siècle.* Paris: Rivages, 1988.

Dal Prà, Laura. "Il gesto del silenzio: Segreto, meditazione e ascesi nell'arte figurativa." Pages 403–19 in *Le forme del silenzio e della parola.* Edited by Massimo Baldini and Silvano Zucal. Brescia: Morcelliana, 1990.

Deonna, Waldemar. "Le silence, gardien du secret." *Zeitschrift für Schweizerische Archeologie und Kunstgeschichte* 12 (1951): 28–41.

Di Benedetto, Arnaldo. Introduction to *Prose di Giovanni della Casa e altri trattatisti cinquecenteschi del comportamento.* Pages 9–34. Turin: UTET, 1974.

Doglio, Maria Luisa. "Ambasciatore e principe: L'*Institutio legati* Ermolao Barbaro." In *Miscellanea di studi in onore di Vittore Branca.* 5 vols. Florence: Leo S. Olschki, 1983. Vol. 3, *Umanesimo e Rinascimento a Firenze e Venezia,* part 1, pp. 297–310.

———. "Le 'Istituzioni' di Mario Equicola: Dall' 'institutio principis' alla formazione del segretario." *Giornale storico della letteratura italiana* 99, vol. 159, fasc. 508 (1982): 505–35.

———. "Nota critica." Pages 615–33 in Fulvio Testi, *Lettere.* 3 vols. Bari: G. Laterza, 1967.

Eisenbichler, Konrad and Philip Sohm, eds. *The Language of Gesture in the Renaissance.* Special issue of *Renaissance and Reformation/Renaissance et Réforme* n. s. 10, 1 (1986).

Eymard d'Angers, Julien. *Recherches sur le stoicisme au XVIe et XVIIe siècles.* Edited by Louis Antoine. Hildesheim and New York: Georg Olms, 1976.

Guillén, Claudio. "Notes toward the Study of the Renaissance Letter." Pages 70–101 in *Renaissance Genres: Essays of Theory, History, and Interpretation.* Edited by Barbara Kiefer Lewalski. Cambridge, Mass.: Harvard University Press, 1986.

Larivaille, Paul. "Familiari, consiglieri, segretari ne *Il Principe* di Giambattista Pigna." In *"Familia" del principe e familia aristocratica.* Edited by Cesare Mozzarelli. "Europa delle Corti," Centro studi sulle società di antico regime, Biblioteca del Cinquecento, 41. 2 vols. Rome: Bulzoni, 1988. Vol. 1, pp. 27–50.

Lencioni Novelli, Roberta. *Celio Malespini tra biografia e Novella.* Naples: Liguori, 1983.

Neveux, Jean-Baptiste. "Un 'parfait secrétaire' du XVIIe siècle: 'Der Teutsche Secretarius' (1655)." *Etudes germaniques* 19, no. 4 (1964): 511–20.

Nigro, Salvatore S. "Lezione sull'ombra." Pages v–xxi in Torquato Accetto, *Rime amorose.* Edited by Salvatore S. Nigro. Turin: Einaudi, 1987.

———. "Il libro in maschera di un segretario del Seicento." *L'immagine riflessa* 6, no. 2 (1983): 201–15.

———. "Scriptor necans." In Torquato Accetto, *Della dissimulazione onesta.* Edited by Salvatore S. Nigro. Genoa: Costa & Nolan, 1983.

Oestreich, Gerhard. *Geist und Gestalt des früh modernen Staates.* Available in English as *Neostoicism and the Early Modern State.* Edited by Brigitta Oestreich and H. G. Koenigsberger. Cambridge and New York: Cambridge University Press, 1982.

Quondam, Amedeo, ed. *Le "carte messaggiere": Retorica e modelli di communicazione epistolare: Per un indice dei libri di lettere del Cinquecento.* Rome: Bulzoni, 1981.

Rubens, Peter Paul. *Lettere italiane.* Edited by Irene Cotta; introduction by Claudio Mutini. Rome: Istituto della Enciclopedia italiana, 1987.

Vecchi, Alberto. "Motivi per una ecdotica degli epistolari e dei carteggi." Pages 6–32 in *Metodologia ecdotica dei carteggi.* Edited by Elio D'Auria. Atti del Convegno internazionale di Studi, Rome, October 23–25, 1980. Florence: Le Monnier, 1989.

Villari, Rosario. *Elogio della dissimulazione: La lotta politica nel Seicento.* Rome and Bari: Laterza, 1987.

Warnke, Martin. "Der Kopf in der Hand." In *Zauber der Medusa: Europäische Manierismus.* Edited by Werner Hofmann. Catalogue of an Exhibit April 3–July 12, 1987, Wiener Künstlerhaus. Vienna: Löcker, 1987.

5

THE REBEL

Rosario Villari

ESISTANCE TO OPPRESSION and tyranny was an ideal value that
had been accepted and praised in other historical periods, but in
the Baroque age that ideal was obscured by a condemnation and
discredit of rebellion that penetrated deeply into the culture and its collective awareness. During the course of a century—from the "Defense of
Liberty against Tyrants" (*Vindiciae contra tyrannos*) written under the
pseudonym Junius Stephanus Brutus (1579; probably by the Huguenot
Philippe Du Plessis-Mornay) to Thomas Hobbes's *Behemoth* (1679)—a
vast literature on the theme of rebellion was produced, supporting or ne-
gating its legitimacy, proposing revolt or combating it, analyzing the
causes of rebellion or certain of its aspects, giving a general survey of
rebellions, or relating the history of individual uprisings. A more limited
span of some fifty years (1590–1640) stands out within that time span
and in that vast literature (a simple inventory of which would fill a volume) as a period in which negation and rejection clearly prevailed over
justification or discussion of opposing ideas and viewpoints.

This attitude was prevalent in the spirit of the age as well as in the
doctrines and practices of governments, and although it was particularly
rigid, it was not without apparent incoherence and ambiguities. All governments attempted to foment rebellion (insurrectional movements, conspiracies, and terrorist acts) in enemy lands, and it is hardly surprising
that England and France came to the aid of the republic of the United
Provinces, or that Pope Urban VIII, in the wake of the Portuguese revolution of 1640, failed to turn away the bishop of Lamego, the envoy and
messenger of the rebel duke of Braganza, with as much dispatch and deci-
siveness as the Spanish government desired. What does seem surprising,
on the other hand, is that such an ideologically conservative age, which
seemed to preclude both ideological preparation for change and challenge

to formal, legitimate power, should have ended, in the decade from 1640
to 1650, in nearly universal revolutionary crisis. Furthermore, the two
events that framed the Baroque period were the beginning of the Netherlands rebellion and the Portuguese independence. For many years Spanish
diplomatic and governmental records continued to refer to William of
Orange and the duke of Braganza, the heads of the two new independent
states, as rebels and their countries as rebel nations, but outside the Habsburg domains contemporaries had a less negative view of the two events.
Some remarked that when entire national communities were called "rebel," it was one way of recognizing the legitimacy of a rebellion backed
by general consensus.

It is nonetheless true that in the late sixteenth century and the first
decades of the seventeenth century, condemnation of rebellion was a
dominant characteristic in culture and thought. José Antonio Maravall
has maintained that Baroque culture as a whole was a response, urged by
the ruling classes and by governments, to the threat of rebellion and social
protest. In Maravall's view, the enormous growth of cultural manifestations directed toward the common people can be explained by a need for
widespread preventive measures and a desire to condition popular opinion. Thus Baroque culture was a government culture working in the interests of political stability and public tranquility that managed to impose
itself and gain common acceptance, drastically thrusting aside (more than
had been true in past times) notions of opposition, protest, or subversion,
whether open or clandestine. A thesis as radical as this, applied to a broad
cultural movement that was unified but not univocal, necessarily elicits
doubts and reservations today, even though it is supported by a traditional
interpretation of the Baroque age as a period of widespread conformity
and authoritarian reaction. Strong pressures exerted from on high and a
widely diffused sense of living in a period of exceptional apprehension
and turbulence, brought on by the growth of the urban population, economic crisis, social conflict, and a shared feeling of instability, can offer
only a partial or very generic explanation of a tendency toward rigid cultural uniformity and a nearly universal acceptance of principles that excluded the hypothesis (or even the very idea) of resistance to power. One
trait characteristic of the period was its need to consider "means for en-
tertaining the people" and "how to avoid riots and rebellions." Giovanni
Botero, whose name necessarily comes up in any discussion of Baroque
political culture, stated this explicitly in 1589:

> Because the common people are by nature unstable and long for novelty
> they will seek it out for themselves, changing even their government and
> their rulers if their prince does not provide some kind of diversion for them.

Knowing this, the wisest rulers have introduced various popular entertainments which exercise the powers of the mind and the body and which are
the more effective the better they succeed in doing this. (*Reason of State,*
III, 1; Waley translation, 76)

Botero cites approvingly the ceremonies, festivities, and celebrations
with which Cardinal Carlo Borromeo had seen fit to "entertain the multitudes of Milan ... so that the churches were filled with people from
morning to evening, and no people was ever so happy, so contented, and
so tranquil as the Milanese of those days" (Waley translation, 75). Theater was another way to mobilize cultural spectacles, and Botero preferred
the gravity of tragedy to the frivolity of comedy. There were other and
more persuasive ways, however, to prevent popular unrest and provide
for the edification of the people than public entertainments and pleasing
fantasy. The obsessive repetition of maxims, images, and formulas presented a baleful vision of rebellion; the atrocity and the spectacularly public nature of punishment and repression were even more forceful means
to the same end. Here the collaboration between juridical culture and
power played an important role in finding or inventing ways in which "the
people should be treated," and public opinion encouraged harsh measures
by concurring on the need to mete out the cruelest sorts of punishment
to rebels and to inculcate terror by example.

Still, the conservatism of governments and the ruling classes and their
overall cultural and propagandistic activities are not a sufficient explanation of the horror of change and novelty that so strongly stamped the
entire epoch, conditioning the thought of people whose independence of
judgment was unquestioned, and even the ideas and the psychology of
opponents to the status quo. There were some in the Baroque age who
claimed the right to defend, *armata manu,* the positions, interests, freedoms, and privileges of social groups or communities, but such demands
tended to be based on proclamations of obedience and loyalty to the sovereign rather than on resistance to a tyrant, as had been the case earlier.
This was one of the paradoxical outcomes of the new course of politics
in the Baroque period. Those who did not follow that approach and who
continued to attack the majesty and authority of the king head-on appeared to be (and in part were) shadows and ghosts from the past.

The term "rebel" is to some extent ambiguous. Even though the term
was applied, in the sixteenth and seventeenth centuries, specifically to persons who fomented political change (and, by direct assimilation, to the
heretic), it was also used in connection with all forms of protest and insubordination, and even for criminals, bandits, and all manner of social
deviants—people who had little or nothing to do with political subversion or heresy. Still, even if the age was obsessed with the presence of the

rebel (in the broadest and most generic sense of the term) in its midst, that would not be sufficient reason for including him in a gallery of Baroque types. Millenarianism, egalitarian utopias, and a variety of forms of basic protest including "social" banditry and hunger riots were intensely and frequently present in the Baroque period, but there was little that distinguished such manifestations from their counterparts in earlier or later periods. The decision to include the rebel among the typical figures of the Baroque age in the present volume presupposes at least a reconsideration, if not a reversal, of a generic, summary, and, on occasion, misleading portrait. There were moments when rebellion—with all its contradictory and multiple aspects, propositions, tendencies, and outcomes—succeeded in crossing the difficult threshold into politics and, by that token, succeeded in influencing the dynamics of society and institutions and, in exceptional circumstances, even contributed to their renewal and their development. Thus it is possible (and even necessary) to distinguish in the *mare magnum* of rebellion in the early modern period manifestations that had at least a potentially political content.

In spite of deliberate attempts on the part of the more direct representatives of power to confuse the issue where rebellion was concerned, for immediately political ends or in order to enhance the "reputation" of governments and governing groups, Baroque culture made the appropriate distinctions and kept them in mind when it judged the many specific instances of rebellion. Purely social protest, ranging from the urban riot to the peasant *jacquerie* and brigandage tinged with varying degrees of social purpose, was quantitatively extremely important in European history of the late sixteenth century and the first half of the seventeenth century, but it was not per se judged to involve a "change in the state." In spite of widespread interest in and attention given to the more elementary forms of protest, anticonformism, and subversion, and in spite of the endemic frequency of such manifestations, rejection and fear centered on the figure of the political rebel. He served as a focus for the broadly diffused resistance to change and mistrust of novelty that inhabited both the culture and the shared mentality of the Baroque age.

During this long period, the Spanish monarchy was the state most stricken with anxieties and internal lacerations. It was not Spanish culture, however, that initiated the new phase in the demonization of the rebel: the epicenter of that movement was late sixteenth-century France. There was good reason for this, for France had undergone a catastrophic experience unique among European monarchies. Thirty years of revolts and civil wars had wounded the nation to the heart, pushed it to the brink of ruin and dissolution, and torn its political fabric asunder. "The signs of our misfortunes will remain forever in France," David Rivault, the future tutor of Louis XIII, wrote in 1595. Condemnation of rebellion had a central position in the renewal of political and religious ideas that followed the assassination of Henry III in 1589 and accompanied the early years of the reign of Henry IV. The spread of that condemnation to the rest of Europe is a topic that has been little studied, but it is evident that when the problem arose in the political literature of the other European countries during those same years, writers, beginning with Justus Lipsius and Botero, referred constantly, directly or indirectly, to France's experience of revolution and to ways in which the promoters of the restoration and renewal of the French monarchy interpreted that experience. Enormous tasks confronted France: putting an end to the period of the Wars of Religion, opening the way to the political and moral reconstruction of the nation, and proposing new ways in which different churches could coexist and new relations between sovereign and subject could be established. Sweeping ideological and political efforts to reach those objectives presupposed a radical critique and perhaps the liquidation of doctrines that for thirty years had provided an ideological screen for violence and for the revolutionary movements that in three decades had unhinged the power and authority of the sovereign.

In all its variants, the theory of the legitimacy of rebellion against a tyrant that had been elaborated during the course of the sixteenth century, on the example of ample medieval and humanistic precedents, was theocratic in inspiration. In France that theory was taken over by the Huguenots after the massacre of St. Bartholomew's Day, and it was expressed with full intensity and dynamism in the *Vindiciae*. Its theocratic inspiration was consonant with Catholic extremism, however: Jean Boucher, Guillaume Rose, and other Catholic theologian-politicians readily transferred it into the camp of the Catholic League, the bitterest adversaries of Henry IV. With the publication of Juan de Mariana's *De Rege et Regis Institutione* (1599), the theory, expediently revised, became quasi-official doctrine among the Jesuits.

When Henry of Navarre fell heir to the throne, the most authoritative Huguenot opponents of monarchy became staunch supporters of hereditary rights and converted to the absolutist concept of sovereignty, but their antimonarchic propaganda had left deep traces that were not easy to brush away. Both the author of the *Vindiciae* and François Hotman, in his *Franco-Gallia,* had attempted to add to the religious justification of rebellion an autonomous juridical and political basis in the theory of the elective origin of the monarchy and the preeminence of the Estates General over the sovereign. Catholic theoreticians too had modified the rigidly aristocratic nature of their original theory, thus enlarging its potential influence well beyond the terrain within which and for which it had arisen.

The great antirevolutionary campaign that developed in France in reaction to the disasters of the Wars of Religion was conducted above all by the so-called *Politiques,* a party opposed to both the League and the Huguenots. The *Politiques* provide an interesting example of collaboration between political power and culture and of a convergence around a common objective of men of divergent practical experience and ideological positions. Some of the major figures in this movement were Pierre Charron, a friend of Montaigne's and the author of the well-known *Traité de la sagesse;* Daniel Drouin, whose *Miroir des rebelles* can perhaps be considered the first text in Baroque literature specifically and systematically dedicated to revolution; the group of Parisians who wrote the famous *Satyre Ménippée* on the occasion of the Estates General convened in 1593 by the leaders of the Catholic League; David Rivault, who has already been mentioned; Gabriel Chappuys, secretary to Henry IV, his interpreter in Spanish and a translator of Boccaccio, Ariosto, Castiglione, and Niccolò Franco; and Jean de Baricave, a doctor of theology, canon of the metropolitan church of Toulouse, and author of a thousand-page treatise. Michel Roussel, the spokesman for the Sorbonne, and William Barclay, a Scot who had emigrated to France and was professor of law at the University of Angers (it was he who coined the term *monarchomachus*), enlarged the scope of the campaign by extending its discourse beyond the confines of French political culture to include George Buchanan and Juan de Mariana.

The demonstration that the "monarchomachist" texts were based on an erroneous and arbitrary interpretation of Holy Scripture obviously played a major role in the campaign of the *Politiques,* but their best arguments lay in the obvious destruction that rebellion had brought to France and in drawing connections, on various levels of intensity, between the French experience and the phenomena of rebellion that other European countries had experienced during the sixteenth century.

The assassinations of Henry III in 1589 and Henry IV in 1610 defined two moments of particularly intense polemics. The principal arguments of the counter-revolutionary offensive had already been elaborated and firmly established by 1590. The assassination of Henry III, unlike that of his successor, was not an isolated episode; it occurred at the climax of revolutionary agitation, immediately following an uprising in Paris and the Day of Barricades fostered by the Catholic League in May 1588, when the sovereign had been forced to flee from the capital and his prestige and authority had fallen to their lowest point. The *Satyre Ménippée,* published in 1594, offered a gallery of portraits of the leaders of the rebellion—members of the aristocracy and the ecclesiastical hierarchy and major protagonists in the final phase of the civil wars. These men—the duke of Mayenne, the archbishop of Lyons, the rector of the Sorbonne, the ill-famed, part-noble, part-brigand governor of Pierrefonds, and the papal legate—provided an impressive series of portrayals of brutal egotism, arrogance, injustice, demagoguery, and disloyalty to the nation. The work was immensely popular, not only thanks to the literary talents of the authors of that "king of pamphlets" (as the *Satyre* was called in the nineteenth century) but also because the work gained credibility and force from the deplorable conditions in the country, the outcome of the rebellion, the evident decline of ideal and religious values, widespread anarchy and terror, and the presence of Spanish militia in the capital. "O Paris," the pamphlet exclaimed, "You are no longer Paris but the lair of ferocious beasts, a fortress of Spaniards, Walloons, and Neapolitans, a refuge and an asylum for thieves, murderers, and assassins. Will you never reclaim your dignity and remember what you once were?"

The patriotic scorn and civic passion that made the *Satyre* a classic of political literature and a landmark in French national awareness were not so much directed at condemnation of the theory of rebellion as they were aimed at unmasking the various rebels and denouncing the contradiction between their stated principles and their actual behavior, their declared goals and the results of their acts. Daniel Drouin's *Miroir des rebelles* was quite different in its orientation. Its force of conviction was based on an attempt to draw general conclusions from the particular experience of France, or, more precisely, to establish a close connection between an evaluation of the French experience and a general and theoretical condemnation of rebellion. Drouin considered rebellion within a panorama reaching from the history of the Hebrew people to medieval and early modern Christian Europe, discussing in passing the Greek world and the Persian, Roman, and Turkish empires. It was in its dimensions as part of universal history that the full significance of the history of France in the preceding thirty years should be seen. Drouin's panoramic survey concluded:

> It is to you, my French nation, that I have attempted to speak in this book
> ... because nowhere in the world today is there a people more dedicated
> to sedition than you. . . . Heed me well, miserable rebels and persecutors of
> your own nation. . . . With what argument, with what pretext do you continue to offer armed resistance to the Crown? In truth you have none, and
> there has never been a rebellion more unmotivated than yours.

The judgment that pervaded Drouin's historical survey and his reconstruction of nearer and more recent events was that rebellion was always fated to fail and punishment was ineluctable. He presented this inevitable and perennial outcome as a sign of God's intention to support legitimate power, even when that power was in the hands of pagan and idolatrous kings: "If faithless rebels ignorant of the ways of salvation have not been spared by the vengeful hand of the Omnipotent, who chose to maintain

pagan and idolatrous sovereigns in their kingdoms, what will become of
the Christians who brazenly rise up against their lords?" Proclaiming that
"God is always on the side of legitimacy," Drouin's work used the theme
of failure to give historical support to the theory of the divine origin of
royal power that was the common denominator and the positive theoretical basis of the entire counter-revolutionary campaign. The argument
seemed to men of the sixteenth century less abstract and less founded in
a priori reasoning than it does to us. What made the figure of the rebel of
the Baroque age tragic—his eagerness to avoid being branded as a rebel,
even in contradiction with his own acts and his own goals; his attempts to
connect himself at all costs to a constitutional legality and an established
tradition—depended largely on the conviction that rebellion was fated
to fail. Although the Protestant Reformation suggested that successful
revolution was possible, on the more strictly political and social plane
failure was the rule.

Drouin attributed the unavoidable failure of rebellions to divine will,
but he also gave more immediate reasons for the high probability, even
the mechanical necessity, of failure and punishment. Drouin made it clear,
in a complex typology of rebellion that included both great peasant uprisings "with no other heads than thieves and brigands" and urban uprisings
(Paris riots in particular), that the true danger came from "the Great."
Popular uprisings, rural and urban, purely social protests, and hunger
riots, per se, were unlikely to affect the stability of the state. They became
dangerous only if "the Great" used them as means to serve their own
ends. This was what had happened during the Wars of Religion: "The
Greatest had the greatest guilt." Drouin concluded from this that the common people must be punished in the severest possible manner in order to
prevent them from being led astray or from being used and manipulated
in support of high-level political designs. "If today rebels were punished
in this exemplary fashion," Drouin suggested after listing a number of
atrocious tortures inflicted on those who had attempted rebellions in the
past, "there undoubtedly would not be such a large number of them: the
fear of such torture would urge them to abandon the party of sedition."
The ruler's true and just indignation, Drouin continued, should nonetheless "fall upon the Great, who are usually the cause of so many tumults
and seditions . . . considering also the fact that the punishment of great
persons, inflicted publicly, inspires greater fear in the commonality and
serves as a better example than if a thousand of the lesser were hanged.
Justice inflicted on one of the Great terrifies an infinite multitude of the
small."

As an action promoted and inspired by the nobility, and in particular
by the great lords, rebellion seemed, and in general was, violence in defense of particular interests and an unjust defense of archaic privileges

that worked against the overall interest of the nation and against a political and social equilibrium guaranteed by the monarchy. Its retrograde
content was what weakened rebellion. Furthermore, any revolutionary
act could achieve even limited efficacy only if it had popular support—a
support that the Great had indeed ceaselessly cultivated and organized
during the civil wars. This demagoguery was considered an utterly nefari-
ous attack on civil coexistence and on society because it unleashed brutish instincts and barbarity; at the same time, it was a sign of wishful
thinking and unreason because nothing was more fragile and illusory
than popular support, which would inevitably collapse before long.

We see here all the elements of the Baroque model for the interpretation of rebellion. In the complex relationships among religious
movements, aristocratic opposition, and popular agitation, emphasis on
subversive tendencies among the nobility and denunciation of the exploitation of religion were certainly nothing new. Past events had often been
interpreted in a similar vein. For example, no less a personage than the
ambassador of the Venetian Republic in Paris had asserted that the French
civil wars had arisen because the Cardinal of Lorraine could brook no
equals and Admiral Coligny and the House of Montmorency would recognize no one superior to them. The *Politiques* worked to fit the various
components of the revolutionary experience into a systematic analysis
that suggested an overall judgment of the phenomenon of rebellion in
contemporary society and that made it possible to find analogies and confirmation in other historical events. What occurred in France, as we have
seen, influenced the political theory of Botero and Justus Lipsius. Botero
referred frequently to France: he spoke of "the great troubles in France,
the sound of which has been heard over here"; France's rulers and her
soldiers had "reduced to extreme poverty what was once a flourishing
kingdom"; France was "deserted and coming to ruin." It is not impossible
that what Botero had to say about the subversive tendencies of Italian
nobles and about instances of noble rebellion in Italy was directly connected to the positions of the French *Politiques*. Botero stated:

> There is both good and bad in the feudal lords of a kingdom. The bad is
> their authority and power, which are suspect to the supreme ruler as pres-
> enting possible sources of aid or refuge to any rebels against his authority
> (which happened in the kingdom of Naples, where the Princes of Taranto
> and Salerno and the Dukes of Sessa and Rossano all played this part). (*Rea-
> son of State*, IV, 5; Waley translation, 86)

Lipsius, too, considered "the factions of the nobles," "the discords
among important and powerful men," and their penchant for "putting
everyone under their sway and healing their own wounds with the misfortunes of the Republic" to be the cause of "universal ruin" and the worse

ills of the state. His Italian translator, Ercole Cati, a gentleman from Ferrara, commented in 1618:

> Without seeking other examples of the nature and effects of factions, it is
> quite enough to consider here the strange events that have occurred in
> France and in Flanders owing to conspiracy and the aversion of these coun-
> tries against their true and legitimate Princes, under the pretext of freedom
> of conscience and religion, but in fact among the largest number of the
> greatest and most powerful Lords out of resentment, hatred, and special
> envy of one house for another, to drive the other out of authority and power
> . . . and, finally, when there is thought to be an interregnum, some, in order
> to occupy a parcel of the kingdom for themselves . . . others, another [par-
> cel], and still others to take entire possession of the crown.

Lipsius's position on the question of tyrannicide was perfectly consistent with the campaign of the French *Politiques*. Although Lipsius recognized that insurgency against tyranny and wiping it from the face of the
globe required "men of the highest courage" and that "the Greeks attributed divine honors to those who killed tyrants," he asserted that the problem was best and most prudently resolved by tolerating tyranny. Power
comes from God; civil war is worse than tyrannicide; submission softens
the hearts of tyrants, and change might bring something even worse:
"Thus I conclude that one must put up with the character of Princes."

The revival of the counter-revolutionary campaign in 1610 was primarily theoretical, and it added little to the stock of notions already acquired. In the climate of high popular feeling that followed the assassination of Henry IV, the connection that had been established between
parricide and rebellion ratified a condemnation that had already met with
broad consensus in public opinion and the national consciousness and
become a paradigm of European political culture. Juan de Mariana's *De
Rege et Regis Institutione* was condemned and publicly burned on the
instigation of the Parlement de Paris and the Sorbonne. The *Vindiciae*
were mentioned on that same occasion—further confirmation of the
broad variety of opinions and orientations that were treated as theories
of tyrannicide. Jean de Baricave was persuaded that the "good" French
had not yet done all that they must to eradicate that poisonous plant.
What he meant was that a solution to the problem required radical refutation of the principles on which the theory of legitimate tyrannicide was
based. The thousand pages of his treatise are thus a painstaking and wearisome comparison between all the affirmations contained in the *Vindiciae*
and Holy Writ, with an occasional incursion into classical literature. Baricave exaggerated not only in the prolixity of his arguments but also in his
claim that his work was novel. It was true, however, that discussion of
principles and citation of facts were much more thoroughly intermingled

in the polemics of the preceding years than they were in the decrees and pronouncements of the Parlement de Paris and the Sorbonne after Ravaillac's assassination of King Henry IV. Even Charron had referred to concrete experiences in political life in a brief text that he wrote in 1589, published in 1606. He recalled in that work that he had been tempted by the League and had joined its cause (as had the great theoretician of absolutism, Jean Bodin), and he remembered his state of mind as a rebel, contrasting it to the disposition necessary for comprehending reality or for wisdom: "I was always as if in anger," Charron wrote, "in a feverish state of continual emotion, and in that manner I learned, to my own cost, that one cannot be both agitated and wise." There is also a clear echo of practical experience in a defense of monarchy that Gabriel Chappuys wrote in 1602, when Henry IV had consolidated his power and the two parties of rebellion had been defeated. In his analysis Chappuys made use of an interpretive criterion borrowed from humanistic culture (it also owed much to the *Satyre Ménippée*) that shifted emphasis away from the religious and political causes of revolt and proved extremely successful in the Baroque age. He stated that the malefic divinity of revolt was ambition, and its natural weapons were the base instincts of the populace and the plebeian penchant for turmoil and violence. Even the theory of popular sovereignty was merely instrumental, because it was ambition that incited men "to flatter the people and persuade them, against all reason, that it was up to them to reproach kings, make them toe the line, and lay down the law for them." It was precisely on the point of popular sovereignty that Chappuys noted contradictions and ambiguities in the *Vindiciae*. Chappuys wondered who was responsible, according to that famous treatise, for liberating the state from tyranny, the people or the Great?

> At first, on pages 103 and 106 of his book, Brutus gives the people all power over both kings and the Great; but then, on pages 210, 212, and 213, he takes it away from them and transfers it to the Great, declaring that the people must take no initiative, even in cases of manifest tyranny, if the Great are not in agreement with the King.

This was a burning question because the Catholic version of the theory was extremely sensitive on this point and tended to grant initiative to the politico-religious community, even to the individual subject. One of the best-known Catholic texts in support of rebellion was the *Apologie pour Jean Chastel* (the student who had attempted to kill Henry IV in 1594).

On another point Chappuys introduced—with great circumspection—an argument based on natural law that Charron had used in his *Discours*. The people could not give offense to the sovereign, but they could defend themselves from an iniquitous act on his part; they could not "shirk the subjection and reverence owed the king," but they could resist offense. It was "against nature" that an inferior take vengeance on a superior and bring punishment on him, but self-defense was part of the order of nature. Several decades later, Thomas Hobbes pointed out the inconsistency inherent in the notion of passive resistance, asserting that such ambiguities and concessions, which could be found in "official" culture but also in the works of the supporters of absolutism, had done much to prepare the way for rebellion in England.

This was certainly not Chappuys's intent, and he saw no need to make theoretical concessions to his adversaries. Rather, his distinctions were prompted by the difficult task of trying to give condemnation of rebellion the universality it needed as a guarantee of its validity. The revolution occurring in the Low Countries was a quite different matter from the Wars of Religion in France, in spite of their many points of contact, particularly as regarded the role of religious and political extremism and certain centrifugal, particularist tendencies. The *Politiques* in France were capable of categorical denial of the use of revolutionary means and of refusing to see any affinity between their ideological positions and those of William of Orange, but they were unable to put the two experiences completely on the same plane. Drouin saw the revolution of Flanders as a religious war, described the disasters and massacres that came out of it, and theorized (writing in 1592) about the inevitability of its failure. According to him, the Netherlands had "rightly" suffered the harsh punishment of the duke of Alba's terrible repression because they should have learned a lesson from their neighbors, "principally our own unfortunate France." At the same time, however, Drouin's anti-Spanish bias undermined the coherence of his argument. He recognized that discontent had been prompted by the pride and tyranny of the Spanish, "who, to tell the truth, are very rude and insolent to those whom they have subjugated." Furthermore, his description of disasters stressed the inhumanity of the duke of Alba's repression, and Drouin ultimately conceded that "even God was angered by the Spanish" and had enabled the confederacy to win several important battles. For his part, Chappuys followed up his 1602 treatise, *Citadelle de la royauté*, with a *Histoire générale de la guerre de Flandre* in two volumes (Paris: Robert Fouët, 1611), a work that bore witness to his keen interest in the question and, more important, that acknowledged the success that the "rebels" had obtained with the Twelve Years' Truce signed in Antwerp and the contribution of the late, lamented, and much-loved Henry IV to bringing about that truce.

The French *Politiques* limited their reactions to the revolutions in Flanders to a display of uncertainty. A fuller comprehension of its novelty (which, incidentally, other sectors of European culture also failed to show at first) would have weakened their counter-revolutionary campaign. What is more, even at a later date (on the eve of revolutions in England and Portugal), William of Orange seemed an exception that proved the rule. In a survey of the political scene in Europe written in 1638, Henri de Rohan noted in his *De l'intérêt des Princes,* significantly, that William had been the only one in a century to have had the honor of founding a state.

William of Orange published his *Apologie* in answer to the proclamation in which Philip II declared him a rebel and a "disturber of the state of Christendom, and specially of these low Countreyes" and promised a sizable reward and even a noble title to anyone who would remove that "publique plague" from the world. In rejecting those accusations William appealed to the constitutional traditions (the initial contract between sovereign and subjects) of the territories that formed the Low Countries, but without asserting any universal concept of independence and national identity. But whereas in other sixteenth-century revolutionary texts constitutional traditions were identified with the privileges and powers of the nobility, considered the interpreters and the sole representatives of the political nation, William conceived such traditions in broader terms as rights and freedoms of the community as a whole. In the religious field as well, William's claim to liberty was not restricted to support of the confessional practice of his coreligionists alone. In the name of that patriotism William rejected both the "absolute bondage" that Spain was attempting to impose on the Netherlands and the accusation, made in Philip II's proclamation, that his political rise was the result of demagogic exploitation of popular uprisings that had attempted to place his acts within the framework of the anarchical and particularist tradition of noble rebellion. William told the Estates General of the United Provinces that the king of Spain was

> depriving you altogether of your auncient privileges and liberties, that they may dispose of you, your wives, and your children, and handle you, as his officers have done the poore Indians, or at least as they do the people of Calabria, Sicily, Naples, and Millaine, whilest they remember not, that these countreis [were not] atcheived by conquest, but come for the most parte by the way of patrimonie, or els such as willingly gave up them selves unto his predecessours, under good and lawfull conditions. (*The Apologie,* edited after the English edition of 1581 by H. Wansink, p. 54)

The true rebels, traitors, and oath-breakers, William continued, were thus those lords (that is, members of the Netherlands aristocracy) who, in their enjoyment of political prominence and military command, had failed to oppose those who were trampling the rights and the constitutions of their country.

They upbraide me, with the great credit that I have amongst the people. . . . I confesse then, that I am, and that I wil al my life long be popular, that is to saie, that I will pursue, mainteine and defend, your libertie and your priviledges. . . . True it is, that five or six ill advised persons [have] gathered together, being the enimies of your libertie, whose . . . tyrannie . . . would be more cruell . . . than that of the Spaniardes hath bin. . . . For what other thing is the common wealth, than the good of all the people. (P. 119)

William thus presented a concept of the national political community different from and broader than the one found in sixteenth-century tradition in either its humanistic and patriotic version or its politico-religious version. William's proposal to involve the population in politics anticipated a line of thought that emerged, not without difficulties and setbacks, during the revolutionary crisis of the mid-seventeenth century. The novelty of William's statements is evident if we compare his *Apologie* with another well-known apology that sprang from the secular and humanistic tradition of writings on tyrannicide, the *Apologia* written by Lorenzino de' Medici, the assassin of his kinsman, Alessandro, duke of Florence (1537). Giacomo Leopardi, who included a portion of Lorenzino's *Apologia* in the prose volume of his *Crestomazia italiana* as testimony to the political eloquence of the sixteenth century, coupled Lorenzino's name with William's for their common struggle to liberate their people from tyranny:

> Meraviglia è colà che s'appresenti
> Maurizio di Sassonia alla tua vista,
> Che con mille vergogne e tradimenti
> Gran parte a' suoi di libertade acquista,
> Egmont, Orange a lor grandezze intenti
> Lor patria liberando oppressa e trista,
> E quel miglior che invia con braccio forte
> Il primo duca di Firenze a morte.
>
> *(What a marvel it is that Maurice of Saxony presents himself to your view, who acquired liberty for his own subjects with a thousand shames and betrayals, Egmont, Orange, intent on their grandeur, liberating their oppressed and downtrodden homelands, and that best of men whose strong arm sent the first duke of Florence to his death. [Paralipomeni della Batracomiomachia, canto 3, stanza 27])*

The similarity between Lorenzino and William was in reality only superficial. A heightened individualism, a literary and intellectual conception of the homeland, an aristocratic exclusiveness, and a fondness for conspiracy gave Lorenzino's text an idealistic and political stamp more akin to an aristocratic and urban version of feudal rebellion than was true of William's apology. What counted most for Lorenzino was the nobility of the individual act. He was quick to blame the ignorance of the people of Florence for the fact that his act produced few results and had no political resonance; he complained that even in a circumstance as extraordinary as the assassination of Duke Alessandro, no one in Florence "except for two or three behaved, I do not say as a good citizen, but as a man."

The new patriotism of William of Orange's *Apologie* failed, for the moment, to have a wide hearing for a number of reasons. It was taken more as a polemic against Spanish "imperialism" than as a potential broadening of the idea of homeland that could also be applied to countries not under foreign domination. The ideal cast of the *Apologie* corresponded only imperfectly to the concrete experience of the Flemish revolution and, in particular, to the religious extremism and political particularism that played such an important role in revolutionary activism. Furthermore, the multiplicity of the territories that made up the Low Countries, their unique traditions, and the spirit of autonomy of the various cities and provinces were difficult to reconcile, in the late sixteenth century, with the idea of a genuine, solid national community. Finally, as has been noted, juridical and political formalism worked against universal acceptance of the independence that William envisioned: what was valid for Flanders in virtue of an initial compact might not be true (or, more simply, was not true) of Naples, Portugal, or the West Indies. The "myth" of the Flemish revolution was created later, when Holland's economic and political character had taken shape and its international role had been well established. The affirmation of that myth may perhaps have coincided with the start of the Thirty Years War and the renewal of hostilities between Spain and Holland. There was something analogous to William's ideas in another *Apologia* (dedicated, not by chance, to Maurice of Nassau, William's son and successor), put out by Bohemian rebels in the aftermath of the defenestration of Prague.

The French "model" of rebellion in the late sixteenth century more nearly resembled experiences (which varied in intensity, however) in other countries of Western Europe. England and Scotland and Spain and its Italian dominions had seen moments of political tension in which great lords of an anarchic and almost medieval spirit, at times abetted by popular protest, had made it difficult for the monarchy to establish firm power. This was how the counter-revolutionary ideological offensive achieved its goals and became part of European culture in the Baroque era. The figure of Brutus lost the nearly uncontested power of suggestion that it had acquired in humanistic culture. Praise of tyrannicide was taken as an attack on the basic values of the political community rather than as an expression of liberty. Pride, inchoate ambition, scorn of the collectivity, untrustworthiness, and rejection of the rules of honor even in personal relations—these were the traits suggested by the figure of the rebel, traits that experience seemed to confirm and hostile propaganda tended to amplify well beyond the facts, extending them to persons who lent themselves poorly to that judgment and those definitions. Immorality, unbridled sexual appetite (conceived at the time as libertine conduct or homosexuality), and indifference to religion might on occasion complete the picture. At every opportunity, public opinion was urged to apply to the rebel a variety of accusations that often had nothing to do with politics. The objective was to overpower opposition and eliminate political criticism, to present the rebel as a common bandit, an outcast for his own personal reasons, and a deviant from universally recognized and accepted norms of behavior.

These elements, which were already contained *in nuce* in Philip II's proscription of William of Orange, can also be found in varying combination and in more explicit form in the accusations of rebellion or suspicion of rebellion of the following century. The only slight note of sympathy (which had little or no effect when it came to practical application of "rigorous" methods of repression) appeared in attitudes toward protest movements among the poor and the hungry when it was certain that they involved no hidden motivations and that political exploitation was out of the question. "He is a poor starving wretch," the Neapolitan chronicler Scipione Guerra quoted a courtier as saying when he freed from the hands of the police a man who had insolently insulted the viceroy. All seventeenth-century manuals on good government noted that governing bodies had a moral obligation to see that essential foodstuffs were plentiful, to discourage speculation, and to control prices in the interest of checking the "resentment" and the "desperation" of the common people.

"The very Name of Treachery and Rebellion is infamous," Tommaso Campanella stated, and his own experience gave him reason to think it true. In his works there is no sign of any theoretical justification of tyrannicide, although he did note the political utility of the concept of the divine origin of royal power. Preachers persuade the people, Campanella stated,

> that it is agreeable to the Will of God that Obedience should be yeilded to the King; and that by suffering Afflictions, they shall be rewarded by God himself; withal often inculcating into their minds Humility, and other the like Vertues; but grievously threatning all Theeves, Murderers, Whoremon-

gers, and Seditious persons, declaring what Punishments, both from Men, and God himself, continually hang over their heads: on the contrary, comforting, and encouraging the Good, and promising them all manner of Happinesse. And so by this meanes, the words of these men being greedily hearkened unto by their Auditors, overcome, and captivate their Minds and Affections. (*On the Spanish Monarchy,* Chilmead translation, 105)

Instead, Campanella offered an abundant store of reflections on how to ward off or repress rebellion, incitements for the repression of heresy, and advice to the king of Spain on how to win back Flanders. His evaluation of William of Orange, borrowed word for word from Botero's *Reason of State,* seems less than positive, although it implies a grudging recognition of William's political skills: William was "a man . . . more fearful than a Sheep, but more crafty than a Foxe." Still, Campanella's contradictions on the question of Flanders are more obvious than those of the French *Politiques.* His advice and exhortations to the king of Spain were accompanied by statements that offered a harsh assessment: "The Spanish are hated by all nations," he stated. "The Low-Countrymen do more detest and abhor to be subject to the Spaniards then they love their own life." "Spanish commanders . . . cruel by nature . . . would make use of Blowes rather than of Fair Words." In the chapter on "Flanders and Lower Germany" of his *De monarchia Hispanica,* Campanella echoed the *Apologie* of William of Orange and went beyond simple hispanophobia: "I shall here lay down for an Observation, that those that are put to fight in their own Country, for their Wives and Children, *pro Aris et Focis,* as the Ancient Romans were used to say, are alwaies wont to fight more stoutly, than those that make war upon a forreign Country."

When Francis Bacon appeared before the House of Commons following the unification of the kingdoms of Scotland and England to argue in favor of the naturalization of the Scots (a move that would give them equal political and civic rights) and to stress the need to respect Scots laws and traditions, he showed proof of a particular sensitivity to the question of the laws and traditions of local or national communities. To emphasize how easy it was to rally the people to the cause of a demand for autonomy he recalled the episode of the revolt of Antonio Pérez in Aragon: "Only upon the voice of a condemned man out of the grate of a prison towards the street, that cried *Fueros,* which is as much as liberties or privileges, there was raised a dangerous rebellion, which was suppressed with difficulty with an army royal" (Bacon, *Works,* 3:320). Neither Campanella nor Bacon (who counted Antonio Pérez among his friends and colleagues) contributed anything new to the construction of a theory of the legitimacy of rebellion. Both men, however, demonstrated particular sensitivity—and we are in the early seventeenth century—to the drawing power of a form of patriotism that may indeed have alternated between particularism and a more modern defense of national identity and national interests but that was already moving away from strict association with the conservative and elitist constitutionalism of the nobility.

In the secret instructions that he prepared for King Philip IV in 1624, Count-Duke Olivares spoke of the spirit of rebellion among the grandees as a thing of the past. Philip's predecessors had taken care to diminish the power of the great lords and make sure they would no longer "raise their heads." Little remained of the serious troubles of the past save a few recurrences in provinces where great lords were still *poderosos*. The problem was no longer posed in traditional terms. What Olivares most feared was that nobles or members of the middle class might "make themselves popular" by taking on political leadership of cities' and provinces' resistance to the directives of the central government, organizing that resistance and promoting convergence among various social forces around common interests and objectives. This, he insisted, would cause irreparable harm. For that reason, Olivares argued, "it would be supremely appropriate, in the cities, to punish severely those who attempt it, with grave harm to the service of Your Majesty. . . . I cannot say how those men have concealed and still conceal their actions today; what is certain is that they give it to be understood publicly that they are defenders of Your Majesty's people." The count-duke had in mind real events and real people who were part of an opposition that he had to deal with if he was to govern. Among others, he was probably thinking of Mateo de Lisón y Viedma, the *procurador* for Granada, a leader of the opposition at the time of the Cortes sessions of 1621 and 1623, and a man who continued to create difficulties for Olivares in the years to come. Some time ago Jean Vilar, a scholar of seventeenth-century Spanish political thought, published Lisón's account of a conversation with Olivares in 1627. The following excerpt elucidates not only the case at hand but also the direction taken by attempts to construct a dignity for resistance and opposition at the height of the Baroque era.

> Then [Olivares] turned to me and said to me: "Your Grace must believe he knows everything and has great understanding. Instead, you know nothing and understand nothing. A man who puts himself against the resolutions taken by His Majesty with the advice of such prudent counselors and ministers must be of humble origins."
>
> I said to him: "I beg Your Excellency to treat me well. No other person in the world would dare say that to me. I draw my origins from ancestors who conquered cities and lands for our Kings, who defended their king-

doms, and who spilled blood and sacrificed their lives in their service. And in what I do I think only of serving His Majesty."

He spoke again, saying that what I was doing was no service to the King, nor defense of anything, but destruction of everything, and that the enemies of the monarchy could not have done as much harm by invading these realms with an army as I have done by perturbing and obstructing the service of the King, and that for that reason I went far beyond the limits of my functions by writing and speaking licentiously of matters of government and of Ministers as great as those of His Majesty, that I would have the punishment that I merited, and that His Majesty had already ordered the collection of materials against me and the deliberations that the Council of State and president Francisco de Contreras had drawn up in order to remove me from the Court.

I answered him that there was little need to worry so much about an ant like myself, nor to collect so many papers, because the lowest doorkeeper of the Court would suffice to punish me.

He said to me that I was not even an ant, not even half an ant, but that I was capable of understanding that I must be punished so that my punishment might serve as an example and an object of fear for many.

I said that whatever punishment was inflicted on me would be a great reward for me because it would be given to me for having defended my homeland and done my duty.

He said that it was my duty to be a gentleman [*un hombre de bien*]. I responded that I had known my duties from when I first came into possession of reason, and I fulfilled them as it was necessary. His Excellency might say what he wanted, but it was not just to treat in this manner those who defended kingdoms and cities, and that this meant preventing them from defending themselves because no one, treated in this manner, would dare to speak up.

Lisón y Viedma's arguments and his terminology were common to all opposition groups and movements from Spain to Bohemia and from Catalonia to Portugal, Italy, France, and England. He defended "constitutional" rights and denounced the violation of a contractual relationship between subjects and the crown; he claimed that the government had no right to impose taxes without the consent of the subjects and the approval of the institutions that represented them; he defended the dignity and the overall utility of an opposition inspired by defense of the general welfare. One seeming change from the preceding century was that (with the notable exception of England) the religious justification of opposition had lost its bite and its wide appeal. Another was an increased tendency to emphasize obedience to law and respect of principles of justice and "equality" whose realization was the task of the monarchy. In reality, the tendency of Lisón y Viedma and many other opposition figures to "make themselves popular" and to have a more unified and "democratic" conception of the community to which they belonged were a marked departure from traditional forms of aristocratic opposition. Such men were often limited by their inability to reach beyond the horizons of local interests or deal in depth with the sovereign's large-scale policies and designs. Nonetheless, their appeal to public utility and general welfare, although debatable from that point of view, was not merely a means to an end. That was why it laid the foundation for a new and genuine political coalition in the revolutionary crisis of the 1640s.

The old, anachronistic, noble form of rebellion did not disappear from the political scene during the Baroque era. In France it was one of the *disgrâces* that, as Rivault had predicted, the civil wars of the sixteenth century bequeathed to the next century, and it reemerged with particular virulence in the Fronde. Religious extremism, which had played such a large role in France and in Flanders, and social egalitarianism, with its deep and powerful medieval roots, were also present and active, though on the Continent their role was relatively marginal. There was a new figure, however, who restored dignity to rebellion and transferred it out of pre-absolutist logic to a logic that operated within the dialectic of absolutism. Lisón y Viedma provided a small-format, local, even localist prototype of this new figure. More fully representative of the new category were such men as Pau Claris in Catalonia, Argyle in Scotland, Matthias Thurn in Bohemia, and the duke of Braganza in Portugal. Recalling twenty years of civil wars in England, Thomas Hobbes found an appropriate term (which he intended negatively) for people of this sort that could, differences aside, be applied to other countries as well: they were "democratical gentlemen" (*Behemoth*, 34). Hobbes was persuaded that rebellion in England had arisen from a revival of monarchomachist doctrines that had spread outward from the universities. He also gave some credit to the influence of Greek and Roman political literature "in which books the popular government was extolled by the glorious name of liberty, and monarchy disgraced by the name of tyranny" (*Behemoth*, 3), to the diffusion of currents of thought favorable to religious liberty, and to an admiration for the prosperity of the Dutch Republic after its revolt against Spain. Following a traditional canon, Hobbes credited ambition with being the motive force of rebellion: "Yet certainly the chief leaders were ambitious ministers and ambitious gentlemen; the ministers envying the authority of the bishops, whom they thought less learned; and the gentlemen envying the privy-council and principal courtiers, whom they thought less wise than themselves" (p. 23). The universities were responsible for the crisis, even from a psychological point of view.

For it is a hard matter, for men who do all think highly of their own wits, when they have also acquired the learning of the university, to be persuaded that they want any ability requisite for the government of a commonwealth, especially having read the glorious histories and the sententious politics of the ancient popular governments of the Greeks and Romans. (P. 23)

The universities, "the core of rebellion," had been for England "as the wooden horse was to the Trojans." Since they could not be done away with, they must be thoroughly reformed; and what Hobbes meant by reform was essentially that they must teach that it was men's duty to obey the king's laws and that "the civil laws are God's laws, as they that make them are by God appointed to make them" (pp. 58, 40, 58).

The connection drawn by Hobbes between culture and rebellion was an important aspect of the political and ideological crisis of the mid-seventeenth century, but it was not cast in the rigidly doctrinaire and religious terms of the preceding century. The "democratical gentleman," with his fervid religiousness and his appeal to traditional contractualism, did not aspire to the creation of a theocracy or an aristocratic regime of the pre-absolutist sort; he was different from the major leaders in the Wars of Religion in France and from the lords of antimonarchical conspiracies in the rest of Europe. Although Hobbes had no adequate explanation for the political and ideological bases of rebellion, he nonetheless touched on a fundamental point—the relationship between monarchy and national consciousness and the imbalance that had been created in that area. "But the people," he stated, "were corrupted generally and the disobedient persons esteemed the best patriots" (p. 4). He wondered that the House of Commons and then the House of Lords, under pressure from popular riots, could have accused the earl of Strafford of high treason and sentenced him. How could he have been guilty of treason against the king when the king himself, who was fully capable of understanding and expressing his wishes, did not think it treason? "It was a piece of that Parliament's artifice, to put the word *traitorously* to any article exhibited against any man whose life they meant to take away" (p. 67). In reality, even before the rebel claimed the title of "defender of the homeland" (and every country had such a hero—a sign of the times that has often been undervalued), political polemics rang out with evocations of his opposite, the "traitor to the homeland." When one country after another took up the accusation, revolution was at the gates.

On the eve of the revolutionary crisis, Gabriel Naudé, a collaborator of Cardinal Mazarin's and an admirer of Campanella, noted the new, broader dimension of the relationship between culture and revolution.

Accumulating social tension led him to predict the worst. He wrote in 1639:

> Certainly, if one considers well the current state of Europe, it is not hard to foresee that it will soon be the scene of similar tragedies [revolutions against the state]. Many long and devastating wars have contributed to the ruin of justice; the excessive number of colleges, seminaries, and students, along with the ease with which books are printed and circulated, have already weakened the sects and religion.

Naudé had little doubt that "more new systems have been created in Astronomy, more novelties have been introduced in philosophy, medicine, and theology, [and] a greater number of atheists have come out into the open . . . than in the last thousand years." He saw revolution as a natural movement in history and in society: "The overthrow of the greatest empires often occurred without anyone thinking about it, or at least without having any great preparations made." He thought it his duty, however, to sound a warning, repeating and exaggerating one of the major lessons that Baroque culture had drawn from its rethinking of sixteenth-century experiences, and he devoted some of his most sonorous pages in the *Considérations politiques sur les coups d'Estat* to violent invective against "the plebs." Potential rebels preparing to occupy the European political stage must know that in order to take on that role fully they would need to raise up the people in order to turn and dispose them to their own ends, but they must also be aware of the risks that course would involve. Following the example of Charron, Naudé portrayed the common people as not only violent and credulous but verbose and flighty:

> [They] approve and, at the same time, disapprove, run from one extreme to the other, believe lightly, rebel immediately, whine and murmur always: in short, everything that *le plèbe* [the common people] think is nothing but vanity, everything they say is false and absurd; what they condemn is good, what they approve is bad; what they praise is infamous, and everything they do and take on is nothing but pure folly.

Hobbes's "democratical gentlemen" stopped short of Naudé's polemic excesses, but they too were persuaded of the dangers that accompanied popular uprisings and the anarchy and barbarity such events could create. They were aware of phenomena of collective suggestion and they knew how easy it was for impostors and demagogues to stir up collective emotions. They were conscious of the inconstancy and the ephemeral nature of plebeian enthusiasms. Unlike Naudé, however, they concluded that the politically aware citizen with an interest in the common good had a civic and moral obligation not to withdraw from popular protests. In his

Instructions to a Son, written after the Restoration, Archibald Campbell, marquess of Argyle and one of the leaders of the Scots rebellion of 1638, recognized that the "popular furies" would never have come to an end if "Superiours" had not intervened. The people would soon learn to evaluate their strength, and they would conclude—with everything that realization would inevitably imply for the overthrow of social order—that their strength was superior to that of the nobility. Thus, one should not remain neutral in a "general Commotion"; indeed, anyone who did so risked being judged infamous (here Argyle solemnly cited one of Solon's decrees; *Instructions,* 7–8). Long-standing tradition has read this statement as an invitation to use one's authority to calm or repress uprisings; it might also be interpreted as a somewhat contorted and hidden way to argue for a political involvement aimed at guiding and giving direction to just popular protest. Argyle's meaning is clear from his own case, given his role in Scotland's struggles and the confirmation he gave of his positions in a statement he made as he awaited capital punishment:

> Those Princes then begin to lose their estates, when they begin to break the ancient laws, manners and customes under which their subjects have lived. . . . Our intended Reformation . . . had the whole stream of universal consent of the whole nation. . . . Nothing is impossible or unfeasible for an enslaved people to do against Tyrants and Usurpers. (*Instructions,* 136, 176–77)

Political leaders in Catalonia, Portugal, and Naples used analogous attitudes and justifications to establish a connection with popular movements that exploded in their respective lands, moderating them and giving them political direction, in order to arrive at their own objectives of political reform and independence. Thus the "democratical gentlemen" and the bourgeois who took on functions analogous to theirs shared the preoccupation concerning the people's blind fury and political incompetence. Nonetheless, they believed that now one could count on expectations of justice and political and social equilibrium that the monarchies themselves had created and encouraged, on a wider diffusion of political culture and information (and its corollary, a greater impatience, as Naudé noted, with "court intrigues, the cabal of factions, the masking of special interests"), and thus on the hope of establishing better communication between their proposals and popular hopes. The events of the decade from 1640 to 1650 were to offer partial confirmation of that hesitant and contested faith and to strengthen a general tendency of changed attitudes concerning rebellion. Consensus and inducement began to take the place of hatred and opprobrium. No longer necessarily synonymous with injustice, abuse of power, anarchy, and sacrilege, rebellion could begin to be conceived of as an act of liberation. The protagonists of this new phase, from Masaniello to Cromwell, may have differed enormously in their roles and in their political and ideological inspiration, but they were alike in making their positions understandable and even in arousing enthusiasm.

BIBLIOGRAPHY

Sixteenth- and Seventeenth-Century Primary Sources:

Apologie ou Defense du . . . prince Guillaume . . . Contre le Ban & Edict publié par le Roi d'Espaigne, par lequel il proscript le dict seigneur Prince . . . Présentée à Messieurs les Estats Generauls des Païs Bas. Leiden: Charles Sylvius, 1581. Quoted from *The Apologie of Prince William of Orange against the Proclamation of the King of Spaine.* Edited after the English edition of 1581 by H. Wansink. Leiden: E. J. Brill, 1969.

Bacon, Francis. "On Seditions and Troubles." In his *The Essayes or Counsels, Civill and Morall.* London: John Haviland for Hanna Barret, 1625. Consulted in Bacon, *The Works.* Edited by James Spedding, Robert Leslie Ellis, and Douglas Denon Heath. 12 vols. London: Longman, 1857–74. Vol. 6, part 2 (1858).

———. "A Speech . . . in the Lower House of Parliament, Concerning the Article of Naturalization" (1607). In Bacon, *The Works,* vol. 10 (1868).

Barclay, William (Guilelmi). *De regno et regali potestate adversus Bucananum, Brutum, Boucherium et reliquos monarchomachos, libri sex.* Parisiis: G. Chaudiere, 1610.

Baricave, Jean de. *La Défence de la monarchie françoise, et autres monarchies . . .* Toulouse: Bosc, 1610.

Botero, Giovanni. *Della ragion di Stato libri dieci: Con tre libri delle cause della Grandezza e Magnificenza della Città.* Venice: Gioliti, 1589. Quoted from *The Reason of State and The Greatness of Cities.* Translated by P. J. and D. P. Waley. New Haven: Yale University Press, 1986.

———. *Le relationi universali.* Venice: Niccolò Polo, 1602.

Brutus, Stephanus Junius (pseudonym). *Vindiciae contra tyrannos: Sive, de principis in populum, populíque in principem legitima potestate.* Edinburgh [Basel?], 1579.

Campanella, Tommaso. *De Monarchia Hispanica discursus.* Amstelodami: L. Elzevirius, 1640. Consulted in the Italian edition of his *Opere.* Edited by Alessandro D'Ancona. Turin: Cugini Pomba, 1854. Quoted from *Thomas Campanella, an Italian Friar and Second Machiavel: His Advice to the King of Spain . . .* Translated by Ed. Chilmead. London: Printed for Philemon Stephens at the Gilded Lyon in St. Pauls Church-Yard, [1660].

Chappuys, Gabriel. *Citadelle de la royauté contre les efforts d'aucuns de ce temps, qui, par escrits captieux, ont voulu l'oppugner . . .* Lyons: Benoist Ricaud, 1595.

———. *Histoire generale de la guerre de Flandre . . .* Paris: R. Fouët, 1611.

Charron, Pierre. *Discours chrestien: Qu'il n'est permis ny loisible à un subiect, pour quelque cause et raison que se soit, de se liguer, bander, & rebeller contre son roy.* Paris: David Le Clerc, 1606.

Discours très-véritable touchant les droicts de la Couronne de Boheme. Paris: Sylvestre Moreau, 1620.

Drouin, Daniel. *Le miroir des rebelles . . .* Tours: Claude de Monstr'oeil et Jean Richer, 1592.

Hobbes, Thomas. *Behemoth, or, The Long Parliament.* Edited by Ferdinand Tönnies; introduction by Stephen Holmes. Facsimile of the 1889 edition. Chicago and London: University of Chicago Press, 1990.

Hotman, François. *La Gaule françoise.* Cologne: Hierome Bertulphe, 1574.

Instructions to a Son by Archibald, Late Marquis of Argyle, Written in the Time of his Confinement. London: D. Trench, 1661.

Lipsius, Justus. *Politicorum sive Civilis Doctrinae libri sex.* Lugduni Batavorum, 1589. Italian translation, Venice: Angelo Righettini, 1618.

Mariana, Juan de. *De Rege et Regis Institutione libri III.* Toleti, apud P. Rodericum, 1599.

Medici, Lorenzino de'. "Apologia" (1537–48). In his *Aridosia e Apologia.* Edited by Federico Ravello. Turin: UTET, 1926.

Naudé, Gabriel. *Considérations politiques sur les coups d'estat.* Rome, 1639. Available in Italian translation as *Considerazioni politiche sui colpi di Stato.* Translated by Piero Bertolucci. Turin: Boringhieri, 1958.

Olivares, Conde-Duque de. "Instrucción secreta dada al rey en 1624." In *Memoriales y cartas del Conde duque de Olivares.* Edited by John H. Elliott and J. F. de la Peña. 2 vols. Madrid: Alfaguara, 1978–80. Vol. 1, *Política interior: 1621 a 1627.*

Pérez, Antonio. *Relaciones.* 2d ed. Paris: 1598.

Rivault, David, sieur de Flurence. *Les Estats esquels il est discouru du prince, du noble & du tiers Estat, conformément à notre temps . . .* Lyons: Benoist Rigaud, 1595.

Rohan, Henri de. *De l'interest des princes et estats de la Chrestienté.* Paris: Pierre Margat, 1638.

Roussel, Michel. *L'Antimariana, ou refutation des propositions de Mariana . . .* Rouen: Jean Petit, 1610.

Satyre Ménippée, ou, La vertu du Catholicon selon l'édition princeps de 1594. Edited by Charles Read. Paris: Librairie des bibliophiles, 1876.

Modern Works:

Bercé, Yves-Marie. *Révoltes et révolutions dans l'Europe moderne (XVIe–XVIIIe siècles).* Paris: Presses Universitaires de France, 1980. Available in English as *Revolt and Revolution in Early Modern Europe: An Essay on the History of Political Violence.* Translated by Joseph Bergin. New York: St. Martin's Press, 1987.

Caprariis, Vittorio de. *Propaganda e pensiero politico in Francia durante le guerre di religione.* Naples: Edizioni Scientifiche italiane, 1959.

Di Rienzo, Eugenio. "Saggezza, prudenza, politica: Stabilità e crisi nel pensiero politico francese del Seicento." In *La sagezza moderna: Temi e problemi dell'-*

opera di Pierre Charron. Edited by Vittorio Dini and Domenico Taranto. Naples and Rome: Edizioni Scientifiche italiane, 1987.

Elliott, J. H. "Revolution and Continuity in Early Modern Europe." *Past and Present* 42 (1968): 35–56. Available in Italian translation in *Le origini dell'Europa moderna.* Edited by Mario Rosa. Bari: De Donato, 1977.

Forster, Robert, and Jack P. Greene, eds. *Preconditions of Revolution in Early Modern Europe.* Baltimore and London: Johns Hopkins University Press, 1970.

Koenigsberger, H. G. "The Organization of Revolutionary Parties in France and the Netherlands during the Sixteenth Century." *Journal of Modern History* 27, no. 4 (1955): 335–51.

Maravall, José Antonio. *La cultura del Barroco: Análisis de una estructura histórica.* Esplugues de Llobregat: Ariel, 1975. Available in English as *Culture of the Baroque: Analysis of a Historical Structure.* Translated by Terry Cochran. Minneapolis: University of Minnesota Press, 1986.

Marchi, Gian Paolo, ed. *Testi cinquecenteschi sulla ribellione politica.* Verona: Libreria Universitaria, 1978.

Mousnier, Roland. *L'assassinat d'Henri IV: Le problème du tyrannicide et l'affermissement de la monarchie absolue.* Paris: Gallimard, 1964. Available in English as *The Assassination of Henry IV: The Tyrannicide Problem and the Consolidation of the French Absolutist Monarchy in the Early Seventeenth Century.* Translated by Joan Spencer. London: Faber & Faber, 1973.

Salmon, J. H. M. *Renaissance and Revolt: Essays in the Intellectual and Social History of Early Modern France.* Cambridge and New York: Cambridge University Press, 1987.

Vilar, Jean. "Formes et tendances de l'opposition sous Olivares: Lisón y Viedma, *defensor de la patria.*" *Mélanges de la Casa de Velázquez* 7 (1971): 263–94.

Vivanti, Corrado. *Lotta politica e pace religiosa in Francia fra Cinque e Seicento.* Turin: G. Einaudi, 1963.

Zagorin, Perez. *Rebels and Rulers 1500–1660.* Cambridge and New York: Cambridge University Press, 1982.

6

THE PREACHER

Manuel Morán and José Andrés-Gallego

PREACHING AND REFORM

I T MIGHT SEEM PARADOXICAL that Benedetto Croce, a severe critic of the Baroque, would use emblematic language for a vivid evocation of the preacher, but, as Hilary Dansey Smith reminded us in a recent study, Croce exclaimed:

> Who can recall the seventeenth century without seeing in his mind the figure of the preacher, dressed in black like a Jesuit, in white like a Dominican, or with the rough habit of the Capuchin, gesticulating in a Baroque church before an elegantly dressed audience?

Croce's insistence on the regular clergy (there is no mention here of the parish priest), on gesticulation, and on Baroque ornamentation all stress the paradigmatic role of the preacher in the post-Tridentine world.

Preaching was of course not per se exclusive to the Baroque age. For nearly two thousand years it had been the habitual means of communication for spreading the Gospel, and in times of doctrinal confusion it was used even more widely. One of those periods was the seventeenth century. In the great religious crisis of the sixteenth century, the participation of a large number of groups of common people in the wars of religion contributed to the spiritual desolation and the material ruin of the majority of Europe's most committed Christians and was one of the principal reasons for the rupture of the spiritual unity of the Continent. It not only separated Catholics from Protestants but also created disunity among Protestants.

The Protestants had no doubts about the instrumental value of preaching: notions such as the free interpretation of Scripture and justification by faith alone led naturally to putting greater emphasis on the ministry of the Word than on sacramental functions. It was imperative that doctrine be transmitted by persons of the highest learning and who were considered most capable of correct interpretation of the Bible. Some more radical sects—the Anabaptists, for example—explicitly counseled that policy. If in the early days of the Protestant Reformation some had dreamed of an earthly Jerusalem in which each individual might interpret the Old and New Testaments according to his or her honest knowledge and understanding, by 1600 there were fewer who thought in those terms. Most thought it a dangerous—even physically dangerous—course to allow a free interpretation that might elicit religious, social, and political notions conducive to revolution, as had indeed happened in the sixteenth century. In fact, in Germany (Protestant Germany, that is) the ideal of literacy took hold somewhat later than scholars used to believe: in order for people to have direct understanding of the Bible they had to be able to read it, and experience taught that explaining Scripture to them was less risky.

After the mid-sixteenth century, Catholic strategy turned to its dual missionary task of bringing stragglers back into the fold and strengthening the spiritual loyalty of those who had remained faithful to Rome. The profound crisis set off by Luther had shown, among other things, that people's faith was weak, presumably because of deficient teaching. Beyond the Channel an overwhelming majority of the population of the entire island—England, Wales, and Scotland—had broken with the papacy and seemed none the worse for it; moreover, the doctrines of the Anglican Church began to resemble those of some of the other great currents of Protestantism. It was clear that the Reformation had surprised those Christians who were without an adequate understanding of the fundamentals of the faith, and that the situation called for action. One result was that the Council of Trent not only determined doctrine on such important matters as the sacraments but also elaborated a genuine program for the teaching of right doctrine based on the training of priests, preaching, and catechistic instruction.

Preaching was the topic of one of the early sessions of the Council of Trent (the fifth, in 1546). One result was the publication on June 17 of that year of an important decree, the *Super lectione et praedicatione*, followed later by the fourth chapter of the *Decretum de reformatione* approved during the twenty-fourth session in 1563. Pastors must instruct their flocks in "that which everyone must know in order to gain eternal salvation; announcing, with brevity and clarity, the vices they should flee and the truths they should practice, so that they may succeed in avoiding the pains of hell, and obtain eternal happiness."

THE HEIGHT OF RHETORIC AND THE REFORMED CHURCHES

One consequence of all this was that for more than a century rhetoric took on a singular importance in the culture of the West. Already important in the Middle Ages, rhetoric was studied even more intensively with the advent of the classical Renaissance, but its apogee came under the Reformation. James J. Murphy has listed 193 works of ecclesiastical oratory published between 1500 and 1700 (and it is probable that there were many more), and Debora Shuger has observed that such works were brought out at a quickening pace until the next to last decade of the seventeenth century, which means that the desire for better expression increased over time.

Thorough examination of all the tendencies in sacred oratory is impossible in the context of the present work, but if we are to understand what motivated the average preacher we need to examine a few basic notions. Now what we notice most is the "gesticulating" Baroque preaching reliant on dramatic effect, and contemporaries were just as sensitive to grandiloquence as we: theoreticians long discussed the relative merits of the "plain style" and the "grand style" in preaching. This was not merely a question of aesthetics, nor was it a simple choice between a "popular" and a "cultivated" style. Both styles were based, at least in part, on classical Latin and Greek didactic texts: some of the more striking expressions in the "grand style" were taken from Cicero, while the "plain style" preferred Seneca and the "Attic tradition," because the major Hellenistic texts used more sober forms than did the Roman texts.

Later authors, especially from the eighteenth century on, have held that this duality reflected something deeper: the "plain style" inspired by Seneca sought to persuade by appealing to reason and the intellect, man's noblest part and the trait most typical of humankind; the Ciceronian style encouraged the use of adjectives and aimed at superficial effect. And since the Baroque age preferred the latter style, its preaching was necessarily, a few exceptional cases aside, inflated, theatrical, and sensational.

This is not the way it was. In the first place, during the sixteenth and seventeenth centuries many authors of instructional and doctrinal texts (among others, Carlo Borromeo in Italy and Fénelon in France) insisted that preachers must address their listeners in a grave and sober manner. The weightiest preachers of the age persisted in a preaching style that aimed at "illuminating" and explicating rather than swaying its listeners' emotions. That tendency was perhaps best expressed in St. Vincent de Paul's *Petite méthode*, a highly influential method that eschewed both the search for rhetorical effect and the *pastorale de la peur*. Lalmy agreed: "The flourishes and ornaments of rhetoric are not appropriate to grave and solemn subjects"—which was precisely the preacher's subject matter when he spoke about God and the saints. In the second place, even Baroque high style had its own meaning and cultivated its strictly anthropological and learned roots. Preachers were to be "voices of God, instruments of divine goodness, trumpets of Christ," Diego Valadés wrote in his *Rhetorica Christiana*, a work published in 1574 and read throughout Europe and the Americas. Even for Protestant theologians, *fiducia* was a matter not only of intellectual consent but also of joy, truth, and confidence—that is, of attitudes that pertained to the will. Moreover, the will had to be molded through preaching: if a preacher tried to kindle or quicken his listeners' faith, he had to move their will as well.

It must be noted, however, that the dominant rhetoric (or rhetorics, since there were more than one) was based on an underlying conception of the life of the spirit that emphasized emotion more than intellect. That conception was already present in the Bible, and it was much in evidence during the Middle Ages. In substance, it reflected the predominance of Augustine's vision of humankind over that of Thomas Aquinas, and after the Reformation it persisted in a number of Christian confessions.

Thus it was not just the Church of Rome that emphasized emotion in preaching. Some Protestant authors of the sixteenth and seventeenth centuries agreed with the greater part of Catholic writers on this point. Their ranks included authoritative scholars such as the Germans Bartholomaus Keckermann and Andreas Gerhard Hyperius (whose work was widely known in John Ludham's translation of 1577) and the Spaniard Luis de Granada, the author of an *Ecclesiasticae Rhetoricae* (1576) that was among the most widely read works of the age. Even the Anglican "metaphysical" preachers active in the late sixteenth and early seventeenth centuries started from the same biblical tendency to link the soul with the heart more than with the mind, and their sermons reflected that orientation. John Donne exclaimed in one of his sermons, "Marke my heart, O Soule, where thou dost dwell."

THE CONSEQUENCES: "MAGNITUDO" AND "PRAESENTIA" AS MAJOR CRITERIA

Still, as the Ciceronian tradition dictated (*ut probet, ut flectet, ut delectet*), oratory should not be reduced to dialectic alone; it must not only train the intellect but also stimulate the will and encourage positive sentiments. In a passage that may seem brusque out of context, Luis de Granada gave a good illustration of this concept:

> The rude and ignorant multitude has to be won over with long speeches: in order for it not only to know and comprehend but also do what we would want, it is important to terrify and disturb it, not only with syllogisms but

also with vivid representations and a great storm of eloquence. This requires an argument not brief and limited but harsh, impetuous, and abundant.

To this end the Catholic Reformation made intensive use of art. Decorative exuberance, a tendency to hyperbole, centrifugal motion, rupture with the formal equilibrium of the Renaissance, and other elements of the new style were used to elicit fervor and marvel in the contemplation of heavenly things. Baroque architecture and music clearly display their dependence on the shaping dictates of the Catholic Reformation, as seen in the symbolism of the dome of St. Peter's or the distribution of space in the Chiesa del Gesù. Even leaving aside church buildings of such exceptional grandiosity, there was a growing trend toward increased church size in cities large and small, not always for demographic reasons. The place of worship was expected to provide religion with an appropriate setting; solemn masses, Lenten sermons, and preaching throughout the liturgical year required vast spaces that could hold great crowds, or at least all the inhabitants of the parish.

The Reformed churches preferred a more subdued style. In seventeenth-century England, the Restoration brought to the Anglican Church a noticeably anti-rhetorical reaction in favor of the "plain style"—a reaction that fostered a more natural, clear, and didactic communication with the faithful. This was, for example, the attitude of one major Anglican theorist, James Arderne, in his *Directions Concerning the Matter and Stile of Sermons* (1671). Not all preachers adopted Arderne's criteria, however. Aside from his work and that of a few others, rhetorical theory aroused less interest in Great Britain than on the Continent, and of the 193 works on the subject that James Murphy lists as having been published between 1500 and 1700, only sixteen were written in English. Although universities in Britain were Anglican, students were equally apt to study texts from other Protestant sources (Keckermann's works, for instance), or Catholic texts such as those of Nicolas Caussin, and references to those authors in seventeenth-century documents indicate that in practice the precepts of the "grand style" were followed as well as the "plain."

Such precepts were just as clear on the theoretical justification of an exaggerated style in Protestant authors as in their Catholic counterparts. Keckermann recommended appealing to people's emotions, perhaps echoing ideas expounded in Luis de Granada's *Ecclesiasticae Rhetoricae*. "Emotion," Keckermann stated, "can be elicited in two ways, through *magnitudo* and *praesentia* or, to speak more clearly, through grandiosity and hypotyposis"—that is, by an elevated subject matter and by the use of lively images.

Some writers clearly preferred *magnitudo,* identifying it with a reliance on conceits, which Baltasar Gracián, a Jesuit, defined thus:

> Conceits are the life of style, the spirit of discourse, and they have as much perfection as they do subtlety; but when a heightened style is combined with the loftiness of the conceit, the work becomes complete. One must strive to have the phrases embellish the style, the objections give it vivacity, mysteries make it redolent; reflections [must make it] profound, exaggerations lofty, allusions clever, fervor pungent, transmutations subtle; ironies may give it salt, crises gall, paronomasia grace, maxims gravity, comparisons fecundity, and analogies high relief. But all this with a grain of wisdom so that everything will smack of good sense.

The rhetorical figures that Gracián described approvingly—metaphor and syntactical inversion—were devices that a good many other authors admired as well.

RHETORIC AND THOUGHT

If we fail to take into account the strong hold that these logical and anthropological approaches had on people's minds we cannot understand some things that historians often think they can explain by attributing them to hypersensitivity. For example, we cannot see why the spirit of the Council of Trent could not have been propagated with a less inflated, more austere aesthetic; one closer to the spiritual renewal to which the Catholic Reformation aspired.

Moreover, the age's undeniable fondness for gesture did not derive from theory alone. The Baroque has to be considered not only as a phenomenon within the intellectual and aesthetic sphere and as an emanation of the Counter-Reformation but also as a way of understanding the world and as the living expression of an epoch. That was why the preachers, men animated by pastoral zeal, at times true artists but always men of their times, simply molded the old message reaffirmed by the Council to fit into forms provided by the world in which they themselves were immersed.

They were also successful when they preached in that manner. Undoubtedly they matched the mentality of the majority, or at least with the mind-set of many of the faithful who flocked to hear them. There is no other explanation of the rich spiritual harvests reported by so many writers—the conversions garnered by St. Vincent de Paul among the convicts in His Most Christian Majesty's galleys, for example, or such initiatives as the creation of the famous Congregation of the Holy Name of Jesus among the criminals incarcerated in the prisons of Seville, which sought to combat the prisoners' use of blasphemy and oaths by making them pay fines. The Congregation's annual festivity, organized by its members, was attended by the authorities and the general public, and it included celebration of the mass (with much music) and a long sermon preached by a local Jesuit of renown.

Sacred oratory was so effective that its style even influenced popular secular literature. For example, the morose picaresque hero Guzmán de Alfarache was simply a preacher who had missed his vocation, and the famous novel narrating his life is full of more or less camouflaged sermons. The authors of the equally famous *autos sacramentales*—short allegorical dramas on religious subjects that were extremely popular in some parts of Europe and the Americas—combined scenic effects and conceits in order to create the special supernatural atmosphere they wanted to communicate. It was no accident that the most famous of these authors, Calderón de la Barca, who was also a court chaplain, defined the *autos* as

> sermones
> puestos en verso, en idea
> representable, cuestiones
> de la Sacra Teología,
> que no alcanzan mis razones
> a explicar ni comprender.
>
> *(Sermons put into verse, into representable ideas, questions of sacred theology that my arguments can neither comprehend nor explain.)*

"Culteranismo" in Preaching: Paravicino

High style spawned exaggerations of various sorts. We can get an idea of how far these could be taken from one of the most eminent examples of *culteranismo* in preaching—an elegant style, Baroque to the point of being incomprehensible. Legend tells us that the friar Félix Hortensio Paravicino y Arteaga won instant fame when, during a visit of Philip III to the University of Salamanca, the preacher who had been charged with giving the sermon fell sick and was replaced by the young Trinitarian friar. His bravura and his fine manners are reported to have pleasingly surprised the king, and someone in the royal retinue suggested to the friar that he follow the king to Valladolid. In reality this tale was pure fantasy, an embellished version of the truth for the use of posterity. Philip III visited Salamanca only once, in 1600, when Paravicino was most probably still working toward his bachelor's degree. The more prosaic truth is that when Paravicino's talents began to be recognized (notwithstanding a weak voice that spiteful critics always mentioned), the superiors of his order sent him to Madrid to pursue his career. He was a success in the capital: a good humanist and a better bibliographer, he frequented literary circles and his distinctive and pleasing ways made him welcome in good society. He soon became indispensable as a court preacher. Paravicino was undeniably an innovator and a poet of extreme sensitivity, although somewhat too self-satisfied (he called himself "the Columbus of a literary new world"). He is also known for his use of a rhetorical subgenre, the "funerary panegyric." One sentence from a sermon dedicated to Philip III illustrates the tone of such works, which were obviously composed well in advance: "Heaven," he declared, "took from you your precious companion, not only as a resplendent architrave for its best gate (since St. John saw that all twelve were of pearl) but as a crown (in the aspect, if not the form, of a halo) to your conjugal fidelity." In common parlance, the king's wife, Doña Margarita of Austria, had died.

Even in his own day Paravicino had adversaries: in the comedy *El príncipe constante* Calderón let drop a few amusing allusions to the *emponomio horténsico*, thus arousing the ire of the friar, who took the sally as an offense to the king and to religion. The anonymous author of a sonnet entitled "Al padre Hortensio" was more explicit:

> De aquel lenguaje crespo e intrincado,
> escuro y con cuydado escurecido,
> entro transposiciones escondido,
> gocé hora y media de un silencio hablado.
>
> *(Thanks to that artificial and tangled language, obscure and carefully concealed, hidden among the transpositions, I enjoyed an hour and a half of spoken silence.)*

As its style became increasingly refined, *culteranismo* in oratory fell into discredit, whether people realized that preaching the Gospel was something more than an exercise in skill, or whether those who practiced that type of oratory (and they were legion in Italy, France, Spain, and Portugal) were unable to maintain the high pitch imposed by the inventors of the style. Diego de Estella asked:

> Tell me what profit can be drawn from spending an hour turning Our Lady into a castle whose principal tower is faith—*collum tuum sicut turris eburnea*—made of ivory. They made Our Lady into a merlon, and afterwards a barbican, and she was the castle. What doctrine and what reformation of customs, nay, what benefit, comes from all this?

As always, there was only a small step from the sublime to the ridiculous. This did not mean, however, that metaphors had to be eliminated, even less that sermons must be syllogistic and follow an absolutely regular structure. Even the *ratio studiorum* of the Jesuits approved toward the end of the sixteenth century admitted "pious tricks" in sacred oratory. All things considered, what was important was to move people's souls, and an exaggerated didacticism could do just as much harm as ridiculous images. "Who can fight against sins if he is preoccupied and governed by the rules for well-rounded periods?" asked the Jesuit Nicolas Caussin in his *De eloquentia sacra et humana* (1619).

PATHOS IN PREACHING

Culteranismo and concettism (represented, respectively, by Paravicino and Gracián) were not the only ways in which Baroque preachers expressed themselves. A search for visual and dramatic effects—perhaps more pertinent to the figurative arts but still necessary to a verbal recreation of the supernatural—led to a descriptive naturalism as a means of appealing to the public's basic emotions. This naturalism, however, was often furthered by artifice of an obviously theatrical sort. Diego de Arce, for example, attempted to dissuade his hearers from sin by these words on the effects of syphilis:

> A sadness of expression, a yellowing of the face, a stuffed-up nose, a fetid breath, an uprooting of the teeth from pus-filled gums, a pain in all the members, a humor that torments the joints, an inability to walk or to sit down without crying out in pain, and, finally, a repugnant aspect of the whole body.

Basically, however, the themes most typical of the Baroque repertory were glimpses of optimistic states—felicity or the glory of the other world. Thus, although a multitude of texts in both France and Italy insisted on sin and fear—*le péché et la peur*—many others contributed to a genuine "culture of hope." The fact remains, however, that in both pastoral writings and the sermon, the path to paradise typically associated thoughts of celestial beatitude with thoughts of hell. "What is this life that we breathe here below?" asked Charles Drelincourt in 1639 in a sermon on *La vanité du monde*—a question that had already become a commonplace and would continue to be one for another three centuries. "It is nothing but a breath in our nostrils, a vapor that appears for a certain time and then vanishes: it is vanity itself." Manuel de Guerra y Ribera made the same point in a sermon for Ash Wednesday, 1679: "What is the world? Nothing more than an obvious deceit that creates a fallacious spectacle: appearances that bewilder more than delight." Honorato de Camús illustrated his preaching by putting a series of head coverings—berets, wigs, helmets, crowns—on a skull that he kept close to hand, thus reinforcing images and situations pictured in his sermon. Other preachers used other objects.

The preachers who became known for purifying the "grand style" and reforming sacred oratory used similar techniques. A historian of our own century, Emilio Santini, has described a preaching mission of the Jesuit Paolo Segneri, perhaps the leading Italian preacher of the seventeenth century. According to Santini, Segneri walked about

> dressed in a ragged habit, barefoot, begging. . . . With staff in hand, his breviary under his arm, the small crucifix of the Jesuit on his breast and rosary beads at his belt, he went forth to meet the parish priest, the groups, and the countless people who asked to be blessed by him and prostrated themselves at his feet. He would then throw himself on his knees, after which, intoning the liturgy, he would lead the multitude into church, where he gave his first discourse.

The preaching mission lasted an entire week, from Monday to Sunday. Aside from masses in the morning and the evening, on Wednesdays, Thursdays, and Fridays he led nighttime penitential processions. Purely spectacular elements were rife in his sermons. As Santini tells us,

> Toward the end of the sermon he would often place a crown of thorns on his head and began to strike the flesh of his naked shoulders with an iron rod. Not content with this, he would beat his breast hard with a round cork stuck with pins and needles set into a tin box, making great quantities of blood flow before crowds who wept and implored forgiveness. In many places the people too scourged themselves. . . . The effect was tremendous: general confessions, innumerable conversions, peace made between one family and another or one village and another, the prohibition of gaming and obscene songs.

Emotive preaching was extremely effective, even though another seventeenth-century Jesuit, Daniello Bartoli, described it as proof of oratorical aberrations:

> A most worthy preacher climbed up to the pulpit on Thursday of the second week of Lent, his face like that of a man in terror, almost as if he had come out of Hell, and from his mouth, with a tone of voice horrible to hear that came right from the heart, he gave no other preaching but a solemn recitation of the reading of the Gospel for that day: *Mortuus est . . . dives et sepultus est in inferno* [The rich man also died and was buried and in Hell; Luke 16.22]. Three times he repeated this and then got down from the pulpit. . . . Many conversions ensued.

This was not—the notion bears repeating—a preaching of imminent disaster to fit a "culture of death"; rather it was, up to a point, the antidote to a civilization that was both frivolous and violent. Although the sermon *alla cappucina* or the *discours pathétique* were among the most representative aspects of Baroque pastoral methods, it would be a mistake to overestimate their diffusion. In reality, even in its own time, this style was just as much criticized for its lack of doctrine as was the sermon in the *culterano* style.

Some Italians so disliked the magniloquence and the gesticulations of the "pathetic" preaching that was widespread in their country that they thought it of foreign origin, come from Spain by way of the Society of Jesus and Naples, which some considered the Mecca of bad taste in preaching. Some even sustained that it was not only Spanish fashion but also the difficulty of expressing oneself in a foreign language that made foreign preachers gesticulate more. In an attempt to get their meaning across when words were insufficient, they used all possible rhetorical images to move their auditors' souls. Without entering into a discussion that smacks of an antiquated nationalism, we can say that not only in Spain and its dominions but in France, Italy, Catholic Germany, and even among Anglicans and other Protestants, preaching was no stranger to artificial arguments and grotesque appeals to the listeners' emotions, whether the preacher was speaking of life or insisting on the inevitability of death.

THE FIGURE OF THE PREACHER

Whose task was it to teach the Gospel? The Council of Trent took a clear stand: it was the duty of bishops to preach in their churches on Sundays and feast days. The questionnaires that aided bishops in the preparation of the *relationes* that they were expected to send to Rome from time to time or to take along on their visits *ad limina* explicitly mentioned preaching by bishops: had preaching occurred? How, and when? This directive, which aimed at assuring orthodox transmission of the divine Word, was an obvious precaution to take in the early years of the Counter-Reformation, when good preachers were rare. It did not in and of itself guarantee the purity of the bishops' doctrine, however. The church continued to be the only institution in which there was a certain degree of social mobility, in the sense that there was a greater probability that a man of modest origins could make his way by personal merit within the church than in society at large. More typically, however, and even without the frequent instances of nepotism, the advantages that came with better access to studies, personal contacts, and family prestige tended to fill high clerical posts with people of noble extraction who were not always characterized by pastoral zeal or theological depth.

Still, the Council of Trent's model of the preaching, reform-minded bishop flourished. Two outstanding examples of that model were Carlo

Borromeo and Juan de Ribera (two men who were also felicitous examples of nepotism), and the influence of the model on the episcopate of the time is evident in such men as St. Francis de Sales, Cornelio Musso, Pierre de Bérulle, and Francesco Bossio.

Preaching represented only a small part of the Catholic Reformation's pastoral program for bishops. The bishops' primary duties really consisted in supervision of the diocesan clergy. They were to see to it that preaching took place on prescribed days—Sundays and feast days and at least three times a week during the fast periods of Lent and Advent—but above all, they were to make sure that the clergy was capable of carrying out its tasks, a responsibility directly connected with the pressing problem of training for the priesthood and, in particular, the preparation of parish priests.

The training received by secular preachers was no different from that of preachers among the regular clergy and, in the last analysis, the two were grouped together. Like the monks and friars, priests studied in a school annexed to a cathedral or a monastery (or as a *sommaia* in a university). More often, they received instruction in the rudiments of the Latin liturgy from their own parish priests or from a grammar teacher. In nearly all cases, the secular clergy was insufficiently prepared, which was undoubtedly the main reason for the poor reputation of its lower ranks, who were pictured as undisciplined, ignorant, and given to less than exemplary conduct.

The Council of Trent's most promising remedy to these problems was diocesan seminaries. The training that these schools offered was specifically oriented toward creating a professional attitude about the fulfillment of the pastoral duties of preaching, conducting the liturgy, and administering the sacraments. The seminary was supposed to reduce the numbers of a parasitic clergy with a vested interest in the traditional system, but, as we have seen, application of the Council's decree came late. France, which had emerged exhausted from the Wars of Religion, began to found the better part of its seminaries only during the latter half of the seventeenth century; in England during the brief reign of Mary Tudor, Reginald Pole was too busy trying to keep things calm to found seminaries; in Spain, although a few seminaries were founded immediately, others came quite late, even in the eighteenth century. This was also true in Italy, however much the great institutions of Rome and Milan worked to furnish priests for poorer localities, even entire regions, that had no seminaries.

During the seventeenth century and even as late as 1700, the majority of parish priests had not attended a seminary, and not all their superiors understood the need for a higher doctrinal and moral standard. Antonio Fino recalled that the bishop of Aversa justified the delay in setting up prebends for the study of theology and in compiling a penitential—both of which were fundamental for training priests—by arguing that courses on theology were available in the monasteries and that Naples was so nearby that all the clergy flocked there *prompto animo* to seek instruction. His explanations did not persuade the Congregation of the Council. Toward the end of the seventeenth century there may have been a better supply of priests and of better-prepared priests, to judge from the number of parish libraries and an increased assiduity in preaching, but the process was gradual and results varied greatly from one diocese to another. In the 1620s it would not have been difficult to find others like one beneficed priest in Ferreira, in Portugal, who praised the sermon of a Jesuit missionary by commenting: "The preachers do their job talking to us about the woes that derive from sins and exhorting us to abandon them, and we do ours by holding on to our sins."

SERMON ANTHOLOGIES

Thanks to printing, preachers could call on auxiliary materials—manuals on eloquence and collections of sermons usually organized to follow the liturgical calendar—that could bridge the gaps in their own training in doctrine and oratory. After the Council of Trent, many works containing sermons for Lent, Advent, saints' feast days, Sundays, and funerals and other special occasions were reprinted and translated into all the major languages of Europe. At times the titles of these anthologies clearly reflect the prevailing mentality: there was nothing odd about titles such as *La Trompette de Sion* by Gilbert Primrose, a Protestant (Bergerac, 1610); *Discursos predicables sobre los cuatro rios del Paraíso* by Juan de Mata, a Catholic (Granada, 1637); or *La honda de David con cinco sermones o piedras* by the Portuguese Timotheo de Ciabra Pimentel (Barcelona, 1631). Other works had purely descriptive but interminable titles such as *Sermón en que se da aviso, que en las caydas públicas de algunas personas, ni se pierda el crédito de la virtud de los buenos, ni cesse, y se entibie el buen propósito de los flacos* by Luis de Granada (Lisbon, 1588).

Texts on rhetoric by Luis de Granada and Agostino Valiero, the popular manuals of Estella and Francesco Panigarola (*Modo di comporre una predica*), and, even more, the sermon collections of Musso, Nicolas de Dijon, Antonio Vieira, and Cristóbal de Avendaño continued to have an extraordinarily wide circulation until the appearance of the new style of the French school of the age of Louis XIV. A significant example of the broad use made of such works is the anecdote related by Jean-Pierre Camus, bishop of Belley, who one day heard a foreign preacher give a sermon that he himself had composed and published.

It is difficult to judge the real influence that such printed texts had on the activities of the secular clergy, especially the rural clergy. In practice, the parish priests' preaching (nearly always at the insistence of their bishops) was usually limited to brief homilies at high mass on Sundays. These were simple sermons based on commentary on some maxim in the Gospel readings for the day, a technique that the great orators disdained. Naturally, these simple homilies have almost never been passed on to posterity, which makes it difficult to evaluate their efficacy. One interesting note is that at times they elicited interruptions from parishioners who felt they were being singled out for personal reprimand. This is clear from the Constitutions of Salamanca of 1654, which set fines up to one hundred maravidíses for this sort of spontaneous outbreak in church during the sermon. We can understand the prudence of Philippe Gorreau, the parish priest of Villiers-le-Bel, who considered excessive familiarity with his parishioners risky.

GREAT OCCASIONS . . .

For these reasons, parish priests made wide use of the decree of the Council of Trent that enabled them to call on a substitute capable of offering higher-quality preaching. This was current practice in the cities and towns during Lent and Advent, periods in which preaching was to take place daily or, at the least, three times weekly. Although collective manifestation of religious sentiment was an integral part of daily life in the seventeenth century, emotion was much more intense in the high points of the liturgical cycle, the days that prepared the great feasts of Christmas and Easter. Lent was particularly propitious for fulfilling the annual duty of confession and communion. Solemn processions, popular devotions, and, above all, attendance at sermons created a climax of penitential emotion that broke the monotony of more mundane activities.

Lenten preaching occurred in small towns and villages as well as in the big cities. The account books (in Spain, the *libros de fábrica*) of rural parishes often mention payments made to Lenten preachers, who were almost always members of the regular clergy, especially from itinerant orders such as the Dominicans and Franciscans.

Similar preaching campaigns also took place in the Reformed churches, differences in liturgy (which reflected theological differences) aside. The institutional framework for preaching in Anglican London was much like that of any Catholic city of Europe or the Americas. In London as in Spain, France, or the Italian states, the most important sermons were delivered before the royal court, by the most eminent ecclesiastics. Next in importance came open-air sermons given from the pulpit at St. Paul's Cross, near the Cathedral (many of them to justify royal decisions concerning religion), and the sermons at St. Mary of Bethlehem Hospital, which were offered every Monday, Tuesday, and Wednesday as a means for inducing the wealthy to be generous toward the poor. Noteworthy sermons were also delivered at the universities. Finally, services at St. Paul's Cathedral included sermons, and the rector or the vicar usually preached on Sunday in the various parish churches of London, as did the parish priest in Tridentine Catholic churches. On solemn occasions orators of greater importance, fame, or skill were invited to speak.

English preachers sought striking effects much like their Continental counterparts, as an extract from a sermon by John Donne, one of the leading "metaphysical" preachers, will show:

> Christ might well say, *Father, forgive them,* which is the first room of this glorious Palace. And in this contemplation, O my unworthy soule, thou art presently in the presence. No passing of guards, no ushers. No examination of thy degree or habit. The Prince is not asleep, nor private, nor weary of giving, nor refers to others. He puts thee not to prevaile by Angels or Archangels. But lest anything might hinder thee from coming into his presence, his presence comes to thee. And lest his Majesty should dazell thee, thou art to speake but to thy Father. (*Sermons,* 5:234)

... And the Specialized Preacher

The sermon was a great event. Such an important spectacle obviously could not be entrusted to an incompetent, so cathedrals and the major collegial churches took pains in their search for people to fulfill this specialized function, and in a few cases they paid them generously. In Santiago de Compostela a committee composed of members of the cathedral chapter, the prior of the Dominicans, and the guardian of the Franciscans met toward the beginning of the summer to work out the list (*la tabla*) of sermons for the year. In Toledo the chapter was called into plenary session some months before Lent to choose a preacher from among possible candidates who were often famous specialists from elsewhere. In the cathedral of Metz the choice of a preacher for major events was reserved to an assembly of the "three orders," which on several occasions called upon a celebrated local canon, Jacques-Bénigne Bossuet. Bossuet's predecessors included eighteen Jesuits, eight Franciscans of various sorts, four Minims, two Augustinians, and one or two members of other orders.

The number of regular clergy among the preachers was by no means unique to Metz, as demonstrated by a satirical *Historia del famoso predicador fray Gerundio de Campazas, alias Zotes,* published in Spain nearly a century later. The author of this work, the Jesuit José Francisco de Isla, explained why his hero should be a friar:

> You will not deny me that the number of preachers who are honoured with the most noble, the most holy, and the most venerable distinction of Friar

is much greater than those who are known by the title of Father or the epithet of Don. For one of these there are at least twenty of the others; because the mendicant fraternities, not clerical—who all use it—and the monkish—some of which use it and others not—are beyond comparison more numerous than all the societies of the regulars, into which it has not been introduced. Those of the secular clergy who exercise the ministry of preaching, it is evident, cannot be compared in number to those who exercise it amongst the professed religious." (Anonymous translation, London, 1772; p. 18)

There were what might be called legal reasons for the large number of friars among the preachers. One of the chief motivations for the founding of the mendicant orders was to have the friars go from place to place preaching the Word of God. They had a special status recognized by the Holy See, which meant that they had acquired certain rights. There were good reasons why the first decree regarding preaching put out by the Council of Trent in 1546 considered preaching part of the parish priests' duties but chapter 4 of the *Decretum de reformatione* in 1563 dropped all mention of parish priests. In the interim there had been complaints and protests.

There was an even more important reason for the greater prevalence of the regular clergy (friars in particular) over secular clergy among preachers: one of the most striking characteristics of Catholic spiritual renewal before the Council was that the regular clergy had become exceptionally skilled at preaching. During the seventeenth century a number of new orders arose, and reformed versions of the traditional religious orders were formed in a desire to return to the orders' original spiritual rigor. The new orders that had sprung up—Theatines, Barnabites, Camillo de Lellis's Ministers of the Sick, above all, the Jesuits—spread everywhere at the side of the Dominicans, Franciscans, Benedictines, Carmelites, and others. Forty-nine of the preachers invited to Rome to preach in the Apostolic Palace between 1573 and 1660 were Jesuits, while the Capuchins played an essential role in preaching to the common people. The pastoral activities of the regular clergy, which initially had simply been supplemental to those of the secular clergy, eventually became indispensable to the bishops, absolving them of some tasks directly related to the cure of souls, preaching and catechism in particular.

THE FIRST REQUISITE: A KNOWLEDGE OF THEOLOGY

This apostolic fervor could at times be associated with a mastery of the accumulated knowledge of many centuries. Conventual schools and their specialized ecclesiastical libraries provided the regular clergy with the intellectual preparation required for its evangelical mission. Diego de Estella stated in his *Modus concionandi* that books were "the instruments and the tools of their trade" for preachers, and the Society of Jesus, as a recent institution, naturally exhibited a special sensitivity to sacred oratory when it endowed its libraries.

Faithful to their pedagogical model of *ratio studiorum,* the Jesuits elaborated their own methods for the training of preachers based on the study of authors of classical antiquity (Cicero in particular, but also Aristotle and Quintilian) and, after 1660, on the manual of Cipriano Soárez.

It is risky, in the current state of scholarship, to speak of "schools" of oratory corresponding to the various religious orders. Obviously, each order had a style of preaching that to some extent reflected its particular charismatic vocation: we can expect to meet the Capuchins on country roads or find optimistic exhortations in sermons of the disciples of St. Francis de Sales or St. Vincent de Paul. Such generalizations are too vague to use as the basis for connecting a given mode of preaching with a given order, even when the orders did have a characteristic theological orientation. The Dominicans had reservations concerning the Immaculate Conception that prompted hostility toward them in Andalusia, where that *opinión pia,* widespread throughout Spain even before it was confirmed by Alexander VII, was professed with particular ardor. This was an exceptional case, however, because high theology rarely entered into ordinary preaching, which generally remained rooted in everyday experience, more out of respect for the prime criterion of adapting one's discourse to the listeners' comprehension than out of any perverse desire to exclude the people from theological debate.

This did not prevent the preacher from being knowledgeable about or deeply versed in doctrine. He was not expected to be an expert in speculative theology, but he might still find it opportune to pursue theological studies—in moral theology in particular, since its function was to condemn vice, correct behavior, and teach virtue. Even Carlo Borromeo, who was competent *in utroque iure* (in Roman and canon law), strove to fill in the gaps of his philosophical and theological knowledge. Preconditions were often imposed, perhaps to eliminate doubt about the preachers' intellectual pretensions: the discalced Carmelites of Alcalá, for example, needed to study logic, physics (natural science), metaphysics, and theology for three years or have a degree in canon law before they were permitted to preach. Among the Capuchins approval to preach was given by the provincial definitor, who did not always grant it. For example, when Friar Agustín María de Granada requested permission to preach in 1595, the answer he received was, "May he remain in peace in his friary of the Pardo."

Naturally, a certain ease in handling Scripture and tradition (defined by the Council of Trent as all of revelation) was a part of the knowledge anyone who was to preach on such matters would have to possess. He would also find useful some familiarity with decrees of the councils, papal bulls, the writings of the doctors of the church, and other authoritative texts.

The preacher had to have mastered Latin, Greek, Hebrew, and Italian, but his knowledge also had to cover all disciplines that he might need to be familiar with, if for no other reason than to avoid hilarity on the part of practitioners of those disciplines should he speak of them. As Diego de Estella stated, "It will be difficult to describe the storm at sea that struck the apostles without knowing what it means to lower sail, to bail, or to steer"; Francisco Terrones recommended that the preacher cultivate "all the arts, all the sciences, in short, a complete encyclopedia, none of which would be superfluous."

Above all, however, preachers needed to know doctrine. Innocent XI insisted on this point in a bull of 1680 prompted by widespread complaints, and he cautioned that preaching must be founded on the Gospel more than on any other sort of text. In a similar vein, Luis de Granada, in his widely read and much admired *Ecclesiasticae Rhetoricae* of a century earlier, quoted a great many Latin authors but also included many texts of the fathers of the church, St. Cyprian in particular. During the seventeenth century knowledge of doctrine was one of the major aspects of a reform movement founded on the preaching and writings of the Jesuit Paolo Segneri and (to a lesser extent) those of Bishop Bossuet, the great reformer of sacred oratory in France.

Much was required of the beginning preacher, but if he was tempted to lose heart he could draw comfort from Terrones's remark that "a preacher with all these qualities has never been seen." Nor had anyone ever seen the grotesque orator that some critics had described, exaggerating common faults to make their case. Daniello Bartoli, a Jesuit, presented a "typical" preacher busy preparing his sermon in these terms:

> The good man will be seated at a table surrounded by books, silently bent to his task. . . . Two or three descriptions have to be put in it, whether the Gospel for the day lends itself to them or not. If he lacks the ingenuity to do them himself he will rob them from poets, from novels, or from academic discourses, piles of which lie on his table. . . . The art and the ingenuity come in transforming, or at least costuming, these descriptions, so that what was a Venus in the poem becomes a Magdalene in the sermon. . . . When the descriptions are dressed up, the next thing is to find a couple of Devices and Emblems of free-ranging invention . . . that he can explain, opening fields to be exploited by the imagination and giving the hearers matter for delight. . . . Next, some text of Scripture is needed, which can

also be interlarded, but more than any other, the Canticles of Solomon, a book of most high mysteries and reputed, like Mount Sinai, to repel beasts who will fear being stoned. For one's reputation and in order to appear as someone who knows much, a passage of theology is needed, but of the most subtle and fine, taken from the questions of the first part, where God one and three is debated. . . . Finally there have to be three or four paradoxes that at first sight seem heretical but then, as they gradually become clear, are found to be mysteries. . . . Once the discourse has been composed in this manner, what remains is to recite it, and one seeks to do so with such a swift tongue that the ears of the listeners, like lame men in a race, are wearied by following it.

THE "CURSUS HONORUM"

Learning required time (Terrones wryly remarked, "In a few years one cannot learn much"), and in that age the novice preacher was urged not only to read printed manuals and absorb manuscript instructions but also to learn by imitation. An aptitude for studies was not enough if he did not also have some innate ability and a pleasing way of talking.

In other words, personal endowments were a second and important element in a successful preaching career. When they analyzed the practical effects of preaching, the theorists drew a distinction between the natural qualities of the preacher and his acquired abilities, and they agreed that natural qualities were a gift of the Holy Spirit. When asked what was the best way to preach, Luis de Granada piously repeated the lesson of his master, the mystic Juan de Avila: "Love our Lord very much." The supernatural aside, however, the efficacy of preachers undoubtedly varied greatly. After all, the preacher was an "instrumental cause"—a notion that Catholic doctrine could not ignore in a theological context dominated by the duality of grace and freedom. That was why the Council of Trent had prudently prohibited the preaching of regular clergy "if they have not been examined and approved by their superiors as to their life, customs, and knowledge, and if they have not obtained their superiors' permission." It was a given that a religious would have to obtain the bishop's permission to operate in diocesan churches. The preacher must also be "well born" and not be "monstrously ugly or terrifying of face," since for many of the faithful that would diminish the value of his doctrine. Finally, he had to have a robust constitution and a good voice, although there were a number of exceptions to that rule on the practical level.

When he had finished his apprenticeship, the preacher moved on to the second phase of his career, which was, precisely, preaching. This might seem obvious if the treatises had not explained why they advised the novice to put what he had learned into immediate practice: "If exercise is lacking," the Augustinian friar Bartolomé Carranza stated in his *Aliquot documenta ad concionandum*, "the intelligence becomes obtuse, the tongue thickens, the soul becomes discouraged and timid."

When eventually it came time to retire, veteran preachers were usually called on to fill positions of responsibility in their own orders; thus they had little time for other activities. The years usually took their toll on preachers, but there were notable exceptions: when Philip II went to Lisbon to be crowned king of Portugal, he met Luis de Granada, who, as the sovereign himself said, was "rather old and toothless" but who nonetheless still had enough energy to preach.

Preachers on the whole agreed that preaching would be unrewarding work if one discounted its supernatural motivation. Undeniably, a good professional enjoyed renown and prestige in secular circles and might also be named preacher to the king; nonetheless, seventeenth-century Spanish and French kings were so lavish with that title that in 1677 Charles II of Spain drastically reduced the numbers of his own royal preachers to three religious, members of each one of the three orders in his realm. Moreover, most of the "preachers to the king" held their title *ad honorem* and without remuneration.

Monetary rewards were rather low: Terrones wrote, "You give a hundred reales to the physician who is killing you, a hundred ducats to the lawyer who makes you lose a thousand in revenue, and to the preacher you give a 'God be with you.'" Things were different in special circumstances—during Lent, for example, but even more, for the funerals of persons of high rank, infrequent as they were. The city of Madrid spent 1,100 reales for the delivery and subsequent printing of the sermon given at Philip III's funeral, but this was a modest sum compared to the cost of the 120 feet of mourning drapery, the allegorical devices, and the architectural decoration of the catafalque constructed for the occasion.

There were other disadvantages: the public in the major cities tended to be demanding. The preachers complained that city-dwellers were so accustomed to evaluating the quality and execution of sermons that a preacher could never rest on his laurels. One Portuguese Augustinian, Diego López de Andrade, protested: "Even if the preachers lose sleep and deserved rest, even if they study many books of all sorts, it is hard to find even one with whom the public declares itself fully satisfied."

Moreover, there was always a chance that some ignorant or hostile listener might complain to the Inquisition. Terrones, who had been a censor of the Holy Office in Granada, declared that "if the inquisitors were to convene all the preachers denounced by malevolent listeners there would no longer be anyone left to talk from the pulpit." When a denunciation was followed up, the members of the tribunal usually acted with clemency, since they were fully aware that the preachers' failings were more apt to come from oratorical passion than willful heterodoxy.

In their passion, some certainly went too far. Diego de Estella stated that the reasonable preacher would prudently moderate his language, "even if he is speaking of Luther." Once in a great while there was a case like that of Charles Hersent, a truly picturesque personage who was expelled from the Oratory in France for his ferocious diatribes against monks and Jesuits. At one point during the Thirty Years War, Philip IV admonished the superiors of the orders and warned them against making political statements—criticism of the pope and of royal fiscal policies—which were, however, beginning to be heard from some Spanish pulpits.

The preacher's social ascendancy came in large part from his real power to correct his listeners and call them to fulfill their duties, a particularly delicate task when his remarks were directed at princes and notables. Even then, public opinion tended to overestimate the preachers' influence in palace circles. For their part, the preachers (Terrones, for one, who was obliged to preach to Philip II in private) tended to deny that they had any such influence or at least to stress the negative aspects of preaching to such august hearers. One example of this may have been Nicolas Caussin, preacher to Louis XIII but not fond of Cardinal Richelieu, and whose preaching career ended when he was exiled. Another was the Capuchin friar Juan de Ocaña, a man whose simple demeanor gave him such an air of devotion that the Jesuit Gonzalez Pereira was moved to pious thoughts ("his eyes turned to the earth, his hood drawn to his mouth, his foot on his own beard"), and who was banished from Madrid in 1637 but returned four years later and preached "very fine things" to the king. Another Capuchin, José de Madrid, was imprisoned in 1678, Buenaventura de Carrocera tells us, "for a sermon he gave in the palace." For the preacher, preaching was truly a double-edged sword.

PREPARATION OF THE SERMON

Within certain limits, the technique of composing a sermon sounds oddly familiar to anyone in the academic world or who has been party to an academic search. According to accepted seventeenth-century theory, the preparation of a sermon, like that of a scholarly lecture, was broken down into phases of *inventio, dispositio,* and *memoria.*

An occasional or a beginning preacher could seek the help of such tools as the *Prediche* of Gabriele Inchino (Venice, 1607) or the *Despertador Christiano* of the theologian José de Barcia y Zambrana (Lisbon, 1684), works that offered sermon outlines and even lead sentences to spur the imagination. A more experienced orator would begin by consulting his own materials: sets of "file cards" classified by subject matter, in the case of Carlo Borromeo, or notes, full or schematic, taken on daily encounters, personal meditation, and, especially, reading. One of the advantages of owning a good library was to be able to spend the months from Easter to October (when little preaching was done) concentrating on studies, taking care to note in the margins appropriate passages that could then be translated and arranged in alphabetical order. One court preacher—Terrones—had a scrivener do this task for him, thus saving him the time and trouble.

After collecting notes from Scripture, the fathers of the church, devotional works, and (in moderation) secular literature, the preacher might spend long hours meditating on the texts he had read and absorbing their contents. The next task was to give form to what would become his sermon. Luis de Granada noted:

> One must seek the best time and place for this meditation. The best hours are those of dawn or those of the night, when the domestics are not making noise and no din distracts our thoughts. Likewise, the solitude and darkness of the place give light for the mind's wanderings. But a consecrated place, especially the one in which the Holy Eucharist is kept, is appropriate above all others.

Luis de Granada's advice seems in contrast with the (perhaps more secular) practice of Terrones, who organized his material while he was dictating (and even so, he usually needed a week to finish a sermon), not to mention the practice of Paravicino, who wrote in a normal hand when he began to compose, but whose writing became illegible when he was carried away by inspiration, with disastrous results for the posthumous editions of his sermons.

Often a professional preacher would write out his sermons ahead of time, even some months beforehand, or at least prepare a detailed outline. Doubtless the process varied according to the solemnity of the circumstances and the time available. The famous Portuguese preacher Timotheo de Ciabra Pimentel managed to give sixty-eight sermons in one Lenten period, and during those forty days he must have had time for little else than a notable effort of memory. Last-minute changes almost always had to be made to adjust a sermon to its hearers: "What sense is there in preaching in a convent of nuns on the qualities required of a good bishop, or in a friary on the Feast of the Magdalene against the use of personal ornaments and cosmetics? However, such things have been seen."

The technique most frequently recommended as a way to learn a sermon well—a task that terrified many aspiring preachers—was to write it down or, even better, to prepare an outline. Reading from the pulpit was not admissible, and reciting by heart was considered fitting only for beginners and better avoided by the experienced preacher, particularly since the points contained in a sermon often had to be repeated in different ways until even the dullest listener grasped them. Thus the most common practice was to get the scheme of the sermon well fixed in mind—its formal structure, exempla, ideas—and commit that scheme to memory, leaving the rest to improvisation.

What a preacher did in the hours before his sermon was dictated by individual temperament. Some—the Dominican Tomás Trujillo, for example—suggested giving a last look at the sermon, but others preferred to follow Aristotle's advice, "It is good to sleep a bit," and not worry.

The Preacher in the Pulpit

Baroque religious practice held that sacred oratory was appropriate to any place that need might dictate. During popular preaching missions, preaching in the streets reached the most recalcitrant of the faithful and facilitated the participation, open or camouflaged, of penitent heretics. Although missions were exceptional events, preaching was present in nearly all situations—and all calamities—of collective life. According to one report in 1559, "all of Castile was depopulated" when people flocked to the auto-da-fé that preceded the execution of the theologian Pedro de Cazalla in Valladolid, an occasion at which the Dominican Melchor Cano spoke for an hour on the highly appropriate scriptural text: "Beware of false prophets, who come to you in sheep's clothing but inwardly are ravenous wolves" (Matt. 7.15).

For the person condemned to death the sermon delivered at the foot of the gallows was obviously an unrepeatable opportunity to make his peace with God, but the spectators—who might easily include the condemned person's companions in crime—might also draw a moral lesson from the drama taking place before their eyes. The Jesuit Pedro León calculated that about twenty thousand people heard him preach when four famous highwaymen were shot to death with arrows on the high road outside the Andalusian town of Carmona. Many analogous occasions might be cited, such as the same Father León's sermons in the prisons and the prostitutes' districts of Seville, or those of the Capuchins in the public squares of Bologna during the plague epidemic of 1630.

Félix Amat recalled with admiration, a century and a half later, the Recollect friar Francisco Solano, a preacher of exquisite Baroque sensibilities active in Lima:

> Sometimes he would enter a courtyard in which plays were performed when a performance had already begun. Jumping suddenly onto a bench or even

onto the stage, he would draw out a crucifix and, crying out and weeping, would urge the audience to consider the dolorous tragedy of Calvary. On an occasion so apparently inopportune, he would speak with so much enthusiasm and love of God, in such a lively and fervent manner, that the listeners passed from licentiousness to devotion, from vanity to piety, from sensual and worldly gaiety to holy contrition of the spirit.

We must of course remember that the place that was by far the most propitious for listening to a sermon was a church, and it is significant that a new sacred architecture arose after the Council of Trent that permitted the faithful to hear and see the preacher from any position in the church. Since this was less true of churches built in earlier times, any orator unfamiliar with the premises was well advised to inspect the church beforehand and try out the acoustics from the pulpit if he wanted to use his voice most effectively.

Although he added little to the theory of gesture and diction, the Baroque preacher made good use of those resources to achieve the sort of persuasion that could arouse more than formal acceptance from his hearers. The manuals advised naturalness and moderation (with a dose of conservatism perhaps greater than was true of actual pulpit practice), but they also left much to the discretion of the preacher. As Terrones wrote, "It is necessary to adjust one's voice and mode of reproach to suit the audience: with the vulgar, loud cries and violent gestures; with nobles, a graceful voice and effective arguments; with sovereigns, a voice almost in falsetto and an attitude of humble submission."

Appropriate head and arm movements formed a language that complemented speech, even though theorists—borrowing from Latin norms—advised abstention from too realistic an interpretation of the theme treated: "When speaking of a cripple who approaches Jesus to ask to be cured, the preacher should not carry on as if he himself limped; when making a comparison with people who knife one another, he must not stab and slash nor crouch in the pulpit."

As Hilary Dansey Smith has observed, this advice may seem absurd today, but some writers of advice make it clear that it was not superfluous at the time. A good dose of mimicry and a little ostentation were a sure hit with an illiterate public. The preachers often exaggerated, however: "Some," Luis de Granada wrote, "bend double or, crouching, hide in the pulpit, or seem to rise in the air and come right out of the pulpit."

Other habits that the preacher was exhorted to learn to control were tugging continually at the sleeves of his habit, pulling his collar, hanging his handkerchief on the edge of the pulpit, and constantly rubbing his knuckles. On the other hand, satisfying such natural needs as coughing, wiping one's brow, or spitting (Terrones was proud of his continence where spitting was concerned) was to some extent tolerated. Preachers were advised to avoid physical problems by restricting their diet.

THE PARTS OF THE SERMON

When the moment came to begin his sermon, the preacher mounted the pulpit before the waiting crowd. At times an assistant seated on the pulpit steps might take notes of the more significant passages—notes that would serve, if the preacher had no draft version, for eventual publication of the sermon. The sermon itself, usually constructed on roughly the same model as the classical oration, was composed of a preamble, an exposition, a confirmation or demonstration, and a peroration or epilogue.

The beginning was a delicate moment. If the preacher was not careful, the preamble—that is, the *divini auxilii imploratio* (imploration of divine aid) culminating in an Ave Maria, an important element in heretical times, and the introduction of the topic—might turn into a miniature sermon. An experienced preacher would limit the time he spent on these preliminaries because he knew that he had only an hour before the public would begin to show signs of impatience. (Sermons delivered during a mission might be longer, and in Italy they could, on occasion, last as long as an hour and a half, but with an intermission for the preacher to catch his breath.) The orator would also do well to concentrate on winning his hearers' good will. As Luis de Granada stated, "Many attend sermons more out of habit than any desire to profit from them, others out of pure curiosity, others yawning and paying no heed, thus they leave unfed and empty-handed." The preacher was also advised to avoid the temptation of remarking on the small number of people present or complaining that he had been invited to preach with little advance notice. He should use a moderate tone of voice in his preamble. If not, as Terrones said, "the game will flee." This was also good advice for the preacher's health, since it was generally accepted that raising one's voice put sudden strain on the arteries, and that getting overheated in a drafty church was a poor idea. The orator should bare his head only in the initial salutation, unless the host was exposed; as God's representative, he should not remove his biretta even if he was preaching to the king, nor should he remove it every time he mentioned the names of Jesus or Mary, for fear that it would be distracting and create confusion if everyone present imitated him.

Announcing the topic of his sermon at the start and giving notice of its major segments would help his hearers to follow him. This was indispensable in some cases, since the longest part of the sermon, the demonstration, would probably contain difficult concepts or comparisons that might befuddle the audience if they lacked a clear point of departure. In any event, the public had to arrive on time for the sermon and needed to follow it attentively if they were to grasp the substance of the preacher's "proofs," especially if these were anything like the arguments used by Manuel de Guerra y Ribera in his commentary on the Gospel text, "And when evening came, the boat was out on the sea, and he was alone on the land" (Mark 6.47):

> The principal reason is still missing. Love is a finger, but not the hand: because it is unnecessary to give the hand to the loved one; it will be enough to give him a finger. So that this just attribution of rewards becomes clearer, it should be observed that the Son is the arm of the Father and the hand of his eternal power, and the Holy Spirit is the finger, for which reason one should not give one's hand to the will but to the intellect; to love one gives only a finger, and to the intellect the hand and the arm are given, because a finger is the least gage of an entire body, and a small prize that can be given to a loved one, but the hand should be given only to someone who is prudent.

An experienced preacher would thus give speculative "proofs" (not too many of them, however, and avoiding questions better reserved to specialists) at the beginning of his demonstration, when those present could be presumed to be relatively fresh.

It was preferable to have some logical connection between one's arguments, but if this proved difficult the connection should not be forced. José Climent, a bishop with Jansenist sympathies, may have been right to criticize a famous orator "who in a sermon in San Isidor ruminated at length on the Latin name of the saint, dividing it into 'Isis' and 'Dorus' and pulling arguments for his sermon out of what the poets had said about those false gods." And if one of the "proofs" were less than convincing, it would be better to hide it in the middle of the demonstration.

Up to this point, our preacher had accomplished the dual task of exposing some doctrinal points (thus satisfying the necessary didactic portion of the sermon) and warming up his hearers psychologically, which he had to do if he was to move them and provoke in them a desire for betterment. He now turned to *magnitudo*—that is, to the technique of dwelling on the enormity of the things, good and bad, that could be seen as connected with his argument. Here was where the preacher could raise his voice and make use of all his rhetorical skills—descriptions, comparisons, allegories—and even a dramatic trick or two in order to get the desired result. To judge from the testimony of Jean-François de Régis and Baltasar Gracián, one common technique was to read a letter sent from heaven or hell; the custom of holding a dialogue with a skull or a crucifix was even more widespread. As we have seen, dialogue lent itself to individual variants: Emilio Orozco Diaz recalled the case of the Jesuit Juan Bautista Escarlo, who, preaching in Valencia during Lent 1643, "showed a skull as if it were that of a famous courtesan who had lived in the city."

The demonstration usually ended with some striking thought or dramatic effect that the preacher had held in reserve for its great emotional power. Few of these could have been as spectacular as the one described by the Portuguese Antonio Vieira in a sermon given on Sexagesima Sunday 1655:

In a sermon on the Passion, the orator, when he gets to the scene of Pilate, tells how they made Christ a king in jest. He says that they took a purple cloth and threw it over his shoulders, and the audience listens with rapt attention; he says that they wove a crown of thorns and fastened it on his head, and everyone remains spellbound; then he says that they tied his hands and gave him a reed as a scepter, and the hearers still listen in silence with bated breath. At this point a curtain opens and the image of the Ecce Homo appears, and then you see everyone throwing himself to the ground and beating his breast, weeping, crying out, howling, and striking himself.

At that point the preacher, without letting this emotional climax abate, would launch into an epilogue that usually consisted of a repetition of his most effective arguments, amplified if need be. He would speak "with stronger, more significant, and even hyperbolical expressions [delivered] more rapidly and in a higher tone of voice, with more tension and sentiment, with apostrophes, questions, and exclamations about what had been said and demonstrated in the sermon, until he finished in glory and beauty" (Terrones).

PREACHING IN RURAL AREAS

If preaching had been limited to the cities and towns, the Catholic Reformation would never have reached most seventeenth-century Europeans. The cities contained many parishes and many monasteries, but only a small proportion of the population lived in them. The problem of the imbalance that existed between the distribution of people and the distribution of pastoral resources was attacked by internal missions, a technique that had been used in other periods but that developed extraordinarily in the Baroque age. In this itinerant evangelization, groups of preachers whose activities were concentrated in rural areas instructed the people and rekindled their faith by sermons and the inculcation of pious practices. Since the secular clergy was far from being capable of this sort of task, missions fell to the lot of the monastic orders and the new congregations.

According to whether missions were primarily aimed at reconverting Protestants or elevating the spiritual condition of Catholics, they put greater emphasis on catechizing or on penitential activities, but the dividing line between the two types was less clear than might be supposed. The common enemy, after all, was Satan, and this guiding idea was reflected in a effort toward the conversion of all souls that made few distinctions in practice between heretics and simple ignorant folk. The Capuchin Nicolas de Dijon expressed an opinion common in his time when he stated that ignorance, more than superstition, was the principal flaw in the religious life of rural society, even though country folk, unlike their city counterparts, showed a willingness to learn and become better. In the early seventeenth century much of France and the Empire was considered mission territory, not only because of doctrinal deviations found there but also because of a general lack of instruction. That did not mean that religious culture was much more evolved in the parts of southern Europe that had not been affected by the Protestant contagion: Father León stated that in some inaccessible parts of Alpujarras no sermons had been preached for some time and the people did not even know what preaching was. "There were women under twenty years of age who, since they had never heard anyone cry aloud in church before, hid and covered their faces fearing punishment when we raised our voices to preach" (Pedro Herrera Puga). In Italy, Paulucci di Calboli recalled that in certain parts of the Kingdom of Naples many people, when asked who was God, responded that it was the pope, the local lord, or even the missionaries who were catechizing them (Carla Russo).

The Capuchins and the Jesuits, who initiated the missionary movement and marked it with their intense dedication, stressed conversion of the heart over that of the intellect. In practice this led to a predilection for spectacular and, if you will, Baroque, effects (Bernard Dompnier). The Congregation of the Mission founded by St. Vincent de Paul in 1625 cultivated instead a more catechizing brand of evangelism that was deliberately lacking in the emotional paraphernalia then in vogue. The Congregation, which originated in a campaign to missionize in the feudal possessions of the Gondi family, spread rapidly to the rest of France, to Italy, and to Poland.

Whatever specific institution he was connected with, the missionary usually had a functional status that differed from that of the ordinary monk or friar. This was clear in the Capuchin order, where the title of "missioner," even outside the friary, was distinct from that of "preacher," and both titles were not necessarily accessible to all members of the order. The general chapter of 1698 sought to avoid abuse of the notion that had cropped up in some provinces that "all or nearly all preachers claimed to be missioners without having the necessary talents" (Buenaventura de Carrocera). What these talents were is easily deduced from the missionaries' special mode of life. They were expected in all circumstances to conduct themselves as much as possible in conformity with conventual life and the rules of the order: they were to travel always by foot, to keep silence or speak of supernatural things, to set a good example at all times, to live soberly, not letting themselves be won over by worldly curiosity and—obviously—to avoid the company of women.

Members of the Congregation had to arise at four in the morning to recite the office and meditate; their morning was taken up with the sermon and with hearing confessions; in the afternoon they had doctrinal preaching ("great" and "small" catechism), after which came more hours in the confessional that often lasted well into the twilight hours. They kept busy: during the first six years of the Congregation the missioners of St. Vincent (who numbered only seven until 1631) preached in 140 missions of two or three weeks each, and in the eighteen years of his activity, Renault de Legendre, one of the French fathers who set up the Congregation's Rome house, participated in 106 missions.

This pace, along with a precarious diet, difficult travel, and exposure to climatic rigors, explains why some missionaries died prematurely, as did Cosimo Galilei, a nephew of Galileo Galilei, who died of galloping consumption in Naples at the age of thirty-six (Luigi Mezzadri). Furthermore, if their missionary work took them to Protestant lands, the missioners always ran the risk of violent death at the hands of some fanatic: this was the fate of Marc Roy, a German Capuchin charged by the Congregatio de Propaganda Fide (Congregation for the Propagation of the Faith) with the responsibility of extending the missions into the Grison mountains. Taking on such arduous tasks required going well beyond a purely human conception of the mission, which was what explained the missioners' prestige among the people. We can agree with Pedro de Lepe, the bishop of Calahorra, who contrasted the missioners' preaching with the more refined and artificial preaching of the day. As Antonio Domínguez Ortiz has said, the missioners' preaching "pays no attention to a brilliant appearance but rather to the salvation of souls."

How was a mission conducted? First, missions tried—wisely—to avoid being a financial burden on the areas in which they intended to preach, which often had been impoverished by exploitation. Expenses were covered by endowments, which could come in many kinds. For example, the Jesuits who were entrusted with giving sermons on Pentecost Monday and Tuesday in San Martín de Prados were paid out of a bequest from the parish priest that produced a revenue of twenty-seven *ferrados* of grain, thirteen of rye, and two hens. A much larger sum was the annual pension of two hundred ducats given by the count of Altamira to the Dominicans of Santiago to have missions conducted in his domains, a duty at first carried out by the Jesuits but whose charge was revoked, for unknown reasons, in 1639 (Aureliano Pardo Villar). Father Vincent Huby noted that in the diocese of Tarascon the parishes were the beneficiaries, from the second half of the seventeenth century on, of a fund that made it possible to hold missions every few years. In many cases it was bishops who paid the expenses, either with a single payment or by appropriate endowments, so that their pastoral visits could be preceded by missions. At times the prelates attended the sermons, although that tended to worry the faithful: according to Luigi Mezzadri, in Fiordini "the people were afraid that the missioners might denounce scandals to the bishop."

Missions might be held at any time of the year except (for obvious reasons) Lent and Advent. They were rarely held in the late summer, the harvest season, when no one would have time for such devotions. In the other periods, the three or four members of the mission team preached, without stopping and with little variation in their repertory, in places that could be reached on foot from their order's house.

In general the missionaries were well received because their programs brought an interruption of the monotony of peasant life and a welcome change in mental habits. On each of the fifteen or thirty days of the mission there were sermons of various sorts—catechizing, doctrinal, and of course moralistic—in which the preachers spoke on Last Things and the disastrous consequences of a sinful life spent in turning one's back to God. The Congregation's members (also called Lazarists) tended to reduce the inherent drama of such topics by speaking on them early in the morning, but, as we have seen, it was more common practice to emphasize their more terrifying aspects and even to use nonverbal techniques to compensate for the rural public's limited receptivity of a more intellectual discourse. The semi-darkness of the church on a winter evening with candle flames flickering in the drafts was the best setting for the more dramatic sort of delivery, which was eventually known as "preaching Capuchin style."

The missionaries' primary role as preachers did not exclude other activities more or less connected with the institutional vocation of their order. When during the autumn of 1614 the Jesuits Gaspar de la Peña and Pedro León held a mission in the area of Aracena, they not only preached and confessed all day long but visited prisons, schools, and hospitals and even managed, according the report quoted by Herrera, to "make friendships, some of them of great importance." The Capuchins usually organized solemn Stations of the Cross and eucharistic functions like forty-hour vigils, and their missions ended with an impressive procession in which friars and penitents made their way through the streets shouldering heavy crosses.

The most evident proof of the success of a mission was the number of the faithful who took part in the sacrament of penance—that is, confession. For that reason the missionaries, who had received the local bishop's permission to absolve reserved sins, would devote a particularly long time to private auricular confession. That provided anyone who usually abstained from confession out of personal animosity toward the local parish priest with a good opportunity to settle accounts with God, and doubtless the general atmosphere of conversion typical of missions accentuated the urge to seek purification. Long lines of people waited before the confessional, and anxious penitents might arrive at all hours asking to be freed from a "serpent" (the term *culebrón* often enters into the reports of Spanish missioners) that had arisen from a long lethargy.

If the population collaborated in the mission as desired, an atmosphere of spiritual renewal would reign during its final days. This fervor was expressed (and this was no small achievement) in reciprocal pardons for offenses great and small, in the righting of irregular marital situations, and in a general reform of mores. This was the moment to break with a concubine or right an egregious injustice before a village astonished to see its most notorious sinners as penitents. The local houses of prostitution were closed and their lodgers promised to mend their ways. The women might even be present among the weeping throng that bade farewell to the brothers at the end of the mission.

It was among the contrasts of the Baroque age that everyone knew that these spectacular results would be short-lived and that soon, even in a few weeks, the village would go back to its old ways. Because they too were aware of this, the missionaries sought to make their spiritual conquests as long-lasting as possible. Knowing that permanent improvement required strengthening the rural clergy, St. Vincent de Paul turned his energies to that problem. Others attempted to establish penitential confraternities and congregations (such as the Escuelas de Cristo or the Third Order Franciscans) and to encourage such pious practices as the Stations of the Cross and the Rosary. Finally, anticipating future practices, much use was made of printing. Bishop Barcia y Zambrana, who promoted a number of missions, distributed to the faithful of his diocese pamphlets with such titles as *El jardín florido del alma* or *La prática del Santísimo Rosario*. As the Capuchin friar Manuel de Jaén explained, "What is preached is soon forgotten, whereas what is printed lasts a long time."

But the diffusion of religious culture in the Baroque era by means of the printed book is in every way part of another story.

BIBLIOGRAPHY

Bibliography on the preacher as a human type is in fairly short supply; on the other hand, there is a wealth of works on rhetorical theory and on preaching as a collective phenomenon. One seldom finds overall views, on the national level, of the preacher or of preaching, although these do exist concerning rhetoric, which is not the specific topic of this chapter. Above all, there are very few works in which the three themes are treated comparatively from an interconfessional standpoint. This list is limited to works that have furnished ideas and information for the present chapter.

Alarcos, Emilio. "Los sermones de Paravicino." *Revista de Filología Española* 24 (1937): 162–97, 249–319.

Bayley, Peter. *French Pulpit Oratory, 1598–1600: A Study in Themes and Styles, with a Descriptive Catalogue of Printed Texts.* Cambridge and New York: Cambridge University Press, 1980.

Benassar, Bartolomé, et al. *L'Inquisition espagnole, XVe–XIXe siècles.* Paris: Hachette, 1979; Verviers: Nouvelles éditions Marabout, 1983.

Black, Christopher. "Perugia and Post-Tridentine Church Reform." *Journal of Ecclesiastical History* 35 (1984): 429–51.

Buenaventura de Carrocera. *La provincia de frailes menores capuchinos de Castilla.* Madrid. Vol. 1, *1575–1701* (1949).

Calvo Poyato, José. "Religiosidad y calamidades en tierras de Córdoba a finales del siglo XVII." *Hispania Sacra* 39 (1987): 185–200.

Campanelli, Marcella. "La biblioteca di un parroco meridionale alla fine del Seicento." *Archivio Storico per le Province Napoletane* 103 (1985): 285–353.

Casas, Elena, ed. *La retórica en España.* Madrid, 1980.

Croce, Benedetto. *Storia della età barocca in Italia: Pensiero-poesia e letteratura-vita morale.* Bari: G. Laterza e figli, 1929.

Davies, Horton. *Like Angels from a Cloud: The English Metaphysical Preachers, 1588–1645.* San Marino: The Huntington Library, 1986.

De Rosa, Gabriele. "Il francescano Cornelio Musso dal concilio di Trento alla diocesi di Bitonto." *Rivista di Storia della Chiesa in Italia* 40 (1986): 55–91.

Domínguez Ortiz, Antonio. *La sociedad española en el siglo XVII.* 2 vols. Madrid: Consejo Superior de Investigaciones Científicas, 1963–70. Vol. 2, *El estamento eclesiástico.*

Dompnier, Bernard. "Les missions des Capucins et leur empreinte sur la réforme catholique en France." *Revue d'histoire de l'Eglise de France* 70 (1984): 127–47.

Estudios sobre el Barroco. Special issue, *Revista de la Universidad de Madrid* 11 (1962).

Fernández Alvarez, Manuel. *La sociedad española en el Siglo de Oro.* 2 vols. Madrid: Gredos, 1984; 2d ed. rev. and aug., 1989.

Fino, Antonio. "Chiesa e società nelle diocesi di Terra di Lavoroa sud del Volturno in età postridentina (1585–1630)." *Rivista di Storia della Chiesa in Italia* 35 (1981): 388–449.

Goyet, Théodore, and Jean-Pierre Collinet, eds. *Journées Bossuet: La prédication au XVIIe siècle.* Actes du colloque, Dijon, December 2–4, 1977. Paris: Nizet, 1980.

Guidetti, Armando. *Le missioni popolari: I grandi Gesuiti italiani.* Milan: Rusconi, 1988.

Heal, Felicity, and Rosemary O'Day, eds. *Church and Society in England: Henry VIII to James I.* Hamden, Conn.: Archon Books, 1977.

Herrera Puga, Pedro. *Sociedad y delincuencia en il Siglo de Oro*. Madrid: Catolica, 1974.

Herrero García, Miguel, ed. *Sermonario clásico: Con un ensayo sobre la oratoria sagrada*. Madrid: Escelicer, 1942.

Homenaje a D. Pedro Sáinz Rodríguez. 4 vols. Madrid: Fundacion Universitaria Españo, 1984–86.

Julia, Dominique, and David Rice McKee. "Les confrères de Jean Meslier: Culture et spiritualité du clergé champenois au XVIIe siècle." *Revue d'histoire de l'Eglise de France* 69 (1982): 61–66.

Lebrun, François, ed. *Histoire des catholiques en France: Du XVe siècle à nos jours*. Toulouse: Privat, 1980.

Lopez Santos, Luis. "La oratoria sagrada en el Seiscientos (un libro inédito del P. Valentin Céspedes)." *Revista de Filología Española* 30 (1946): 353–68.

Luigi da Gatteo. *La peste a Bologna nel 1630*. Forlì: Poligrafico Romagnola, 1930.

Martí, Antonio M. *La preceptiva retórica española en el Siglo de Oro*. Madrid: Gredos, 1972.

Martinez, B. "Las librerías e imprentas de los jesuitas (1540–1767): Una aportación notable a la cultura española." *Hispania Sacra* 40 (1988): 315–88.

Martorell Téllez-Girón, Ricardo., ed. *Anales de Madrid de Léon Pinelo, Reinado de Felipe III, Años 1598 a 1621*. Madrid: E. Maestre, 1931.

Menéndez Pelayo, Marcelino. *Historia de los heterodoxos españoles*. 4th ed. 2 vols. Madrid: Catolica, 1986–87.

Mezzadri, Luigi. "Le missioni popolari della Congregazione della Missione nello Stato della Chiesa (1642–1700)." *Rivista di Storia della Chiesa Italiana* 33 (1979): 12–44.

———. *Vincent de Paul: 1581–1660*. Translated by Jean-Pierre Bagot. Paris: Desclée De Brouwer, 1985.

Murphy, James J., with the technical assistance of Kevin P. Roddy. *Renaissance Rhetoric: A Short-Title Catalogue*. New York: Garland, 1981.

Pardo Villar, Aureliano. *Los domínicos en Santiago: Los apuntes históricos*. Madrid: Consejo Superior de Investigaciones Cientificas, 1953.

Petrocchi, Massimo. *Storia della spiritualità italiana, secoli XIII–XX*. 3 vols. Rome: Edizioni di storia e letteratura, 1978–9. Vol, 2, *Il Cinquecento e il Seicento* (1978).

Pierrard, Pierre. *Le prêtre français: Du concile de Trente à nos jours*. Paris: Desclée, 1986.

Problemi di Storia della Chiesa nei secoli XVII–XVIII. Atti del V convegno di aggiornamento, Associazione italiana dei professori di storia della chiesa, Bologna, September 3–7, 1979. Naples: Edizioni Dehoniane, 1982.

Ribera, S. Juan de. *Sermones: Primera transcripción de los originales autógrafos, notas y estudio preliminar por Ramón Robres Lluch*. Valencia: Comercial, 1987.

Rusconi, Roberto. *Predicazione e vita religiosa nella società italiana da Carlo Magno alla Controriforma*. Turin: Loescher, 1981.

Santini, Emilio. *Eloquenza italiana dal Concilio tridentino ai nostri giorni: Gli oratori sacri*. 2 vols. Palermo: Sandron, 1923–28.

Savignac, Jean-Paul. *Historia de la Iglesia.* Madrid: Palabra. Vol. 2, *La Iglesia en la edad moderna.* Translated by Pedro Antonio Urbina. 2d edition (1988).

Shuger, Debora. "The Christian Grand Style in Renaissance Rhetoric." *Viator* 16 (1985): 337–66.

Smith, Hilary Dansey. *Preaching in the Spanish Golden Age: A Study of Some Preachers of the Reign of Philip III.* Oxford and New York: Oxford University Press, 1978.

Terrones del Caño, Francisco. *Instrucción de Predicadores: Prólogo y notas del p. Félix G. Olmedo.* Madrid: Espasa-Calpe, 1946.

Transmettre la foi: XVIe–XXe siècles. Actes du 109e congrès national des sociétés savantes, Dijon 1984. 2 vols. Paris: Comité des travaux en histoire et science, 1984. Vol. 1, *Pastorale et prédication en France.*

7

THE MISSIONARY

Adriano Prosperi

THE APOSTOLIC MANNER AND
THE "JUDICIAL" MANNER

The supreme office of the pope embraces everything that can pertain to the
health of souls, but no thing more than the safeguard of the Catholic faith,
there being two operations necessary concerning it, one to keep it within
the faithful, constraining them as if with penalties to keep it firmly, the
other to spread it and propagate it among the unbelievers; therefore two
manners of procedure have thus far been taken in the holy Church, one
judicial, hence the office of the Holy Inquisition has been instituted, the
other moral, or rather apostolic, hence missions of workers among the
peoples who are most in need are sent continually; and to that end a number of seminaries and colleges have been made to instruct those who are to
be sent and to go in support of the new converts.[1]

THE LETTER OF JANUARY 15, 1622 , announcing to all the papal
nuncios the creation of the new Congregatio de Propaganda Fide
(Congregation for the Propagation of the Faith)—immediately
shortened to "di Propaganda," in a bureaucratic simplification destined
for lasting success—set up a double standard. It was one thing to have
dealings with the *fedeli* and quite another to deal with the *infedeli*. The
faithful were the subjects of rulers who recognized the authority of the
pope; the "infidels" were all the rest—that is, the non-Christian populations of the Americas, Asia, and Africa, but also the subjects of Protestant
rulers. This distinction failed to cover all cases, however, since even in the
lands of Catholic princes there were some subjects who, although not
Catholics, could not be treated as heretics: "In the Catholic provinces
there can be found Hebrews, and on occasion in the ports and in the
public squares or in borderlands there are heretics, schismatics, and infidels." Since the church could not use the Inquisition in such places, it had
to resign itself to the arts of persuasion.

This sort of language might seem startling at a time when all of Europe was sated with the horrors of the religious war that was later called the Thirty Years War. Nonetheless, it was one of the most important results of the lively polemics that had taken place during the sixteenth century over the use of violence in religious matters—polemics that had moved in different directions according to whether they concerned extra-European nonbelievers or European heretics, but that, for the moment, seemed to have arrived at a working agreement. It was a distinction that for some time was not too carefully made; indeed, many in the Catholic camp were tempted to lump together all the "others" and apply the same violent coercion to all. Only a few decades earlier, in the mid-sixteenth century, the Spanish theologian Alfonso de Castro had argued the legitimacy of the use of violent force against heretics and the justice of a war of conquest to Christianize the West Indies. Similarly, the jurist Marquardus de Susannis argued the legitimacy of forced conversion of Jews where they had hithertofore been permitted to maintain their religious identity within Christian society (decidedly not the case in the Iberian Peninsula and the Spanish dominions), a notion supported by Pope Paul IV in both theory and practice.

The papal encyclical of 1622 juxtaposed two manners—gentle persuasion and violent force—and showed that they complemented one another, but one belonged to the past and the other looked to the future. When, in the seventeenth century, missionary work seemed the church's most urgent task, the Inquisition had by and large completed the most challenging part of its work. Heresy was no longer a pressing problem in Catholic countries: there were still heretics, of course, but they were no longer considered a serious threat. Capital punishment was applied only in the most extreme cases, and normally they too could be resolved with an expeditious abjuration, for which pre-printed bureaucratic forms were available. The problem of witchcraft remained, to be sure, but it seemed that the need for true religion to do battle with the alternative religion of the devil was fading, leaving in its wake a highly complicated situation that the inquisitors attempted to decipher with a good dose of coolheadedness and skepticism. Their relations with the faithful entrusted to their guidance involved, among other things, patient investigation and persuasion. In short, truth seemed less evident to the inquisitors of the seventeenth century than it had to their predecessors at the time of the all-out combat of the Protestant Reformation.

Doubt and perplexity reigned. The comforting certitude of the self-evidence of truth that had existed during the violent battles of the Reformation had now disappeared. When the impulse for general reform passed from a clash of ideas to the governance of society, it lost its way in a tangle of possible directions. Theological battles had become a matter

for specialists and no longer prompted the ingenuous, even confused, enthusiasms of the past. Anyone charged with the direction of moral conduct (or simply with reflection upon it) had to renounce the grandiose
and fascinating simplicity of evangelical models for more tortuous paths.
Human behavior seemed complicated, difficult to understand and to
guide. Moral theology wandered in the thickets of casuistry; the search
for good groped through the maze of identification of the lesser evil. All
of European Christendom seemed affected by the new malaise. Even in
the Protestant world the straight path seemed less evident and the strong
voice of conscience seemed flawed by doubt and perplexity; casuistry,
both as a moral discipline and a guiding thread through the labyrinth of
choice between good and evil, found willing listeners well beyond the
borders of Catholicism.[2]

This was why gentle persuasion seemed the better course, and why
missionary work was more attractive. The missionary's tasks had always
been accomplished by peaceful means. Moreover, at a time when the
harsh theological polemics of the Reformation had been watered down
by a complex and wearisome academic specialization in controversy, the
task of addressing distant interlocutors who were totally extraneous to
quarrels among Christians—the "infidels"—had all the irresistible fascination of exoticism.

Exoticism, like the science of persuasion, was communicated primarily through words, and words—the spoken word of the missionaries who
addressed "infidel" populations and the written and printed word of their
fellow religious who reported on the missions and propagandized them
in Europe—reigned supreme.

There is an Italian proverb that states, "Tra dire e fare c'è di mezzo il
mare" (literally, "The sea stands between saying and doing"), and indeed
all the seas and oceans of the world lay between Europe and missionary
lands. The power of words eliminated distance, however, and when the
missionary order applied it to interpreting images from the new worlds it
reached new heights. Daniello Bartoli's writings offer a striking example
of that power.

Bartoli never saw the things he wrote about. He spent his life "for
more than thirty years . . . in a little room, between a crucifix and a pile
of books, manuscripts, and documents, writing intrepidly but patiently."[3]
Nonetheless, his books opened up vast horizons to his readers' imaginations.

Bartoli himself tells us how he worked: everything he wrote was
based on authentic reports from people who witnessed or participated in
the events he related. Bartoli was not alone, though: there were many
others who were attracted by the allure of travel and adventure literature
and who let their imaginations take fire from eyewitness accounts and

observed exotic lands over the missionaries' shoulders. Bartoli might well have asked the same rhetorical question that Ludovico Antonio Muratori asked a century later: "How is it that I have succeeded in discoursing on such distant and strange lands, confined in Modena without ever having set foot outside Italy?" Bartoli might also have agreed with Muratori's answer: "I respond that if not with my own, I have gone to Paraguay with the feet of others, and with the eyes of others I have visited those fortunate missions, with the result that I can give a full account of what I shall say."
Bartoli, too, had walked with the feet of others:

> And thus in this as in all the rest, I relied on the faithful memoirs of men . . . [who] lived in China, by the grace of God, not for some ten or fifteen months closed in a castle as if in prison, but familiar with the whole breadth of that kingdom, and this for twenty, thirty, forty, and more years spent not only in the labors of the apostolic ministry but also in nights of long and wearisome study of the letters and the sciences proper to that country, until they became teachers [*maestri*] to the very masters of the land. And of these have I, for my use and profit, large quantities of original writings, as well as spoken reports from other eye-witnesses who have come from there and from China, from Macao to Peking—that is, from one end to the other.[4]

Reporting on the missions could not be separated from telling about missionary practices, and the men who had labored for religious conversion had also produced writings. In Bartoli's times that went without saying. For decades, the printing presses had turned out an incessant flow of new collections of "Letters" and "Reports" that made available to every category of reader travel narratives and reports on the experiences of European missionaries throughout the globe. Bartoli went out of his way, however, to note that his sources were the "original writings": the versions of those writings that had appeared in print, in fact, were not the raw texts of the letters sent by the missionaries but the result of a complex editing process that involved selection and censorship and that was designed to provide readers with a certain image and keep careful control over their reactions. In other words, it was a propaganda operation. To cite one example: the forty letters sent from China by two missionaries between 1583 and 1584 were winnowed down to eight published letters.[5]

Still, when Bartoli set to work on the extraordinarily rich store of original papers held in archives, the bond that he established with the protagonists of his history was something more than a historian's connection with his source materials. The deeper tie between missionary work and the work of the historian of the missions became clear in Bartoli's emphasis on the "long and wearisome study" that occupied the missionaries' nights.

The heroic exercise of letters and learning was the true point of encounter between the historian of the missions and the missionaries. Bartoli, closeted in his study as if in life confinement, saw in the Jesuit missionaries in China the harmonious combination of apostolic and literary labors that he himself could achieve only on a less heroic level. But if days dedicated to "apostolic ministry" were wearisome, nights dedicated to "bone-wearying" study were even more so. The book was the instrument that made it possible to understand the world and lead others to understand it. Another Jesuit, Antonio Possevino, a man so expert in books that he elaborated the bibliographical canon for post-Tridentine Catholicism, wrote that God was the author of a book—the world—and the professor at whose "celestial school" one must study.[6]

Describing the world was an old problem, however, and anyone who chose to do so had to take into account a long tradition that had undergone a surprising revival in the sixteenth century. What should one see? And how should it be described? The models were as varied as the sorts of travelers. Some writers had attempted to draw up exhaustive guidelines. Toward the end of the sixteenth century, for example, Albrecht Meier, a German, worked out and published a *Methodus describendi regiones* that offered an orderly listing of various points that the writer should keep in mind: customs, social practices, economic exchanges, systems for the administration of justice and the collection of taxes, holidays, rites and ceremonies, pastimes and entertainments, and so forth.[7] The travelers that Meier had in mind were by and large the same as those whom Antonio Possevino listed in an introduction to the study of geography: "the sailors, the merchants, the soldiers,"[8] but Meier also included scholars and gentlemen in search of instruction.

In short, there was a widespread demand for geographical knowledge waiting to be satisfied. The missionaries had for some time written histories of "different" peoples—at least since Giovanni da Pian del Carpine's *Historia Mongolorum*. The merchant writers had been interested in profits and in trade goods (there are a number of references to textiles and precious stones in Marco Polo's *Liber diversorum* or *Delle maraveglie del Mondo* that show proof of his keen mercantile eye); the preachers of the Christian faith did not so much replace that tradition as they added to it their own curiosity about religious beliefs. There was little room for ethnographic information, however, in the literature on the discovery of the Americas. For one thing, it was more urgent to describe the abundant "harvest" of souls that awaited the evangelizers. Above all, the peoples and the customs that travelers encountered were singularly different, so different that it seemed they could only be described in negative terms by listing all the familiar things they lacked: clothing, laws, commerce, money, kings, letters, and learning. This remained the predominant attitude in descriptions of the "savage" peoples of the Americas from the earliest accounts of voyages to Montaigne's reflections and Shakespeare's reworking of the theme.[9]

Things changed considerably when the scene to be described was the Far East. There missionaries felt encouraged to provide descriptions to satisfy their readers' curiosity about a world that was indeed different, but that could be read according to familiar models. Furthermore, some readers in positions of authority could impose wishes of their own. Cardinal Marcello Cervini, for example, asked Ignatius of Loyola to pass on to Francesco Saverio a request that the latter supply information in his letters on such questions as: "Como andan vestidos, de qué es su comer y bever, y las camas en qué duermen, y qué costa haze cada unos dellos. También, quanto a la región, donde está, en qué clima . . . y qué costumbres" ("How they dress, what they eat and drink, what kind of beds they sleep in, and what does one cost. Also, as for the region, where it is, in what climate . . . and with what customs").[10]

The Society of Jesus later specialized in gathering, organizing, and circulating just that sort of information. A sizable print literature, the result of a process of selection from the enormous mass of data contained in the Jesuits' letters, established a long-lasting relationship between the Society and the public and fed the latter's appetite for things marvelous and exotic. Bartoli's work was the culmination of a century of collective efforts.

One result of those efforts was to stimulate the imaginations of young people who dreamed of adventure and aspired to martyrdom for the faith. Entire generations of aspiring missionaries were recruited by such means. Some—St. Luigi Gonzaga, for one—died before their dream could be realized. Above all, many other religious took on more modest tasks in the European headquarters of the orders, consoling themselves by projecting what they were doing onto the backdrop of the exotic scenarios described in letters from the Indies. One Jesuit, Silvestro Landini, wrote, "I read no other books. . . . These letters are quite enough for me. . . . They have given me so much joy that in this world I would want no more, and so much confusion . . . seeing myself so far [from being] comparable to those most holy souls."[11] We can see traces in Landini's words of the ways in which this sort of literature was received and of its function as both escapist and inspirational literature.

When Bartoli set off on his writing career, however, the idea of martyrdom for the faith no longer dominated missionary literature. Mystical yearnings had been duly channeled and controlled; as the general movement for renewal in Christian life spread and became institutionalized, anyone still intent on promoting utopian projects (like one Jesuit from Parma who wanted to "reform Christianity and convert the infidels and the heretics")[12] had been eased out. In the missionary lands themselves, the task at hand was a slow, patient, long-term effort that depended more upon study and learning and less upon religious ardor and evangelical example to open a breach in societies and cultures as complex as those of Japan and China.

By that time, there could be no doubt about the basic substance of the missionary ideal. Nonviolent conquest could only be achieved through the construction of a didactic relationship, through teaching, and through affirmation of the superiority of the missionaries' knowledge. From his earliest works, Bartoli "defended and corrected" the man of letters, and another Jesuit of the age and a famous missionary, Paolo Segneri, wrote a series of works to offer models of human conduct—the educated penitent, the educated confessor, the educated parish priest, the educated Christian—all "instructed" in a faith that had become an encyclopedia of varied and complex disciplines. Of a later generation than Bartoli, Segneri championed missions within the Catholic world rather than missions to the outside world, and his works touched a high point in the affirmation of persuasion and instruction rather than force to inculcate faith. All of Segneri's activities as a preacher and a writer were devoted to realizing an idea deeply imbedded in the history of missions: instruction in things of the faith must be directed not only at the "infidels" but at all Christians in need of it. And those who needed it most were the illiterate and the peasants.

Before gentler methods of persuasion could prevail, however, the missions had to come to terms with the basic principle that lay behind the institution of the Inquisition and that sanctioned its use of force on the recalcitrant: the conviction that religious truth was one and self-evident. It was the capital problem of the *compelle intrare*—that is, of whether or not extra-European populations should be forcibly constrained to convert to Christianity—that set off the furious debate in the sixteenth century in which Bartolomé de las Casas played such a major role.

MISSIONARIES AND ETIQUETTE

The use of force was taken for granted in the conquest of the Americas. Jurists, theologians, and philosophers might debate the question, but it was clear to everyone that the Christian missions depended on the governing structures that the Spanish armies had created. In India, Japan, and China missionaries could operate independently, counting on their own capabilities alone. But how were they to use those capabilities? The problem was much discussed, and often bitterly. A closer look at one example may make this clear.

Toward the end of the year 1583 there was a great commotion in the

Jesuit college of Goa. A trip to Europe was being planned for a group of young Japanese noblemen, and the father who held the post of provincial visitor, Alessandro Valignano, had much to do.

The voyage of the young Japanese was a great event: they were to constitute visible proof of the great success of the Jesuits' missionary presence in Japan and, at the same time, provide Japan with an opportunity to open its eyes to Catholic Europe. Unlike the various groups of American "savages" that had been exhibited in European cities as trophies and curiosities, the Japanese were to return to Japan immediately. Valignano's instructions to that effect left no room for doubts: their testimony was indispensable to the credibility of the Jesuit missions in Japan. For that reason it was important to filter their impressions. The young men must be accompanied by guides wherever they went so that they would see only what they should see—that is, all possible expressions of the power, pomp, and wealth of the Catholic world and none of its poverty or seamier sides. The voyage as cultural instruction was thus born complete in all its parts—guides, fixed, inflexible routes, and concealment of all that might give the tourist a disagreeable impression.

The voyage took place, after long and painstaking preparations, and the group was received with elaborate ceremony in all the Italian cities it visited. The Japanese noblemen made their entry into Rome on March 10, 1585, and the city, which ten years earlier had been the site of the extraordinary Baroque celebration of the Jubilee, had a new opportunity to display the magnificence of an urban structure increasingly called upon to exhibit the undisputed sacrality of papal power and its sway over the Catholic world. The organizers did not limit their efforts to planning solemn entries and triumphal decorations that—grandiose as they were—could have a full effect only on eyewitnesses. The trip was accompanied and followed up by a constant stream of printed matter that the Jesuits orchestrated with care to present the reception of the delegation as an official diplomatic mission to subject Japan to obedience to the pope.[13]

The religious triumph that was exhibited as having been achieved was in reality far from the truth, and there was bitter discussion about what to do next, especially when Alessandro Valignano reached Japan. One stage in that debate took place in the houses of the Society of Jesus in the Far East even before the delegation of young Japanese left for Rome. In those final days of 1583, Father Valignano and Father Francisco Cabral, the two highest-ranking Jesuits in the Far East, sat down in their respective quarters, Valignano in Goa and Cabral in Macao, to write long letters to the same man, Claudio Acquaviva, the general of the Society.[14] The contents of their two letters revealed radically opposed views on missionary programs and methods but also profound differences of character and a high degree of personal hostility. Despite the pious protocol of Jesuit epistolary style, both men made it clear to their general in Rome that each found the other insufferable. Thus behind the Society's compact facade lay violent conflict among the men who had organized the publicity display of the visit of the young Japanese.

It was not the first time that the two men charged with the Japanese missions of the Society had disagreed, or that their discordant voices had reached Rome. This time, however, there was a special reason for the two simultaneous letters. A treatise written by Valignano on Japanese "ceremonies" and containing his thoughts on relations between missionaries and the local society was to accompany the "embassy" of the young Japanese nobles on their way to Rome.[15] Valignano had intended to carry this work to Rome himself so that he could defend its contents in person, but when word reached him in Goa that he had been appointed provincial, he was obliged to give up the trip and commit his arguments to a letter. As for Cabral, his letter simply repeated old accusations and complaints. He had already protested on several other occasions about the methods that Valignano had introduced, and he had even requested to be removed from his post to live in peace and devote his thoughts to his soul.

The disagreement between the two men touched on an entire gamut of problems regarding missionary activity in Japan. This was already clear in 1580, when Valignano had requested a consultation, which took place at Bungo. The questions that Valignano, then visitor, put on the agenda included the structure and internal organization of the missions, their financing, the establishment of colleges, the eventual naming of a bishop, and, last but not least, "ceremonies." The latter term referred to a series of rules about social relations: how to dress, how to greet people, how to receive visitors and pay visits, and more. Disagreement focused on these "ceremonies." Valignano insisted on respect of his "Book of Rules" or, as it was more commonly called, his "Ceremonial" (*Il cerimoniale per i missionari del Giappone*), but there was an immediate battle over its application. Thus the only way to silence criticism was to have the opinion of the general of the Society. His approval was forthcoming, but not without reservations. The "Rules of Office" that were put into effect in 1592 were the result of long negotiations. Valignano's text, which had sailed the Pacific to reach Rome, met with the same fate as other documents reflecting the early missionaries' ethnographic and anthropological interests (another famous example is the work of the Franciscan Bernardino de Sahagún). A forgotten relic of a decisive stage in Europe's relations with other worlds, Valignano's text resurfaced only in 1946, when European domination in Asia had come to an end. The disappearance of this text is enough to suggest that the rules that Valignano proposed may have been more than "simply a brief and practical guide."[16]

One fundamental aspect of Italian culture in the early modern age was, as is known, the elaboration of codes of conduct within a predetermined context. Baldassare Castiglione's *Il cortegiano* springs immediately to mind for the princely court. The effort to define a common terrain of practical regulations that a variety of interlocutors could share met with a success that by itself demonstrates the importance of the question. The basic task was to define the range and extent of an individual's duties to society. Such works introduced a new notion of personality that insisted on flexibility and willingness to adapt to others, but it also led to a new justification of social domination, since only those who were skilled in using such rules were recognized as members of the elite. Anyone who failed to respect them was branded as a "peasant" or a "savage"—categories that were considered nearly interchangeable. The mix of formal duties and real powers that was created by the knowledge and practice of such codes of conduct made them irresistible. The names invented to define such codes gave rise to the most solemn terms used, in both early modern and contemporary times, to justify the right of one part of society or the world to dominate and lay down the law for the rest. In this manner formal rules for proper conduct, or *civilitates* (which in Italy took the name of the dedicatee of Giovanni della Casa's famous *Galateo*), became the norm underlying "civilization." The success of such terms was linked to a pedagogical and catechistic literature produced by authors as renowned as Erasmus. Although Giovanni della Casa found fame with his *Galateo*, he was also the author of a lesser-known treatise, *De officiis inter potentiores et tenuiores amicos*, whose title explicitly stated the need to identify signs of domination and distance between "superiors" and "inferiors"—that is, between the dominators and the dominated.[17] Just as Giovanni della Casa's title referred explicitly to *officia*, or social duties, the Society of Jesus spoke of "Regole degli uffizi" when it debated and made changes in Valignano's text.

What linked civility, civilization, and duties—an affirmation of domination and a respect for rules—is obvious but difficult to put into words. Clearly, contemporaries found it hard to do so. Alessandro Valignano referred to widespread awareness of such a connection in the opening lines of his treatise: "One of the most important things needed in Japan in order to do what the Fathers propose concerning conversion and Christianity is to know how to treat the Japanese in such a way that, on the one hand, they [the Fathers] enjoy authority and, on the other, that they show much familiarity, uniting these two things in such a way that the one not hinder the other but join together so that each has its proper place."[18]

The elaboration of norms of conduct, to which first Italian culture and then European culture in general devoted so much attention between the sixteenth and the seventeenth centuries, is in many ways a well-known story. It is safe to say that from that time on, the importance of rules of "civility" became a rightful and permanent part of the upbringing of the cultivated classes. It is less often noted that the debate about rules of conduct and the elaboration of those rules were reflected in two areas that might seem remote from secular, humanistic culture—Protestant religious polemics and missionary work. References to I Corinthians 9, where Paul speaks of being "all things to all men"—that is, of adapting one's discourse to different groups of hearers in order to lead them to Christ—often give an indication of this interest in conduct. The passage was obligatory reading for anyone who intended to continue the work of the apostles, but it was also meditated and discussed at length by others who had experienced the lacerations of religious differences within Christianity. Here adaptation was an obligation of the "strong" in faith, who were called upon to respect the needs of the "weak." I Corinthians 9 was read along with or in opposition to Galatians 2.11–13 on St. Paul's "insincerity," and the "adaptation" to others of the first letter was presented as a more acceptable version of the "simulation" of the second.[19] Concrete situations gave rise to theory, and in real life relative strength was what usually made people conceal or modify their own "truth."

Must one "adapt" to people whose religious ideas were different from one's own? And in such "adaptation," which of one's own convictions could be left (provisionally) in the shadow? The question was discussed time and again during the age of the Reformation, as everyone knows. It is less well known that techniques of "accommodation" and of simulation and dissimulation were tested all over the world. Conquerors and conquered alike had to ponder the question of adaptation, the first to consolidate their victories and the second to make their defeats less ruinous. The theoretical problem was the same, however: how much simulation and how much dissimulation were necessary to save one's own truth or to win over to the truth those who did not yet possess it or were not yet willing to accept it? For the vanquished, the question was a matter of survival as soon as they had been defeated, but for the victors it arose somewhat later, when they discovered that winning and winning over the population were not the same thing. What is astonishing is that the problem arose at roughly the same time throughout Europe and the world. While in Europe the Anabaptists were discovering techniques of simulation and dissimulation, a Nahuatl text suggested the need to "accommodate" to the conquistadors and to construct sanctuaries to house the Castilian gods.[20]

The lesson in adaptation that Europe had learned from religious conflict was readily applied to techniques for the cultural conquest of extra-European populations. One theoretician of simulation, the heretical and Nicodemian priest Paolo Rosello, elaborated on his ideas about adaptation in an imaginary dialogue with Cardinal Gaspare Contarini:

[Contarini]: "One must have the greatest regard and much respect for the place in which one speaks of and debates about penitence and [one must] choose the persons, because in fact one must not speak always in the same way of this virtue, for the reason that it must be taught differently among Gentiles [i.e. pagans], in the synagogues and among Jews, and, finally, among Christians and in the holy and sacred church."

"I did not think," I then said, "most reverend Monsignor, that one should have this respect of places or persons, for which reason I would be most grateful if you would content me with further explanations."

And he responded willingly, saying, "Know, Rosello, that I have no other desire than to show you, with brevity, that I do not speak vain words. I say, therefore, that if penitence is to be taught among the Gentiles, or among persons who live like the Gentiles, it must be taught according to the works of the law written in their hearts and according to the conscience, which is everyone's faithful witness. It follows that those people, because they do not recognize either the law of Moses or the Gospel of Christ, must therefore be constrained by the illumination of the Word alone, which shines splendidly in their darkness by the splendor of the divine light that shines over each one of them—that is, by the gifts of creation and of our condition, somewhere in which the image and semblance of God shines forth, some trace nonetheless remaining even though its sign was corrupted by Adam's fall. . . . All children of Adam . . . by the operation of the law written in their hearts, if they do not do naturally those things which that law of nature seeks, they immediately feel inner remorse that accuses them, with which they must be led to penitence. . . . If one is to teach penitence among Jews, who accept only their Moses, damning and reproving our Christ, then one must teach penitence according to the order and decree of the law, never going beyond the norm prescribed in the letter of the law. . . . That perfidious and recalcitrant people can only be persuaded by the decrees of Mosaic law, which they read every sabbath in their synagogues."

. . . .

"What you say, Monsignor," I then said, "I believe to be true. But among Christians, how is one to teach penitence?"

And he immediately responded, "Know, Rosello, that among Christians the way to teach penitence is to turn it into grief . . . over faults and failings committed, so that it generates in us solicitude, sorrow, satisfaction, fear, desire, revenge, and all this not according to the gifts of nature, nor according to the threats of the law, but according to the moans and the sobs of the spirit. . . . And this alone is true and proper penitence."[21]

The terms that Rosello used here—pagans, Jews, true and proper Christians—served to define categories (and inclusive categories) within Christianity itself. The three levels could also be seen as placed within three periods of time: the age of the Father, of the Son, and of the Holy Spirit. In short, Rosello used a range of arguments that lent themselves to suggesting and supporting forms of adaptation and simulation and that offered the possibility of reading between the lines in various ways. But he took his categories and his arguments from traditions solidly rooted in current theological language.

Valignano was aware of these problems. He may have had occasion to read the writings of Paolo Rosello during his student years in Padua, since they were written and printed not far from that city and not long before. Valignano's student years were even more turbulent than was normal for young people living in a university city, since he had been involved in a violent crime of passion and only escaped an extremely severe sentence because he belonged to a powerful Neapolitan noble family.[22]

An exemplary religious conversion gave Valignano personal experience with repentance and led him to seek a career in the Society of Jesus and its missionary undertakings that his escapade in Padua might otherwise have denied him. There was a recent example in his own social circle: the voice of conscience had moved a kinsman, Marquess Galeazzo Caracciolo di Vico, to a stupefying change of allegiance. Exiled for his faith, Caracciolo's innate qualities led him to become head of the Italian church in Geneva. Once Valignano had become a Jesuit he too found himself rapidly elevated to a position of responsibility, and in a part of the world even farther from home, where he was squarely faced with the problem of how to deal with the "Gentiles." After his arrival in Japan, Valignano "spent the entire first year as mute as a statue," as he wrote the general of the order in 1581, reflecting the stance and almost the words of Francesco Saverio.[23] Then, after long reflection, he proposed his rules.

The missionary's first objective was to "acquire authority," and the best way to do so was to adopt the social model most authoritative in the culture but also most consonant with the model of the religious in the European setting. For Valignano, that model was to be taken from the bonzes of Zen Buddhism—a decision that shaped the rules in his *Cerimoniale* regarding gravity of demeanor, ways of treating inferiors, and the etiquette of receiving or making visits. Christian preaching was to strive to resemble contemplative meditation in the style of Zen; the missionaries should not be seen "outside of the house" practicing "mortifications of any sort"; nor should they "be sent on pilgrimage disheveled and badly dressed as if poor . . . because with this they destroy and diminish the reputation of religion among the Japanese."[24]

The ritual of the tea ceremony became more important than the sacred rites of Christianity. Discourtesy became the unpardonable sin: one needed to "know how to deal with men with appropriate modesty and edification, treating them in conformity with each one's estate and with the courtesy and urbanity in use in the country . . . because some things appertained to some and not to others." This was a golden rule with which Valignano knew that his Roman confreres would agree. In fact, he responded to the objections raised by his superiors by placing a note at the beginning of the first chapter of the second version of the *Cerimoniale* that stated, "If this is true everywhere, it is even more true in Japan."[25] Except that in Japan the rules were different from the ones everyone already knew, which meant that they must be mastered before they could be applied. And in Japan those rules were based on the principle of exact recognition of social differences. This meant that if the Jesuits wanted a place on the upper levels of society, they needed all the attributes of that station, including such material attributes as servants, horses, and residences. They also needed to observe a particular style in their social relations that was not precisely in tune with the message of the Gospels. For example, they were expected to treat the lower classes of society—the poor or vagabonds—with scorn. Here was where the problems began.

"Accommodating" oneself to others, in the interpretation that the Society of Jesus gave the notion, was a means necessary to obtaining the end of "winning them over to Christ." As Father Juan Alfonso Polanco wrote in his *Industriae*, this method involved withholding one's own point of view, "approving what deserves approbation and tolerating and dissimulating some things that were better not clearly said or done."[26] In essence, this was fiction, a trick played in order to win the game. If anyone objected that tricks and fictions were reprehensible in such a noble cause, the ready response was that recourse to human trickery was the consequence of the silence of God. The same God whose miracles had made straight the way of the first apostles now seemed to have decided to let his new apostles take care of themselves, and no extraordinary gift of tongues helped the missionaries to understand or make themselves understood in the Babel of languages of the new worlds. Besides, what else could they have been expected to do? Father Claudio Acquaviva, general of the Society of Jesus, pondered these thoughts anew as he scanned the text of *Il cerimoniale* and wondered where things had begun to go wrong.

Acquaviva's negative reaction was significant because it showed, paradoxically, the full extent of Valignano's success. His efforts to master a "different" culture had made him unrecognizable to his own superiors. Valignano's decision to imitate the style of the bonzes of Zen Buddhism may well have been a means to an end and only a mask to aid in simulation and dissimulation, but the mask had blotted out the features of the face behind it. The general of the order—the very man who should have been the most expert in the art of deciphering hidden meanings—no longer recognized his own men, and he recoiled in dismay before the turn that accommodation was taking.

It was not the vociferous objections of Valignano's adversary, Cabral, that most struck the general. Men like Cabral were highly respectable and their Christianity was a basic ingredient of conquest. But the general could not have hesitated long in his choice between the two. Cabral and Valignano had in common only the undeniable prestige of their families, and Cabral's surname immediately connected him to the warrior elite that had built Portugal's colonial empire. Religious conversion had led both men to the Society of Jesus, but whereas Cabral had come into the order from a career that had accustomed him to military command and armed conquest, Valignano had behind him the murky story of amorous passion and violence of his university years. The polemic that set the two men against one another reflected the different styles of their past experience. Cabral treated others with soldierly firmness; he demanded that the upper ranks of the Society be filled with "iron men" (*de hierro*), and he recalled with pride that in his twenty-nine years in Japan he had been constrained to obey the orders of a superior for only three years.[27] Nothing was more foreign to Cabral's makeup than tricks and "accommodations"; his Christianity was proud and intransigent, and he offered his poverty and humility to the scorn of the Japanese without calculation of the consequences, trusting that the very differentness of his inassimilable values would attract the "Gentiles."

As he judged the controversy from Rome, the general could not have remained undecided very long: Valignano's language was his own. Paul, I Corinthians 9, is cited immediately in Acquaviva's letter of response. Still, he must have meditated on his answer for several days, since he withdrew into the confines of Sant' Andrea al Quirinale while the solemn festivities welcoming the young Japanese nobles to Rome were in full swing. Valignano's basic principle seemed to him just,

> because, since God our Lord no longer gives aid with miracles and gifts of prophecy, and those peoples depend so highly upon exterior things, we have to accommodate ourselves to them and "enter with theirs in order then to come out with ours." Up to a certain point, my dear Father, this seems to me a most prudent counsel, because even the Apostle became all things to all men in order to win them over to Christ.

"Up to a certain point," however. "Accommodation" was a means, religious conquest was the end, and the end justified the means. The religious conflicts of the sixteenth century had taught the need for simulation and dissimulation in religious matters; in the following century that precept was to be adapted to questions of state and of politics.[28] What was at stake was relations with the power structure; specifically, overcoming unfavorable odds. But where did acceptance of forms end and giving in on content begin? And how could Christianity, the religion of a man-

God derided and crucified, be made to fit with the pomp and ostentatious display necessitated by a decision to "accommodate ourselves to the customs and the concepts of the Bonzes"? Everyone knew that it was impolitic to insist too much on the symbol of Christ crucified: the experience of missionaries in other lands had shown the wisdom of a prudent silence or deliberate ambiguity on that point. In those same years, Matteo Ricci, who later became the most famous representative of the method of "accommodation," was discovering how difficult it was to explain the man on the cross to the Chinese, and he had become resigned to speaking of Christ as "a famous saint from our land." Acquaviva would have been well aware of this, but he complained of it anyway: "Now whoever preaches this doctrine, I know not why, is long obliged to hide the virtue of the Cross and the imitation of Christ, who preached for God [and] who both taught and showed by example voluntary poverty and scorn of all worldly things."[29]

Acquaviva's response is a singular document. It shows him horrified by the foreseeable outcome of the process of "accommodation," but it is also proof that the only other alternative to that strategy was a return to the prophetic model that would reduce religious conquest to heroic witness to the Gospel, to "the cross, struggles, and scorn." The arguments that sprang to the general's pen have an archaic savor: "Therefore I desire that we take great heart, for if we live in conformity with our profession, our Lord will come to our aid more than could be promised by our prudence."

The idea that there was any choice was illusory, however: where the Europeans did not have military superiority and cultural supremacy, the only way to guarantee any sort of hearing to the bearers of the Christian message lay with the strategies of "accommodation." These were strategies that did not yield immediate results: Matteo Ricci wrote from China in 1595, "May Your Reverence not ask me how many thousands of souls I have converted." There was bitter irony in his words, since Ricci had just permitted himself a complaint about the lack of results: "Poenitet me patientiae, qua eos [labores] pertuli, poenitet etiam fructus in sterilissimo deserto" ("I am unhappy to have borne those labors patiently; I am also unhappy with the harvests gathered in a most sterile desert").[30] Comments of this sort were obviously not written for publication; printed works gave invigorating reports of the extraordinary advances of Christianity in Japan and China. They might even hint at miraculous divine intervention paving the way for the missionaries and making them capable of understanding and making themselves understood in exotic languages. In reality, things were quite different: "It is so difficult to learn their letters," Ricci confessed, "that we cannot extend our operations, and twice, when I had instructed a companion sufficiently to have him go elsewhere, it was the Lord's will to take him from me by death; thus I need to wait for another companion."[31]

At times such bitter thoughts took the form of dreams. Matteo Ricci tells of one dream that he had while he was making his way to Nanking:

> I was standing, made melancholy by the sad outcome of my attempt, and the travails of the journey, when it seemed to me that I met a man I did not recognize, who said to me: "So it is you who have just been traveling through this land, seeking to destroy its ancient laws and replace them with the Law of God?" And I, astonished that this person could penetrate so deep into my heart, asked in return: "Be you devil or God?" And he replied, "Not the devil but God." So I threw myself at his feet, weeping, and said, "If you, my Lord, know this, why up to now have you given me no help?"[32]

In short, there were no miracles. This meant that before anyone could preach the Gospel and even think about making converts he must find a place for himself in that alien society and make himself acceptable within it. The habit not only made the monk but was decisive: the clothing in which one appeared before the inhabitants of those remote lands was more important than public profession of Christian virtues.

This explains the missionaries' rapid change of costume. Although at first Ricci dressed "in the Chinese fashion, leaving the square biretta in memory of the Cross," he soon removed even that last remainder of European clerical garb and wore "an extravagant biretta, pointed like a bishop's, in order to make myself totally Chinese."[33] That headgear may have been extravagant from the European readers' point of view, but it had a precise meaning for the Chinese: after mature reflection, Ricci had decided to present himself as a man of letters. Accommodation was a flexible strategy that demanded constant attention to local rules: if Valignano had persuaded the Jesuits in Japan to imitate Buddhist bonzes, in China that choice was an error because, as Ricci soon discovered, "in China, the name of bonzes is in very low repute." Thus, as he wrote, "I decided to leave off the name of bonzes and put myself in the dress and the status of a preacher."[34] The word "preacher" may not be the most accurate term for what Ricci was attempting to describe, but it was certainly the term most likely to appeal to superiors in Italy who needed to know about and approve his activities. At this point, the game of reflected images, of masks, and of verbal filters had to be played simultaneously in the East and in the West. Within the limits of the possible, the sort of conflict that had been set off in Rome by Valignano's *Il cerimoniale* was to be avoided at all costs. Just such conflicts multiplied, however, in the famous "question of rites."

Many might have accused such systems of hypocrisy, but, as even one author of Romantic culture had to admit, it was a special variety of "systematic hypocrisy" that was "a product of upbringing" and that stood in contrast to a character "without any moral standards whatever." [35]

What Valignano proposed in Japan and Ricci in China was doubtless promising; no other approach was as attentive to the way others thought, nor more flexible in circumscribing rough points and differences. Its validity may perhaps be measured better by the resistance that it encountered, both in China and in Europe, than by the consensus it inspired. Acquaviva's perplexity was only a forewarning of turbulent reactions in Europe that were still to come. A much larger tempest was set off in 1641, when the rival missionary orders, the Franciscans and the Dominicans, appointed themselves guardians of doctrinal orthodoxy and complained to the Congregation for the Propagation of the Faith that the Jesuits had mishandled the Chinese missions. In substance (and simplifying to the extreme), the complex affair of the so-called "Chinese rites" involved whether or not Christians could pay to the dead the honors and rites of Confucian tradition that the Jesuits claimed were completely "civic" and not religious. The controversy was a bitter one, not so much (or not only) because of institutional competition for primacy in missionary work, as because of the seductive appeal of ideological purity and the threat of dangerous concessions within orthodoxy.

For a long time, Europeans knew only their own side of this story. At the time, the contending parties produced a flood of treatises and a mountain of documents of all sorts, which have led historians to reconstruct the history of the question of rites as one of bitter theological contention and petty rivalry within the inner sanctum of the Roman curia and the headquarters of the major orders, with Portugal, which was intent on keeping control over the personnel of the missions, paying close heed. Increasing uncertainty and resistance in Roman circles led to repeated condemnations, on the part of the Holy Office and the popes, of the ways in which the Jesuits had handled "rites," but that was not the only threat to their missionary activities. When Chinese sources became available for examination, it became clear that the Jesuits' attempts at openness to Chinese culture had met with profound resistance on the part of the Chinese. [36] In the end, inquisitorial intransigence won over the missionaries' openness, a victory in which the Inquisition was an instrument in the internal struggles among the forces safeguarding the citadel of orthodoxy. The acts of the Mezzabarba legation report a dialogue between the emperor of China and the papal legate on the errors that Matteo Ricci had committed that makes interesting reading. [37] The only posthumous recompense that remained to the idea of "accommodation" and its champions, by then long gone, was the smiling irony of the emperor as he amused himself by embarrassing the rigid and obsequious Italian monsignors, asking them why they allowed the depiction of things that did not exist, such as angels' wings, and how the pope, who had never been to China, could decide and judge questions regarding Chinese rites.

SEDUCING PRINCES AND SERVING THE PEOPLE

It was discovered early on that the same campaigns for religious conquest pursued in distant lands needed to be waged within the "Christian Continent," and by the mid-sixteenth century it had become normal to speak of "these Indies" or "the Indies in these parts" in connection with labors of preaching and catechizing in rural areas of Catholic countries or in areas of Europe infested with heresy.[38]

By the 1630s the analogy between European peasants and American savages had become firmly established. When the Dominican Francisco de Vitoria lectured on matters pertaining *de Indiis* in his courses at Salamanca, he posed the question of whether the obvious stupidity of the populations of the Americas and the barbarity of their mores might not support the theory that they were "by nature slaves." His answer was that "even among our own people we can see many peasants who are little different from brute animals."[39] This image of the peasant was new in that phase of Spanish culture, but it soon became a commonplace.

While Vitoria was drawing his instructive parallel between peasants and savages, the Franciscan bishop Antonio de Guevara, in a contemporary "best-seller" that enjoyed particularly wide circulation in Italy, portrayed the peasant as a brutish being of monstrous appearance—"an animal in human form"—who nonetheless revealed an intelligence and an eloquence worthy of the gods.[40] Guevara's Italian readers included a steward for the Medici family, who used the work to defend the importance of peasant culture, and the famous author of *Le sottilissime astuzie di Bertoldo*, Giulio Cesare Croce. Guevara's peasant, as one scholar has pointed out, "inaugurated a new course, modifying, in a drastic restoration, an image that had circulated with nonchalant frequency in the late Middle Ages"—the image of the "impious and bestial" peasant.[41] The peasant's rough and bestial appearance was discovered to conceal a humanity that attracted increasing interest as the need to dominate it grew clearer. "Savages" in Europe and abroad were to keep company for some time, at least for the way they were regarded by the dominant classes in Europe and by their religion.

At first, within Europe as in the Indies (a term applied to all extra-European lands), the *missio* was defined as the sending, by persons in authority, of clergy skilled in preaching in the aim of restoring (or instituting) the orthodox model of religious life. The pressing need for initiatives of the sort began to be felt when mounting criticism of the clergy, encouraged by the Protestant Reformation, went beyond safe limits and, above all, when Protestant ideas threatened to take hold in Italy. The person who is often cited as the first, the most knowledgeable, and the most impassioned missionary to the *Indie di qua* [the Indies here; European territories] was a Jesuit from Sarzana, Silvestro Landini, a man who began his career in the mountains of the Garfagnana hunting out heretics and arguing with the local clergy on such questions as grace and free will. In Spain, where the Protestant Reformation had never made great inroads, the most pressing problem was the conversion of the Muslim minority. In fact, one of the first to speak of *otras Indias* was Father Cristoforo Rodriguez, who worried much about the difficult conversion of the "Moriscos."[42] The notion and the image of the Indies was encouraging; it implied an easy and abundant harvest of souls, to be gathered according to the stereotypes of missionary culture of the age. It also was a consolation to those who were left doing lesser tasks than an idealized apostolate in distant lands.

Thus the *missio* was, as it always had been, a responsibility entrusted to religious by higher authorities—by the pope, or by bishops or bishops' vicars called upon (especially in Italy) to exercise tighter control over their dioceses in the immediate post-Tridentine period. When a missionary had accomplished his task, his superiors delivered a certificate to him. In the case of Landini, Isidoro Chiari, the bishop of Foligno and a former Benedictine abbot, wrote an enthusiastic recommendation calling Landini "not a man but an angel of God."[43] The priests of the various dioceses that Landini and his missionaries visited were notably less enthusiastic: in the Lunigiana in 1548 "the priests, congregated in multitudes . . . with fists, with their eyes ablaze, drawing arms, and many other improprieties," attacked Landini. He reported that they poked their "halberds at my breast" and threatened "to split me down to my feet."[44] What had aroused the bishop's enthusiasm was probably just what made the priests furious: Landini's insistence on such devotional practices as frequent communion and on thorough knowledge of the catechism undermined longstanding rules and traditions. This sort of conflict was inherent in the institutional model of the *missio* in that the mission set someone sent by the central authorities and endowed with extraordinary powers against those who held traditional power within the local community. Otto Hintze spoke of similar clashes between the "commissary" and the "officials."[45]

Where missionaries were concerned, however, there were other ingredients in the mixture. First, the local clergy was often nonexistent, especially in out-of-the-way places in the mountain areas or the islands. Moreover, the missionary's trip to such places, although it could not be compared in length or danger with a voyage to the real "Indies," was sufficiently adventurous to make the traveler feel that he was in foreign

parts and to open his mind to different ways. Landini's reaction on crossing the strait between Genoa and Capraia was not very different from the
report of the voyage from Salamanca to Ciudad Real made by Bartolomé
de las Casas and his fellow Dominicans a few years earlier, between 1544
and 1545. Landini reported:

> When it pleased our Lord, we took off toward Corsica. One night, on the
> high seas, high waves being raised, the mast broke, and the captain cried
> out, "We are all dead." I at that moment had completed the "Te Deum
> laudamus" because I had spent the entire night putting the house of my
> soul in order in the hope of sure transit out of this miserable life, and I was
> prepared to give absolution to all my fellow friars on the ship. The waves
> were leaping over both the prow and the poop.

All sea voyages involved assaults from nature and from men, anguish in
the face of dangers, an apostolic yearning for martyrdom, and sailors who
might swear and blaspheme but when danger loomed crowded around
the clerics. Voyages also called for acts of courage: Bartolomé de las Casas
commanded the elements to silence, and one of Landini's companions,
Father Emmanuel, displayed his "magnanimity" by shinnying up the
mainmast in the middle of the storm.[46]

The inherent appeal of travel literature found an ally in the heroic
aura surrounding the struggle for the conquest of souls in campaigns for
conversion and in the personalization and symbolization of nature that
went along with those campaigns. The missionaries and their companions
felt the presence of angels, the Madonna, and demons who accompanied
or assailed them in their difficult travels. Such companions may have
helped them to be more open toward new things and more acutely perceptive of all that was new in the places and persons they encountered.

Leaving familiar things behind them gave these travelers the impression of extreme contrasts in both nature and humankind. Landini found
on the island of Capraia "errors, superstitions, [and] idolatries," but he
also found "the earthly paradise in many delights of spiritual goods . . .
the primitive church in [the inhabitants'] frequentation of confession and
communion every day." He was also moved by the terrible poverty of the
population, however, and he spoke of children who went barefoot, even
in winter, and slept on the bare ground and of people fifty years old "who
have never eaten their fill of bread."

Not many years after, other Jesuits were called upon to give assistance
and perform inquisitorial services in the merciless Spanish campaign
against the Waldensians in Calabria. Here again, in spite of their explicit
charge to uproot heresy, and in spite of reiterated calls to duty from the
grand inquisitor, Michele Ghislieri (later Pope Pius V), the predominant
tone in their letters was compassion for the multitudes who had been

"butchered and quartered . . . burned and thrown off towers . . . slaughtered in the countryside." Their heresy apart (or, as one Jesuit wrote, "apart from the plague"), the Jesuits found the Waldensians "admirably instructed regarding good moral conduct," unlike the Catholics of Cosenza, whom they judged to be "people as accustomed to evil . . . [and] without justice and government as if they all dwelt in the woods."[47]

Woodland savages, on the one hand, and, on the other, people admirably predisposed to receive the Gospel: the same contrast can often be found in contemporary evaluations of the people of the distant "Indies." But by this time strategies had changed in the campaign for spiritual conquest, both at home and abroad. The *peregrinatio* as an occasional incursion, even when backed by arms, no longer solved the problem of spiritual conquest: "Weapons can force bodies but not opinions; heterodox doctrines are uprooted from hearts with right doctrine and Catholic persuasion . . . with much humility, charity, and love." Father Rodriguez came to this opinion during the campaign against the Waldensians in Calabria, and his opinion was confirmed far to the north, with the failure of the expedition of Emanuele Filiberto, duke of Savoy, against the Waldensians who had settled in the valleys of the Alps. The conclusion was equally valid for the entire missionary movement, however. Once again, *vincere* was one thing; *convincere* quite another.

This did not mean repudiation of the use of force. That would have been unthinkable in a period in which Europeans everywhere were taking up arms to settle their religious differences. Catholics in particular expected such conflicts to give a new and powerful impulse to the missions. As in Calabria, where the army had paved the way for gentler persuasion by the Jesuits, in France during the Wars of Religion and in the Empire the first hint of trouble brought a call to arms. Before the Thirty Years War the Jesuit Jakob Rem spoke for many others in his expectation of a *bellum cruentum, sed sacrum* that would end in the triumph of the Catholic cause and lend *magnum incrementum* to the Church of Rome. Rem reproached fellow Jesuits eager to be sent to the Indies because he was persuaded that a war was imminent that would open up great possibilities for missionary work in Germany.[48] The methods of gentle persuasion could thus be grafted onto an abrupt initial break. But this still would not solve the problem of deeply rooting the "holy faith" once it had been imposed by force. At that point, discourse returned to the art—and the artifice—of people skilled at moving hearts and training minds.

It was inevitable that methods and instruments should tend to become the same in the "Indies" at home and abroad. The field of missionary work was still organized and unified by the networks set up by the major religious orders, through which men and initiatives still circulated. When Diego de Valadés published his manual on sacred oratory, he quite naturally drew upon his experiences as a missionary as the basis for his advice to preachers everywhere.[49] Furthermore, Valadés's suggestions for the use of images in New Spain concurred with the Jesuit Gaspar Loarte's proposals, during those same years, for the improvement of instruction in the catechism in Catholic Europe. Such instruction was to be organized along two lines: first, the arts of "accommodation" and of simulation that had been developed for countries of "high" culture not under the military domination of Christian rulers—China and Japan—were reserved for the dominant classes and, in particular, for the sovereigns of the non-Catholic states of Europe; second, the didactic techniques developed for the *rudes* of the Americas were put to use in the internal missions aimed at the people of rural areas in Catholic countries.

It seemed obvious in those years that rulers must be won over with all available techniques. The first of these was direction of conscience. To dominate the conscience of princes meant governing through them, and since the end in view was the laudable one of assuring soul's salvation for entire populations of the governed, all means were to be considered good. The Theatine saint Father Andrea Avellino not only devoted much of his time to correspondence advising, encouraging, and guiding the princes and noblewomen of his day but found it absolutely obvious that it was his moral duty to concentrate his energies on such persons, because "from the health of the Princes is born, in great part, the health of the peoples."[50] Once armed hostilities had ceased, there was an entire catalogue of techniques available for winning over the defeated ruler. For example, the Jesuit Lorenzo Forero, noting the failure of the Thirty Years War, suggested subtler ways to conquer the people's hearts. Clever men should be placed in positions near the rulers, gain their confidence, and bring them to Catholicism. If the prince were already "Christian" (by which Forero meant Catholic), an attempt should be made to institutionalize control over his conscience. Thus in Bavaria under the Wittelsbachs, a Catholic stronghold in German lands, the Jesuits suggested to William V in 1583 that he establish a *mensa conscientiae* on the Portuguese and Spanish model—that is, a council that would rule on the propriety of all such major political moves as declaring war, imposing new taxes, and so forth.[51]

The Jesuits were thought particularly skilled in such matters, but they had no monopoly on them. In the confessional age, the ruler's religion was so important a matter that many people cultivated the art of guiding the "Christian prince." Where the Jesuits reigned supreme, however, was in educational policy. The Jesuits' memorandum to Duke William V of Bavaria suggested that the sons of "heretical" nobles be brought to the court, attracted by the advantages of learning languages and the arts of

war along with the young Catholic prince. It also proposed offering schol-
arships and good professional posts to young male bourgeois of the "heretical" cities and towns near the borders of the Bavarian state. The system of Jesuit secondary schools (that is, "colleges") for the training of the
elites of Europe covered the entire Continent. It is hardly surprising that
Antonio Possevino suggested "the remedy of the Seminaries" as the best
way to win over to Catholicism the Russia of Ivan the Terrible. Learning,
which had opened doors for Matteo Ricci in China, was also a means for
controlling the upbringing of the elite; hence it was a way to gain a foothold in countries where Catholicism was not an officially accepted religion and await future developments.

Culture played an important role in missionary activities on the other
end of the social scale with the conquest of the lower classes in Catholic
lands. In theological terms, *fides implicita* needed to be distinguished
from *fides esplicita*, since theological knowledge was complex, and only
a very small number of Christians were capable of penetrating mysteries
of the faith. But what was the nub of belief indispensable for salvation? In
one chapter of his *De procuranda Indorum salute*, José de Acosta argued
vigorously against theologians who held that unsophisticated (*más rudos*)
Christians needed only "implicit faith" and did not need to believe explicitly in Christ.[52] The most pressing problem for missionaries had become
ignorance. Dramatic reports came in from rural Europe: peasants were
not even able to state how many gods Christians had. Someone in Bavaria
claimed that they were seven, like the sacraments; in Eboli, in the Kingdom of Naples, some said there were a hundred, "others a thousand, still
others higher numbers."[53] The situation was so serious that even exceptional individual efforts were insufficient; it called for a permanent organization and an efficacious strategy.

The *missio* needed to be organized and institutionalized. Around
1590, the Jesuits, who had discovered the importance of *reducciones* in
New Spain, transferred the model to Italy. It was then decided that "several missions will be instituted in all provinces." Furthermore, in the instructions of Claudio Acquaviva, the general of the Society, to the Jesuits
setting off *ad missiones*, there was an eloquent shift in the meaning of the
term "mission." Rather than a charge or an individual responsibility, the
"mission" had become primarily a place. Acquaviva suggested the possibility of permanently staffed places for missions, and he stated explicitly
that their purpose was to combat ignorance.[54] How that was to be done
was less clear. The general's instructions offered a basic solution, to which
variations could be added from place to place, that spelled out the missionaries' duties from their initial visit to the community church to their
meeting with the parish priest (for the collection of information on the

chief sins rampant among the population) to the organization of lessons on doctrine (in the afternoon) and preaching and hearing confessions (in the morning).

These basic procedures could be carried out stressing, as need dictated, either the goal of moving sinners' hearts to repentance or that of educating their minds to grasp the concepts of the catechism. The printing press furnished the principal tools for schooling: printed images and, in particular, single printed sheets that inculcated precepts of doctrine and religious practice along with rules of etiquette. The most obvious aspect of the missions, however, was penitential preaching. Here the missionaries were called upon to remedy a grave want in Tridentine Catholicism: at a time when the religious orders were discredited and suspect, a reorganization of diocesan structure had put preaching to the people in the hands of clergy trained in the seminaries. It was soon obvious, however, that the preaching of the parish priests had serious deficiencies, and that it paled before the effectiveness of the preaching during the major Advent and Lenten cycles that was the specialty of the Franciscans and the Dominicans. Similarly, the Council's rigid reaffirmation of the obligation to make individual confession was insufficient to resolve all the problems connected with that fundamentally important moment of control and encounter between the clergy and the people.

Penitence and the organization and control of the sense of guilt remained a question central to Christianity in the early modern age, as the Lutheran Reformation demonstrated. The resolution of guilt in a brief, habitual, and secret act left unsatisfied the communitarian and social aspect of penitence and conversion. It was not by chance that the Society of Jesus, the order that did more than all others to guarantee the secrecy of individual confession and that perfected and disseminated the confessional elaborated by the bishops of the Catholic Reformation (Gian Matteo Giberti and Carlo Borromeo), was also the order that rediscovered the importance of the "general confession" as a turning point in Christian life and in the overall reorganization of the penitent's social relations. This occurred, what is more, on the planetary scale and among a body of the faithful that ranged from the Indians of Peru to the peasants of Europe. The Jesuits' study of matters of conscience, their skill in stimulating and controlling emotions through the use of the spiritual exercises of Ignatius of Loyola, their mastery of oratorical techniques, and, last but not least, their use of the visual and the theatrical arts all contributed to their success.

The mission offered an ideal framework for applying to the faithful of rural areas the powers and artifices of sacred oratory, as the specialists had worked them out. Complex theatrical effects were orchestrated to fit with the unified time frame that began with the arrival of the missionaries and ended with their departure. This drama often began very quietly, but it culminated in a crescendo of "general confessions" that left the religious wrung out but happy, and it ended with the missionaries' departure amid tears and manifestations of high enthusiasm. The church was a theatrical space, but other spaces were readied and decorated as well, and ritual routes in the form of processions connected them in obligatory progression from one to the other.

Processions often went in a particular direction, for example, from the city or town toward the country area that stood in need of benediction and inclusion within the city's sacred space. Always and everywhere, their order of march reflected an ideal and eternal order that was a projection of the real community. As in the parable, the first and most important members of the community competed with one another to become last in a great show of humility and penitence, with the result, of course, that even in penitence they reaffirmed their primacy. Penitence signaled the cancelation of humankind's offenses toward God, but also and especially the obliteration of offenses within human society—all thanks to the mediation of the religious. The "peaces" between one Christian and another that sealed the successful mission were the climax of all the dramatic tension that the preachers had so artfully constructed. They were a structural element in missionary work that continued unchanged throughout the missionary movement from Landini's missions to the Tusco-Emilian Apennines in the mid-sixteenth century to Segneri's famous missions.

The preachers used a broad range of theatrical resources, and the missionary's reputation was linked to the success of such techniques. Paolo Segneri was so renowned that he was called to Bavaria to repeat the "performances" for which he had become famous in Italy. (The fact that he did not speak the Bavarians' language and had to have interpreters is further proof, if such is necessary, of the preeminence of gesture over speech in this sort of preaching.)

During one mission of Segneri's to the Modenese Apennines in 1672 he had a "woods" church built out of tree trunks and branches. The site of this church, which was to serve as the point of arrival for processions, was deliberately chosen, following a tactic of substitution, to occupy a spot in which pagan plant worship was rumored to have survived. As the procession wound its way from the real church in the village to the woods "church," advancing along an ideal "conversion" path, it passed by a series of tableaux of scenes from sacred history.

In his processions, which grew longer day by day, he represented the circumcision of Our Lord, the Presentation of the same, the Taking in the garden, the Flagellation at the pillar, the *Ecce homo,* Christ on the cross between the two thieves, and among these [scenes], holy mysteries with Herod, Caiaphas, and Pilate, a great throng of Pharisees and Scribes.[55]

The commentator went on to remark, like a spectator at a well-performed play, "and everyone played his part well, but some individuals admirably."

The director and star actor was the missionary, who sought to give a dramatic dimension to every moment of a sojourn within the community that was supposed to leave a permanent mark. How were people to be persuaded to leave off their "bad habits"? One of Segneri's favorite techniques was the Jesuit tactic of substitution: if someone were enslaved by a guilty passion for gambling at cards, Segneri suggested that "as a gift he be given playing cards, and whoever gives back the cards with the promise to gamble no more at such games should be given in exchange a medal with plenary indulgence at the point of death." The idea was not new. Speaking of the Indians of the Americas, Acosta had suggested that generous use be made of rosary beads, holy water, holy images of various sorts, and all the sacred bric-a-brac that from that time on flooded the entire Catholic world.[56]

Still, the most emotional moment in this theatrical performance was undoubtedly the sermon on penitence, which was preceded by public scourging:

Undoing the belt of his outer garment with one sweeping gesture and throwing it neatly over his left arm . . . with his right hand grasping a whip made up of close-set strips of iron that another brother standing by handed to him, he begins to beat himself energetically and keeps it up for some time, thus reducing the audience to such a state of commotion that whatever he preaches to them, all that can be heard is moans and wrenching sobs, all that can be seen is weeping.

This was the moment for the *coup de grâce:* his hearers' resistance crumbled when he launched into a dialogue with a skull passed to him on cue by another assistant:

When, finally, he asks the other brother for the mirror of his own miseries— that is, a horrifying dead man's skull—taking it in his left hand and looking fixedly at it, he begins (as if that poor soul could hear) to speak with it, to interrogate it, to dialogue and moralize with it in its state of damnation. O! here is contrition for a life badly lived! O! here the place is filled with sound! O! here voices resound crying for mercy, promising restitution, promising peace, promising penitence![57]

This was all pure theater, and the spectator reporting on it was so aware of its drama that his comments centered more on the speaker's skill at holding his hearers spellbound than on the preacher's sanctity. The commentator's parenthetical "as if that poor soul could hear" was more a remark on verisimilitude than an expression of doubt concerning survival after death.

It should be said, however, that the intense theatricality characteristic of the missions was not a technique required by the missionaries' superiors. Quite the contrary. Although the Jesuits were indeed one of the orders most apt to use drama as a means of acculturation in their extra-European missionary activities, the congregations of the Society often expressed reservations about such techniques and attempted to tone down exuberant "holy representations" that included devils in chains, *danses macabres,* and fireworks.[58] The people who were the target of the missions were by no means passive. Moreover, the very success of the preaching campaigns, with their promises of pardon and pacification within the community, gave new life and new form to ancient expressions of popular culture to which the missionaries had to find "accommodations."

The wide gamut of accommodations that the missionaries found they needed to make was matched by the equally vast world of social practices that they discovered. A survey of everything that the missionaries listed under the categories of "abuses" and "superstitions" is a good place to start for anyone who wants to study the culture of the lower classes during this period. The missionaries viewed such customs, if not with open disapproval, at least with a sense of their own superiority, as in this report from the Valsesia:

> When they carry the dead body out of the house, they light some straw, and they go along the roads crying, "May the spirit go where the body goes." They do a tricenary for the souls of the dead, and they go to the dead person's place, and when they get there they take their heads in their hands and begin to weep uncontrollably, with so many outcries that it is something laughable. They keep all the dead exposed in caskets and the heads in certain boxes, and the women go there often, take them up, wash them, and then begin to cry out so much they seem mad.[59]

The missionaries usually showed less condescension and more pity and sympathy before the miserable poverty in which the people lived—conditions that worsened during the course of the eighteenth century. Their concern was not only a normal reaction to increasingly bad living conditions; it also sprang from the divorce, already in progress, between the functions of spiritual assistance and the needs of cultural conquest that had given rise to the missions. There was also a growing gap between the rural world and the urban world, one that differed, however, from the division of the previous century. Before, the city had unified a dispersed, suspect, and feared rural world by lending it urban religion; now country religion needed to be safeguarded and was proposed as a model for cities that were in the process of becoming dechristianized. When St. Alfonso Maria de' Liguori founded the Congregation of the Most Holy Redeemer, he stated that his goal was "to help the people scattered in the countryside and in rural hamlets," and in his works he showed a consistent mistrust of city society.[60] Naturally, St. Alfonso had to graft his own work onto the robust trunk of the historical experience of the Society of Jesus, the order that had left the strongest mark on the mission as a decisive part of religious life. There were other orders and congregations, however, that during the course of the seventeenth century made human solidarity toward the poor, the defenseless, and the wretched an integral part of their missionary work.

The name that springs to mind in this connection is that of St. Vincent de Paul. The wide use of the italianized version of his name—Vincenzo de' Paoli—reflects the profound roots that the Congregation of the Mission put down in Italy, both through its own efforts and those of such others as St. Leonardo da Porto Maurizio, who took inspiration from the Vincentine model.[61] The simple style of these new missionaries, their ability to listen to the people rather than mesmerize them and inundate them with oratory, and above all their focus on bettering the living conditions of the poor and their vow to assist peasants (*rusticani*) introduce us to a world of thoughts totally different from the one that had produced earlier missionary strategies.

The question of propagation of the faith and its infinite complications—the art of dissimulation, the ability to "accommodate" to one's interlocutor as a means to an end, the use of force and trickery—had been raised with dramatic modernity in the context of religious conflicts that tore Europe asunder. Thus a new personage promised to a bright future was born under the time-honored guise of the apostolic preacher. He had many faces: an intellectual with multiple skills, an expert in the art of communication (visual, oral, and by means of print), a prophet, ethnologist, conspirator, spy, subverter of the established order, and a master of the art of taking command of the conscience of others and directing it to ends that, although his own, were connected with the triumph of the reign of God rather than any egotistical personal success and hence justified all means.

Such a man, who was often called an "apostolic man,"[62] possessed the truth and had a divine mandate to spread it. His task was to seize the hearts and thoughts of an entire population and to bring the faithful to the tribunal of confession, where their sins would be washed away and, with his help, the promise of a new life would be implanted in their souls. That "apostolic man" could not be a familiar figure like the parish priest. He needed to pass through people's lives as a providential, dramatic, and exceptional event, imitating and foreshadowing the second coming of Christ. The missionary had to arrive without warning; when his mission had been accomplished he had to leave bearing with him all the sins of the community. This meant that it was inevitable that what, by its very nature, had to seem (if not to be) a meteoric passage was institutionalized in orders, preordained times, and fixed rituals.

The contrast between apparent spontaneity and careful planning is one of the many contradictions in the history of missions, and they deserve to be remembered among the polarities of the Baroque age for this if nothing else. As Leo Spitzer said, "Perhaps 'Baroque man' does not exist; what exists is instead a Baroque attitude, which is a fundamentally Christian attitude."[63] Still, something very modern took form out of the attempt to revitalize and circulate ancient models of Christian life. The discovery that the human conscience was unfathomable, coupled with an imperious need to direct the conscience, enriched the panorama of ecclesiastical institutions with a new presence during the course of the seventeenth century. Above all, however, it was to open the Pandora's box of the relationship between the intellectual and the masses.

NOTES

1. Circular letter to the apostolic nuncios, January 15, 1622, in *Sacrae Congregationis de Propaganda Fide memoria rerum: 350 anni a servizio delle missioni . . . 1622–1972,* ed. Josef Metzler, 3 vols. in 5 pts. (Rome, Freiburg, Vienna: Herder, 1972–76). Vol. 3, pt. 2, pp. 656–58.

2. See Edmund Leites, ed., *Conscience and Casuistry in Early Modern Europe* (Cambridge and New York: Cambridge University Press, 1988; Paris: Editions de la Maison des sciences de l'homme, 1989).

3. Ezio Raimondi, introductory note to Daniello Bartoli, *Scritti,* ed. Ezio Raimondi (Turin: Einaudi, 1977), ix.

4. Bartoli, *Scritti,* 123. On Muratori, see Ludovico Antonio Muratori, *Il cristianesimo felice nelle missioni dei padri della Compagnia di Gesù nel Paraguai,* ed. Paolo Collo (Palermo: Sellerio, 1985), 32.

5. See the "Avvisi della Cina dell'ottantatré et dell'ottantaquattro," published in appendix to *Avvisi del Giappone degli anni 1582, 83, ed 84 con alcuni altri della Cina dell'83 e 84 cavati dalle lettere della Compagnia di Gesù* (Rome: Zanetti, 1586). On this report, see M. Howard Reinstra, *Jesuit Letters from China 1583–84* (Minneapolis: University of Minnesota Press, 1986). A less familiar topic is the use of pictures to communicate ethnographic information, on which see Bernadette Majorana, *La gloriosa impresa: Storia e immagini di un viaggio secentesco* (Palermo: Sellerio, 1990), 21ff.

6. Antonio Possevino, *Coltura degl'ingegni* (Vicenza: G. Greco, 1598), 3.

7. The Latin edition (Helmstadii: Lucius, 1587) was followed two years later by an English version: *Certain briefe, and speciall instructions for gentlemen, merchants, students, souldiers, marriners etc.,* on which see Margaret Trabue Hod-

gen, *Early Anthropology in the Sixteenth and Seventeenth Centuries* (Philadelphia: University of Pennsylvania Press, 1964), 187. On sixteenth-century advice to travelers, see Justin Stagl, "The Methodising of Travel in the 16th Century: A Tale of Three Cities," *History and Anthropology* 4, no. 2 (1990): 303–38.

8. Antonio Possevino, *Apparato all'historia di tutte le nationi et il modo di studiare la geografia* (Venice: Gio. Battista Ciotti, 1598), fol. 239v.

9. The observation on the rhetoric of absence and the reference to Shakespeare's *The Tempest* are drawn from Hodgen, *Early Anthropology,* 196–99.

10. Ignatius of Loyola, Letter of July 5, 1553, in *Monumenta Ignatiana, Epistolae* (Rome: Monumenta Historica Societatis Iesu [henceforth abbreviated MHSI], 1965). Vol. 5, p. 165.

11. Silvestro Landini, Letter to Ignatius of Loyola dated Modena, May 16, 1550, MHSI, *Epistolae mixtae,* vol. 5, *1555–1556,* 698–702. See also Adriano Prosperi, "'Otras Indias': Missionari della Controriforma tra contadini e selvaggi," in *Scienze, credenze occulte, livelli di cultura,* Convegno internazionale di studi, Firenze, June 26–30, 1980, ed. Gian Carlo Garfagnini (Florence: Olschki, 1982), 205–34, esp. 209ff.

12. Giulio Chierici, on whom see the letter of Father Juan Alfonso Polanco of February 19, 1578, MHSI, *Polanci complementa,* 2 vols. (Madrid: 1917, reprint Rome: MHSI, 1969). Vol. 2, p. 473.

13. See, for example, the title *Relatione del viaggio et arrivo in Europa, Roma e Bologna de i serenissimi Principi Giapponesi venuti a dare ubidienze a Sua Santità* (Bologna: A. Benacci, 1585). This was a famous episode and has been treated in a number of studies. See Adriana Boscaro, "Giapponesi a Venezia nel 1585," in *Venezia e l'Oriente,* ed. Lionello Lanciotti (Florence: Olschki, 1987), 409–29. The press campaign carried on by the Jesuits in Japan is less well-known: a report appeared in Japan under the name of the young people who went to Rome (but which was really written by the Jesuits) in which the same process of idealization that had been applied to Japan in Europe was directed toward the image of Europe in Japan. This text was entitled *De missione legatorum Iaponensium ad Romanam Curiam, rebusque in Europa, ac toto itinere animadversis dialogus, ex ephemeride ipsorum legatorum collectus, et in sermonem latinum versus, ad Eduardo de Sande Sacerdote Societati Iesu* (In. Macaensi Portu Sinici regni in domo Societatis Iesu . . . anno 1590). My thanks to Alessandro Arcangeli for providing me with a reproduction of this text.

14. The fundamental study on Valignano's missionary work is Josef Franz Schütte, *Valignanos Missionsgrundsätze für Japan,* 2 vols. (Rome: Edizioni di storia e letteratura, 1951–58); available in English as *Valignano's Mission Principles for Japan,* trans. John J. Coyne, 2 vols. (St. Louis: Institute of Jesuit Sources, 1980–83).

15. This text was rediscovered by Josef Franz Schütte and has been published as Alessandro Valignano, S. J., *Il cerimoniale per i missionari del Giappone,* ed. Josef Franz Schütte (Rome: Edizioni di storia e letteratura, 1946).

16. Valignano, *Il cerimoniale,* Schütte introduction, 81.

17. Giovanni della Casa, *De officiis inter potentiores et tenuiores amicos,* in *Prose di Giovanni della Casa e altri trattatisti cinquecenteschi del comportamento,* ed. Arnaldo Di Benedetto (Turin: UTET, 1970), 136ff.

18. Valignano, *Il cerimoniale*, 120–21.

19. On the connection between the two passages, see Albano Biondi, "La giustificazione della simulazione nel Cinquecento," in *Eresia e riforma nell'Italia del Cinquecento: Miscellanea I* (Florence: G. C. Sansoni; Chicago: The Newberry Library, 1974), 8–68.

20. This text appears in Serge Gruzinski, *La colonisation de l'imaginaire: Sociétés indigènes et occidentalisation dans le Mexique espagnol XVIe–XVIIIe siècle* (Paris: Gallimard, 1988), 147; available in English as *The Conquest of Mexico: The Incorporation of Indian Societies into the Western World, 16th–19th Centuries*, trans. Eileen Corrigan (Cambridge, U.K.: Polity Press, distrib. Blackwell, 1933).

21. *Discorso di penitenza raccolto per Messer Paolo Rosello da un ragionamento del Reverendissimo Cardinal Contarini* (Venice, 1549), 13v–15r.

22. Schütte, *Valignanos Missionsgrundsätze*, vol. 1, pp. 36–50.

23. Valignano, *Il cerimoniale*, 19.

24. Valignano, *Il cerimoniale*, 155–57.

25. Valignano, *Il cerimoniale*, 282–85.

26. MHSI, *Polanci complementa*, 1969 reprint, vol. 2, pp. 829ff.

27. "Yo va en viente y nueve años que estoy en la Compañia . . . solo los tres fuy súbdito y todos los demás tuve siempre cuidado de otros," Letter of resignation sent August 30, 1580; see Schütte, *Valignanos Missionsgrundsätze*, vol. 1, pt. 2, p. 500.

28. See Rosario Villari, *Elogio della dissimulazione: La lotta politica nel Seicento* (Rome and Bari: Laterza, 1987).

29. Josef Franz Schütte has published the letter of Claudio Acquaviva dated December 24, 1585, in appendix to Valignano, *Il cerimoniale*, 314–24; see also 320. On the question of the Crucifixion, see Johannes Bettray, *Die Akkomodationsmethode des P. Matteo Ricci in China* (Rome: Apud Aedes Universitatis Gregorianae, 1955), 365–82, and Jonathan D. Spence, *The Memory Palace of Matteo Ricci* (New York: Viking/Penguin, 1984), 246–47.

30. Letter of Ricci to his fellow Jesuit Girolamo Benci, Nanking, October 7, 1595, in Matteo Ricci, *Lettere del manoscritto maceratese*, ed. Chiara Zeuli (Macerata, 1985), 47–52, esp. p. 49.

31. Letter of Matteo Ricci to his father, Giovanni Battista Ricci, from Shaozhou, December 10, 1593, in *Lettere*, 43–46.

32. Letter to Girolamo Costa from Nanking, October 28, 1595, in Ricci, *Lettere*, 53–76, esp. 64; quoted from Spence, *The Memory Palace of Matteo Ricci*, 81–82.

33. Letter to Benci, October 7, 1595, in Ricci, *Lettere*, 47–52.

34. Letter to Costa, October 28, 1595, in Ricci, *Lettere*, 65.

35. See M. E. Saltykov'-Shchedrin, *Gospoda Golovlevy* (Leningrad, 1934), consulted in Italian translation, *I signori Golovljòv*, trans. C. Coisson (Turin, 1946), 174–78; quoted from *The Golovlevs*, trans. I. P. Foote (Oxford and New York: Oxford University Press, 1986), 115.

36. For a description of the polemics and the negative reactions set off in the Chinese intellectual world by the proposals of the Jesuit missionaries, see Jacques Gernet, *Chine et christianisme: Action et réaction* (Paris: Gallimard, 1982); avail-

able in English as *China and the Christian Impact: A Conflict of Cultures,* trans. Janet Lloyd (Cambridge and New York: Cambridge University Press; Paris: Editions de la Maison des sciences de l'homme, 1985).

37. See Giacomo Di Fiore, *La legazione Mezzabarba in Cina (1720–1721)* (Naples: Istituto universale orientale, 1989).

38. See Prosperi, "'Otras Indias,'" 205–34.

39. Quoted from Anthony Pagden, *The Fall of Natural Man: The American Indian and the Origins of Comparative Ethnology* (Cambridge and New York: Cambridge University Press, 1982, rev. ed. 1986), 97.

40. See Antonio de Guevara, *Libro llamado Relox de Principes, o, Libre aureo del Emperador Marco Aurelio* (1531), a work frequently reprinted and translated.

41. Piero Camporesi, "Mostruosità e sapienza del villano," in *Agostino Gallo nella cultura del Cinquecento,* Atti del convegno, Brescia, October 23–24, 1988, ed. Maurizio Pegrari (Brescia: Moretto, 1988), 193–214, esp. 197. The Tuscan steward for the Medici family was Cesare Frullani of Cerreto Guidi, the author of *Gl'avvenimenti del lago di Fucecchio e modo del suo governo,* ed. Anna Corsi and Adriano Prosperi (Rome: Istituto storico italiano, 1988), esp. 68.

42. The letter in which Landini states that "this island will be my India" was written in 1553 from Corsica: MHSI, *Epistolae mixtae, ex variis Europae locis ab anno 1537 ad 1556 scriptae . . .* (Matriti, 1900), 115ff. The Cristoforo Rodriguez letter was written in 1556: MHSI, *Litterae quadrimestres,* vol. 5, p. 296: "Juzgo in Domino . . . que abriría el Señor aquí otras Indias, convertiendo á tanta multitud de ánimas de moriscos que, según sus muestras y obras, se van al infierno."

43. The document is dated May 14, 1549, and is reproduced, in Spanish, in MHSI, *Litterae quadrimestres.* Vol. 1, p. 156.

44. Landini, letter of February 7, 1548, in MHSI, *Litterae quadrimestres.* Vol. 1, p. 81.

45. See Otto Hintze, "The Commissioner and His Importance in the General History of Administration: A Comparative Study," in Hintze, *The Historical Essays of Otto Hintze,* ed. Felix Gilbert with Robert M. Berdahl (New York: Oxford University Press, 1975).

46. Parts of a report on the voyage of Bartolomé de las Casas by Fray Tomás de la Torre are given in José Luis Martínez, *Passageri delle Indie: I viaggi transatlantici del XVI secolo,* trans. Monica Lavino and Edda Cicogna; ed. Ernesto Franco (Genoa: Marietti, 1988). Landini's letter on the trip from Genoa to Corsica is dated March 16, 1553, and can be found in MHSI, *Epistolae mixtae, ex variis Europae locis ab anno 1537 ad 1556 scriptae,* vol. 3, *1553,* 165ff.

47. See Mario Scaduto, S. J., "Tra inquisitori e riformati: Le missioni dei Gesuiti tra Valdesi della Calabria e delle Puglie," *Archivum Historicum Societatis Jesu* 15 (1946): 1–76, esp. 9–12.

48. Jakob Rem, *Vaticinia,* in the collection *Jesuitica 1081* of the Hauptstadtsarchiv München, "De bellis quibusdam," 2. After Rem's death in 1618, his followers interpreted the outbreak of the Thirty Years War as a realization of prophecy, remembering Rem's statement: "Brevi apud nos quoque Indiae erunt et non sufficiet numerus nostrorum" (*Vaticinia,* 3).

49. This is clear in the title of his treatise: Diego de Valadés, *Rethorica christiana . . . exemplis suo loco insertis, quae quidem ex Indorum maxime deprompta sunt historiis* (Perugia, 1579).

50. Andrea Avellino, letter to Ottavio Farnese, in *Lettere scritte dal glorioso s. Andrea Avellino a diversi suoi divoti* (Naples, 1731). Vol. 1, p. 197.

51. According to Forero, Protestant rulers should have at their side men "qui sibi dextre et ingeniose ad illos accessum parent, et clam mysteria fidei catholicae illis instillent" (Hauptstadtsarchiv München, *Jesuiten 81*, 273–76). The Jesuits' memoranda can also be found in the Hauptstadtsarchiv in Munich under the title, *Acta cum duce Bavariae 1583*, 9–16. There is an extensive literature on the history of Bavaria in the age of the Counter-Reformation, a summary of which can be found in Hubert Glaser, ed., *Um Glauben und Reich: Kurfürst Maximilan I: Beiträge zur Bayerischen Geschichte und Kunst 1573–1657*, 2 vols. (Munich: Hirmer, 1980).

52. "Contra un error singular que dice que los cristianos más rudos se pueden salvar sin la fe explícita en Cristo"; Acosta, *De Procuranda Indorum Salute*, in his *Obras*, ed. Francisco Mateos (Madrid: Atlas, 1954), 550–52.

53. The quotation from a report by Scipione Paolucci, S. J., on the ignorance of the peasants of Eboli is taken from Carlo Ginzburg, "Folklore, magia, religione," in *Storia d'Italia*, 6 vols. (Turin: G. Einaudi, 1972–77). Vol. 1, *I caratteri originali*, pp, 657–59. The quotation on the Bavarians is taken from a manuscript report of 1614 in Hauptstadtsarchiv München, *Jesuiten 1*, pp. 1ff.

54. The 1590 document is in the Archivio Romano della Compagnia di Gesù, *Inst. 40*, fols. 137r–138v. See also *Ordinationes Praepositorum Generalium: Instructiones et formulae communes toti Societati . . .* (Rome: in Collegio Romano eiusdem Societatis, 1606), 195–202: "Finis harum Missionum est auxilium tot animarum, quae ex ignoratione rerum ad salutem sua necessariarum, in statu peccati, cum aeternae damnationis periculo, versantur." In 1647 the decision was taken to name a prefect of the missions for every province: see Carla Faralli, "Le missioni dei gesuiti in Italia (secc. XVI–XVII): Problemi di una ricerca in corso," *Bollettino della società di studi valdesi* 138 (December 1975): 97–116. On the tendency toward permanent residence in the missions, see Mario Rosa, *Religione e società nel Mezzogiorno tra Cinque e Seicento* (Bari: De Donato, 1976), 245–72. On "reductions" in Paraguay, see Girolamo Imbruglia, *L'invenzione del Paraguay: Studio sull'idea di comunità tra Seicento e Settecento* (Naples: Bibliopolis, 1983).

55. [Lodovico Bartolini], *Relatione delle missioni fatte su le montagne di Modona dalli molto R. R. P. P. Paolo Segneri e Gio. Pietro Pinamonti della compagnia di Giesù l'anno 1672* (Modena: Andrea Cassiani, 1673), 7.

56. "Que en vez de los ritos perniciosos se introduzcan otros saludables, y borrar unas ceremonias con otras. El agua bendita, las imágenes, los rosarios, las cuentas benditas, los cirios y las demás cosas que aprueba y frecuenta la santa Iglesia, persuádense los sacerdotes que son muy oportunas para los neófitos, y en los sermones al pueblo cólmelas de alabanzas": Acosta, *Obras*, 565.

57. [Bartolini], *Relatione delle missioni*, 12. On Jesuit theatricality and the use of drama in the teaching of the Society of Jesus, see Marc Fumaroli, *Héros et orateurs: Rhétorique et dramaturgie cornéliennes* (Geneva: Droz, 1990); in Italian

translation as *Eroi e oratori: Retorica e drammaturgia secentesche,* trans. L. Zecchi (Bologna: Il Mulino, 1990).

58. "Caveatur item, ne—quod iustam reprehensionem habet—in omni actione producantur Daemones, mendici, potatores, blasphemi, pueri leviculi, choreae mortuales, ignes artificiales, explosiones fistularum" (Minutes of the congregation, 1622: Hauptstadtsarchiv München, *Jesuiten 84,* fol. 37.

59. Martino Signorelli, *Storia della Valmaggia* (Locarno: Tipografia Stazione, 1972), 417.

60. Giovanni Orlandi, "S. Alfonso Maria de Liguori e l'ambiente missionario napoletano nel Settecento: La Compagnia di Gesù," *Spicilegium Historicum Congregationis SS.mi Redemptoris* 38 (1990): 5–195.

61. There is an extensive bibliography on St. Vincent de Paul and the Congregation of the Mission. See, for example, St. Vincent de Paul, *Correspondance, entretiens, documents,* ed. Pierre Coste, 13 vols., plus 1 vol. tables and 1 vol. supplement (Paris: J. Gabalda, 1920–70); Luigi Mezzadri, "Le missioni popolari della Congregazione della Missione nello Stato della Chiesa (1642–1700)," *Rivista di storia della chiesa in Italia* 33 (1979): 12–44; Giorgio F. Rossi, "Missioni vincenziane, religiosità e vita civile nella diocesi di Tivoli nei secoli XVII–XIX," *Atti e memorie della Società Tiburtina di storia e d'arte* 53 (1980): 143–210.

62. Amid an endless literature on the subject, see, for example, a manual written by a Capuchin friar, Gaetano Maria da Bergamo, *L'uomo apostolico istruito nella sua vocazione al confessionario per udire spezialmente de Confessioni generali, nel tempo delle missioni e de' giubbilei ...* (Venice: Gio. Battista Regozza, 1727).

63. Leo Spitzer, *Cinque saggi di ispanistica,* ed. Giovanni Maria Bertini (Turin: Giappichelli, 1962).

8

THE NUN

Mario Rosa

PREFACE

ALTHOUGH FEMALE MONASTIC INSTITUTIONS in the sixteenth century remained much as they had been during the preceding century, the Council of Trent initiated significant changes, which were reinforced by the regulations pronounced by Pius V in 1566 and 1571 and reiterated by Gregory XIII in 1572. With the imposition of the cloister, or "enclosure," the life of religious communities—within the convent and in its relations with the outside world—took on elements that continued to be typical throughout the age of the Counter-Reformation. Everywhere in Catholic Europe the church faced the basic problem of gaining acceptance for its reforms, enclosure chief among them. It began a slow, difficult process of dismantling or eroding long-standing customs and ways of life inappropriate to the new climate and of imposing religious practices and habits, individual and communitarian, more consonant to the new ideal of a stricter observance of the rules. It was to be a long struggle, made of clashes and compromises between convents and bishops; between bishops and male religious orders that were often unwilling to turn over to the bishop traditional forms of direction of the female convents under their guidance; between the nuns' families of birth, who sent surplus daughters to the cloister in the interests of conserving their patrimony, and the ecclesiastical authorities; between local political powers jealously holding to their ancient autonomous rights and churchmen attempting to apply the Tridentine and Roman directives.

This was the historical background for the figure of the nun during the Baroque age—a figure rich in external contrasts (which can only be touched on here) and internal ones. For instance, a hierarchy of values and relationships that pertained in the secular world tended to be reproduced within the convent: professed nuns whose social origins and sizable dowry granted them prestige and surrounded them with consideration might have a private cell and enjoy support from other family members within the cloister that set them off from the poorer lay sisters. Or there were marked differences between nuns willing to accept the reforms and the disciplinary process being put into effect and others who opposed them in various ways.

Strict observance was a return to an earlier, more ascetic and austere form of religious life that occurred in the sixteenth century and, in particular, during the first half of the seventeenth century, after the first post-Tridentine reform moment had run its course and produced disappointing results. Strict observance was especially notable in the Iberian Peninsula, where the older orders gave rise to impetuous "discalced" movements for reform that reached back to "barefoot" origins. The reform struck male religious orders first, in Castile in particular. There were soon discalced Carmelites (1562) linked to the extraordinary personalities of St. John of the Cross and St. Teresa, discalced Augustinians (1566), and discalced Trinitarians (1597). The movement also touched female orders, where it confirmed the continuing expansion, even in a spiritual sense, of the congregations, but where it also emphasized the contrast (by that date generally accepted) between monastic institutions in which the religious lived, and would continue to live, "most comfortably" and the reformed institutions, and between convents that continued to operate as schools and to maintain ties with the world despite enclosure and others that were places of harsh asceticism and mystical contemplation.

The Spanish model (which was not restricted to St. Teresa's Carmel) was soon "exported," and it had a powerful influence not only in the Hispanicized lands across the Atlantic but also in Italy and France and throughout Catholic Europe. At nearly the same time, however—that is, between the very end of the Wars of Religion and the Fronde—an antithetical (or at least complementary) model was being elaborated and developed in France. The French model proved highly successful, and with its Spanish counterpart it formed a gigantic ideological and religious ellipse that encircled female monastic life throughout the age of the Counter-Reformation. The female religious state in France of the *Grand Siècle*—a society more dynamic than that of Italy or Spain during the same period—was not really based on the founding of reformed branches of the old orders, although St. Teresa's Carmelites were widely imitated and exerted an enormous influence on religious life among the aristocracy and the nobility "of the robe." Rather, what was unique in France was the founding and diffusion of a number of new congregations. One of these, founded in the late sixteenth century, was the Ursulines, an order with simple vows and a dedication to active social involvement, based on the Italian model of St. Angela Merici and transplanted into France. The Ursulines' strongly pedagogical vocation made the order synonymous with schooling, particularly with the education of the offspring of the bourgeoisie of ancien régime France. Another new order, the Congregation of Notre-Dame, founded in Lorraine in 1597, was also dedicated to teaching, but on a more aristocratic level. Other orders included the Congregation of the Visitation of Holy Mary founded (in 1610) by St. Jeanne-Françoise de Chantal and St. Francis de Sales, whose sisters were "vowed and sacrificed to the Divine Majesty," and, as a response to the acute social needs created by the Thirty Years War, the Congregation of the Daughters of Charity founded (in 1633) by St. Vincent de Paul and St. Louise Marillac.

Throughout Europe and, to some extent, in the New World, monastic institutions tried various combinations of the more severe Spanish model and the more flexible French model through the seventeenth century and into the early years of the eighteenth century and beyond. They underwent (at some risk) the crisis of Quietism, a movement stressing direct colloquy of the soul with God through "quiet" (that is, passive) prayer that seemed (particularly in female institutions) to question the sacramental and hierarchical mediation of the church. By the mid-seventeenth century, however, although female monastic institution still varied enormously, they seemed to have reached some sort of stability. In their more direct and strident forms, at least, relations between the convents and the outside world were increasingly mediated by the supervision of the bishops and by the presence of spiritual directors and confessors. Convents seemed to settle into a more tranquil routine. Within them discipline was more strictly enforced, thanks to firmly consolidated models of Counter-Reformation monastic spirituality and to an increasing acceptance of communitarian rules on the part of the female religious. Little by little, the new discipline gradually paralleled the penitential practices and the "dark night of the soul" of the mystical experience or else it replaced those practices with a well-regulated regimen of daily devotions and a more peaceful and continuous "exercise" of Christian virtues. A sizable literature sought to define this new face of the female religious in the difficult phase that opened up at the height of the turbulence of the Baroque seventeenth century and that moved, adopting new elements of "modernization," toward new perspectives reflecting ongoing changes in European society, changes that increased during the eighteenth century and that became even greater after the break of the French Revolution and the advent of the contemporary age. Although the jagged progress of the overall historical process might seem to have a certain linearity, it is not an easy task to outline all the various moments and phases of those vicissitudes. I have had to make a difficult choice, rejecting a typological or sociological description of the "average" nun during the Baroque age in favor of a series of "portraits" of the ones who were in some sense exemplary. I hope that these portraits will help focus on specific conditions and will perhaps even throw light on aspects of the topic that the present examination must necessarily leave aside.

Spaces and Times of Enclosure

There were weighty consequences to enclosure that ran throughout monastic life during the Counter-Reformation. Cloistering was a form of incarceration whose rigor was felt not only by the nuns directly subjected to it but also by kin and friends, who were quick to complain of the clergy's attempts to weaken the nuns' ties to their families of birth. Admittedly, enclosure was not easily achieved; long-standing customs remained in force, and more lenient practices on the part of certain bishops and ecclesiastical superiors worked to counter some of the more severe papal decrees. Still, it was generally agreed that nuns had to be separated from the outside world and isolated from its attractions. The ecclesiastical hierarchy eventually viewed this new moral and religious ideal in terms of rigid discipline, and it took enclosure as an essential element in the reform of female monastic institutions. Nothing illustrates this better, looking beyond individual instances and specific rulings, than the decisions of the Congregazione Romana dei Regolari (the Congregation of Religious) and its rulings on the specific cases and questions put to it by various convents during the first half of the seventeenth century. Its responses provided an emblematic expression of a mentality and a way of operating that—thanks to the fact that such responses were also juridical precedents—was destined to acquire a more general normative value.

The first task of the Congregation was to establish tighter control over persons who, for a variety of reasons, might enter a convent or be present within its walls. These might be ecclesiastical personnel such as chaplains and, even more, confessors; important personages who were frequent visitors within the cloister walls (and who at times arrived accompanied by a large retinue); widows, married women, or unmarried elderly women temporarily lodged in the convent; women of a humbler sort who had been given refuge when calamity or war struck; the many workers, architects, master artisans, and others who maintained or enlarged the convent buildings and whose presence reflects the intense activity in ecclesiastical construction during these years. There were also musicians, singing masters, and music masters whose moves from one church or convent to another (along with prohibitions of *canto figurato*—polyphony) enable us to map the major centers for music in Italy. Last but not necessarily least, there were workers, bookkeepers, auditors, administrators, and stewards, all of whom were involved in the management of the holdings of the various female institutions. The guidelines laid down to facilitate the work of the Congregation of Religious included detailed descriptions of the cases in which verbal communication or conversation should be forbidden within the convent or should be subject to strict rules. Aside from a general entry under *Clausura* (enclosure, the cloister), there were specifications under *Casi riservati* (cases reserved to the bishops' authority), *Parlare* (speaking) *Parlatorio* (parlatory), and *Rappresentazioni* (performances). These were not abstractions or theoretical cases of which the Congregation was taking note, but specific occurrences and concrete moments in religious life. The Congregation was explicit, on the one hand, about its mistrust of the religious charged with the direction of the female monastic institutions; on the other hand, it stressed duties of obedience to the local ordinary. In Sulmona in 1618 and in Borgo San Sepolcro in 1627, for instance, the Congregation outlined, under the heading "Obedience," rules resembling those of military strategy to "constrain the nuns to recognize the bishop as their superior." The Congregation noted that "when pleasant means are insufficient," this was to be done

> with more serious remedies, such as closing the parlatories and the gates to them, but also all the other places by which provisions can be furnished them and giving them only bread and water, calling, if need be, on the secular arm, and if that is not enough, [by] putting the leaders of the sedition under lock and key, always beginning with the weakest convent and the one that has the least aid, because when one cedes another will more easily follow its example.

Parlatories and gates were real spaces but also symbolic spaces between the outside and the inside. The church hierarchy and the Congregation of Religious, speaking for the church, insisted on that fact with obsessive intensity, almost as if to give tangible confirmation to an ironclad condition of separateness. The bars of the parlatory grate "must be made closer together," the Congregation ordered in 1629 in a decision regarding a convent in Lecce, "so that the nuns can in no way reach their hands through it to touch the hand, the finger, or any other part of a person from outside the convent." The same Congregation had decreed in 1617 that "the gates must be perpetually locked, nor will they ever be opened except in cases of specific necessity." Rulings in 1619 and 1639 specified that the gates must be closed "with two locks and two keys, one on the outside and the other on the inside." Not even this seemed sufficient to guarantee enclosure. What, for example, if indiscreet glances should pass over the convent walls? The Congregation had an answer ready as early as 1605: windows that overlooked the cloister must not be left open. Later specific orders were given to wall up all windows or openings in bell towers or churches contiguous to convent buildings. A ruling in 1612 regarding L'Aquila, which seems dictated by experts on bricklaying rather than by an ecclesiastical committee, stipulated that the bricks in the openings must not be staggered, leaving peepholes, but must rather be laid down in full courses. And what if the nuns themselves were to cast a furtive glance over the wall? A ruling of the Congregation of 1627—we are at the beginning of the new age of Galilean science—prohibited, "under pain of severe penalties," the use of *occhiali lunghi* (spyglasses) turned, we must suppose, not toward the investigation of heavenly spaces but toward more terrestrial curiosities.

Whether the convents welcomed enclosure or suffered it, their internal order was the result of an unending struggle, on the part of individual nuns and of the entire community, to satisfy an obsessive observance of the daily schedule of prayer and work. Obviously, much time was devoted to individual and community prayer, to ascetic and edifying reading, individual and collective, to divine worship and sacramental practices (the Eucharist in particular), and to meditation and spiritual exercises under the guidance of spiritual directors and confessors (who were, for the most part, regular clergy and Capuchin friars, and whose importance in female conventual life should be emphasized once and for all). Various sorts of prayer occupied about one-third of the day, and prayer was interrupted by hours of manual and domestic work, by meals, and by moments of recreation, which could be severe and simple in the "reformed" monasteries or could take forms more open to such worldly interests as music or art in other institutions. Work was the prime element in female conventual life. It was a means for avoiding all dangerous opportunities for leisure. Frequently it provided a way to round out the convent's sometimes meager sources of revenue with embroidery, the manufacture of small devotional objects, or the preparation of sweets, marmalades, and, above all, syrups, medications, and salves. On occasion these items found a ready reception outside the cloister walls, as did a famous salve made by Mother Agnès de Sainte-Thècle, Jean Racine's aunt, which was sold at the Abbey of Port-Royal.

The sovereign virtues of the nun were silence and muted speech, measured and discreet gestures (if not absolute immobility during periods of meditation), control of the body according to a precise code of behavior, and, if possible, control over the soul's intentions. But all this was what "should be," an ideal to strive for, which on occasion might be breached by floods of words and random gestures, as with the mystical "raptures" of St. Maria Maddalena de' Pazzi, whose fellow nuns took turns following her around the Carmelite house in Florence diligently noting her fleeting visions. On a humbler plane, the ideal was shattered daily by innumerable minor infractions that the nuns were expected to report, along with their own failures to observe the rules and "obediences," during a once- or twice-weekly "faults chapter" conducted according to carefully delineated procedures meting out punishments to be applied publicly in the refectory. The dominant idea behind this overall process of control, which was assimilated into a continual striving for self-discipline, was the male and clerical notion (reinforced by the Counter-Reformation) of the weakness and fragility of women and their need for guidance, in combination with a genuine obsession with female chastity. Indeed, the seventeenth-century "reforms" put much more stress on the vow of chastity than on vows of poverty and obedience, and female monastic establishments were generally regarded as places more for the conservation of virtue than for the practice of sanctity.

When enclosure, with all its practical and symbolic valences, had become the very condition of female conventual life, the nuns' sentiments and impressions were exacerbated by their isolation from their families and from intellectual pursuits, on the one hand, and by mortification and condemnation of the flesh, on the other. For many of them, however, neither being kept incessantly occupied in prayer or manual labor nor continual repression of their inner impulses—what the ascetic literature of the age defined as the struggle of the spirit against a perverse nature— could wipe out or sublimate all the memories, desires, or regrets that arose from comparing their past experience and their present condition. Such sentiments were even heightened by solitude, and they were often expressed, in the terms most familiar to both the nuns and their confessors and spiritual directors, as illusions, obsessions, or even diabolical possession, which contemporary treatises on devotional questions or exorcism portrayed in the fearsome form of wild beasts and monsters lurking in the depths of the human heart, waiting for their chance to assail it. There is an entire first-person "spiritual" literature or literature "of confession" crammed with such worrisome phenomena, ranging from the tormented analyses of Sister Jeanne des Anges after the events of Loudun to the mystical heights reached by St. Veronica Giuliani. Insistent and daily self-discipline was not enough to liberate a nun from a hovering Enemy ready to clutch her. The body, the source of all temptation, had to be dominated more harshly by forcing it to withstand long night vigils— and the nighttime hours harbored insidious and subtle snares because the Counter-Reformation sensibility peopled the night with both images of terror and refined aids to salvation. Or the body should be subjected to prolonged periods of abstinence and fasting (to the point of anorexia), to repeated mortification and merciless scourging, practiced individually or in common, or to the hidden torments of the hair shirt. St. Veronica Giuliani wore a habit "all full of thorns, which I called my embroidered dress"; the blessed Maria Maddalena Martinengo, a Capuchin, counted among her "usual little recreations" embroidering the instruments of the Passion "with the needle threaded with silk . . . into her own flesh, nice and big, as chalice-covers are embroidered, not without bleeding."

Although death to the world was frequently taken in its most absolute sense, these implacable mortifications were not for all nuns, but the less fervent sisters still did not have an easy time following the paths of the conventual life. Overwhelmed by scruples or exposed to the fear—and often the terror—of sin instilled in them by preachers and confessors and by a literal interpretation of ascetic and normative readings, nuns were often prone to neuroses, if not to mental disturbance. It is no coincidence that the first half of the seventeenth century—the period of the female orders' return to observance and of a stricter establishment of enclosure—also saw a genuine epidemic of diabolical possessions. or that violent internal conflict broke out among nuns (the Ursulines of Loudun, for instance) who sought shelter in the convent more than rigorous discipline and who were capable of following the letter of their Rule but were incapable of more exalted ideals. The Congregation of Religious had recommended extreme caution and prudence when it came to exorcisms to free nuns from diabolical possession, and it suggested, on more than one occasion, that such measures be carried out "with the least fuss possible." Eventually, when the major phenomena of possession were on the wane, the Congregation opted for a position of wise skepticism that opened the way to a cautious, rational evaluation of the phenomena themselves. It also encouraged more meditative, less controversial forms of piety that, despite the explosive appearance of Quietism, were the forms more characteristic of female religious piety during the latter half of the seventeenth century. As the Congregation observed in 1639:

> When after much time no good result is seen from exorcism, the ordinary should not permit further exorcism of the nun . . . and must think that the vision of Demons supposed [by the nuns] is simple opinion or phantasm, from which in any event they can easily liberate themselves by standing in the grace of blessed God and frequenting the sacraments.

Indeed, nuns would do better to seek help not in penitential practices and mortification of the flesh but in what the age called the "holy sweetnesses of Heaven." It is significant, moreover, that the body that had been treated to such fiercely punitive practices was also very much present in devotions to the Virgin Mary and to Christ. The body was present in "affective" devotions to the body of the Virgin, in particular in elements characterizing the Virgin as Mother (the breast, the arms, the mouth); in devotions involving the body of the Infant Jesus, which were particularly popular in Benedictine, Franciscan, and Carmelite convents; in devotions to the body of Christ on the Cross or, more accurately, to the Blessed

Wounds, a sort of sacred dismembering or "pious heraldry," as one scholar dubbed it, much in vogue during the seventeenth century. Such practices tended to sublimate the nuns' human instinct of maternity in the divine maternity of Mary, and to soften mortification of the flesh by contemplation of the Savior's sufferings. The result was a "tender" piety parceled out piecemeal and inevitably accompanied by a large number of prayers and devotional acts—special Rosaries, brief prayers, triduums, and novenas—all carefully tallied and couched in a highly sensual, passional language and images. While her devastating crisis of diabolic possession was taking its course, reaching (with the aid of her new and extraordinary confessor) a mystical crisis that was to have triumphant results, Sister Jeanne des Anges wrote, "Father Surin advised me to do a novena of communions in honor of St. Joseph and promised me he would say nine masses to the same effect." Suffering brought her to a miraculous turning point:

> Then I had the vision of a great cloud around the bed on which I was lying, and on my right I saw my good Angel. He was of a strange beauty, like a young man of about eighteen, with long shining blond tresses that fell on the left shoulder of my confessor. . . . I also saw St. Joseph in the form and figure of a man, with a face more resplendent than the sun and with long hair. . . . I approached and he put a hand on my right side, where the pain has always been most intense. It seems to me that he made an unction on that part of the body, and soon after I felt that I was returning to my outer senses and was completely cured.

"Sensible" devotion—to use a particularly nice contemporary term—seems to be a constant in the religious expressions that were in use in the seventeenth century. Sister Jeanne des Anges described her daily practice of adoration of the sacrament of the Eucharist thus: "The divine presence was at times so sensible to my heart that I remained in rapture before its divine Majesty and my internal senses lacked the strength to support the waves of love that I felt." Still, "sensible" inner devotion was the privilege of few, as were the harshest mortifications of the flesh and the highest and most overwhelming summits of contemplation. Most nuns had to be content with cultivating more accessible, more external "sensible" pious practices. One of these was the devotion to the Sacred Heart, initially—at the very end of the seventeenth century—invested with a strong penitential charge and linked, thanks to the visions of the Visitation sister Marguerite Marie Alacoque, to the mystique of royal power. Able Jesuit writers soon gave devotion to the Sacred Heart a more attractive and familiar *douceur*, which was not the least of the reasons for its lightning-swift success both inside and outside cloistered walls.

"BUT TO GIVE YOU A BETTER GIFT, I SEND YOU A ROSE"

Undeniably, the new post-Tridentine discipline intended the conventual state to cut off ties with the world and, if possible, even family relations, and to destine the nun to a life of renunciation, prayer, and sanctification. In reality, the condition of the voluntary—more often, the forced—recluse frequently heightened her feeling for her family. Such feelings might be bitterly resentful, as in the case of the Venetian nun Arcangela Tarabotti, where they were filtered, as we shall see, through a complex literary structure; or they might be affectionate, as in the case of Sister Maria Celeste Galilei, and expressed colloquially in letters to her great and unhappy father.

When Virginia Galilei became a nun in 1616, taking the name of Sister Maria Celeste, she and her sister Livia (also illegitimate), who took the name of Sister Arcangela, entered the Convent of the Poor Clares of San Matteo d'Arcetri, neither a rigorous order nor a wealthy convent. For the entire decade from 1623 to 1633—at least these are the dates of the letters that have come down to us—Sister Maria Celeste wove a fragile web of relations with the outside world out of her own worries, small daily happenings, modest gifts to her father, her brother Vincenzio, or the children of the family, and concerns for her father's health and for his affairs (concerns that quite naturally intensified during Galileo's trial in Rome and after his condemnation). "Several little fish made of marzipan" sent from the nearby convent would appear on the dining table of Galileo's villa at Bellosguardo, or "a little quince preserve, seasoned with poverty—that is, made with apples," while wine, yarn, and "other loving little things" (*altre amorevolezze*) made their way to San Matteo from Bellosguardo. Little embroidered collars and cuffs, a gift from Sister Maria Celeste to her uncle Michelangelo Galileo for his "little children" (*fanciullini*), were accompanied by an affectionate gift to Maria Celeste's sister-in-law, Sestilia Bocchineri, of a valuable rosary made of agates that she had received from her father some time before. Sister Maria Celeste discreetly suggested that in return a scudo or two might be sent back "for needs"—that is, to pay for the private cell that Maria Celeste, who already suffered from the illness that was to lead her to an early death, hoped to occupy. A musical instrument, a theorbo (*chitarrone*) that Galileo had given his daughters some years before (perhaps less a gift to Arcangela than to Maria Celeste, who taught *canto firmo* to the novices and had daily duties with the choir) was replaced by two new, up-to-date breviaries that included the new saints added to the calendar by recent Counter-Reformation canonizations because the old breviaries, "being instruments that we use every day," were worn thin.

Despite her narrow monastic world, Sister Maria Celeste made ready use of her father's technological knowledge and his extraordinary manual dexterity. A clock (*oriolo*) made its way back and forth between Arcetri and Bellosguardo for repairs. When she asked for its return, Maria Celeste explained that "the sacristan who calls us to Matins is fond of it"; once she had it back, she assured her father that it was working well, its failure "having been my fault, because I put it a bit off kilter." Sister Maria Celeste also turned to her father, with polite timidity, for waxed cloth to cover the frames of the windows in the large cell in which she and the other sisters usually worked: "But first it would please me to know if you [*Ella*, the most polite form of address] would be happy to do me this service. I do not doubt your affection, but because the job is more one for a carpenter than a philosopher I have some trepidation." Her father's health was of particular concern to her: she advised him (probably during Lent in 1626) "not to stay in the orchard until better weather arrives," and during a wave of plague in 1630 she was sufficiently worried about the danger that she sent him two small jars containing a paste made of dried figs, hazelnuts, rue, salt, and honey "proven to be an admirable defense" and a vial of the miraculous waters of Sister Orsola da Pistoia— singular examples of the popular pharmaceutical products that persisted and flourished at the dawn of the new scientific age.

Sister Maria Celeste was also sensitive to more difficult problems of a greater import. She did her best to patch up disagreements between her father and her brother Vincenzio. She worked to improve her community's financial situation, relying on her father's fame to approach the archbishop of Florence and the grand duchess. She was aware of her father's scientific activities, requesting an *occhiale* from him—an instrument that Antonio Favaro thought to be a microscope but that was more likely to have been a spyglass. (This may have been during the very years that the Congregation of Religious prohibited the use of such instruments among nuns.) She also asked to borrow a copy of his *Il saggiatore*. More than anything else, however, Sister Maria Celeste's letters show a mixture of affection and piety. In the dark months of Galileo's second trial, when good news followed bad and it was difficult to know what was happening, she first expressed her faith "in the happy outcome of your transactions, for that is how my wishes and my love have made me foresee them." Later, she spoke happily of the explosion of joy that ran through the convent, where "all were overjoyed on hearing of your fortunate successes." Still later she wrote, stricken by the "sudden and unexpected . . . new travail" of Galileo's condemnation, to advise him, in "full awareness of the fallacy and instability of all things in this terrible world [*mondaccio*]," not to "pay much attention to these squalls, but rather to hope that they will soon be calmed and changed to just as much satisfaction for you."

But Sister Maria Celeste was far from inactive during this time. During her father's trial she kept the keys to the nearby Villa del Gioiello (which Galileo had rented in 1631), and she worked, with the aid of trusted helpers, to remove Galileo's papers so they could not be confiscated. After his condemnation she dreamed ("fabricating castles in the air") of trying to apply for a papal pardon, working, in female style, to approach the pope's sister-in-law through the wife of the Tuscan ambassador in Rome. Once Galileo's condemnation had been read, the most she could do was to accept the obligation that her father had imposed on her of weekly recitation of the seven penitential psalms. She wrote that she hoped that this would help him "in some slight way" and that she was persuaded "that prayer, accompanied by the duty to obey the Holy Church," was efficacious, but also that she prayed "to remove this thought from you." What had happened had left its mark, however, and prudence was called for. Stopping at Siena before his return to the Gioiello, Galileo had begun to write again. Sister Maria Celeste wrote that she was overjoyed that he "found [himself] occupied by things so much to [his] taste as writing," but she added, in a letter written October 8, 1633, "for the love of God, may they not be matters that will have the same fortune as past ones already written."

Sister Maria Celeste died on April 2, 1634, after a short illness. In a famous letter Galileo, who, after his return to the Gioiello, had often taken the road to the convent to visit his daughter, gives us the measure of a very human relationship unchanged by the passing years. Galileo wrote to his friend Elia Diodati:

> I had been staying fairly quietly here, with frequent visits to a nearby convent where two daughters whom I loved very much were nuns—in particular the elder, a woman of exquisite intelligence, singular goodness, and very fond of me. She, by an accumulation of melancholy humors that occurred during my absence, which she found burdensome, finally developed a precipitous dysentery, and within six days she died, being thirty-three years of age, leaving me in extreme affliction.

On his return to the villa from the convent the day before the death of Sister Maria Celeste, Galileo had found an order from Cardinal Francesco Barberini to desist, under pain of imprisonment by the Holy Office, in his request to have the prohibition to set foot in the city of Florence lifted. He may have thought back to a very different letter, sent many years earlier by Sister Maria Celeste on December 19, 1625. It had accompanied the gift of a bit of candied citron that had not turned out as well as she wished, "for [the citron's] being somewhat withered," and two baked pears for Advent. She had added: "But to give you a better gift I send you a rose, which, since it is an extraordinary thing in this season, may be welcome to you."

AN INDICTMENT OF THE RELIGIOUS LIFE
AND THE LOVE OF LETTERS

Sister Maria Celeste's affection for her family and her serene patience stand in strong contrast to an indictment of forced placement in a monastic institution that emerges from the sizable literary production of Sister Arcangela Tarabotti, a Benedictine nun in the Convent of Sant'Anna di Castello in Venice. Her case is an anomaly. By her "political" and lay writings, she does not fit the cliché, repeated in his day by Benedetto Croce, of the seventeenth-century woman of letters as a nun and an author of mystical (or in any event religious) works.

Arcangela Tarabotti came of a good Venetian family. Constrained to take the veil in 1620 in the interests of social strategies that she later attacked forcefully in her writings, she maintained constant relations with the world outside the monastery until her death in 1652. Her acquaintances and contacts included Venetian patricians and French diplomats, but also intellectual libertines, members of the Accademia degli Incogniti such as Girolamo Brusoni and Loredan (Gian Francesco Loredano, to whom she dedicated her *Lettere familiari e di complimento* [1650], a work that testifies amply to her secular interests). One work that stands out among her endeavors is *L'inferno monacale*, which was unpublished during her lifetime but undoubtedly circulated in manuscript and has only recently been published in its entirety.

L'inferno monacale is a work full of biblical quotations that Tarabotti committed to memory while reading her breviary, of reminiscences of Italian literary texts (from Dante to Petrarch, Tasso, and Guarini) and Latin classics, and of a fair number of allusions to libertine literature. Among its other virtues the work places the problem of Tarabotti's culture into the more general framework of the female conventual culture of the age. Tarabotti's cultural background was not the typical baggage of piety; rather it was secular, the culture of an autodidact, more reliant on the compilations of excerpts that were popular among people of middling culture (and in convents, which, for understandable reasons, offered only limited library resources) and on anthologies for school uses or religious and moralistic purposes than on any firsthand acquaintance with primary sources. Nonetheless, her reading allowed Tarabotti to inject a broad variety of scholarly references into a literary production that was aimed—the *Inferno monacale* in particular—at portraying the collective drama of the overwhelming majority of the more than two thousand women whose lot it was, in mid-seventeenth-century Venice, to be cloistered, without a vocation, in the thirty convents of the city, all for the benefit of a state interested in controlling the economic and social interests of the elite. These women, in Tarabotti's words, had been closed "in the belly of a chimerical and foul animal," trapped in a situation "not unlike the infernal abyss," in a "theater in which most baneful tragedies are played" and where trickery had laid out for many "unfortunate women" the bleak meanders of a "perpetual labyrinth."

Sister Arcangela Tarabotti's writings were, as we have seen, an anomaly, unique in the seventeenth century. In a century that preferred a literature "of entertainment," nuns fond of cultivating letters usually produced works of piety or devotional poetry. Among the latter, one voice that stood out from the rest was that of Francesca di Gesù Maria, a Poor Clare, whose exemplary biography (*La vita;* 1660) was written by Andrea Nicoletti. It appeared only a few years after Sister Francesca's own *Pie e divote poesie,* a collection published in 1654, shortly after her death, and reprinted on several occasions. Born Isabella Farnese, the daughter of Mario Farnese, lord of Farnese and Latera, small fiefs near Viterbo, and of Giove, near Terni, she entered the convent of San Lorenzo in Panisperna in Rome as a boarder to be schooled. She became a professed nun in 1609, taking the name of Francesca, and was soon imitated by her sister Vittoria, who took the name of Isabella.

It seems that the two sisters, Sister Francesca in particular, found convent life insufficient to their religious needs. After a period characterized by mortifications and mystical phenomena that led to a serious illness, Sister Francesca left San Lorenzo, and we next find her in 1618 in Farnese, where she founded a new conventual community. Behind the edifying gloss that her biographer, Nicoletti, put on his saintly heroine, in his book and elsewhere we may glimpse family strategy, given that Sister Francesca's father did much to aid the new foundation. For some time, Sister Francesca lived an exemplary hermit's existence in a straw hut built in a remote corner of the convent grounds in Farnese. It seems clear that she tried to propose, against her father's wishes, that the community follow the model of the Carmelites of St. Teresa of Avila. After the original constitution dictated by her father, two other constitutions were proposed, but Francesca refused to discuss them, let alone accept them. This brought her to a period of inner "contradictions" during which, as she related:

> There was in my soul a nearly continuous presence of the most holy Humanity of Jesus Christ, in imaginary fashion, and with so much beauty that I was much in love, but with a most keen, most tender love; therefore I sought a thousand ways to give vent to that sweet and loving torture.

A great many of the "Rime amorose al medesimo Signore" written by Sister Francesca and sung by the community sprang from that "sensible" devotion—a devotion pruned of the sensual images that we have encountered in Sister Jeanne des Anges and that derived ultimately from Franciscan roots.

The definitive constitutions of the monastery were drawn up in 1625. They took inspiration from the rule of the Urbanist Poor Clares (a relatively relaxed rule chartered by Urban IV in 1263), a compromise that Francesca must have found unsatisfactory because even after her election as abbess in 1624 she continued to follow the model of St. Teresa, combining the ideal of solitude and an irrepressible commitment to the active life and monastic reform. Francesca's fame as the "founder" of a convent (which gave her biographer another opportunity to compare her with St. Teresa) and her social status soon took her to Albano (in 1631) to superintend the foundation of a new convent of Poor Clares of strict observance, the Convent of the Conception, under the patronage of Caterina Savelli, princess of Albano and feudal lady of the territory (and a distant relative of Francesca's).

Francesca went next to the nearby town of Palestrina to reform a convent of Urbanist Poor Clares under the protection of Cardinal Barberini. One might theorize that the 1630s were a decade, if not of a generalized program for reform of convents near Rome, at least of an attempt, in which the Roman nobility took an active part, to reorganize a number of Franciscan institutions in the area and put them on a more austere basis. Indeed, Sister Francesca and her birth sister, Sister Isabella, who had come to help her, were responsible not only for such "reform" but also for the rebuilding of the Convent of Santa Maria degli Angioli in Palestrina, a project funded by Barberini munificence and completed in 1642.

When the "family" convent in Farnese was abandoned in 1640, the nuns were temporarily placed in the convents of Albano and Palestrina to await the construction of a large convent in Rome in the Rione Monti, to be dedicated, like the convent in Albano, to the Immaculate Conception. Once again the Barberini family contributed support and funds, along with the Rondinini and Peretti families, a confirmation of the prestige that Sister Francesca enjoyed in Roman high society of the time. The new convent, completed presumably around 1643, became the mother house of the small "reformed" congregation, and it was there that Sister Francesca spent the last eight years of her life—a period of intense activity governing the convent, punctuated by frequent ecstatic experiences and harsh mortifications. The rigidity of such penitential practices was mitigated—for all the sisters as well as for Sister Francesca—by the aid and the liberating effects of song, a matter that deserves fuller reflection in the context, here and elsewhere, of the cloistered life. The constitutions of the Convent of the Immaculate Conception in fact specified that an hour and a half a day were to be devoted to singing the many spiritual songs composed by Francesca, Isabella, and some of the other nuns in the convent.

The central portion of one such song, the "Alma mia giubilo, e festa," sings with warm abandon of the madness of divine love:

Andarò d'amor piagata
Ogn'hor più forte gridando
Giesù mio sempre chiamando
Quasi cerva ars'e assetata
Non più in me, ma trasformata
Nel mio Sposo e mio Fattore
Fatta pazza per amore.

*(I shall go, wounded with love, every
hour loudly crying, Jesus mine! ever
calling out, like a doe, burning with
thirst and my thirst slaked, no more in
me, but transformed into my Spouse
and my Maker, made mad for love.)*

With these lines we enter into the heart of Sister Francesca's *Pie e divote poesie* (called *Poesie sacre* in later editions), a work that still awaits an adequate critical edition. For the most part in the tradition of Lauds and, as we have seen, inspired by the Franciscan devotion to the humanity of Christ, the songs evoke Christ's infancy (as in the fresh "Care sorelle, deh giubiliamo": "Dear sisters, let us exult") or weep for his Passion (as in the intense "Al Monte, anima mia": "To the Mountain, my soul"). Although she followed the traditional models of the Lauds, Sister Francesca added her own note of insistent affectivity that pervaded the serene moments of the nuns' sacramental life and their joyful meditations. There are "Hor che l'anima mia stringe al suo seno" ("Now that my soul clings to his breast") for after communion; "Dolcezza degli Angeli e de' Santi" ("Sweetness of the Angels and of the Saints") and "Vergine dolce e pia" ("Virgin sweet and pious"), for contemplation of the "sweetness" of Jesus and the Virgin Mary; "All'amor tutte, all'amor" ("To love, everyone, to love"), to celebrate the "joy" of the religious state. Some songs contain moments of greater tension, as in one song devoted to seeking the hidden God: "Dove sei, buon Giesù, dove t'ascondi" ("Where are you, good Jesus; where are you hiding?"); others have an impetuous strength: "Quando sarà, Signore" ("When shall it be, Lord?") and one of her finest compositions, "O bellezza divina, in cui mirando" ("O beauty divine, on which gazing"). The last two songs stand in strong contrast to the spiritualized Petrarchism of "Hor che sciolta da cure e da pensieri" ("Now loosed from cares and worries") and from the measured Baroque taste of penitential compositions such as "Per piangere i peccati della vita passata" ("To weep for the sins of past life").

As Benedetto Croce once noted, the fact that the nuns of Francesca's convent added a translation of St. John of the Cross's famous "Noche obscura del alma" to the 1679 edition of Sister Francesca's *Poesie* throws a singular light on both the literary experience and the spiritual experience of this group after Francesca's death, in an intellectual climate so strongly imbued with Quietist currents as the late seventeenth century was. At closer inspection, the Quietist crisis seems indeed to have altered the more archaic and, one might say, traditional schemes of the collection and to have given a special cast to Sister Francesca's life, which we know only from Nicoletti's biography, a work with a message that merges her history with that of the institution, celebrating her as its "founder," and that gives a highly edifying picture of her as "holy nun." There was probably more to her life than that. For one thing, her biographer cleverly avoided discussing the ways in which song sublimated the "sweeping flames of divine love" burning for hours in Sister Francesca with a spiritual tension that reached out toward totalizing and exclusive mystical experiences that she only occasionally realized. For another, the biographer thought not even worth mentioning one striking episode in Francesca's life. On her deathbed Francesca entrusted the supervision of her institution not to the Roman prelates and princes who had made it possible and promoted it but to Father Filippo di Gesù, a Discalced Trinitarian of the Congregation of Spain.

KNOWLEDGE AS TRANSGRESSION

The history we are pursuing is at times predictable; at other times it can be surprising. The scene now shifts from convents in Latium, papal Rome under the Barberinis, and the exploitation of Sister Francesca's passion for reform to New Spain under the Spanish viceroys and the poetic experience of Sister Juana Inés de la Cruz. If Sister Francesca Farnese's life was to some extent an enigma, that of Sister Juana Inés was even more of one. The works of many biographers and scholars—from the first *Life* written by the Jesuit Diego Calleja to the psychological introspections of Ludwig Pfandl (1946) and the more recent historical reconstruction by Octavio Paz (1982)—have examined the life and cultural history of Sister Juana Inés as she straddled a fine line between a cultivated literary practice whose worldly and courtly values were, in principle, prohibited to a nun and an orthodoxy embodied in a bureaucracy of prelates and confessors in the singular social setting of colonial Spain during the second half of the seventeenth century.

Born in 1648 the illegitimate daughter of a well-born Creole woman and a Biscayan knight who soon disappeared from the picture, Inés seems to have been gripped early in life by an extraordinary intellectual curiosity. She was taken in by wealthy maternal relatives in Mexico City at an uncertain date and spent a number of her school years with them. Around 1664 her reputation for learning gained her entry into the splendid and brilliant court of the viceroy's wife, the marchioness of Mancera. Here courtly etiquette (the *galateos de palacio*) with its Platonic but worldly rituals was the basis for Inés's first poems of courtly love. Soon, however, the lack of support from a family of her own and the absence of a dowry opened quite different doors for her—the gates to a convent. She spent a brief time as a novice in the Discalced Carmelite Convent of San José, but its harsh discipline sent her to an order known for its much gentler rule, and in 1669 she took her final vows in the Hieronymite Convent of Santa Paula, taking the name of Juana Inés de la Cruz.

Around 1680, after some years of relative silence, Sister Juana Inés entered into a happier period for nearly a decade, a period that coincided with the tenure as viceroy of the marquess of La Laguna, whose wife, the countess of Parades, offered the nun long years of generous protection. A work entitled *Neptuno Alegórico,* a description of the triumphal arch erected facing the Cathedral of Mexico City in celebration of the entry of the new viceroy—a structure that she called "an Ocean of Colors, a Political Simulacrum"—was the elaborate ticket for Sister Juana Inés's return to the courtly practices that she may indeed never have given up. Nothing in that "Ocean of Colors" was directly political. This singular "hieroglyph," as she called it, used motifs borrowed from Góngora, and in Sister Juana Inés's work his thicket of emblematic and metaphorical allusions mingled with a neo-Platonic hermeticism borrowed from the *Oedipus Aegyptiacus* of the Jesuit Athanasius Kircher (one of her favorite authors). The esoteric key to the triumphal arch was Neptune's descent from Isis, and it aspired to be an archetype of highest knowledge, profane and divine. The compositions written by Sister Juana Inés for the La Lagunas, a body of works that amounted to about one-fourth of her entire poetic output, were in reality labyrinths of conceits. They served as a verbal emblem of an unspoken political relation and, in this particular case, of a privileged means of communication between the convent and the palace of the reigning power.

Much has been written about the relationship between the nun and the countess of Parades and about the loving friendship for a woman called Lysi that Sister Juana Inés manifested in poems written in the terms of the codes of courtly love. There is no doubt that there was a complex bond between these two exceptional women, a bond sublimated by Platonism and conditioned by their very different roles—the vicereine who inspired the nun to write the *auto sacramental* (allegorical play) *El divino Narciso* and who saw to the publication of the first volume of the work, and the cloistered poetess who identified with the goddess Isis, mother, virgin, and the inventor of writing:

> De alto Numen agitada
> La, aunque virgen, preñada
> De conceptos divinos
> Pitonisa doncella
> De Delfos.

> *(Stirred by high Numen [deity],*
> *Pitonisa, maid of Delphos,*
> *although virgin, impregnated*
> *with divine thoughts)*

Sister Juana Inés was also capable of an extremely lucid grasp of the nature of her own contradictory and secret passions:

> Este amoroso tormento . . . que empieza como deseo
> Y acaba en melancolía.

> *(This amorous torment . . . that fills like desire and ends in melancholy)*

Although she read theological and mythological texts avidly, loved music, and displayed a keen curiosity about science and unusual phenomena, and although she lived in a cell that she transformed into a library and a sort of *Wunderkammer* (as we can see from the portraits that we have of her), Sister Juana Inés had a taste for symbolic and emblematic culture that makes her seem to us singularly old-fashioned in the 1680s, her mature years. In a closed society dominated by a fear of the Inquisition and distant from the centers of new philosophic and scientific thought in Europe, her "modernity" was composed more of intellectual intentions reelaborated on the basis of centuries of tradition. They were old schemes rather than new cultural acquisitions. Her world was extraordinarily suggestive, but it was a fragile world that lived by the favor of the Palace and the tacit consent of the church. That world shattered the moment the church sensed a change in the conditions perpetuating that long tolerance. That was precisely what happened when Viceroy La Laguna and his vicereine left New Spain in 1688 and when Juana Inés fell under the lengthening shadow of the rigorist archbishop of Mexico City, Francisco de Agujar y Seijas.

Sister Juana Inés remained active despite such difficulties. Above all, in 1692 she published a longer and more ambitious poem, "Primero sueño," written around 1685, which treated the traditional religious theme of the soul's pilgrimage in an original and to some extent startling manner. Mingling reminiscences of Cicero and Macrobius with the *iter exstaticum* of the ever-present Father Kircher, the work began with an extraordinary image of night as a dark pyramid rising out of the earth:

> Piramidal funesta, de la tierra
> Nacida sombra.

Both allegory and confession, the voyage without apparitions, guide, or revelations was not an ascent toward God but rather a confrontation of individual solitude in face of the universe and a revelation that the supernatural world had vanished. Sister Juana Inés's vision of a non-vision, as has been pointed out, has an extraordinary modernity, particularly in comparison with the many Baroque "visionary" excesses in which the annihilated soul was absorbed into the divine. Although Sister Juana Inés's vision shared that literature's contemplation of the prodigious machinery of the universe and its yearning for knowledge, her poem expresses her desire for free and rational conquest.

As Octavio Paz has persuasively shown, it is dubious, to say the least, that the "Primero sueño" can be taken as an expression of Sister Juana Inés's intellectual crisis or the first step in her "conversion." The fairly sudden change in Sister Juana Inés was instead prompted by a violent attack connected with events surrounding the appearance of the *Carta atenagórica* (1690), a work that she addressed to the bishop of Puebla, Manuel Fernandez de Santa Cruz (who was represented in the work in the guise of a nun, Filotea de la Cruz). At the time, Fernandez was conducting a somewhat murky anti-Jesuit polemic (and of which Sister Juana Inés may have been the unwitting cause) against the pro-Jesuit bishop of Mexico City, Agujar y Seijas. Sister Juana Inés next wrote an imprudent "Respuesta a sor Filotea de la Cruz" in 1691, a work that circulated in manuscript before its posthumous publication in 1700 and that offered an impassioned defense of open intellectual anxiety. Not only did the "Respuesta" effect a break between Sister Juana Inés and her less than enthusiastic protector, Agujar y Seijas; it also broke the delicate equilibrium that had been painstakingly maintained until then. The break could not have been either rapid or painless, however, since it was not until 1694 that Sister Juana Inés wrote a "Petición" to implore pardon for her faults and signed (with her own blood) a final but not wholly explicit protestation of submission. The petition and the declaration of submission did the trick, however, especially when, later in that same year, Sister Juana Inés sent Archbishop Agujar y Seijas all her books and the scientific instruments in her collections, to be sold by him and the proceeds to be distributed to the poor. She kept for herself only three devotional books and some hair shirts.

Sister Juana Inés soon disappeared from the scene. Her death in an epidemic only a few years later, in 1695, spared her a life of exemplary penitence (and perhaps swift posthumous hagiographic immortality); instead, the Baroque exaggerations of her *Fama y obras póshumas* (1700) won her such celebratory titles as the "Mexican Phoenix of Poetry" and the "Tenth Muse." Neither a woman suffering from a neurotic repressed "masculinity," as Pfandl would have it, nor the first feminist in the Americas, as Dorothy Schons considered her to be, nor even the "converted" saint of a later tradition of Catholic studies, Sister Juana Inés, of all the literate nuns of the Baroque age, was perhaps the one who gave the loftiest—and certainly the most tormented—response to a social prohibition that kept her, as a woman and as a nun, from satisfying her unquenchable thirst for knowledge in the same way that her male counterparts could. The finest praise of her came from her first biographer, Calleja. Rather than evoking the presence of God at the dying nun's bedside, as was the custom in the usual edifying literature, he said—and he may not even have been conscious of the extraordinary resonance of his words—"como un fiel amigo estuvo a su lado todo el tiempo, hasta el ultimo aliento, su clara inteligencia" ("like a faithful friend, her clear intelligence remained always by her side until her last breath").

MYSTICISM AND POLITICS IN SEVENTEENTH-CENTURY SPAIN

The nuns of the Baroque age were writers, but they were also capable of following the complex threads of politics from inside their convents. This was the case of the Spanish mystic Sister Maria de Jesús de Agreda, who left more than six hundred letters in a thick file of correspondence with King Philip IV between 1643 and 1665, Spain's terrible years of rebellions, invasions, and military defeats between the fall of Olivares and peace with France.

Born Maria Coronel y Arana in 1602 of parents of the minor nobility in a small town on the borderlands between Old Castile, Navarra, and Aragona, she made up her mind in 1618 to turn the family house—with her parents' consent—into a Discalced Carmelite convent named for the Immaculate Conception and placed under a rule even more severe than St. Teresa's. Her mother and her sister subsequently joined the convent, while two brothers and her father entered the Franciscan order. Taking the name of Maria de Jesús when she took her final vows in 1620, she went through a long period of contemplation on the Carmelite model, frequently interrupted by moments of ecstasy and characterized by even more frequent experiences of the phenomena of being in two places at one time. During such "flights" to Mexico she added to scourging and more usual penitential practices the normally male missionary ministry of preaching in the indigenous language. Her earliest writings seem imbued with a christocentric piety, but after 1627, when she became mother superior of her convent, Maria de Jesús ran it even more firmly after the Teresan model. Following the completion of a new convent building in 1633, her marian ecstasies intensified, to the point of dominating her existence. When in the course of these bouts of ecstasy the Virgin in person implored her to write her biography, Maria de Jesús produced *La Mística Ciudad de Dios,* the first part of which was published in 1681, three other parts following later. The work appeared in French translation in 1695, when Bossuet attacked it with flaming words and it was condemned by the Sorbonne. It was prohibited by Rome for excessive mariology, but thanks to the efforts of the Franciscans, who used the work in their preaching on the Immaculate Conception, it continued to be a best-seller throughout the eighteenth century.

Maria counted a number of important persons among her acquaintances, and her fame had become so great that in 1643 Philip IV, who had taken personal command of the government after the fall of Olivares, stopped at Agreda to meet her on his way to Saragosa at the head of a military expedition to halt the French invasion that was spreading through Catalonia. This meeting was the start of the epistolary colloquium between Maria and her sovereign, an exchange that involved both spiritual and political guidance and that was to continue for twenty-two years. One singular aspect of their correspondence was its "synoptic" structure: the nun's responses were put on the same sheet as the royal missives, written in the wide margin that Philip had deliberately left blank, in the Spanish fashion.

Maria's first suggestions to the king in the difficult period "after Olivares," when all of the *válido*'s kin save a nephew, Luis de Haro, were swept out of office, counseled prudence and vigilance. During the course of the year 1644, a year that brought modest Spanish victories and the death of Queen Isabel, Philip found time to read *La Mística Ciudad de Dios* in a manuscript copy that Maria had sent him, and he acquiesced to her explicit request that he encourage the church in Rome to put forth a solemn declaration in favor of the Immaculate Conception, a topic that took up a considerable amount of space throughout their correspondence. From the first exchanges in their relationship, however, a problem arises for us. Since Maria seemed so well informed not only about military events but also about the workings of the Spanish system of government and the relative importance of its various parts, had she been influenced politically, consciously or unconsciously? One thing is certain: beginning in 1635, Maria was in communication with Francisco de Borja, whose uncle Fernando had ambitions to succeed Olivares. She continued to display a loyalty toward the Borja clan, to oppose the king's confidence in Luis de Haro and work against de Haro's political ascent, and to urge the king to take the reins of government into his own hands, if necessary surrounding himself with wise counselors but avoiding the hampering presence of an omnipotent minister. Her reasons for sympathizing with, if not participating in, the conspiracy of the duke of Hijar (1648) to stir up a revolt among Andalusian nobles are less clear. Perhaps Maria's willingness to give heed to an aristocratic rebellion based in a tradition of Aragonese autonomy (feelings that she later freely admitted to Philip IV) was another form of opposition to the centralizing and pro-Castilian politics of de Haro and an attempt to bring the sovereign back to what she considered his more direct responsibilities.

Their correspondence reached its dramatic height in October 1646, when the death of Prince Baltasar Carlos left Spain with no heir to the throne, and when the military situation in Flanders and in Italy seemed to be taking a turn for the worse. After the king had paid another visit to Agreda, Maria spoke to him through the mouth of the dead prince, an "emissary of God" whom she had heard in a vision. In a number of letters written during the year 1647 she insisted on her role as "confessor," a role in which she was able to assuage some of the sovereign's grief over the loss of his heir and some of his worries about the political situation. She remained powerless to counter de Haro's growing influence or to bring the sovereign back to what she viewed as his duties. It is highly probable that persons or groups hostile to Maria attempted to take advantage of this state of affairs to destroy the prestige that, in spite of all, she continued to enjoy with the rather weak king. In a letter dated August 20, 1649, Maria alluded indirectly to dangers threatening her, declared that she had burned papers in her possession, and begged the king not to show to anyone papers of hers in his possession (probably a reference to the *Mística Ciudad de Dios*). Thanks to efficacious mediation on Philip's part, no penalties were inflicted either on the nun herself, interrogated by the Inquisition in March 1650, or on her work, though it was scrutinized with severity.

Around the mid-1650s, the situation turned bleak again. Fears concerning the perils threatening the crown and a denunciation of the blindness of the world that Maria had expressed in a letter to Borja in January 1656 were focused, on Assumption Day (August 15) of that year, in an apocalyptical vision in which it is difficult to disentangle her exhortation to Christian princes to make peace from a warning not to compromise with heretics. There were, in fact, secret negotiations in course between Spain and France (which failed, at least for the moment) of which Maria must have had some sort of word. In her role as the spokesperson of an irreversible political crisis, Maria echoed sentiments that had profound roots in Spain. Because they emerged from within the confines of the cloister, her thoughts were amplified; they seemed to reflect the opinions of sizable groups of people (political, military, diplomatic, and ecclesiastical) who obstinately refused to see as a victor the French enemy who had humiliated Habsburg power by compromising with Protestant "heretics" at the Peace of Westphalia. The history of Maria's disappointments seemed to be repeating itself, but soon, converted to arguments in favor of peace, she took on a new role at the center of a political and diplomatic circle and corresponded not only with the king and with Borja but also with de Haro.

Luis de Haro's sudden death led Maria to urge the king, once again, to assume direct command of the state. An important letter of November 25, 1661, which denounced the capriciousness and the corruption of the judicial system and painted a gloomy picture of heavy taxes, poverty, and depopulation, and the continuing devaluation of the money probably had some influence on a series of royal pragmatics enacted shortly after in an attempt to reorganize the sectors of Spanish society that needed it most. The kingdom was still adrift, however. The Spanish armies suffered continual defeats at the hands of the English and the Portuguese (1663–64); the court was split by quarrels between the "French" party and a "German" party headed by the new queen, the youthful Mariana of Austria; dynastic succession reposed insecurely in a weak and sickly child, the future Charles II. The best that Maria could do was to entrust the sovereign's fate into the hands of divine grace, which she did in her last letter (March 27, 1665). Her death on May 24 of that year came only a few months before "her" king was lowered into his solemn tomb at the Escorial on September 18.

"UN GRAND ET VASTE PAYS, PLEIN DE MONTAGNES [ET] DE VALLÉES"

The strong missionary spirit that was expressed only on the level of desire in the case of Maria de Jesús de Agreda became actual works with the Ursuline sister Marie de l'Incarnation. She lived a singular life. Born Marie Guyart in Tours in 1599, the daughter of a family of well-off bakers, she was given a good education, and at a very young age she married a master silk-worker, Claude Martin, with whom she had a son, Claude, but who left her a widow in 1619. In this period of Marie's life, economic difficulties mingled with her first visions and her relations with the Reformed Cistercian monks of the Abbey of Feuillans, near Tours. She divided her time between embroidery, care of the sick, and, at the suggestion of her spiritual adviser, reading the *Introduction à la vie dévote* of

St. Francis de Sales and the works of St. Teresa of Avila. In the five years or so from 1625 to 1631 she became a successful businesswoman who ran the largest transport company in Touraine, a task turned over to her by her sister, also named Claude, and her brother-in-law, Claude's husband, Paul Buisson, a man who was nearly illiterate.

Further mystical experiences (which were studied some time ago by Henri Brémond) now alternated with the sagacious direction of a shipping business that operated not only over the roads and along the waterways of France but beyond, on the Atlantic to the New World, in the wake of French colonization in the age of Richelieu. In a suggestive mixture of violent asceticism and active involvement, Marie moved between two worlds, between penitence and work, pious meditations and letters of exchange. Her obvious competence and the network of relations that she established during those years were no obstacle to her vocation. They were even a stimulus to her decision in 1631 to join the Ursulines who, like the Cistercians of the Abbey of Feuillans, had recently settled in Tours. She placed the upbringing of her son into the hands of the Jesuits, and after two years of novitiate took her final vows in 1633, choosing the name Marie de l'Incarnation. Her spiritual guidance was entrusted to two Jesuit confessors, Father De La Haye and Father Dinet, under whose direction she wrote the *Entretiens spirituels, ou, Relations d'oraison,* parts of which were later published by her son Claude.

Between 1633 and 1635 Marie reached inner peace, according to the hagiographic reconstruction of her life, but the vision of "un grand et vaste pays, plein de montagnes [et] de vallées" ("a great and vast land, full of mountains and valleys") where her true vocation was to be found (and which Father Dinet identified as Canada) seemed to open awesome new perspectives to Marie, at the time director of novices. Underlying Marie's vision there undoubtedly lay France's efforts to colonize the New World and the Jesuit propaganda in support of that policy. In an atmosphere of interest and, in many ways, profound excitement, Marie finally crossed the Atlantic in 1639, accompanied by two other Ursulines and three sisters Hospitallers, in a voyage made possible by the support of the Jesuits, the Compagnie des Cent Associés (which held the monopoly of the fur trade in the French colonies of the New World and supervised its colonization), and such court personages as the duchess of Aiguillon, Richelieu's niece, and even the queen, Anne of Austria, with whom Marie remained in correspondence.

In the years that followed, the small mission gradually increased in numbers thanks to recruits from France, while Marie gave herself over to working among the women and girls of both French families and Native American families (Algonquins, for the most part). She sent many letters (some six hundred) to her son, her family, and friends between 1639 and

1672, which her son published, in a first edition, in 1677. Her letters, together with the Jesuits' reports, are documents of exceptional interest, not only for Marie's missionary activities in Quebec but also for information on the early stages of the economic, social, and political life of the region, long subjected to the danger of attack from the Iroquois and the target of an aggressive English colonial policy. Although Marie always had urgent practical responsibilities as mother superior and book-keeper—duties that she handled with the same dispatch that she had displayed when she ran the family transport business—she not only drew up special constitutions for the Ursulines of Quebec (1645) but ceased only at her death her intense activity as a "missionary" writer. Aside from her letters, she wrote a second autobiography (1653–54), and later, after she had learned the local languages, she produced a Huron catechism and three Algonquin catechisms (1662), an Algonquin dictionary (1667), a compendium of sacred history in Algonquin, and an Iroquois dictionary and catechism (1668), unfortunately all lost.

During the last decade of Marie's life the Compagnie des Cent Asso-ciés gave up its control of the North American territories and the colony passed under the direct control of the crown of France under Louis XIV. As the population increased, and in particular as young women began arriving from the homeland, encouraged to migrate by matrimonial poli-cies backed by the crown, Marie's problems grew: there were many young French women that the Ursulines were expected to educate or to take in (under a variety of titles) until they made more permanent arrangements. There were also, and above all, young Indian girls to be gallicized and christianized, and Marie and the other sisters soon learned from the "suc-cesses" of the Jesuit missions that the wiser course dictated adaptation to local cultures.

With France far away, Marie's life came to merge increasingly with the life of her new homeland. This was true even on the linguistic level, and her son Claude, now a learned Benedictine intent on erecting a monu-ment to his mother's memory by publishing her letters, was constrained by a France under the sway of the Académie to "correct" his mother's "Canadian" French. Marie's last letter was to her son. In it she described a rare celestial phenomenon, a perihelion (the moment when a planet reaches its position closest to the sun) that had occurred the previous spring. Many others of the letters she wrote contain descriptions of the "wonders" of the "young" land in terms that indulged in a taste for natu-ral and scientific phenomena perhaps borrowed from the Jesuits. Still, the way in which Marie was described by Bossuet and Fénelon—the great adversaries in the age of the "twilight of the mystics" in late seventeenth-century France (in agreement for once)—was perhaps more consonant with her work. In the "Teresa of our day and of the New World" an old experience had been joined to a new, as yet unconquered, reality in a land in which infinite mystical spaces and immense natural landscapes accompanied both the personal adventure of the Ursuline from Tours and French political and commercial hegemony.

"TOUT LE RESTE N'EST RIEN"

In 1622 Sister Virginia Maria de Leyva, the "nun of Monza," watched the demolition of the wall that had blocked the door to her cell, a room three *braccia* wide and five long in the Convent of the Convertite di Santa Valeria in Milan in which she had lived as a recluse for fifteen years, receiving the meager fare allowed to her through a small aperture that also let in a beam of light for reading the liturgy. She had been subjected to this harsh confinement in punishment for her criminal relation with Gian Paolo Osio. We know that Sister Virginia did not interrupt her life of penitence at this alleviation of her confinement because we have an edifying life of the nun sketched out (but never completed or published) by Cardinal Federico Borromeo, a man who not only had been personally involved in her discipline but also was acutely sensitive to the female conventual condition in general. Giuseppe Ripamonti described the same Sister Virginia, a few years before her death in 1650, as "an old woman, bent, emaciated, thin, venerable: to see her it was hard to think that once she could have been beautiful and brazen."

I have no intention of repeating here the entire story of the "nun of Monza." This tale of a young woman forced to enter a convent and the tragic outcome of her transgression of conventual discipline became literature thanks to Alessandro Manzoni, and later biographers and novelists have continued to find her story fascinating. What matters here is to emphasize that although her punishment was harsh, it was not unusual in terms of the disciplinary measures of the age. The decisions of the Congregation of Religious record many similar cases. For example, at nearly the same time as Sister Virginia's release from her confinement, the Congregation permitted a nun in Pistoia to leave the locked cell in which she had been imprisoned for twenty-nine years "for a sin of fragility," and some years later, in 1661, the singular existence of Sister Benedetta Carlini came to an end after thirty-five years of harsh incarceration. The abbess of the Convent of La Madre di Dio in Pescia (and the subject of a recent study), Benedetta had been accused of sexual transgression (lesbianism), but above all of reiterated transgression of the convent's statutes by her claims to miraculous favors and by her notoriety.

We catch only a glimpse of these seventeenth-century nuns as they appear in the pages of the trial records, with their personal histories swallowed up by the somberness of their sentences or by the anonymity of

a long incarceration. They were women first sacrificed to family patri-
monial strategies and then guilty of an irrepressible thirst for terrestrial
love, like Sister Virginia Maria, or, like Sister Benedetta, of an overween-
ing need for an autonomous psychological space. Their stories enriched
the myth, outside the convent, of the nun as perverse, corrupt, or, at best,
unhappy—a myth that the time-honored tradition of the novella absorbed into contemporary libertine literature, along with adventurous or
scandalous stories of ribald defrocked friars, and that later made its way
into the serial romance. But it was precisely that myth, stripped of all
"loose" or unhealthy connotations, that gave rise, in the late 1660s, to a
truly extraordinary literary case that was to intrigue critics and scholars
for three centuries. Rather than turning a religious figure from real life
into an artistic creation, as Manzoni did later with the lady of Monza, it
made fiction credible as history.

La Fontaine wrote in *Les amours de Psyché*, "Aimez, aimez: tout le
reste n'est rien" ("Love! Love! All the rest is naught"); Molière has a character in *Monsieur de Pourceaugnac* exclaim:

> Aimons-nous donc d'une ardeur éternelle.
> Quand deux coeurs s'aiment bien,
> Tout le reste n'est rien.
>
> *(Let us then love one another with an eternal ardor.
> When two hearts love truly, all the rest is naught.)*

Both works appeared in 1669, and the identical utterances make it unlikely that pure coincidence was involved. Indeed, it is highly probable
that both La Fontaine and Molière intended a sly allusion to a text that
both they and their readers had held in hand and that was enjoying an
immense success in the *salons* and in the conversation of *précieux* and
précieuses.

The preceding January the pliant Parisian printer-publisher Claude
Barbin, who sold *romans à clé*, satires, and pamphlets from his stall in
the Palais de Justice, had published *Les lettres portugaises traduites en
françois*. Portugal was fashionable in France at the time, as Spain was to
be among nineteenth-century French writers and artists, not so much out
of a taste for the exotic as because of the war that the French armies had
conducted on the Iberian Peninsula, which had ended in 1668 and had
resulted in Portugal's independence from Spain. This slim brochure was
made up of five letters purportedly written by a Portuguese nun to her
lover, a French officer who had been stationed in Portugal and had returned to France. The letters were a burning appeal that met with no
response; an uninterrupted and passionate monologue moving from surprise at the initial separation to the nun's full awareness that she had been

abandoned. Our sentence comes from the very first letter, which contains the muted cry, "Vous ne trouverez jamais tant d'amour, et tout le reste n'est rien" ("You will never find greater love, and all the rest is naught")—words that, between the anonymous author of the *Lettres,* La Fontaine, and Molière, provide the ideal cipher for an extraordinary moment in French civilization in the *Grand Siècle.*

For our purposes it is unimportant (though it is a question that enters into the continued critical success of this slim work) whether or not the nun, Mariane, can be identified as Sister Mariana Alcoforado, a woman who really lived during those years in the royal convent of the Poor Clares of Nossa Senhora da Conceição of Beja. Nor is it important here whether or not the officer in this love story was the marquess of Chamilly, who appears as an old man in Saint-Simon's *Mémoires.* Various candidates have been suggested as the anonymous author of this work, among them a modest barrister in the Parlement de Paris named Subligny, who was later involved in a polemical exchange between Molière and Racine; even Racine himself, at the time a young man seeking his way (a candidature based on Mariane's supposed resemblance to Racine's heroines); and, as recent studies persuasively argue, Gabriel-Joseph de Lavergne, count of Guilleragues, a noble "de la robe" who later had a distinguished public career and who frequented the *salons* of Mme de La Sablière and Mme de Sablé. Whoever the anonymous author was, what matters is that the five letters that make up the *Lettres portugaises* responded to five questions about love that were debated in the *salon* of Mme de Sablé. The analysis of passion in the letters moves through a gradual loss of all illusions toward a culmination in the last letter, which ends steeped in an utter pessimism in which love is portrayed as a sickness to be torn from the heart. If in the fictional literary work the "nocturnal" silence of a cell in a Portuguese convent had been unexpectedly flooded by the brilliant conversation of a Parisian *salon,* in real life Mme de Sablé, who for some years had retired from time to time to the Abbey of Port-Royal, in the end renounced society to move in the opposite direction, forsaking conversation for silence.

REBELLION AND OBEDIENCE AMONG JESUITS AND JANSENISTS

Witchcraft had been a rural phenomenon, and it had reached its height between the late sixteenth century and the early years of the seventeenth century. Diabolic possession, on the other hand, was widespread in the cities of France under the regency of Maria de' Medici and under Richelieu in a singular, though not surprising, connection between possession and an upsurge of mystical phenomena. Sister Jeanne des Anges expressed both these movements, first as the protagonist of the possessions of Loudun, and later as a mystic and visionary in the same convent. The Loudun episode occurred immediately after a terrible wave of the plague in 1632 that had decimated the city population but left the convent of the Ursulines untouched behind its cloistered walls. The first apparitions of phantasms began in September. They appeared to the prioress, Jeanne des Anges, first, then to another nun, as a vague male form. In October they took the semblance of Urbain Grandier, the parish priest of the church of Saint-Pierre du Marché, a man who had given generously of himself during the epidemic and who was to become the unfortunate "guilty party" of the entire episode.

That the odor of a bouquet of musk roses was what set off the diabolical possessions in the convent is a detail worth noting, as it recalls the importance of the olfactory sense during the seventeenth century. Smells ranging from the odor of sanctity that emanated from the body of a pious nun who had just died to the sulphurous stench that unequivocally signified a diabolical presence were prominent in these and similar experiences. Grandier, accused of being the source of the evil influence, appealed to the bishop of Poitiers and to the Parlement de Paris, but the demoniacal crisis among the Ursulines spread. The exorcists and physicians who spelled one another to try their remedies judged that a few nuns were merely obsessed. Then nine more became possessed, and the contagion spread, with increasingly spectacular manifestations, from the cell of Sister Jeanne des Anges to the convent chapel, then to the parish churches and to the public squares, where it resembled a gigantic Counter-Reformation spectacle. The excitement reached its height in the spring of 1634, when experienced Capuchin exorcists worked more and more feverishly to unmask the Evil One and to guarantee the definitive triumph of the faith in Loudun, a *place de sûreté* whose population was divided between Huguenots and Catholics.

Cases of possession were not new among the Ursulines. The order, of relatively recent foundation, was still hesitating between contemplation and activism, and the sisters showed no great inclination for the rigors of a newly imposed enclosure. Analogous phenomena had occurred among the Ursulines in the preceding decades in Aix-en-Provence (1611–13), and in Pontoise and Paris (1621–22). What was new in Loudon was the violence, the extent, and the long duration of the episodes. It has rightly been remarked that the phenomenon of possession (not only at Loudun) was an expression of rebellion on the part of aggressive and forceful women in an age in which there were women rulers, reformers, mystics, and writers. In the case of the Ursulines, possession affected women who had been educated and were themselves educators. The phenomenon was to create a split between men of the church and men of science. It led the churchmen, in a time of a crisis of certainty, to redouble their efforts to combat unbelief and atheism; it permitted the men of science a glimpse of a path (one beset with difficulties, however) toward doubt, as we can see from their increasingly deliberate attempts to connect the symptoms of possession with natural causes.

Although such "scientific" positions opened the way for the marginalization and, ultimately, the disappearance of the phenomenon of possessions, it may be more interesting for our purposes to follow the Jesuits' operation, through Father Surin, to co-opt mystical anguish and transfer it to the context of the popular mission.

Father Surin, who would later pay a personal price for his relations with Sister Jeanne des Anges in the form of a neurotic obsession, arrived in Loudun in December 1634. He was the one who encouraged the shift (rather, the metamorphosis) of Sister Jeanne from a woman possessed to a witness to the miracles of God, an inspired oracle, and a spiritual guide. During her long and triumphal tour through northern France in 1637, such august personages as King Louis XIII, his queen, Anne of Austria, and Cardinal Richelieu paid homage to her hand, on which the departing demons had traced the holy names of Joseph, Mary, Jesus, and St. Francis de Sales, and to a shift that St. Joseph had coated with an unction that had cured Sister Jeanne of a serious illness. This trip marked the start of a new atmosphere among the Ursulines that brought them into closer relations with the power structure and established their role in seventeenth-century French society regarding the education of girls, in Paris and the provinces but also in the missions of Marie de l'Incarnation in the New World.

The rebellion of the nuns of Port-Royal thirty years later had a quite different effect, since it served as a focal point for the history of French Jansenism. The Cistercian Abbey of Port-Royal des Champs, where enclosure had been reestablished in 1609 through the efforts of Mother Angélique Arnauld, sister of the "Great Arnauld," was located in a damp and unhealthy spot that the community abandoned in 1625 for the more comfortable, though still austere, Paris branch of the order. Later, in 1648, when drainage projects and other works had been completed, the better part of the group returned to Port-Royal des Champs. The Parisian period was marked by the community's relations with Saint-Cyran, who became its spiritual director in 1636, a position that he continued to fill until his death in 1643, and with the "Solitaries" (*solitaires*), a group of learned laymen and clerics who followed the community when it returned to Port-Royal des Champs and whose fate was to be intertwined with that of the abbey when the Jansenist crisis exploded.

As is known, the Abbey of Port-Royal's involvement in the history of Jansenism came to a head with Rome's condemnation (in 1653) of five statements of doctrine taken from Jansenius's *Augustinus*. After Arnauld made his famous distinction between questions of law and questions of fact—that is, his insistence that the propositions, although deserving of condemnation, were not to be found in the *Augustinus*—the resulting polemics were aggravated when the nuns were required to sign a formal acceptance of the condemnation, a move that transformed what had already been a serious problem of ecclesiastic discipline into an enormous problem of conscience. The nuns' refusal to sign the formula became a symbol of resistance, then and after, for the entire Jansenist movement. It eventually transcended the affair itself and was transformed into an appeal, renewed on several occasions, for individual responsibility in religious matters in face of a hierarchic and authoritarian church and an intolerant and repressive political power.

The conflict, only momentarily mitigated by a compromise in 1661, was rekindled in 1664 when, during a dramatic visit to the convent, the archbishop of Paris, Hardouin de Péréfixe, demanded that the nuns sign the formula, an event immortalized in literature as early as Jean Racine's nearly contemporaneous *Abrégé de l'histoire de Port-Royal* and later by Sainte-Beuve in the nineteenth century and in a play by Henri de Montherlant in our own century (1954). When anti-Jansensist hostilities revived, after a decade of relative calm from 1669 to 1679, Port-Royal seemed doomed to slow extinction. The intractable nuns were dispersed, the abbey was prohibited from accepting new professions, and the nuns who had lived through the abbey's highest moments of protest—among them the second Mother Angélique, niece of the first Mother Angélique and who lived until 1684—disappeared one by one, along with such protagonists of the conflict as Arnauld and Pierre Nicole. Jean Racine, the man who, with Pascal, had perhaps best understood the tragic grandeur of Port-Royal, died in 1699. Two years earlier, almost as a last testimony to forty years of struggle, Racine had secretly written his famous *Abrégé*, and his last wishes were to be buried within the confines of the beloved abbey that had always figured, like an indelible watermark, in the fabric of a lifetime of triumphs in the literary world and the court.

Barely ten years later, Port-Royal was again a target of attack in the "Jesuitical" climate of the last years of the reign of Louis XIV, when the Sun King mercilessly wiped out what was regarded as a symbol of obstinate dissent. But the myth of Port-Royal sprang from the ruins of the abbey, relaunched in the post-revolutionary years with unmitigated enthusiasm by Abbé Grégoire as a remembered place of suffering and a call to religious meditation. Beyond the myth, however, it is more appropriate to our interests to return to the image of Port-Royal des Champs and the protagonists of its history as they appeared to their contemporaries of the mid-seventeenth century—that is, in the paintings of Philippe de Champaigne and in the verse of the very young Racine. The limpid but firm gaze of Mother Angélique shines out of her portrait by Philippe, now in the Musée de Chantilly, while the religious atmosphere of Port-Royal shows through in every line and muted highlight of the admirable painting *La mère Agnès et la soeur Catherine de Sainte-Suzanne,* now in the Louvre, a sort of grandiose ex voto that Philippe painted in thanks for the miraculous recovery from illness of his daughter, who was a nun at the Abbey. Racine's evocation of the "holy home of silence" (*saints demeures du silence*) in the second of the seven odes in *Le Paysage, ou, Promenades de Port-Royal,* presumably written around 1657 or 1658, breaks suddenly into high color and music in a refined idyll celebrating the innocent nature of the surrounding countryside. In its darker notes it hints at the power of his mature work:

> Je vois ce sacré Santuaire,
> Ce grand temple, ce saint séjour,
> Où Jésus encore chaque jour
> S'immole pour nous à son Père.
> . . . .
> Je vois ce cloître vénérable,
> Ces beaux lieux du Ciel bien-aimés,
> Qui de cent temples animés
> Cachent la richesse adorable.
> . . . .
> C'est là que mille anges mortels,
> D'une éternelle plainte,
> Gémissent aux pieds des autels.
>
> *(I see that holy sanctuary, that great temple,*
> *that saintly place where Jesus, still, every*
> *day, immolates himself for us in his Father. I*
> *see that venerable cloister, those lovely*
> *places well loved by Heaven, which conceal*
> *the adorable riches of a hundred animated*
> *temples. That is where a thousand mortal*
> *angels, with an eternal cry, moan at the foot*
> *of the altars.)*

DESTRUCTION OF THE BODY AND SOUL'S SALVATION IN THE LATE SEVENTEENTH CENTURY

Chronologically, St. Teresa of Avila belongs to the sixteenth century, but her influence over female conventual spirituality (among other areas) in the seventeenth century was such that anyone retracing the vicissitudes of Baroque mysticism cannot omit at least some mention of the inner experience that she transmitted to her immensely popular writings. Space is lacking here for an adequate review of her influence; the best we can do is note that she provided the most complex and elevated form of conventual experience with an indication of ways to lose the self in the infinite remoteness of divinity. The century teemed with forms of "true" and "false" sanctity, with "living saints" and visionary nuns—cases that were filtered, scrutinized, and at times "authenticated" (a process to which St. Teresa herself was subjected) by the ecclesiastical authorities. In solitude and humiliation of the flesh, in the "exile" that neither intense devotions nor the written words of the breviary or edifying reading matter could remedy, there emerged, forcefully but always painfully—in mystical "suffering"—a radical need in which the space of individual experiences was blotted out in the void of an ineffable absence. As the blessed Maria Maddalena Martinengo wrote, addressing her own soul, it was a leap "into the profound abyss of your nothingness." Such experiences varied greatly in degree and kind, but they appeared continually throughout the seventeenth century. Conventual biographies and autobiographies, which multiplied as the century advanced, sought more and more consciously to fit the characteristics of the cloistered nun into a body of traditional doctrine, adapting to the aristocratic, or at least upper-bourgeois natures of the young women who peopled the convents a patrimony constructed by the fathers of the church and the female mystics of the Middle Ages, by cultivated ecclesiastics and more recent spiritual guides. The "portraits" of one nun or another that emerged from convent chronicles, edifying narratives, or more directly from autobiographies were reappropriated from older models, as has been noted regarding Sister Maria Crocifissa Tomasi. These works were also, and above all, successful attempts to use the interaction between past and present to "construct" a legitimation for behaviors and values that were all the more exemplary for showing how spirituality, experienced in an institutional setting, could be linked with the prerogatives of illustrious birth.

It is within that context that I would like to examine some of the mystical experiences of the later Baroque age. It seems to me, in fact, that between the seventeenth and the eighteenth centuries, when the long crisis of the Counter-Reformation began to be resolved, opening the way to new spiritual horizons, there were ancient themes and long-standing tensions, aggravated in the post-Tridentine age by the narrow confines of the cloister, that were seen in a clearer light and that burst forth to give witness to their difficult transformation. If, on the one hand, we can see signs of ongoing change, on the other we can still perceive the sum of attitudes that inspired the inner life of generations of female religious from the late sixteenth century to Quietism. This was true (among many others) of the nearly contemporaneous cases—comparable yet dissimilar—of St. Veronica Giuliani and the blessed Maria Maddalena Martinengo.

Visions, mystical marriage (1694 and 1697), transfixion (1696), and the stigmata (1697, 1699, 1703, 1726) marked the spiritual career of St. Veronica Giuliani. A nun in the Capuchin convent in Città di Castello from 1676, Veronica was entrusted to the firm direction of her confessors, the Oratorians Girolamo Bastianelli and Ubaldo Antonio Cappelletti, and to the supervision of the local ordinaries, Bishops Luca Antonio Eustachi and Alessandro Codebò, thanks to whom we have the forty-two thick volumes of Veronica's *Diario* (1693–1727) and other scattered writings. The incisive style of one of the latter, a piece prepared for Monsignor Eustachi in 1700, gives a clear notion of her "suffering" of Christ's Passion, the basis of her mysticism. It was a mysticism patterned on the experience of St. Francis of Assisi and, in particular, on the experiences of St. Teresa and St. Maria Maddalena de' Pazzi—that is, a mysticism in the Franciscan, especially the Carmelite, model. Her "suffering" was unremitting. Veronica felt it as a tireless fury driving her toward evermore severe penance. The convent orchard was often the scene of such experiences: "I felt such a yearning," she wrote, "that not even at night could I take rest. I went into the orchard at night, when it was snowing hard, and I remained there suffering for some time. But to what purpose? Suffering invited more suffering."

Following the classical schemes of ascetic and mystical experience, Veronica's diabolical temptations, for the most part nocturnal, continued obsessively for years, as did liberation from them by mortification—a liberation that Veronica definitively achieved some time between 1696 and 1697. She began to be freed from tension and bewilderment on the feast of St. John the Apostle, December 27, 1694, when she had a reassuring vision of Jesus's favorite disciple resting his head on the heart of his divine master. "At that very point," she noted in her *Diario*, "it seemed to me that my soul was also yearning to go take its rest in that Heart. In a twinkling rapture ensued." The same vision had appeared on December 27, 1673, to the sister of the Visitation Marguerite Marie Alacoque in the convent of Paray-le-Monial, when it inspired the new devotion to the Sacred Heart of Jesus. If not the result of direct knowledge of that episode (which is probable, given that Jesuit propaganda immediately publicized the event), Veronica Giuliani's experience gave proof of a devout and "visionary" substratum that was by then common to all Europe of the late seventeenth century.

Although Veronica was eager to describe the "harmony" she now began to feel in her heart, the Lord still eluded her. She expressed her desire to become one with God in 1694, before her first experience of mystical marriage, in the "Lungo lamento al fuggitivo Signore," whose warmth and transparency make it one of the finest passages in the *Diario*. Her act of dedication to Jesus, written in blood (another detail that she shared with Alacoque), and the "contempt, humiliations, and sufferings" that she directed toward her body by pinching herself with hot pincers or wearing her "embroidered" shift sewn with thorns seemed from that date on relieved by the vision of the Infant Jesus "all in splendor and as a living creature," a legacy from the Franciscan emotional tradition and the Carmelites' strong sense of the mystery of the Incarnation. The Infant Jesus appeared to her in a vision at Christmas 1696, when her heart was transfixed by an arrow of love, following the model of St. Teresa; and the following year, in another vision, the Holy Child gave her the "kiss of peace." The latter figures in a mystical tradition running from St. Catherine of Genoa to St. Francis de Sales, whom Veronica—who was not without education, as some exegetes have suggested—must have known, along with Ruysbroek, St. Catherine of Siena, St. Teresa, and St. John of the Cross. Later in 1697, in a vision of Christ crucified contemplated "amid pain and love," her body received the stigmata from "five rays like fire" that issued forth from the wounds of the Redeemer.

In 1697 mystical experiences came in rapid succession. Christ appeared to her in a vision to offer her his Sacred Heart, announcing, "Love itself to comfort love"; next came a second mystical marriage (after the first in 1694) and another experience of the stigmata. These experiences culminated in an ineffable experience of annihilation in God. The path to this complete union (which Veronica figures, still following St. Teresa, as an "inner castle") still did not lead her into the abyss of Quietude. Veronica's intelligence, either thanks to her very personal way of actively reliving her experience of the divine or because of the alert presence and assiduous guidance of her spiritual directors, always remained alive, even when she was filled with a sense of "how much profit it was to the soul to penetrate truly this nothingness of ours, this annihilation." Even when maddened by love, she seems to have continued to "have light" about herself. As she wrote to Monsignor Eustachi:

> Amid the cognition of nothingness and amid the infinite love I clearly discerned that the true path of love was holy humility. This I asked of God with all my heart. He gave me the condition of my nothingness and I perceived that I could do nothing. And with that light of nothingness one comes to walk by the path of humility, which is the road that makes it possible to find true love of God. In fact, it seemed to me that love was the road to humility and humility the road to love.

Thus a new way of thinking opened up for Veronica. She spent the last twenty years of her life absorbed in an ongoing ascetic experience increasingly focused on a dramatic sense of expiation for the souls in Purgatory, nonbelievers, and warring Christian princes, and, more generally, for the church and Christianity, an experience often expressed in the somber tones of suffering and couched in apocalyptical language. Moreover, it was those pursuits that placed Veronica Giuliani within the larger coordinates of the "ecclesiastical" model of the humble and holy nun and the political and religious values proposed by the Roman Catholic Church in the period from the mid-eighteenth century to the mid-nineteenth century, when the church was beset by the growing secularization of society and by the trauma of revolutions. Proof of this can be seen in the introduction of canonization proceedings for Veronica in 1745, the declaration of her heroic virtues in 1796, her beatification in 1804, and her canonization in 1839.

Quite a different portrait emerges from the writings and the inner experience of a Capuchin Poor Clare from Brescia, Sister Maria Maddalena Martinengo, born Margherita Martinengo di Barco (1687–1737). Only some excerpts from her unpublished autobiography, written between 1722 and 1725 and addressed to her ordinary confessor, Canon Giuseppe Onofri, have come down to us. From them we have a first impression of Maria Maddalena patterned on the cliché of the noble girl destined for the convent. After a difficult period in her life that lasted until 1705 or 1706 and in which family strategies may have played a part, Margherita Martinengo chose, of her own volition, to enter the Capuchin convent of Santa Maria della Neve in her hometown, Brescia, where she made her final vows, taking the name of Maria Maddalena, and where she remained until her death. A person of a certain culture, thanks to her education and to family tradition, she was also restless and energetic. The vocation that burned within her demanded severity, almost as if she wanted to blot out her aristocratic origins. She was equally severe in a will to penitence that she turned toward herself and that led her to accept the humblest sorts of tasks (although she was also mistress of the novices, then vicar, and, eventually, abbess in 1632–34 and 1636–37) and to take on physical torments of an almost unimaginable severity.

The charismatic manifestations (ecstasies, mystical marriage, stigmata) with which Maria Maddalena, like Veronica Giuliani, was rewarded in 1713, and which became particularly intense between 1719 and 1721, alternated between a yearning for humility comparable to Veronica Giuliani's and an abandonment in God that in her autobiography takes on peremptory and sweeping tones. She seems to have gone beyond a penitential desire for "suffering": "For some time," she wrote, "I have clearly realized that the only aliment for love is not suffering, mortifying the flesh, fasting, doing vigils; rather, love itself is the aliment of love."

This way of thinking led, as it did in prayer as Quietism defined it, to obliterating any cooperation on the part of the soul and to exalting passivity as the path to nullification in the divine essence. As Maria Maddalena wrote in her *Autobiografia:*

> God is charity and charity is God, and the soul being transformed in God is all fire of charity. This love is thus most sweet, most delicious, and indescribably quiet. . . . The ardor that I feel is at times something insufferable; thus when . . . I feel myself so burned, I shrink into myself, and in the same love I abandon myself so that it will consume me at its pleasure, I being totally quiet, motionless, and barely daring to breathe. To avoid increasing that impetuous upwelling, I do no internal act, leaving love to do its work quietly. In this manner, sensible love can be quieted and essential love kindled.

We are at the limits—or perhaps at the very core—of doctrines and experiences that the church had already condemned, with special consequences in Brescia among Theatines, Oratorians, and the secular clergy, but also among the canons of the cathedral and the directors of conscience in the various convents. The risk was still present and fear still very much alive. If we are fortunate enough to have the portions of Maria Maddalena's *Autobiografia* that have come down to us untouched, the same was not true of other writings that were burned in 1729 by order of her confessor extraordinary, Don Sandri, who accused his penitent (on what grounds we do not know) of hypocrisy and heresy. Thus if Maria Maddalena reached the glorification of beatitude (albeit somewhat late, in 1900), it was thanks to a sanctity built on an explicit censure.

Among the writings that have come down to us there are spiritual dialogues and a few fragments, but also a song collection of some twenty compositions. This *canzoniere,* like the poetical works of Sister Francesca (born Isabella Farnese), still lacks an evaluation of its precise historical and cultural context. Up to now, only the problem of its authenticity has been posed—and rightly so, if nine of the poems attributed to the nun were in fact written by the Oratorian Cardinal Pier Matteo Petrucci, the leading voice in Italian Quietism. The problem of attribution tells us much about a phase of Counter-Reformation spirituality that was reaching its end and giving way, as religious experience and female conventual institutions evolved, to new forms and ideals reflecting new adjustments between the active and the contemplative life—forms that reached their full development in the eighteenth century and that ranged from the enlightened Catholicism of Muratori to the active charity of St. Alfonso Maria de' Liguori.

"THE CORAL, TENDER UNDER THE SEA'S WAVE": THE NUN
BETWEEN COUNTER-REFORMATION AND ENLIGHTENMENT

*La monaca perfetta ritratta dalla Scrittura sacra, auttorità et esempi de'
Santi Padri,* a work written by an Oblate father, Carlo Andrea Basso of
Milan, appeared in 1627 in that city of the Borromeos. The work, reprinted in 1653, drew on the pastoral and disciplinary activities of both
Carlo and Federico Borromeo, and it served the regular and secular
clergy, the church hierarchy, and the nuns themselves (particularly in Italy)
as an ideal thread to connect the post-Tridentine generations with the
generations of the high Counter-Reformation. It furnished an image,
eventually provided with fuller definition in countless forms and examples, of the "perfect nun" dear to the heart not only of Basso but of
the champions of an institutional, organized, and devout Counter-
Reformation. The practice of mental prayer was to be encouraged in convents. In 1612 and again in 1620, the Congregation of Religious in Rome
gave official authorization to the Jesuits to spread this practice in the female conventual institutions of Milan, Palermo, and probably elsewhere.
Throughout the century, the chief instruments for the introduction of that
practice were the *Compendium meditationum de praecipuis fidei nostre
mysteriis* of Father Luis de la Puente, translated into Italian in 1620 as
Compendio delle Meditazioni, and, even more, with the waning of the
Counter-Reformation, the *Ritiramento spirituale* of Father Camillo Ettori
(1685), a work taken from the spiritual exercises of St. Ignatius made
"most easy" for both female religious and the laity that went through a
truly extraordinary number of printings and translations during the
seventeenth and eighteenth centuries.

Between the 1670s and the 1680s a series of works of advice and
counsel doubtless reflected a current situation as they attempted to draw
clear distinctions in the bitter clashes between laxists and rigorists and to
describe the rising tide of Quietism. Controversy about such matters was
echoed by confessors and directors of conscience and found fertile terrain
in female monastic institutions. St. Francis de Sales had proclaimed, "De
la clôture dépend le bon ordre de tout le reste" ("The good order of everything else depends on enclosure"), and in 1681 Jean-Baptiste Thiers, a
rigorist, used that statement as the epigraph for his *Traité de la clôture
des religieuses.* This work carefully detailed the instances in which people
from the outside would be permitted to enter the holy precincts of the
convent and the nuns permitted to leave them. It also offered yet another
sweeping condemnation (after those of the Jansenists and the "devout"
party) of what those who preached austere morals and renunciation saw
as the overly free and easy ways of the great Benedictine abbeys and the

wealthiest convents of the France of the *Grand Siècle*. Spiritual "warn-ings," exhortations, and meditations multiplied in this period, but their titles can be deceiving. Indeed, if the Jesuits had their manuals, there was advice from the other side as well, as in the *Insegnamenti spirituali per la monaca* of the Oratorian Benedetto Biscia, "a little work," as its long subtitle stated, "in which all Souls of whatever state and condition can also draw most solid fruit of the spirit." This work, printed in Iesi in 1683 under the auspices of Cardinal Bishop Petrucci, sought "spiritual solid-ity" through a return, by way of St. Philip Neri, St. Francis de Sales, and Lorenzo Scupoli, to the tradition of Spanish mysticism of St. Teresa and St. John of the Cross. It also reserved special praise for the writings of the same Petrucci, which were soon to attract the condemnation of the Holy Office for their portrayal of the spirit's progress toward annihilation in "most pure God" and in "his most unique center, where alone it will find peace, repose, and joy."

It was certainly not easy to navigate between the reefs of rigorism and Quietism. Two works written during these years stand out as emblematic of perspectives that would find more adequate scope during the following century. It was the task of Giovanni Battista De Luca, a member of the Curia, a cardinal, and a leading figure in the austere institutional reforms of Pope Innocent XI, to point the way—a way that a man like De Luca found congenial, thanks to his intensely "practical" activities within the Roman congregations and his authorship of a large number of practical juridical tracts. *Il religioso pratico dell'uno e dell'altro sesso* (1679), like other works by De Luca, codified practices that had been in existence for centuries. He focused particularly on observation of the rules of conven-tual community life, counseling avoidance of rigorous and violent means of discipline because, as he observed, "since they are women already im-prisoned in perpetuity, the modes of terror and punishment that are prac-ticed among religious of the other sex—incarceration, changing cells, re-moval of voting privileges or responsibilities—are not appropriate." The same moderation appears in his advice to attenuate the rigid dictates of the Congregation of Religious regarding "conversations" among the nuns or among the nuns and the novices or the girls present in the convent for schooling, where De Luca left norms of conduct to a wise, case-by-case discretion that suggested the beginnings of a new form of sociability. There are significant, albeit hesitant, indications of a new atmosphere in this work. One cannot help but be struck by the quiet reason and the strong juridical sense in De Luca's treatment of "persons who voluntarily suffer the sentence—perhaps the greatest after capital punishment—of perpetual imprisonment," especially since these words were written dur-ing the "turning point" years of the papacy of Innocent XI, when severity inherited from the Counter-Reformation was beginning to dissipate. Just as striking was De Luca's appeal to "Superiors and Confessors" to avoid "the harshnesses [and] penances" of the conventual "way of life" and his pleas that they "walk with much urbanity and circumspection, since the rigors that are customarily used, even for good ends, by some Superiors and Confessors filled with unthinking zeal are blameworthy."

Without saying so explicitly, De Luca placed himself at a turning point in the seventeenth-century debate on the relation between the active and the contemplative life in the context of the female conventual population. Although De Luca gave only a partial response to that debate, another writer, Pietro Pinamonti, seemed more clearly aware of transition in his effort to provide an adequate definition of the condition of the female religious. Pinamonti's *Religiosa in solitudine,* published in Bologna in 1695 and often reprinted—it was translated into all European languages, and was still being published in the nineteenth century—gives a clearer picture than De Luca's of the anti-Quietist battle. The *Religiosa in solitudine* gave special attention to France, referring to the recent condemnation of Fénelon, and it recommended the "retirement" to be found in the spiritual exercises of Ignatius of Loyola as an antidote to the "false doctrine" of Quietist prayer. Father Pinamonti, like his fellow Jesuit Father Segneri, was particularly interested in popularizing (and in this case feminizing) tools for meditation and prayer. Paolo Segneri's *Il Cristiano istruito* and Pinamonti's *La religiosa in solitudine* are comparable in their basic pedagogical concern not only to offer "the nuns the way to occupy themselves fruitfully in the Spiritual Exercises," but also to "be of service to anyone who yearns to reform his or her own state with such means." The condition of the female religious was and remained for Pinamonti a separate, more perfect condition, but it was a model that could be transferred and easily imitated in any other condition, thanks to eight- or ten-day retreats focused on the Exercises of St. Ignatius, meditations, and reading, in particular on the life of Christ with emphasis on the more tender and emotional aspects of the Passion. A necessary corollary to this program lay in other pious practices and acts of external penitence including confession, communion, attendance at mass, and frequent prayer before the Holy Sacrament. This approach sought a fragile balance between a concentration on minor devotional acts—which was becoming the prevalent style—and an attempt to anchor devotions in mental prayer, examination of conscience, and a substantive program of ascetic readings under the wise guidance of a director of conscience.

The first step lay in the reliance, encouraged by the Jesuits, on a Guardian Angel and in devotions to St. Joseph and especially to the Virgin Mary. Such practices marked a shift from the inner "sensible" devotion that had been typical of seventeenth-century mysticism to a more external devotion that was still "sensible" because it relied on control of the senses by such techniques to avoid visual distractions and guide the emotions as limiting the light in the cell or the room or repeating a meditation, in whole or in part, until it produced "tears of tenderness." Even Pinamonti's exhortations, rather than insisting on the involvement of the "heart"—a few mentions of the Passion aside—were all modulated to fit with rational references and images. These were often drawn from the scientific apologetics popularized by the Jesuit Daniello Bartoli, and they coincided with a taste in literature that even a writer of the quality of Lorenzo Magalotti found congenial. Pinamonti wrote of crystal "that solidifies into a gemstone" only when exposed to the midday sun, just as the heart will do when long exposed to the rays of faith; of the heart's strength, which wins over all obstacles, never stopping, until it reaches its final goal, "just as a river, which never lets itself be attracted by the amenity of its banks or turned back by defenses, never stops until it reaches the sea"; of the living faith that tempers the heart "with holy hardness against itself" just like "coral, which, under the sea waves, is tender as a plant," but "taken out in view of the heavens becomes as hard as a precious stone." The strength of such images and their metaphorical thrust, in combination with a smooth and persuasive style, expressed a totally new way of understanding the conventual life, and they permitted a shift from the lofty heights of mysticism to a more human construction of the will by following an ascetic path and relying on faith and serenity rather than harshness and solitude.

Thus the way was open for St. Alfonso Maria de' Liguori's *La vera sposa di Gesù Cristo cioè la monaca santa* (1760). Although this work insisted perhaps more than Pinamonti's on the "perfection" of the conventual state, now contested by Enlightenment polemics, it contained the same guiding idea as Pinamonti's work—that is, its stated intent was to offer a work "useful not only for female and male religious, but also for the laity, while it also treats the practice of the Christian virtues that pertain to persons of all estates." Inner and outer mortification, analyzed with discretion, now provided a base for an ethics and a religious conception that could easily flow from the cloister to the world, thus resolving the problem of the relationship between the contemplative life and the active life that had been part of the experiences of St. Teresa and Marie de l'Incarnation, and deciding the question in favor of an ideal of perfection brought down to daily practice and placed within the grasp of everyone. The image of the nun of the Baroque age—destroyed by mortifications and finding sublimation in visions of God—or (the other side of that coin) the image of the nun in rebellion against forced incarceration in a convent was replaced, gradually but inexorably, by what has come to be defined as "Catholicism in the feminine." The two views could be found in the same age: nuns' protests in the name of a thwarted natural liberty were to find a voice in Diderot's *La religieuse,* a work written in 1759–60, in the same epoch as Alfonso Maria de' Liguori's *La vera sposa,* but published only in 1796 during the years of the French Revolution.

Up to the time of the French Revolution and the Napoleonic era, eighteenth-century society underwent vast changes that contributed powerfully to transformations in the image and the ideal of the nun. Widespread secularization affected the order of society, social structures, and people's ways of thinking. Monastic institutions, both male and female, were reformed or suppressed and their premises given over to public use (in the case of convents, and particularly in Habsburg lands, to their use as schools). Some convents maintained a severe conventual discipline, aided by a nineteenth-century enthusiasm for a Romantic version of religious culture. In general, however, the religious congregations that sprang up after the trauma of the French Revolution, that multiplied during the Restoration, and that continued to have an extraordinary success throughout the century and beyond marked a deep historical cleavage with the post-Tridentine age. New proposals arose within the Roman Catholic Church that urged a new social and religious mission for women and that ushered in a new place for women within the active framework of contemporary society.

SELECTED BIBLIOGRAPHY

The paragraphs below follow the order of the sections in the chapter. Primary sources and secondary works are given in alphabetical order within each paragraph.

Antonio Domínguez Ortiz, *Las clases privilegiadas en la España del Antiguo Régimen* (Madrid: Ediciones ISTMO, 1973); René Taveneaux, *Le catholicisme dans la France classique, 1610–1715* (Paris: SEDES, 1980); Jean de Viguerie, *Le catholicisme des Français dans l'ancienne France* (Paris: Nouvelles éditions latines, 1988); Gabriella Zarri, "Monasteri femminili e città (secoli XV–XVIII)," in *Storia d'Italia, Annali,* gen. eds. Ruggiero Romano and Corrado Vivanti (Turin: Einaudi, 1978–   ), vol. 9, *La chiesa e il potere politico dal Medioevo all'età contemporanea,* ed. Giorgio Chittolini and Giovanni Miccoli (1986), 359–429.

Biblioteca Apostolica Vaticana, Borg. Lat. 71, *Breve compendio di decreti et ordini fatti dalla S. Congr. de Regolari spettanti a monache (1604–44);* Raimondo Creytens, "La riforma dei monasteri femminili dopo i decreti Tridentini," in *Il Concilio di Trento e la riforma tridentina,* Atti del Convegno storico internazionale, Trent, September 2–6, 1963, 2 vols. (Rome and Vienna: Herder, 1965), 1:45–83; Jeanne des Anges, *Storia della mia possessione,* ed. Angelo Morino (Palermo: Sellerio di Giorgianni, 1986); Geneviève Reynes, *Couvents de femmes: La vie des religieuses contemplatives dans la France des XVIIe et XVIIIe siècles* (Paris: Fayard, 1987); Mario Rosa, "Regalità e 'douceur' nell'Europe del '700: La contrastata devozione al Sacro Cuore," in *Dai quaccheri a Gandhi: Studi di storia religiosa in onore di Ettore Passerin d'Entrèves,* ed. Francesco Traniello (Bologna: Il Mulino, 1988), 71–98.

Antonio Favaro, *Galileo Galilei e suor Maria Celeste* (Florence: Barbera, 1891).

Giovanni Baffioni, "Liriche sacre inedite di Francesca Farnese," in *Atti e Memorie dell'Arcadia,* 3d ser. 6, no. 2 (1973): 99–197; Benedetto Croce, "Donne letterate nel Seicento," in his *Nuovi saggi sulla letteratura italiana del Seicento* (Bari: Laterza, 1931), 154–71; Francesca Medioli, *L'"Inferno monacale" di Arcangela Tarabotti* (Turin: Rosenberg & Sellier, 1990).

Octavio Paz, *Sor Juana Inés de la Cruz o Las trampas de la fe,* 2d ed. (Barcelona: Seix Barral, 1988), available in English as *Sor Juana, or, The Traps of Faith,* trans. Margaret Sayers Peden (Cambridge, Mass.: Belknap Press, 1988).

René Bouvier, *Philippe IV et Marie d'Agreda: Confidences royales* (Paris: F. Sorlot, 1939).

Françoise Deroy-Pineau, *Marie de l'Incarnation: Marie Guyart femme d'affaires, mystique, mère de la Nouvelle France 1599–1672* (Paris: R. Laffont, 1989).

Claude Aveline, *. . . Et tout le reste n'est rien: La religieuse portugaise avec le texte de ses lettres,* new ed. (Paris: Mercure de France, 1986); Judith C. Brown, *Immodest Acts: The Life of a Lesbian Nun in Renaissance Italy* (Oxford and New York: Oxford University Press, 1986); *Vita e processo di suor Virginia Maria de Leyva monaca di Monza,* presented by Giancarlo Vigorelli, ed. Umberto Columbo (Milan: Garzanti, 1985).

La possession de Loudun, ed. Michel de Certeau (1970) (Paris: Gallimard/Julliard, 1990); Jean Racine, *Oeuvres complètes de Racine,* ed. P. Mesnard, 8 vols. (Paris: Hachette, 1856–73), vol. 1 (1856), 614–27; René Taveneaux, *La vie quotidienne des jansénistes aux XVIIe et XVIIIe siècles* (1973), new ed. (Paris: Hachette, 1985).

Sara Cabibbo and Marilena Modica, *La santa dei Tomasi: Storia di Suor Maria Crocifissa (1645–1699)* (Turin: Einaudi, 1989); Michel de Certeau, *La fable mystique: XVIe–XVIIe siècle* (1982) (Paris: Gallimard, 1987), available in English as *The Mystic Fable,* trans. Michael B. Smith (Chicago: University of Chicago Press, 1992); Certeau, *Il parlare angelico: Figure per una poetica della lingua (secoli XVI e XVII)* (Florence: Olschki, 1989); Metodio da Nembro, *Misticismo e missione di S. Veronica Giuliani, cappuccina (1660–1727)* (Milan: Centro studi cappuccini lombardi, 1962); Giovanni Pozzi and Claudio Leonardi, eds., *Scrittrici mistiche italiane* (Genoa: Marietti, 1988); G. M. Pugnetti, *L'autobiografia della beata suor Maria Maddalena Martinengo contessa di Barco clarissa cappuccina,* supplement to *Commentari dell'Ateneo di Brescia* (1964).

Claude Langlois, *Le catholicisme au féminin: Les congrégations françaises à supérieure générale au XIXe siècle* (Paris: Editions du Cerf, 1984); Georges Claude May, *Diderot et "La religieuse": Etude historique et littéraire* (Paris: Presses Universitaires de France; New Haven, Conn.: Yale University Press, 1954).

9

THE WITCH

Brian P. Levack

O F ALL THE FIGURES OF THE BAROQUE AGE, the witch was the
most feared. The reason for this fear was not readily apparent.
On the surface, the witch does not seem to have constituted
much of a threat. Physically she was old and weak and in some cases
infirm. Her low social and economic status made her dependent upon
the community for financial support. She had neither political power nor
influential connections. Those with whom she associated came from the
same levels of society as she did. She was rarely able to circumvent, much
less withstand, the inexorable forces of the law that pursued her. It appears that she should be pitied rather than feared, and that is how she is
usually treated in twentieth-century historical literature.

Nevertheless the witch was feared, both by her neighbors and by her
political and social superiors. The fear was so great that theologians, lawyers, and physicians wrote treatises with the double intention of exposing
her and encouraging her prosecution. Her neighbors often contributed to
the legal costs of imprisoning and trying her. Witnesses who would be
disqualified from testifying at the trial of any other type of criminal were
allowed to sign depositions against her. Lawyers often refused to provide
her with judicial representation. Magistrates and judges who in other circumstances had a reputation for judicial fairness would do anything to
prevent her acquittal and hence her return to society.

The witch inspired fear for two reasons. The first was her magical
power. The witch was an alleged practitioner of harmful magic, an activity that theologians and lawyers referred to as *maleficium*. By means of
some mysterious preternatural or supernatural power she was allegedly
able to bring misfortune, disease, or death to her neighbors or their animals. Sometimes this harm was directed at the entire community, such as
when the witch caused a hailstorm that destroyed unharvested crops or a
fire that leveled an entire town or village. In maritime regions, especially

in Scandinavia, witches were known to cause storms at sea. More commonly, however, the witch directed her magic at specific individuals, especially those with whom she was on bad terms. The usual form that the harm took was the infliction of disease, resulting in the disfigurement, disablement, or death of the victim. On other occasions witches were accused of causing impotence in bridegrooms, destroying cattle, and stealing property.

The magic that the witch allegedly performed was not the high magic of the Renaissance neo-Platonists. The witch's magic, unassisted by written manuals or philosophical treatises, was of a much cruder variety. Most of it involved the simple recitation of a curse or hex. In some cases it took even less effort, as when the magic was performed by an inherent power in the witch. Some witches could cause harm simply by looking at their victim, a practice suggestive of what we call the evil eye. Others caused misfortune merely by wishing it, without performing any art at all. Occasionally the witch would use some sort of magical paraphernalia, such as a doll made in the image of the intended victim, which was then either pricked or smashed in order to harm the victim. At other times witches sprinkled a black powder or smeared an ointment on people or cattle in order to harm or kill them. Witches who caused storms at sea were reported to have done so by throwing bewitched stones or cats into the water. A common method of causing impotence was by means of ligature—the tying of knots in a piece of thread, rope, or leather.

The second reason that the witch evoked fear, especially among the clergy and the more educated members of society, was that she was considered to be an ally and servant of the Devil. Ever since the days of the early church, Christian theologians had insisted that all magic, whether it served beneficent or maleficent purposes, was performed through the power of the Devil. During the Middle Ages this charge was leveled mainly against learned magicians, especially necromancers who summoned up demons with the intention of commanding them to produce magical effects. Because these ritual magicians were receiving the benefits of demonic power, and because it was assumed that they must be offering demons something in return for their assistance, they were accused of making pacts with the Devil. This branded them as both heretics and apostates, men who had abandoned their Christian faith and had entered into an illicit relationship with the Prince of Darkness.

During the fifteenth century these charges of forming pacts with the Devil began to be directed against the alleged practitioners of simple village magic rather than the more learned ritual magicians. These new heretical magicians, who were now referred to as witches, came from the lower levels of society and were mainly women. They begin to appear in court records during the first half of the fifteenth century in France and

Switzerland. As both the social status and the sex of these magicians changed, so too did the charges of Devil worship that were made against them. Whereas learned male magicians had always tried to command the demons with whom they were dealing, the female witches became the servants of Satan and their role was to obey rather than command. As King James VI of Scotland wrote in 1597, "Witches are servants only, and slaves to the Devil, whereas necromancers are his masters and commanders."

As more and more of these witches were accused and tried, and as lawyers and theologians wrote manuals and treatises about them, a standard learned view of their diabolism developed. According to this stereotype, the witch was first lured into the service of the Devil by a deliberate act of demonic temptation. The Devil himself, often taking the form of a handsome and attractively dressed man, appeared to the witch and offered her wealth, sexual favors, or some other source of human happiness in exchange for her service. When money was offered, the amount was usually pitifully small, and it was frequently reported that the coin was later transformed into a piece of slate stone. The witch and the Devil then entered into an explicit, face-to-face pact during which the new initiate renounced her faith, trampled on the cross, and submitted to rebaptism by the Devil. As a token of her allegiance to the Devil she was given a special mark on her body, which demonologists claimed would neither bleed nor cause pain when pricked. Prosecutors went to great lengths to discover such marks, which became *prima facie* evidence of witchcraft. In seventeenth-century Scotland a number of professional witch finders, known as prickers, specialized in locating these marks.

After the witch had been initiated into her new faith, she was expected to worship regularly at large assemblies, known as sabbaths, along with other witches. At the nocturnal secret gatherings, which allegedly took place in the forests and mountains outside villages and towns, large groups of witches paid homage to the Devil, who usually appeared in the form of a large goat, bull, or dog. Not only did the witches submit to him in the most debased way, by kissing his buttocks, but they also sacrificed unbaptized children to him. After this the witches engaged in naked dancing, promiscuous heterosexual and homosexual activity with both demons and other witches, and excessive eating and drinking. At these repasts the witches ate a variety of repulsive and unsalted foods, including the flesh of infants. A further activity was the brewing of concoctions to be used in the performance of *maleficia*. Sometimes the Devil actually gave powders and ointments to the witches to use in the craft. In some sabbaths, especially those that took place in France, there was a mockery of the Catholic mass in which prayers were said backward, the priest stood on his head, the eucharistic host was made out of black turnip, and the name of the Devil was substituted for that of Jesus Christ in all prayers. After all these activities had been concluded, the Devil swiftly transported the witch home in the manner he had brought her there, which was usually by flight through the air. Sometimes the witches were said to have flown on broomsticks, pitchforks, or the backs of animals, but irrespective of the method of transportation, the power of flight was believed to have come from the Devil.

It should be clear from this description of the sabbath why those who accepted its reality should have lived in deep apprehension of witches. In addition to fearing her magical power, these men feared her moral destructiveness. The witch was an ally of Satan who was actively engaged in the performance and the propagation of evil. She was committed to the reversal of the entire moral order, defying the standards not only of Christianity but of society itself. Her crime was so terrible that it was regarded as a *crimen exceptum,* a special offense that was to be prosecuted with much less restraint than other secular or religious crimes. It is for this reason that some of the most extreme applications of judicial torture, often administered repeatedly until the accused confessed, occurred during witchcraft trials.

The prospect of moral as well as physical destruction was frightening enough, but it was compounded by the fact that the witch allegedly had large numbers of confederates. The reported presence of hundreds, if not thousands, of witches at the sabbath confirmed that society was faced with a collective, conspiratorial challenge to its religion, its moral values, and the social order. The threat, moreover, was pan-European, since it was widely known among the educated elite that witches were being prosecuted throughout the continent. The witch may have been a local figure, known only to the few hundred neighbors she had in a rural village, but in the eyes of the elite she was a truly international personage, capable of flight over long distances (in some cases over the Atlantic Ocean itself), and part of a conspiracy and rebellion that was European in its dimensions. In 1571 a French witch told King Charles IX that there were more than three hundred thousand witches in his realm, while in 1602 the demonologist Henri Boguet used this figure to project a total of 1,800,000 for all of Europe.

The witch, therefore, was an object of intense fear, a fear that was shared by both the lower classes and the learned elite. To what extent was this fear based in reality? Here we need to distinguish once again between the magical and the diabolical aspects of the witch's activity. The witch's magic had a solid basis in reality. This is not to say that all accused witches were practicing magicians or that their magic actually worked. The first proposition is manifestly wrong and the second unprovable. It is simply to say that some witches did actually try to practice harmful magic. In every community there were some women who performed magical rituals. Usually their craft involved what we would call beneficent magic: the recitation of magical formulas and corrupted prayers and the administration of herbs and unguents to cure people and animals of their maladies. It might also have involved the practice of divination in order to discover the location of stolen goods. Now it is quite certain that from time to time some of these village magicians tried to use their powers in order to harm their enemies, or at least they tried to make their enemies fear such use. It was widely accepted by both the educated elite and the common people that those who could cure could also harm their patients, and there are many known instances when healers did in fact use their sorcery for maleficent purposes.

Nor was the practice of such sorcery restricted to the local "wise women." In an age in which virtually everyone believed in magic, the temptation to have recourse to it must have been strong, especially in times of stress. The physical survival of cursing tablets and dolls pierced with needles, together with the evidence that parts of corpses were used for maleficent purposes, suggests that sorcery was a feature of seventeenth-century village life. The percentage of witches who actually were engaged in the practice of such magic is probably fairly small; most of the persons accused of witchcraft were scapegoats of their communities. Nevertheless, the village sorcerer was not entirely a figment of other people's imaginations.

Like the magician-witch, the diabolical witch—the witch who made a pact with the Devil and worshiped him collectively—was not a totally imaginary figure. In an age of frequent famine, rising prices, declining wages, and a general reduction in the standard of living, there were ample temptations for lower-class people, especially women, to seek an arrangement with the Devil in order to improve their lot. Whether such women actually spoke to some kind of supernatural being while making these pacts should not concern us; the important consideration is that they believed they were indeed entering into some kind of pact. The free confession of many witches to having entered into such contracts, coupled with the obvious guilt that some of them manifested at their trials, suggests that they had in fact decided to sell their souls for temporal gain.

Whether any of these women actually worshiped the Devil at the sabbath is much more problematic. The problem is twofold. On the one hand, the accounts we have of these assemblies contain reports of manifestly impossible deeds such as flying through the air. Hence the entire testimony falls under suspicion. On the other hand, most of the confessions to activity at the sabbath are contaminated in one way or another. In most cases the confessions were elicited under torture, which renders them valueless, since they then become statements of what interrogators wished to hear rather than what actually happened. In other cases the confessions take the form of testimony by children or by people under the influence of drugs. In the Basque country in 1610, for example, more than thirteen hundred children confessed to having attended the sabbath. Upon further interrogation by a skeptical inquisitor, Alonso Salazar de Frias, the entire assembly proved to be a chimera. The possibility, moreover, of thousands of individuals converging on a distant point and then returning to their homes without detection or a chance encounter with strangers strains one's credulity.

It is possible that small groups of accused witches did occasionally gather in secret outside their villages. At Neuchâtel in 1582 a traveler stumbled across a group of women dancing around a fire. One of the women, Jehanne Berna, confessed that the gathering was "an assembly of sorcerers" and named three accomplices. Likewise, the possibility that bacchanalian orgies actually took place cannot be dismissed out of hand, although it is unlikely that the women accused of witchcraft were apt to have been participants in such revels. What is extremely unlikely, however, is that the large sabbaths that are frequently described in the accusations and confessions of witches (such as the alleged gathering of one hundred thousand "devotees of Satan" described by Pierre de Lancre in 1612) ever actually took place. Virtually all the evidence we have for such assemblies is clearly contaminated.

It is also extremely unlikely that people accused of attending the sabbath had organized themselves for some other, nondiabolical purposes that were interpreted by juridical authorities as the worship of the Devil. There is no shortage of historical theories that interpret the activities of accused witches in this way. The most famous is that of Dame Margaret Murray, an anthropologist who argued that witches were really members of an ancient pre-Christian fertility cult whose beneficent rites were misrepresented by alarmed clerics and judges as harmful and diabolical. Other scholars, sharing a romantic interpretation of witchcraft, have interpreted the witches' assemblies as organized protests either against the established economic and social order or against patriarchy. One historian has seen the witches' sabbath as the work of goliards parodying the prevailing ecclesiastical order. The problem with all these interpretations is that there is no proof that witches ever gathered in large numbers for any purpose, diabolical or otherwise. The fear of collective Devil worship may have been based on the reality of the secret assemblies of other groups. We know, for example, that heretics did gather in fairly large numbers for the purposes of religious worship, and certainly pagans had done so in the past. But witches, if they ever practiced any craft at all, did so individually or in small groups.

Even if witches did not do most of the things they were accused of, many of them did, in the course of their prosecution, come to believe that they were in fact witches. The most striking illustration of this development occurred in the Friuli, where the Venetian Inquisition prosecuted members of an agrarian fertility cult, the "benandanti," between 1575 and 1650. The benandanti, who wore their cauls around their necks as amulets, believed that they went out at night, while they were in a state of catalepsy, to do battle with the witches. In this symbolic battle the benandanti fought with fennel sticks while the witches used sorghum stalks. Victory by the benandanti would result in successful harvests, whereas failure would portend infertility. Inquisitors, unable to comprehend this set of popular beliefs, assumed that the benandanti were actually witches who were "going out" to the sabbath. Members of the sect vehemently denied this charge, but over the course of some seventy years, as the result of intense judicial pressure (which did not, however, include torture), the benandanti and their neighbors came to believe that they were witches.

A similar process of self-definition often took place in French and Swiss witch trials, where judges or inquisitors managed to persuade some accused witches that they were actually guilty of their crimes. In these trials witches appeared to be genuinely contrite for their sins. The reasons for such contrition can only be conjectured and may have varied from case to case. One possibility is that the accused were in fact guilty of some of the actions attributed to them such as the performance of harmful magic. The confession of a woman from Rosières-aux-Salines in Lorraine to having used witchcraft only to kill people who were angry with her falls into this category. Another possibility is that the accused considered themselves to be sinners and that prosecution for the diabolical crime of witchcraft forced them to come to terms with their evilness. This seems to have been the case when a woman from La Neuveville-les-Raon in Lorraine confessed her crime and begged the judges "to pray God for her poor soul so that it may please God to pardon her faults."

A third possibility is that witches, in the course of their trials, became fascinated with the revelation that they possessed preternatural powers and, once they recognized this, readily admitted their crime. Carl Theodore Dreyer's brilliant film *Vredens Dag* (Day of Wrath), which was based on the trial of Anna Pedersdotter in Bergen in 1590, establishes the plausibility of such a revelation. In the film Anna was tried for having killed her husband by witchcraft, and in fact she had wished him dead shortly before his demise. She was also accused of using her powers to seduce her stepson, and her success in this regard only served to confirm her own sense of guilt. A final possibility is that a woman, recognizing that her situation was hopeless, may have tried to intimidate her prosecutors with the threat of magical retaliation against them. In these cases, such as that of the Scottish witch Jannet Macmurdoch in 1671, the accused accepted and identified with the label that was assigned to her and then used it to defend herself.

Even if some individuals came to believe that they were in fact witches, we still cannot deny that most of the charges brought against witches, especially those charges dealing with Devil worship, were groundless. The witch's crime was in large part imaginary. That being the case, we must ask why certain individuals were falsely accused of it. Why were certain persons singled out, either by their neighbors or by their judicial superiors, for prosecution? Why did some women and men, rather than others, serve as the scapegoats of early modern European communities? Who, in other words, were the witches?

First and foremost, they were women. Here all the data we have from witchcraft prosecutions throughout Europe and the countless images we have from contemporary paintings, engravings, and woodcuts are in agreement. More than 80 percent of all persons accused of witchcraft during the sixteenth and seventeenth centuries were female. In some areas, such as in England, the percentage was even higher, exceeding 90 percent. To be sure, there was nothing to prevent men from becoming witches. Just like women they could practice magic and make pacts with the Devil. In the famous woodcuts illustrating the witches' pact with the Devil in Francesco Maria Guazzo's *Compendium Maleficarum* (1608), the witches were divided in almost equal numbers between the two sexes. Nevertheless, men were only rarely accused of this crime, and when they were, it was often in association with their wives or mothers. Their prosecution did little to challenge the assumption, shared by both the elite and the common people, that the witch was female.

Although this assumption may have been held throughout society, the common people and the elite had different reasons for making it. Among simple villagers the witch was female mainly because she was more likely than a man to practice simple forms of magic. Women were traditionally the white magicians or healers in European communities. They were the ones who knew how to use herbs, ointments, and other magical concoctions to cure the maladies of both man and beast. They were capable, therefore, of using their magical power for maleficent purposes, and the fact that many of their patients did not recover from their afflictions made them vulnerable to charges of *maleficium*. If these healers incurred the anger of their neighbors by charging excessive fees for their services, an accusation of witchcraft might very well be used to keep their financial ambition in check.

If these healers also served in the capacity of midwives, as many of them did, the possibility of suspicion for performing *maleficium* was even greater. Midwives had ample opportunity to harm newborn children, and since infant mortality was very high at this time, they often became the targets of suspicion. At times of great stress they served as the scapegoats of the entire community. In 1587 a midwife and healer by the name of Walpurga Hausmännin from the German town of Dillingen was accused of bewitching no fewer than forty-three babies to death by rubbing them with a magical salve, and to have then compounded this crime by using the bones of the slain infants to manufacture hail with the intention of damaging her neighbors' crops. Of the twelve women accused of witchcraft at Cologne between 1627 and 1630 whose occupations are known seven were midwives.

Even if a woman did not practice as a healer or midwife, she was still more likely than a man to be accused of witchcraft by her neighbors. Her assigned role as cook in the home, her participation in the rituals of childbirth, and her frequent contact with children who were sick gave her both the opportunity and the means to bring about magical harm. It was generally recognized, moreover, that women had greater need of magical power than men. Denied the physical, economic, and political assets of men, women were forced back upon those mysterious powers that both in mythology and popular culture were associated with the witch and the enchantress. And if villagers needed any reinforcement of their suspicions, they would find it in the sermons of the local priest or minister, who was also convinced that witches were females.

The reasons for the clerics' suspicion, however, were in most cases different from those of the witch's neighbors. The clergy, most of whom were educated, were much more concerned with the witch's diabolical than her magical practices. The members of the clerical and ruling elite were more likely to suspect and accuse women of witchcraft because they thought women were more prone than men to diabolical deception and temptation. Using the example of Eve's temptation in the Garden of Eden, clerics had for centuries argued that women were morally weaker than men. According to the *Malleus Maleficarum*, which was written by two Dominican inquisitors in 1486, "a wicked woman is by her nature quicker to abjure the faith, which is the root of witchcraft." The main source of this weakness was women's "carnal lust," which in the minds of these Dominicans was insatiable. The Devil, appealing to this sexual desire, was able to entice women into his service and hence to practice witchcraft. The reports of sexual promiscuity at the sabbath only served to underline the importance of the witch's sexual desire in the minds of the clerical elite.

The frequency of references to the sexual desires and behavior of witches in contemporary treatises suggests that clerics harbored deep fears of sexual temptation, fears that were especially strong among men who had chosen a celibate life. In the case of the *Malleus Maleficarum*, the references to female sexuality were so persistent, if not obsessive, that we can only conclude that the authors were projecting their sexual desires onto women. This same type of projection may have taken place at the parish level at the time of the Counter-Reformation. One of the main features of Catholic reform was a demand that the parish clergy adhere to the strict standards of clerical celibacy established by the church. For many priests, especially those who had been rather lax in this regard, there were bound to be frequent temptations and occasional lapses. One way of dealing with such temptation, as well as with the guilt for backsliding, was to project one's sexual behavior onto female witches, who served as the symbols of sexuality in these communities.

Members of the clerical and ruling elite also had their own reasons for suspecting midwives of witchcraft. As magistrates they shared the concerns of the common people for the death of infants in their communities, and as judges they were particularly concerned about the alarming increase in infanticide and abortion that took place as economic conditions deteriorated throughout Europe after 1550. To them such a crime was more plausible if it was done by a midwife who practiced witchcraft. What bothered them most about witchcraft, however, was the practice of Devil worship, and in this regard the midwife was almost a natural suspect. It was widely believed that witches sacrificed unbaptized babies to the Devil as part of the ceremonies performed at the sabbath. And who would have better access to a regular supply of such infants than the midwife? There was also a fear that the witch would actually baptize the children they delivered as members of Satan's church. In 1728 a Hungarian midwife from Szegerin was accused of baptizing two thousand infants in the name of the Devil. A further reason for the prosecution of midwives for witchcraft was male suspicion and resentment of their exclusive control over the mysteries of childbirth. An accusation of witchcraft was a highly plausible means of expressing that resentment, and it had the added virtue of popular support.

The witch was not only a woman, but also an *old* woman. In the large majority of recorded cases, the witch had reached the age of fifty, which in early modern Europe was about ten years past menopause and considered to be old by one's neighbors. In some areas, such as Essex County, England, the median age of witches was sixty. Occasionally, as in the trial of Collette du Mont on the isle of Guernsey in 1624, the accused was referred to repeatedly as "the old woman." When dealing with the age of witches, the evidence from art lends support to the evidence from judicial records. In many contemporary engravings and paintings the witch is represented as an old, unattractive woman with wrinkled skin and unkempt hair. She is also frequently depicted as being lame, another sign of advanced age. Reginald Scot was on solid ground, therefore, when he asserted that "witches are women which be commonly old."

There are many reasons why witches tended to be elderly. To begin with, witches were generally prosecuted after suspicion of them had mounted over the years, a situation that naturally kept the average age of those tried fairly high. If the witch was a healer or midwife, she was almost old by definition, since it took years to acquire the skill of the "wise woman" and to develop a clientele. A further explanation lies in the fact that older people, especially if they were senile, often manifested signs of eccentric or antisocial behavior that tended to make their neighbors uncomfortable and to invite accusations of witchcraft. The same type of older person would also be more likely to confess freely to diabolical activities as a result of her senility. A final reason for the large number of old witches is that elderly persons were not as strong as younger ones and were therefore more likely to use sorcery as a means of protection or revenge.

The stereotype of the old, unattractive female witch was by no means incompatible with the clerical view of the witch as a woman driven by carnal lust. It is easy to see young and voluptuous witches, such as those who appear in some of the engravings of Hans Baldung Grien and Filippino Lippi, as the embodiment of female sexuality. It is much more implausible to think of the older witch in similar terms, but many contemporaries, especially clerics, saw her precisely in that light. The older witch was, after all, often sexually experienced, and if she was widowed she was independent of male control. It was a common assumption that she had made a pact with the Devil in order to have carnal relations with him and that she engaged in promiscuous sex at the sabbath. To the celibate cleric the sexual passion of the older, unattached witch represented a particularly dangerous form of temptation. In the middle-aged layman it may have aroused fears of sexual inadequacy.

Although the witch was usually old there were frequent exceptions to this rule. Women who were accused specifically of using love magic in order to secure the affections of estranged husbands or the spouses of others were usually younger than the typical practitioner of village magic. A second group of younger witches were children ranging in age from five to thirteen, who either confessed freely or were named as witches by their neighbors. Some child witches were accused simply because they were related to adult female witches, since witchcraft was often believed to run in families. On the isle of Guernsey in 1617 the two daughters of Jeanne Guignon were executed for witchcraft together with their mother. Other children, however, were believed to have practiced witchcraft as a means of revenge against their parents and thus were prosecuted separately.

The most common set of circumstances in which children, and for that matter males, were accused of witchcraft was during chain-reaction witch-hunts. In these operations the first group of suspects, after having confessed under torture, were forced to name their accomplices, who in turn were apprehended and tried. These hunts could become extremely large, involving the prosecution of hundreds of individuals. At Bamberg, for example, more than three hundred persons were executed for witchcraft between 1624 and 1631. Since most of the accusations in this type of witch-hunt came from confessing witches themselves, the victims did not readily conform to the stereotype. At Würzburg, for example, where more than 160 persons were executed for witchcraft between 1627 and 1629, over 25 percent of the victims were children and more than 50 percent were male. The percentage of men and children increased as the hunt progressed and as the courts relied more and more on the accusations of those whom they were prosecuting.

A similar situation occurred at Salem, Massachusetts, in 1692, when a hunt began with the accusation of three old women who conformed to the traditional image of the witch. As the hunt developed—in this case as the result of the accusations of nine demonically afflicted girls—charges were made against a four-year-old child, a number of wealthy merchants, and the wife of the governor of the colony. In this case, as in many of a similar nature, the breakdown of the stereotype led to a skepticism regarding the guilt of the accused and ultimately to the end of the hunt. Another large hunt involving the prosecution of children took place in the town of Mora, Sweden, in 1669. That hunt began when a teen-aged boy accused a young girl and several others of stealing children for the Devil. In the trials that followed a number of children were condemned to death and many others were subjected to noncapital punishments on the basis of testimony by confessing witches that the children had accompanied them to the sabbath at a place called Blocula.

In establishing the profile of the typical witch, the question of marital status is the most difficult to determine. The limited statistical evidence we have indicates no clear pattern, with the percentage of accused witches who were married ranging from 25 to 70 percent from region to region. The stereotype of the old female witch could easily accommodate both married and unmarried women. Both types of women could easily have been involved in the practice of simple magic, and both could have been vulnerable to the sexual or material enticements of the Devil. It does appear, however, that in most communities the percentage of unmarried witches (which includes those who never married, widows, and those who were separated or divorced from their husbands) was greater than the percentage of unmarried women in the general population. To some extent this was simply a function of age. Women tended to live longer than men in early modern Europe, just as they do now, so if witches were generally old women, we would expect a large number to have been widowed or never to have married.

Unmarried women also tended to be poorer than their married neighbors, and as we shall see, poverty was one of the main characteristics of the witch. The large number of unmarried witches, therefore, may simply reflect the fact that they were old and poor. There is no question, however, that the unmarried woman was more vulnerable to the suspicion and accusation of witchcraft than her married neighbor. It was a question of both protection and control. On the one hand, husbands could shield their wives from prosecution by interceding with judicial authorities on their behalf or initiating proceedings for slander or false arrest against their accusers. On the other hand, husbands exercised fairly tight control over the actions of their wives and thus reduced their opportunities for independent action. The solitary woman was an independent social agent, and thus she interacted on that basis with her community. The potential sources for conflict with her neighbors were much greater than they were for the married woman.

There was ample reason for villages and towns to fear the activities of unmarried women in the sixteenth and seventeenth centuries, since their numbers were growing. The percentage of widows in the female population, which usually ranged from 10 to 20 percent, rose at certain times and in certain places to 30 percent. These increases usually occurred after visitations of the plague, which often caused more deaths among men than women, and during periods of warfare, when men suffered more casualties than women. At the same time, the number of women who never married increased from about 5 percent in the Middle Ages to somewhere between 10 and 20 percent in the seventeenth century, a development that coincided with an increase in the age at first marriage. As this change was taking place, the convents, which had accommodated many single women during the Middle Ages, either experienced a decline in membership or were dissolved as a result of the Reformation. This meant that early modern European communities not only contained more unmarried women than they had during the Middle Ages but also had greater difficulty accommodating them. Many unmarried women, to be sure, found places in the patriarchal households of brothers or other relatives, but others opted for an independent existence. To make matters worse, most of these unmarried women were fairly poor, and thus they represented a serious social problem. If men already harbored deep fears of unattached women, their fears were aggravated by the process of social and demographic change.

Although the unmarried woman was more likely to be accused of witchcraft than her married neighbor, the married woman was susceptible to such accusations from her spouse or children. Tensions within families, which were not expected to be resolved by means of lawsuits or domestic violence, sometimes took the form of witchcraft accusations. Not only did husbands occasionally name their wives as witches but children sometimes accused their mothers. In a number of cases adult children and their spouses used witchcraft accusations to retaliate against a mother who disapproved of their marriage. In 1611 in the German territory of Ellwangen, a seventy-year-old woman named Barbara Rüfin found herself accused of witchcraft not only by her husband but also by her son, who resented his mother's opposition to his marriage and her subsequent attempts to poison his wife. As cases like this suggest, witchcraft accusations became one of the many weapons that were used to attack the custom of arranged marriage, a practice that underwent a gradual loss of popularity during the early modern period, when religious reformers insisted upon marital fidelity and when the age at first marriage increased.

The seventeenth-century witch, whether married or unmarried, almost always came from the lower levels of society, and she often required both public and private assistance in order to survive. There is no question concerning the poverty of all but a few witches. They did not, it is true, always rank among the very poorest residents of towns and villages. They were usually not, for example, part of the wandering poor population. Witches were in most cases longtime residents of their communities, as the charges against them for having harmed people ten, fifteen, or twenty years in the past clearly indicate. But as members of those communities they usually had to struggle economically. This meant that they often became involved in disputes with their neighbors over the possession of small parcels of land or over the failure of employers to pay them for their services. It also meant that they frequently asked their neighbors for some kind of charity, especially when public assistance was not available. The demonologist Nicolas Rémy claimed that witches were "for the most part beggars who support life on the alms they receive," while Girolamo Cardano, an Italian physician, referred to them as beggars and "miserable old women."

The burden that these women placed upon resources of towns and villages, especially before a comprehensive and effective system of poor relief was introduced, can be witnessed in England, where villagers frequently claimed that a witch had harmed them because they had refused her a cup of milk, a piece of pork, or a piece of cheese. In these circumstances the witch had asked her neighbors to adhere to the traditional Christian standards of social morality that required one to help those in need. In times of great dearth, however, which were commonplace in the sixteenth and seventeenth centuries, adherence to such standards constituted a great financial burden. The problem was that failure to dispense charity created feelings of guilt, which could only be relieved by accusing the imposing party of witchcraft, thereby freeing the person from the customary obligations of charity. Thus in England witchcraft accusations enabled individuals to justify a new code of individualistic behavior and to discard a traditional social morality.

The poverty and low social status of the witch also made her alleged acts of *maleficia* much more plausible. Because witches were poor, they lacked both political and legal power, and since they were for the most part old and female, they also lacked physical strength. In these circumstances witches had no means of protection except the magical powers that were attributed to them. In this respect they often conformed to the image their neighbors and their superiors had of them. If a witch wished to take revenge upon an enemy or prevent that person from inflicting further harm, she might very well have placed a curse or hex on him. Her purpose might have been simply to neutralize him through fear, but by her actions she had recourse to the powers that she was suspected of possessing.

Although the great majority of witches lived in straitened economic circumstances, a few were relatively well off. Sometimes wealthy witches were accused, just as men and younger women were, in the later stages of large witch-hunts when the stereotype of the witch broke down. Prominent and wealthy men or their wives occasionally became the targets of witchcraft accusations, particularly ones inspired by political motives, as when members of town councils accused the wives of their rivals. There also could be economic motives in bringing charges against such people. When women stood to inherit property, either as only daughters or as widows, they often incurred the hostility of those men who would otherwise have gained possession of their land. In New England almost 90 percent of all witches who were executed came from families that did not have male heirs.

A few witches, such as those at Salem, possessed some modest economic assets, but virtually all of them were uneducated and illiterate. This is hardly surprising in light of the limited educational opportunities that were available to women, especially poor women, in the seventeenth century. The witch's lack of education is of no little importance in understanding the dynamics of her prosecution. On the one hand, it put her at a tremendous disadvantage with respect to her accusers. Ignorant of the procedures by which she was being tried and of the demonological theories that her prosecutors were using to explain her actions, she could easily be intimidated and confused, and she was certainly not equipped to mount an effective defense. On the other hand, the witch, living in the world of popular, as opposed to learned, culture, attracted the hostility of those prosecutors who were determined to reform, if not eliminate, that culture. Many of the witch trials of the seventeenth century can be seen as forms of cultural combat in which learned prosecutors attempted to discredit those beliefs and practices of the common people that did not strike them as religiously orthodox. By labeling the actions and the beliefs of the uneducated witch as heretical and diabolical, they sought to eradicate the superstition of the lower classes. In this way the witch became the victim of a cultural war between the wealthy and the poor, the literate and the illiterate, and the cities and the countryside.

To claim that the typical witch was a poor, old, illiterate, unmarried woman still does not tell us why only a few such women were accused of witchcraft whereas many others of similar description were not. In the final analysis, the most distinctive characteristics of the witch were her personality and her behavior. The witch was a certain type of person who violated the widely accepted standards of behavior in sixteenth- and seventeenth-century communities. The standards that she challenged were of four different types: neighborliness, femininity, morality, and religious practice.

The witch was a bad neighbor. Although she had been a longtime resident of the local community, she did not contribute to its social harmony. Perhaps owing to her poverty and her financially dependent status, she was frequently involved in disputes with her neighbors over property, pasture rights, wages, personal conduct, or public issues. The depositions taken from her neighbors often speak of her sharp tongue and her quarrelsome personality. In an age in which everyone, especially someone from the lower ranks of society, was expected to be deferential, she was outspoken, if not insolent, toward her superiors. Always ready to answer back, she seemed to have a propensity for cursing. It was this trait, of course, that had been one of the sources of her suspicion to begin with; at her trial it only served to confirm that she was in fact a witch.

The behavior of the witch was so unconventional, and her confessions so fanciful, that a few contemporaries as well as some modern historians considered her to be mentally ill. The first scholar to advance this argument was Johann Weyer, the student of Cornelius Agrippa von Nettesheim and the physician to the humanistic Duke of Cleves. In *De Praestigiis Daemonum* (1563) Weyer claimed that witches were poor deluded creatures suffering from melancholy and old age who were deceived by the Devil into believing that they had made a pact with him. There is some merit to Weyer's argument. Many witches claimed at their trials that they were sad or depressed when they were tempted into witchcraft, and it is even more likely that some of them were senile. Certainly many witches were along in years, and their angry, eccentric behavior may have been caused, or at least aggravated, by senescence. It is unlikely, however, that senility can explain the unpleasantness of most witches' behavior. The judicial record, even though it comes from hostile sources, suggests that witches had been acting in unneighborly fashion long before the onset of senility, and many of the accused were far too young to have experienced this malady at all.

It is even less likely that witches suffered from other forms of mental illness. The fanciful nature of their confessions suggests that they may have experienced some form of psychosis, but it is much more likely that those confessions reflect the results of torture and a willingness to satisfy the demands of their inquisitors rather than the deranged condition of the witch's mind. Another possible interpretation of their fanciful confessions is that they were under the influence of mood-altering drugs. Certainly such drugs were widely available in the villages of seventeenth-century Europe. Plants such as belladonna contained atropines that, when rubbed into the skin, could produce dizziness and lightheadedness, while pain killers like the hyoscyamus plant and henbane could produce deep, lifelike dreams. It is possible that some of the statements by witches that they flew to the sabbath were suggested by their experiences while under the influence of such substances. It is less likely, however, that the acerbic personality of the witch can be attributed to the same source.

Whatever the causes of the witch's eccentric behavior, she certainly made her neighbors uncomfortable in her presence, and this in turn led to deep resentment of her. Of course there were different ways of dealing with a bad neighbor. One possibility was to ignore her, but in the environment of early modern European communities this was often impossible. In agricultural villages of two, three, or four hundred persons it was difficult to ignore a woman who actively engaged people in a hostile way. This may help to explain the heavy concentration of witchcraft prosecutions in rural areas and in small towns, which often had populations of fewer than one thousand persons. The large cities rarely were the site of witchcraft accusations, even though the trials were often held there. Almost all prosecutions originated in small, face-to-face communities, just as they do in primitive societies today. The witch was someone whom everyone knew and disliked but who could not be avoided.

If the witch was a bad neighbor, she was also an extremely unfeminine one. Her actions defied all the conventions of proper female behavior that prevailed in early modern Europe. These conventions were defined by men, and they represented deliberate efforts to suppress female characteristics that they found unacceptable. Men in both Catholic and Protestant areas expected women to be obedient, submissive, and self-effacing. They were, in other words, to be "good wives." In making such demands, men assumed that by nature women were not inclined to act in this way, as much seventeenth-century literature would suggest. The witch was the personification of an unfeminine type. She was aggressive, defiant, uppity, and vengeful, and as mentioned above, she was also removed from the immediate control of men. She therefore represented a challenge to male authority as well as to male standards of feminine behavior. By naming her as a witch men and women could indicate their disapproval of such behavior and at the same time discourage others from adopting it. In this way witchcraft prosecutions played a role in the definition of modern femininity.

Part of that definition of femininity was moral in nature. Women were expected to be virtuous and chaste. Those women who were accused of witchcraft, by contrast, had reputations for various forms of moral deviance. This should not surprise us. Witches were believed to be quintessentially evil human beings. They were sinful by nature, having abandoned their Christian faith, entered the service of the Devil, and practiced *maleficia*. It is only logical that villagers would have suspected notorious sinners rather than upstanding members of the community of this crime.

But what types of moral transgressions were witches known to have committed? Very few of them had ever been accused of major crimes, and only a small percentage had been prosecuted for petty secular crimes, theft for example. Their offenses, like most recorded crimes of women at this time, were of a more sexual nature. This emphasis on sexual conduct is understandable when one considers the centrality of sexual imagery in contemporary descriptions of the sabbath. In some cases individuals came under suspicion of witchcraft simply because they displayed their sexuality publicly. In Lucerne, for example, a woman and her daughter who were tried for witchcraft were seen sitting in a brook "clutching themselves between their legs," while another was spied running out of the woods with her skirt raised. Many of the Scottish witches prosecuted in the mid-seventeenth century had earlier been brought before the kirk sessions of their parish to answer charges of fornication, adultery, and even abortion. One woman accused in 1661 had been suspected of familiarity with English soldiers during the occupation of the country a few years before. Three other Scottish witches accused during the 1640s, Elspeth Edie, Jennet Walker, and Margaret Halberstoun, were known to have had sexual relations with James Wilson, who was in turn accused and later executed for adultery, bestiality, and incest.

Closely related to the witch's moral behavior was her religious conduct. Just as neighbors were disposed toward suspecting those women of loose sexual mores, they were also suspicious of one who did not adhere to prevailing standards of religious conformity. The Sabbath-breaker, the person who did not attend church regularly, or who was suspected of religious heterodoxy was also likely to incur suspicions of witchcraft. In this regard the suspicion was more likely to come from the local priest or minister than from the witch's neighbors, especially since it was the clerical elite who were most concerned about the witch's worship of the Devil. But evidence of religious nonconformity made the witch vulnerable to popular accusations as well, since it confirmed her rejection of social convention.

One of the charges most frequently leveled against witches, especially in Protestant countries, was "backwardness" in religion. The term naturally suggests Roman Catholicism, and in some Protestant witchcraft treatises attachment to the old religion was considered one of the main characteristics of the witch. In 1584 the skeptical Reginald Scot described English witches as "poor, sullen, superstitious, and papists." It might be tempting to conclude on the basis of such statements that witch-hunts were mechanisms by which Protestant or Catholic communities rid themselves of those people suspected of belonging to the other religious camp. According to this interpretation, witch trials were local manifestations of the wars of religion, which did in fact coincide with the most intense period of witch-hunting. The witch was, after all, considered to be a heretic, and that was how both Catholic and Protestant theologians viewed an adherent to the rival faith. Nevertheless, the witch was not considered to be either a Catholic or Protestant heretic. If she were, she would have been prosecuted for a different crime by either Catholic or Protestant tribunals. In some jurisdictions, such as Cologne, trials for witchcraft increased when those for Protestant heresy (in this case Anabaptism) decreased. The witch's crime was not conversion to a rival religion but apostasy, the rejection of her Christian faith and the worship of the Devil.

Within her community, moreover, the witch was only rarely identified as professing the rival faith. Like most of the members of her village or town, she was at least nominally of the same religion as her neighbors and her superiors. As in so many other ways, the witch was not completely divorced from her community. She never lived in complete isolation from her neighbors, nor was she a newcomer to her village. On the other hand, she was never fully a part of that community and frequently challenged its values. As far as religion was concerned, her backwardness usually involved some residual attachment to the old faith. She might be known to say the old Catholic prayers or practice the old Catholic rituals in one form or another. Since she was old, such behavior would be eminently plausible, especially in areas that had converted from one religion to another in her lifetime. Her religious behavior would attract the concern of her superiors not so much because they were looking for heretics but because they were looking for witches.

The aspect of the old religion that gave them most concern was superstition. Among both Protestant and reformed Catholics there had developed a determination to wipe out peasant superstition—beliefs and practices that had been associated with the old faith but that had fallen out of favor because they smacked of paganism. The magic of the witch was considered to be an example of such superstition. Indeed, one of the many reasons authorities instigated witch-hunts was to root out such corrupt practices. The old women who still said the old prayers or who demonstrated an attachment to unreformed religion was suspected mainly for her ignorance and her superstition, not because she was considered to be a Catholic agent.

This entire discussion of the personality of the witch underlines the importance of reputation in the designation of a person as a witch. The women accused of witchcraft were generally those who had given ample evidence of their intrinsic evil over a long period of time. Except in chain-reaction hunts, when the process of naming accomplices got out of control, there was never much surprise when certain people were arrested for this crime. Villagers knew all along who the witches were likely to be. All it took was a specific crisis to bring both their neighbors and the local authorities to act.

The seventeenth-century witch was therefore a poor, old woman, more often unmarried than not, whose behavior was unneighborly, unfeminine, immoral, and religiously backward. Defying the conventions of both her religion and her sex, she managed to offend and frighten her neighbors and her superiors. The decision to prosecute and execute her can be seen as simply an attempt to rid these communities of such unpleasant and dangerous neighbors. By killing witches, villagers also gained revenge for the magical harm that had befallen them and their loved ones, while at the same time confirming that witchcraft had in fact been the source of their misfortunes.

For the members of the secular and clerical elite, the prosecution of the witch often had a more religious motivation. Since these men tended to define the witch's crime more in diabolical than in magical terms, they often saw her prosecution as a religious duty. The great European witch-hunt cannot be attributed simply to religious fervor, but with both ecclesiastical and secular judges this sentiment clearly played an important part. Men inspired with either Protestant or Catholic ideals viewed the trial of witches as a means of making war against Satan and thereby establishing a godly state and strengthening the kingdom of God on earth. They also prosecuted witches as symbols of the disorder that seemed to prevail in the world.

The need for order is of course a constant in man's nature, and all ages give evidence of efforts to obtain it. During the seventeenth century, however, there was a preoccupation with it, mainly because it was widely believed that the old order had collapsed. Certainly the traditional ecclesiastical order had collapsed at the time of the Reformation, and much of the religious energy of the succeeding one hundred and fifty years was dedicated to its restoration or replacement. Especially among Protestants, who had rejected the entire structure of the Catholic church, the need for a new discipline in home and church was of paramount importance. The political problem was no less critical. The early modern period was characterized by an almost continuous series of rebellions by the lower classes, and the mid-seventeenth century witnessed a number of major upheavals, including the first great revolution of modern times in England. These rebellions were not unrelated to the growing disorder within society. Lower standards of living, rising unemployment, rampant inflation, and the swelling of the population of many towns created unprecedented social unrest and placed unbearable strains on the old governmental machinery. Within society there were frequent challenges to traditional hierarchies and within families a reluctance to accept patriarchal rule. Even the heavens seemed to have lost their order as the medieval Aristotelian and Ptolemaic universe collapsed under the influence of Copernicus's heliocentric model. Symptomatic of this multifaceted crisis of order was a profound sense of impending doom and chaos that characterized much late sixteenth- and seventeenth-century literature.

The witch came to symbolize all this chaos and disorder. As a woman, of course, she was instinctively associated with nature, and as a witch she was associated in particular with the destructive, chaotic side of nature, which was known to bring plague, disease, and famine. Her alleged work, it should be remembered, involved the destruction of crops, the murder of infants, and even the spreading of plague. As a person driven by sexual passion, moreover, the witch represented another dangerous form of disorder. The witch's "bestial cupidity" to which Jean Bodin referred in *De la démonomanie des sorciers* (1580) associated her with the lower orders of the natural world, while the wild, frenzied dances that she performed at the sabbath, the unharmonious music to which she danced naked, and the promiscuous sexual relations in which she engaged all reflected an uncontrolled temperament.

Within her community the witch represented a constant challenge to the ideal of the well-ordered society. To begin with, she was generally outside the system of patriarchal control, and as such she represented a challenge to what was considered a natural hierarchy. She was the antithesis of the ideal of the perfect wife that was central to most conceptions of a well-ordered society. In her dealings with her superiors she was insolent and defiant. In the duchy of Württemberg she was known for her aggressiveness; in the *pays* of Labourd for her effrontery. Even after her arrest she often denied the authority of the court that was prosecuting her and the validity of the beliefs upon which her trial was based. At times she threatened the judges and officers of the court with magical retaliation, a course of action that only stiffened the resolve of her prosecutors to do away with her.

It should come as no surprise that this woman was often referred to as a rebel. Of course she hardly conformed to the stereotype of the rebel. As an old and sometimes decrepit woman she would be the least likely person to mount a physical assault against the established regime. Only in some Habsburg lands were some witches known to be actual political rebels, and most of those witches were male. But in her own magical way the female witch was considered to be as much the rebel as the young rioter, plotter, or even bandit. She was, after all, branded as a heretic and an apostate, and as such she was guilty of *lèse majesté* against God. As a Devil worshiper she was part of what was considered to be an enormous conspiracy against both church and state. Even worse, she was participating in a movement that was trying to turn the world upside down, symbolized by the many rituals of inversion that were performed at the sabbath. If one had any doubts regarding her intentions, there was the reassurance of Scripture, "Rebellion is as the sin of witchcraft" (1 Sam. 15.23). The English theologian William Perkins developed this theme in *The Damned Art of Witchcraft* (1602). "The most notorious traitor and witch that can be," Perkins wrote, "is the witch. For she renounceth God himself, the king of kings; she leaves the society of his church and people; she bindeth herself in league with the Devil." Later in the seventeenth century Scottish royalists, in an effort to discredit the recently defeated Covenanters, asserted in 1661, "Rebellion is the mother of witchcraft."

Much of this talk about rebellion was mere rhetoric. It reflected the fears and the insecurities of a threatened male establishment rather than the activities of the witch herself. As we have seen, most of the charges brought against witches were completely groundless. Witches did not gather at the sabbath, plot the destruction of church and state, or copulate with demons. Very few of them made pacts with the Devil. Most of them did not even engage in the practice of maleficent magic. Witches were the classic scapegoats, victims of the neuroses of both the ruling elite and the impoverished lower classes.

It is as both subversive and scapegoat that the witch has continued to exist, long after the prosecution of witches has ceased and the belief in them has disappeared. At many times in modern history, when a profound fear has gripped the souls of men, authorities have identified deviant or marginal groups in their midst as the source of their troubles; they have accused them of crimes that they did not commit; they have attributed to them a desire to destroy both the moral and the political order; and they have done everything in their power to destroy them. The republican in England during the 1790s, the Jew in Nazi Germany, the Communist in post–World War II America have all taken on the role, and in many cases experienced the fate, of the seventeenth-century witch.

But it would be wrong to see the witch simply as scapegoat and victim. The witch did sometimes embody the "spirit of revolt" that Jules Michelet attributed to the medieval witch in *La Sorcière* (1862) and that Emmanuel Le Roy Ladurie has detected in the mythical content of the confessions of witches from Languedoc. For the witch did often enter a protest against both the policies of the ruling elite in seventeenth-century communities and the judicial practices of seventeenth-century courts. In taking such a stand she had little hope of success. In most countries of Europe acquittals in witchcraft cases were relatively rare. In a few instances, sustained by the determination to establish her innocence, she courageously withstood the excruciating tortures that were administered to her and managed to survive. In the great majority of cases she was executed or banished. Her death or exile was a terrible tragedy, the result of one of the greatest miscarriages of justice in the history of the West. But when we consider the witch's defiance of those authorities who persecuted her, her efforts to withstand the tortures administered to her, and her often persistent denials of her own guilt, we find much to admire as well as to pity.

BIBLIOGRAPHY

Caro Baroja, Julio. *The World of the Witches*. Translated by O. N. V. Glendinning. Chicago: University of Chicago Press, 1964.

Dupont-Bouchat, Marie Sylvie, Willem Frijhoff, and Robert Muchembled. *Prophètes et sorciers dans les Pays-Bas XVI–XVII siècle*. Paris: Hachette, 1978.

Ginzberg, Carlo. *The Night Battles: Witchcraft and Agrarian Cults in the Sixteenth and Seventeenth Centuries*. Translated by John and Anne Tedeschi. New York: Penguin Books, 1985. Originally published as *I Benandanti: Stregoneria e culti agrari tra Cinquecento e Seicento*. Turin: Einaudi, 1966.

Henningsen, Gustav. *The Witches' Advocate: Basque Witchcraft and the Spanish Inquisition (1609–1614)*. Reno, Nev.: University of Nevada Press, 1980.

Klaits, Joseph. *Servants of Satan: The Age of the Witch Hunts*. Bloomington, Ind.: Indiana University Press, 1985.

Larner, Christina. *Enemies of God: The Witch-Hunt in Scotland*. Baltimore: Johns Hopkins University Press, 1981.

Lehmann, Hartmut. "Hexenverfolgungen und Hexenprozesse im Alten Reich zwischen Reformation und Aufklärung." *Jahrbuch des Instituts für Deutsche Geschichte* 7 (1978): 13–70.

Levack, Brian P. *The Witch-Hunt in Early Modern Europe*. London and New York: Longman, 1987.

Midelfort, H. C. Erik. *Witch Hunting in Southwestern Germany, 1562–1684: The Social and Intellectual Foundations*. Stanford: Stanford University Press, 1972.

Monter, E. William. *Witchcraft in France and Switzerland: The Borderlands during the Reformation.* Ithaca: Cornell University Press, 1976.

Muchembled, Robert. "The Witches of the Cambrésis: The Acculturation of the Rural World in the Sixteenth and Seventeenth Centuries." Pages 221–76 in *Religion and the People, 800–1700.* Edited by James Obelkevich. Chapel Hill: University of North Carolina Press, 1979.

Soman, Alfred. "Les procès de sorcellerie au Parlement de Paris (1565–1642)." *Annales E.S.C.* (July-August 1977): 790–814.

Thomas, Keith. *Religion and the Decline of Magic: Studies in Popular Beliefs in Sixteenth- and Seventeenth-Century England.* London: Weidenfeld & Nicolson; New York: Scribner, 1971.

10

THE SCIENTIST

Paolo Rossi

SCIENCE AND "SCIENTISTS"

THE TYPE OF KNOWLEDGE that we call "science" was born in Europe, and it spread with extraordinary rapidity throughout the entire planet. It is now present not only in non-Occidental cultures of extremely ancient tradition (China, Japan, India, Korea) but also among peoples who, only a century ago, were considered "primitive." Either because we are too used to extraordinary things or because we have a weak sense of history, we have reached the point where we feel no astonishment at the truly stupefying fact that scientific knowledge cuts across ethnic groups, civilizations, nations, and religious and cultural traditions. Millions of young people study the same texts. The physics and the genetics studied in a university department in Japan or Australia are exactly the same disciplines studied in Scotland, France, or Italy. All members of the scientific community share a system of norms and a scientific ethos that is (in a measure that varies historically) independent of languages and political or religious creeds. The fact that those norms are at times violated—as the critics and the adversaries of science are fond of pointing out—does not mean that they do not exist or that they are not broadly operative. Above all, it does not stop the great majority of scientists from reacting strongly when those norms are denied or challenged. One commonly accepted rule is the independence of scientific truth from all racial, political, or religious criteria—that is, from all criteria external to science itself. Another limits intellectual ownership of a discovery (which, once made, belongs to everyone) to public recognition of that discovery. Another is a "systematic skepticism" that requires and welcomes verification, which means that all hypotheses advanced and all results deriving from them are subject to continual, unbiased, critical public examination.

The medieval universities offered professional training for a career in the church, in jurisprudence, and in medicine. The ancient world and the medieval world had solid and long-lasting intellectual traditions, particularly in mathematics, astronomy, and medicine. Some scholars have spoken of premodern scientific knowledge as "a science without scientists" because the historical figure of the modern scientist arose in Europe between the late sixteenth century and the end of the seventeenth century. Undeniably, great changes took place during the course of the seventeenth century. Equally undeniably, the term "scientific revolution," by now part of the language, refers not only to the emergence of novelties or discoveries in particular sectors of knowledge but also to the profound transformations by means of which a specific form of knowledge with unique characteristics was constituted—a process that led to defining activities of scientific research as a genuine "profession." Within a complex movement (that has been studied at length) involving ideas and relationships among various communities, the sociology of science—a flourishing discipline in our own century—has discerned two major processes. It has called these processes "institutionalization" and "professionalization." The first term speaks of the ways in which science has constructed institutions of its own (academies, scientific societies; at a later date, laboratories and research institutes) distinct from the traditional institutions of culture. The second term speaks of a shift that took place, for the most part during the nineteenth century, when research activities became a career and the "virtuoso" or dilettante scientist disappeared.

The so-called "fathers" of modern science (Kepler, Galileo, Bacon, Descartes, Harvey, and others) often spoke of science, but they did not use the word "scientist," a word coined in the nineteenth century. To speak of the image or the figure of the man of science during the Baroque age is to raise a series of questions concerning the origins of the modern image of science and some of the basic characteristics of that image. The condition of the "scientist" in the age of Copernicus and Cardano was still that of the medieval intellectual: he was either a man of the church, a professor, or a physician. During the seventeenth century a series of important changes took place. The first scientific institutions arose, and an image of science was proposed that contained some elements that we recognize as "our own."

EMERGENT FIGURES AND IDEAS

The history of science (a discipline that originated in the age of positivism) often projected into the past the image of the nineteenth-century scientist and, as Walter Pagel noted regarding Harvey, it constructed an imaginary personage—a sort of anti-Aristotelian, positivist, patient experimenter who had no resemblance to historical reality. But it is not fair to use hindsight to quarrel with the great achievements of positivist history. In fact, the dynamism of the new ideas and the moment in which they and new figures emerged out of traditional contexts have been largely ignored, even in the most recent history of science, a discipline greatly influenced by logical empiricism and the philosophy of Karl Popper. Scholars have begun from the basis of those philosophical presuppositions and from a widely shared interest in what has been called the logical structure of theories to concentrate more on what was constructed than on the modes and techniques of construction; on styles that had already been realized more than on the emergence of new styles; on fully matured individuals more than on the processes of the rise and formation of ideas.

The emergence of ideas and social figures is a birth, an arrival into life, and the figures who first emerge in history bring with them much of the past and only scattered bits of the future.

A VARIETY OF FIGURES

The most striking thing about the generation of men of science of the age of Peter Paul Rubens (who died in 1640) and Gian Lorenzo Bernini (who died in 1680, at the venerable age of eighty-two) is their enormous diversity. In the thirty years between 1626 and 1657 death came for Francis Bacon (1626), Johannes Kepler (1630), Robert Fludd (1637), Robert Burton (1640), Galileo Galilei (1642), Jan Baptista van Helmont (1644), Bonaventura Cavalieri (1647), Marin Mersenne (1648), René Descartes (1650), Pierre Gassendi (1655), and William Harvey (1657). Francis Bacon was a famous philosopher who published aphorisms instead of treatises, who detested the universities, who was engaged in politics to the point of becoming lord chancellor, and who lived on a magnificent scale (before his trial for corruption) and kept a pack of over a hundred greyhounds. Kepler went to teach mathematics and astronomy at Graz at the age of twenty-three; he became Tycho Brahe's assistant in his observatory at Uraniborg, the first European scientific institution not within a university in which research took place, books were printed, and astronomy was taught. In 1601 Kepler was named imperial mathematician, but he lived a miserable life, making a living drawing up horoscopes, and he struggled for over six years to save his mother, accused of witchcraft, from being burned at the stake. Galileo was a professor of mathematics at Pisa and Padua who aspired in vain to a chair in philosophy. He did not consider making instruments beneath him; he became "first mathematician and philosopher" to the grand duke of Tuscany; he was tried and sentenced for having sustained theses that were judged heretical and was forced to abjure his Copernican convictions publicly, kneeling before the cardinals of the Roman Inquisition. Descartes was a soldier and a ferocious critic of the schools and the universities; he wrote his most famous text in the form of an autobiography and discovered the basic elements of a new and marvelous science in a dream. He lived on a modest independent income, refused to publish his work in physics after he learned of Galileo's condemnation, and ended his days as private tutor to Queen Christina of Sweden. Mersenne was a religious in the order of the Minims who added a vow not to eat meat or dairy products to the usual vows. From his abbey he corresponded with all the scientists and learned men of his time and served as a point of reference for them. Van Helmont was a physician, as was the Rosicrucian magus Robert Fludd. Harvey was also a physician: he studied in Padua, became a member of the Royal College of Physicians, was personal physician to James I, and never abandoned his Aristotelian grounding. Cavalieri was a religious of the order of the Gesuati, the Apostolic Clerics of St. Jerome, and taught mathematics at the university. Gassendi was a priest whose friends and acquaintances included physicians and men of science and a professor of astronomy at the Collège Royal in Paris.

The science of the seventeenth century did not arise only because of the work of great figures. It was constructed, propagandized, and energetically defended by a composite and multifaceted throng—professors and teachers of mathematics and astronomy in and out of the universities, physicians, surveyors, navigators, engineers, instrument makers, pharmacists, alchemists, surgeons, travelers, natural philosophers, and cultivated craftsmen, "virtuosi" who cultivated mechanical philosophy. As A. Rupert Hall has written, the period was a sort of "free age" between the more restricted age of the medieval *magister artium* and that of the doctorate or the Ph.D. of modern times. Becoming a "scientist" in the seventeenth century did not require Latin or mathematics, nor did it require a broad knowledge of books or a university chair. Publishing a paper in the acts of an academy or becoming a member of a scientific society was open to a broad range of people—professors, experimenters, craftsmen, the curious, and dilettantes. Although recent scholarship has quite rightly corrected a too rigid opposition between the universities and the academies, the notion that the universities played a relatively marginal role in the scientific revolution remains valid. It is true that nearly all the great scientists of the seventeenth century (and the eighteenth century) studied in a university, but it is also true that very few scientists spent their entire careers inside, even mainly inside, a university. During the seventeenth century, the universities tended to be closed to discoveries in physics, astronomy, botany, zoology, and chemistry, although they continued to pursue an interest in mathematics and medicine. They remained largely untouched by the doctrines of the new "mechanical" or "experimental" philosophy, which was diffused through books, periodicals, the acts of the academies and scientific societies, and private letters rather than through university courses.

In the 1660s, a private association of like-minded friends known as Gresham College circulated a "Ballad of Gresham College" that stated:

> Gresham College now will be
> The whole world's university;
> Oxford and Cambridge make us laugh,
> Their learning is but pedantry.
>
> *[English version supplied by the author]*

THE LEGACY OF MAGIC

During the age of the Renaissance, the magus and the alchemist wove a tapestry whose borders overlapped the fabric of science and modern technology at several points. The hermetic tradition had by no means disappeared in the early seventeenth century, as evidenced by the violently polemical tone of Bacon's writings between 1603 and 1620, by Mersenne's harsh attacks in the 1620s, or by the quarrels between Mersenne and Robert Fludd and between Fludd and Kepler. The "triadic" arrangements of the manuals of the history of philosophy written by Hegel's followers present imaginary temporal distances, but Campanella's *Metaphysics* was published in Paris the year following the publication of Descartes's *Discourse on Method*. The image inherited from positivism of the triumphal advance of scientific knowledge through the superstitions of magic now seems definitively a thing of the past, and a number of important studies (by Eugenio Garin, Walter Pagel, Frances Yates, Allen Debus, D. P. Walker, Paola Zambelli, and Charles Webster) have clearly shown the extent of the influence of the magical-hermetic tradition on many men who figured prominently in the scientific revolution.

In his defense of the sun's central position in the solar system, Copernicus invoked the authority of Hermes Trismegistus. In the early seventeenth century, William Gilbert appealed to the authority of Hermes and Zoroaster and equated his own doctrine of the earth's magnetic force with the "magical" thesis of universal animation. It is hard to say (if the question even has any sense) whether the *De Magnete* is the last work of natural magic of the Renaissance or one of the first works of modern experimental science. Even if all works on magnetism open with Gilbert's name, his science had nothing to do either with mathematics and mathematical methods or with mechanics as Galileo understood the term. Gilbert thought of attraction as a spiritual force, he held that the magnet had a soul (superior to man's soul), and he understood the Earth as a *mater communis* in whose womb metals were formed.

Bacon violently attacked the "fantastic, tumid, and superstitious" philosophy of the magus and the alchemist and called Paracelsus "a fanatical breeder of phantasms," yet he spoke of matter's "perceptions," "desires," and "aversions" and his thought was strongly conditioned by the language and the models of the tradition of alchemy, particularly in the concept of "forms" that lies at the heart of his physics. When he accepted the thesis that fire can cause substances to appear that did not previously exist, or when he lingered over the difficulties deriving from "contemporaneous introduction of several natures into one body," Bacon was treating the sort of problem typical of alchemy.

Kepler had a thorough knowledge of the *Corpus Hermeticum*. He held that the structures of geometry corresponded to the structures of the universe; he compared the number of the planets and the dimensions of their spheres with the relationship between the five regular or "cosmic" solids spoken of by Plato; his theories on the music or celestial harmony of the spheres were imbued with Pythagorean mysticism. Kepler did not know the principle of inertia and had no notion of centripetal force, so for him a continual and uniform velocity required the application of a continual motor force. The existence of a "soul" in the sun was indispensable to the functioning of the solar system.

The modern world has taken Descartes as an emblem of rational thought. In his maturity he reached the point of radical rejection of all symbolism, but as a young man he thought that the imagination gave better results than reason; he amused himself (as so many sixteenth-century magi had done) with the construction of automatons and shadow theaters; like many followers of magical Llullism, he insisted on the unity and the harmony of the cosmos. These were notions that appeared later (in a different key) in Leibniz, whose "universal characteristic" reflected concepts from the tradition of hermetic and cabalistic Llullism. Leibniz saw his new logic as an "innocent magic" and a "nonchimerical cabala." He was also an ardent reader of works that now could scarcely be called "scientific."

Motifs from solar literature even found an echo in Harvey in his image of the heart as the "sun of the microcosm." Even Newton's concept of space as *sensorium Dei* has been shown to have been influenced by neo-Platonic currents and the Judaic cabala. Newton not only read and summarized alchemic texts but also spent long hours studying alchemy. It is clear from his manuscripts that he had faith in a *prisca theologia* (one of the central notions of hermeticism) whose truth was to be proved by means of the new experimental science.

The notion of truth and progress conceived *also* as a "return" was a prevalent theme. Francis Bacon presented his great reform of knowledge as an *instauratio*, the fulfillment of an ancient promise. The new operative science was to permit the restoration of the power over nature that humankind had lost after the Fall. Bacon thought that the "ancient fables" were not produced in their age but were like "sacred relics and light airs breathing out of better times, that were caught from the traditions of more ancient nations and so received into the flutes and the trumpets of the Greeks."

The idea that knowledge had to be revived, that it was in some fashion hidden in the remote past of human history, that before the philosophy of the Greeks some fundamental truths had been glimpsed but were later wiped out and lost is certainly a "hermetic" theme: it runs through a large part of the culture of the seventeenth century, however, and it surfaces in the least likely authors. One example is the *Regulae* of Descartes, the doughty champion of the superiority of the moderns.

In his *De mundi systemate*, written between 1684 and 1686, Newton traced the Copernican thesis not only back to Philolaus and Aristarchus but to Plato, Anaximander, and Numa Pompilius, and he repeated the thesis of the ancient wisdom of the Egyptians, "who represent, with sacred rites and hieroglyphics, mysteries that transcend popular comprehension." In his *Scolii classici* (recently edited by Paolo Casini), Newton manipulated his authors shrewdly, carefully choosing his quotations to show that the ancient philosophers were aware of the phenomena and the laws of gravitational astronomy. Even if they expressed it symbolically, people in the remote historical past knew that the force of attraction diminishes proportionally to the square of the distance.

Some have gone too far in presenting Bacon and Newton as "hermetic" thinkers, but we cannot deny that Bacon's position concerning "ancient fables" is not easily deciphered and that Newton was firmly convinced that he was rediscovering truths of natural philosophy that had appeared in the remote historical past, had been revealed by God himself, had been concealed after the Fall and the introduction of sin, and had been in part rediscovered by the ancient sages. The great book of nature had already been deciphered. Copernicus, Kepler, and even Galileo conceived of the progress of astronomy as a return.

The metaphor of a tapestry with superimposed or interwoven threads by no means implies that we should follow the lead of some who have been tempted to give up trying to distinguish between the various colors and threads in that fabric. Thinkers of the early modern age accepted from the great tradition of natural magic of the Renaissance one idea of central importance: the knowledge that has nature as its object is not only contemplation and not only "theory." It is also operation, manipulation, intervention. The dominion and control of nature are constitutive ends and are essential to science, and what we call "reality" has something to do not only with what we think about the world, but also with what we do in the world.

This notion is expressed with high literary efficacy—as was his wont—by the Lord Chancellor: Bacon tells us that we must read with humility in the great book of nature; that we need to polish the clouded mirror of the mind and "make ourselves like children," but that we also need to learn to "twist the lion's tail."

KNOWING AND DOING

The idea that knowing the world has something to do with its transformation (or that knowing and doing might even be one and the same) runs through the scientific culture of the seventeenth century. One operative idea in what was commonly known as "mechanical philosophy" was that natural events could be described by means of the concepts and methods of the branch of physics called "mechanics"; another strongly operative idea was, precisely, that the machines and devices constructed by human beings could constitute a "privileged model" for the comprehension of nature.

Devices, machines, and the mechanical arts in general were conceived in ways that had little to do with tradition. In Bacon's eyes the "mechanical arts" contained a knowledge that had formerly existed on the fringes of official science and had been relegated to the world of people who constructed buildings, built ships, and made instruments—the world of mining engineers and of the many craftsmen who applied their skills to a variety of materials. Their activities served to "reveal the processes of nature" and were a form of knowledge. The technical arts (unlike philosophy and all other branches of knowledge) were capable of progressing— that is, they built on their own acquisitions, and at such a rapid pace that "men's desires fall short before they reach perfection." Furthermore, the mechanical arts relied on collaboration and were a form of collective knowledge: in them, "many wits and industries have contributed in one," whereas in philosophy "many wits and industries have been spent about the wit of some one." There was a call to make the methods, procedures, and language of the technical arts topics for reflection and study: the *experientia erratica* of "mechanics" and the dispersed knowledge of those who used their hands to modify nature should be removed from chance and from the harmful influence of the magus and the alchemist and should be made into an organic and systematic *corpus* of knowledge. Throughout the philosophic tradition from Plato to Bernardino Telesio, there had been a rigid separation between theory and practice, knowledge and operation, intellect applied to the world and human intervening in the world. For Bacon it made no sense to ask whether the truths of science derived from the methods used to determine them or from their practical utility. For him, the two "twin human intentions, Science and Power" were one, and if one could say that the test of truth in a method was that it gave rise to works, it was equally true, reading that same axiom backward, that actual works could come only from a true method. Theoretical research and practical activity, understood in these terms, were one and the same, and what was most useful operatively was also what was truest in theory ("ista duo pronuntiata, activum et contemplativum, res eadem sunt, et quod in operando utilissimum, id in sciendo verissimum"). In that sense, practical results were not only beneficial for life but were also gauges of truth ("opera non tantum beneficia, sed et veritatis pignora sunt").

Kepler denied that the universe was "a divine animated being" and conceived it as being similar to a watch all of whose motions "derive from a simple material force." Hobbes wondered, "What is the heart, but a spring; and the nerves, but so many strings?" Descartes considered automatons, which, although constructed by men, "move on their own," and he compared nerves to the "tubes of the machinery of fountains" and muscles and tendons to mechanical devices and springs. For Boyle, the entire universe was "a great self-moving machine" and all phenomena should thus be considered in terms of "the two great and universal principles of bodies: matter and motion." Gassendi stated that we investigate natural things in the same way as we investigate "the things of which we ourselves are the authors."

The only realities available to knowledge were the world of the phenomena, which analysis could reconstruct, and the world of things, which the hands could produce by artifice or the intellect could create as possible entities. We can know machines; we can know the real world to the extent that it can be brought down to the model of a machine. Such notions deliberately reversed traditional approaches to the relationship between nature and "art" (that is, artifice). Art was not (as in a widespread medieval tradition) the "monkey" of nature; it was not "on its knees" before Nature. The products of art were neither different from nor inferior to those of nature. Descartes insisted forcefully on this point: "There is no difference between the machines that craftsmen construct and the various bodies composed by nature." Both Descartes and Gassendi agreed with Bacon's thesis that denied all difference in the essence of natural objects and artificial objects: "The opinion has long been prevalent that art is something different from nature and things artificial different from things natural. . . . Men ought to be surely persuaded of this: that the artificial does not differ from the natural in form or essence, but only in the efficient [cause]."

If the universe was a machine, the ancient image of a correspondence between man the microcosm and the universe as macrocosm crumbled, as did the idea that the universe was created to the measure of man. Within the new conception of the relationship of art and nature there was increasing acceptance of the notion that man is precluded from knowledge of essences and final causes and that such knowledge, outside the realm of science, is reserved to God as the artificer, constructor, or watchmaker of the universe. The criterion of "knowing as doing" and of the identity of knowing and constructing could be applied to man as well as to God. The human intellect had full access to the truths of mathematics and geometry inasmuch as these were constructed truths, but it could never grasp either the hidden essences of things (*quidditates rerum intimae*) nor the secrets of nature (*arcana naturae*); science could be and was intended to be only phenomenal knowledge of the world. We know the "true reasons," Mersenne wrote, "only of those things that we can construct with our hands or with our intellect." Hobbes, who disagreed with Mersenne on many points, was in complete agreement on this one: geometry was demonstrable because we ourselves trace its lines and figures, and political philosophy was demonstrable "because we ourselves construct the state." We can only express hypotheses concerning natural bodies.

The idea of an active, constructive knowledge was to have a decisive influence on thought concerning the social and political world as well as the natural world. Hobbes's statements have quite rightly been compared with what Giambattista Vico had to say about the identity of *verum* and *factum*. In his *Scienza Nuova* Vico saw the world of history as knowable and a legitimate object of science inasmuch as history was made and that world had been constructed by humankind.

EQUALITY OF INTELLIGENCE

For those who cultivated magic and alchemy and for the followers of the hermetic tradition, the texts of ancient wisdom were sacred books containing hidden secrets decipherable only by an elect few "initiates." The truth was hidden in the past and in what was profound, and what was most hidden was most precious. Truth had to be sought; it needed to be deciphered by reaching behind the various means used to keep it hidden from the unworthy. The seeker must always go "beyond the letter" for a message that was increasingly recondite as the search advanced. The borderline between the figure of the magus and that of the priest was difficult to determine. Even when magic emphasized the "naturalness" of magical operations, it never freed itself either from the ambiguous concept of method as initiation or from the image of the magus as an exceptional being and magi as the "elect."

"People's passion for opening schools" seemed to Jan Amos Komenský (Latinized as Comenius), writing around 1630, to be one of the characteristics of the new times. That same enthusiasm was responsible for "the great multiplication of books in all languages so that even children and women can acquire familiarity with them." The movement for universal knowledge—comprehensible to all because communicable to all—became a central and dominant cultural theme. Some convictions concerning human nature, access to truth, and the procedures for gaining knowledge were expressed in terms sufficiently radical to disconcert those scholars who have undervalued the presence of the hermetic tradition and the weight of magical naturalism on culture, including scientific culture. Those convictions arose from within a range of perspectives, and their meanings varied. Independent of their origins, however, they contributed to the affirmation and consolidation of an image of knowledge that stood in strong contrast to the magical and alchemic tradition; they provided an alternative to that tradition and offered a new image of the persons who pursued such knowledge.

Three ideas lay at the center of the new image of knowledge. First: no process of "initiation" of a religious sort was necessary in order to accede to knowledge and to truth. Nor must one scorn the part of human nature that was "only human" or seek to join the elect or the "illuminated." Membership in the human species sufficed. Second: the procedures or "methods" for reaching truth were not inaccessible, secret, uncommunicable, or complicated but rather "modest," "simple," or "humble." Thus verities could be exposed in clear language and were, for that reason, accessible to all (in principle if not in fact). Third: all human beings were capable of acquiring knowledge and perceiving the truth. Rather than revelation or an incommunicable mystical experience, scientific knowledge made explicit potentialities present in everyone. As Antoine Arnauld said in his *Nouveaux éléments de géométrie,* science simply consisted in "advancing what we know naturally."

The truths that are called common notions, Descartes wrote in his *Principia philosophiae,* are the ones that many people are capable of perceiving clearly and distinctly. If some persons did not find those truths sufficiently self-evident, it was not "because one man's faculty of knowledge extends more widely than another's." Inability to perceive truth was caused by prejudices acquired in childhood that were extremely difficult to shake off. I hardly need recall the famous beginning of Descartes's *Discourse on Method,* which affirms that "good sense is the best distributed thing in the world." The faculty of distinguishing truth from falsehood was equal by nature in all humankind. "The diversity of our opinions" did not arise "because some of us are more reasonable than others" but "because we direct our thoughts along different paths and do not attend to the same things." Speaking of himself, Descartes states that he had "never presumed my mind to be in any way more perfect than that of the ordinary man." The notions in his writings were "simple" and in accordance with "good sense," and his method followed "simple and easy reasonings." The doctrine exposing the rules of method was not veiled or covered "to keep it far from the common people" but was adorned and garbed so as "to seem pleasing to human intelligence." Since "all the things which come within the scope of human knowledge are interconnected," if one began with the simplest notions and proceeded step by step, "it does not take great skill and capacity to find them." The exposition of the method must proceed by "clear and common" arguments; when it did, the truths reached "will have course in the world in the same fashion as coins, which are of no less value when they come out of a peasant's purse." If not many men devoted themselves to the search for wisdom it was because they "do not hope to succeed and do not know what they are capable of."

In his comparison of his own philosophy with the one "by which the philosophers' stones are made," Thomas Hobbes stated that "every man brought Philosophy, that is, Natural Reason, into the world with him." Reason, he added, "is no less natural than passion and is the same in all men." The few and first elements of philosophy were the "seeds" out of which a true philosophy could be developed. Those seeds, or first principles, seemed to Hobbes "but poor, arid, and, in appearance, deformed." Addressing his reader as a friend, Hobbes writes that "philosophy is the daughter of your mind; it is still unformed within you." The method he had constructed could be used by all: "If it pleases you, you can use it yourself."

Mersenne, the indefatigable "secretary of cultivated Europe," put the radically antimagical and antioccult idea of the equality of intelligence into a striking maxim: "A man can do nothing that another man cannot also do, and each man contains within himself all that is needed to philosophize and reason on all things."

Even though historians of political thought have not always realized it, the thesis of the equality of intelligence in face of scientific truth had strong political implications. All human beings, Pufendorf said, have within them a principle for self-government, and all men are intelligent beings in their susceptibility to obligations: "I cannot be persuaded that the mere face of natural excellence is sufficient to give one being the right to impose any obligation on other beings, who have, just as he does, an internal principle for governing themselves." The notion of equality before the truth implied a renunciation of the image, present in hermeticism and in many philosophies derived from Aristotle and Averroës, of a clear separation between "philosophers" and "vulgar" people "like beasts" for whom tales of miracles, angels, and devils were appropriate. Such people required fables, as Pomponazzi wrote, "to induce them to good and preserve them from evil, as one does with children with the hope of rewards and the fear of punishment."

After the age of Bacon and Descartes, Hobbes, Mersenne, and Galileo, all forms of knowledge that theorized secrecy in the name of inaccessibility, that envisaged "superhuman" difficulties on the path to knowledge, or that stated that only initiates could know the truth and only the few could reach the *epistēmē* became irremediably and structurally connected with the political notion that the commonality were unable to govern themselves unaided and, like children, needed fables that kept them from the truth.

The idea of the equality of intelligence became an integral and constitutive part of the modern image of science. As is the case with all ideas associated or identified with values, it is not fully accepted even today. When ambiguity and enigmatic language become essential to a philosophy or when philosophy painstakingly avoids linguistic clarity or explicitly condemns clear expression as superficial or mere good sense; when the notion of "looking to the past" and the affirmation of a Hidden Wisdom of the Origins and the image of a Truth at the Beginning of Time become major, guiding ideas and central themes in a philosophy; when philosophers theorize a difference of essence between the elect, "Shepherds of Being" (who can attain Wisdom, attain "instants" of revelation, and foresee and foretell Destiny) and those who remain forever confined within the temporality of daily experience, capable of intellect but totally incapable of Thought; when, finally, all this occurs at one time (as, in our century, among Heidegger's followers), then the hermetic tradition reveals its unspent force and celebrates a belated triumph.

SCIENCE AND THE "MEMORY DOCTORS"

As Ludwik Fleck stated as long ago as 1935, the more a specific field of knowledge is presented as strongly structured, the more the concepts it involves become coherent with the whole, and the more susceptible they are to reciprocal definition and continual cross-reference. That network of concepts gave rise, in the so-called "mature" sciences, to a sort of inextricably interwoven fabric resembling "the structure of an organism" more than a collection of statements. All the parts of that structure fulfill a specific function. Some time after its rise and at the end of a cycle in its development, when a science has settled into its specificity and has become recognized as a unique discipline, the initial phases of its development are no longer readily comprehensible, and its rise comes to be understood and expressed in ways strikingly different from how it was understood and expressed at the start.

Thomas Kuhn has returned to these questions in more recent years to stress the fact that scientists tend to see their activities according to a concept of linear progress. They rewrite their manuals ceaselessly, but what they are rewriting is history "written backwards." Why should one consider valuable something that the constancy and intelligence of generations of seekers have enabled us to abandon? Why should the innumerable "errors" that fill the history of science be placed among things worthy to be remembered? Kuhn concludes that there is a strong tendency in the ideology of the scientific profession to disregard history. "New breakthrough[s] . . . initiate the removal of suddenly outdated books and journals from their active position in a science library to the desuetude of a general depository." Once a solution to a problem has been found, the preceding attempts to resolve that problem lose their relevance and become "excess baggage, a needless burden which must be set aside." In respect to their past, artists and scientists have sharply divergent reactions: "Picasso's success has not relegated Rembrandt's paintings to the storage vaults of art museums." Unlike the fine arts, "science destroys its past."

Affirming a need to forget the past and contrasting science and history are in reality older than Ludwik Fleck thought in the 1930s and Thomas Kuhn stated in the 1960s. Both of these attitudes, along with the rise of a genuine quarrel with history, can be traced back to the start of the early modern period and to the years that witnessed the emergence of the modern image of science.

Galileo contrasted natural philosophers to "historians" or "doctors of memory." The thought of the second group needed continual reference to a guide. Seekers were not blind; they needed no guides: "Should you want to continue in this mode of study, leave off the name of philosophers and call yourselves either historians or doctors of memory, as it is not right that those who never philosophize should usurp the honored title of philosopher." The testimony of others had no value compared to the criterion of truth and falsity: "Adducing much testimony serves no purpose because we have never denied that many have written or believed such a thing; rather, we have said that such a thing is false."

It seemed that one had to choose between being a scientist or a historian; between believing in distinguishing truth from falsehood or citing the testimony of others; between knowing nature or knowing history. Descartes agreed on this point: "We will never succeed in being philosophers if we have read all the arguments of Plato and Aristotle without being able to make a sure judgement of a specific problem. In such a case

we would demonstrate that we have learned history, not the sciences."
History was what had already been invented and put into books; science
was skill in solving problems; it was "the discovery of all that the human
mind can discover." Conversing with those of past centuries, Descartes
stated, was "much the same as traveling. But one who spends too much
time traveling eventually becomes a stranger in his own country; and one
who is too curious about the practices of past ages usually remains quite
ignorant about those of the present." Malebranche agreed: historians
were people with a penchant for "things rare and remote" who tended to
"ignore the most necessary and most beautiful truths."

For Spinoza, the truth and rigor of geometry belonged to a world
that did not depend upon the approval of hearers or upon temporal
events. That rigor and that truth formed a model that could be extended
to all knowledge. Truth implied an absolute irrelevance to contexts and
to events that take place within time. How the truth had been arrived at
was of no importance:

> Euclid . . . who only wrote of extremely simple and perfectly intelligible
> matters, is easily understood of every one in his own language; for to be
> certain of the meaning here, it is not indispensable to have a perfect knowl-
> edge of the tongue in which the author wrote; a very ordinary and almost
> puerile proficiency suffices; neither do we here find it requisite to study the
> life and manners of the author, nor are we interested in knowing in what
> language he wrote, in what age he lived, to whom he addressed himself,
> etc.; neither do we see it necessary to inquire into the fortune of the books,
> nor their various readings, nor by whose advice they were accepted as genu-
> ine. Saying so much of Euclid, the same is to be understood of all who have
> written of things appreciable in themselves.

The model to which Spinoza was looking was structured so that theories did not simply replace one another but rather became integrated on
an ever increasing level of generality. Leibniz thought that in philosophy
one could abandon rivalry between schools and even completely do without schools. Philosophy too would become a form of knowledge capable
of growing by successive integration: "In philosophy the schools will disappear just as they have disappeared in geometry. We see, in effect, that
there are no Euclidians, Archimedians, and Apollonians, and that Archi-
medes and Apollonius did not set themselves the task of overturning the
principles of their predecessors but of enlarging them."

Pascal thought that there were sciences dependent upon memory and
reliant upon authority, and other sciences that put their trust instead in
reason and gave little weight to authority. History, geography, jurisprudence, and theology belonged to the first group, "depend on memory, and
are purely historical." They arose either out of "pure and simple fact" or

were "of divine or human institution." "Authority alone can illuminate us" regarding their arguments, and "one can have entire knowledge [of them] to which nothing can be added." Geometry, arithmetic, music, physics, medicine, and architecture belonged to the second group. They "depend on reason" and had as their aim "the search for and the discovery of hidden truths." In these sciences "authority is useless" and reason alone led to knowledge; in them the mind was free to deploy its capacities; in them "invention can be endless and uninterrupted." Growth, progress, novelty, and invention pertained to the sciences of the second group alone: the ancients had laid down an outline for them, and modern thinkers would leave them to posterity in a better state than they had found them. Nature "is always the same, but is not always equally well known." Truth "does not begin to be when people have begun to know it" but was "always older than all the opinions that have been held."

The term *novus* recurs almost obsessively in hundreds of books on philosophy and the sciences published from the age of Copernicus to the age of Newton: *Machinae novae, Nova de universis philosophia, De mundo nostro sublunari philosophia nova, Novum organum, Astronomia nova, Novo theatro di machine, Discorsi intorno a due nuove scienze, Scienza nuova.* This was the age in which a New World was discovered, a world populated with unknown men, new animals, and new plants; a world in which "a vast number of new stars and new motions that were totally unknown to the ancient astronomers" were discovered and the microscope "produced new worlds and unknown lands to our view." There was a complex relationship between the "rediscovery of the ancients" and the "sense of the new" that was characteristic of the culture of the so-called Renaissance. The rejection of the exemplarity of classical culture (on which all the humanists had insisted) took on strongly polemical overtones and in many cases (as in these lines of verse by Perrot de la Sale) took the form of a rejection of classical culture itself:

> De Grec et de Latin, mais point de connaissance
> On nous munit la teste en notre adolescence.
>
> *(In our adolescence they stuff our heads with Greek and Latin but not with knowledge.)*

"Sell your houses [and] your wardrobe and burn your books," Petrus Severinus, a Paracelsan, wrote in 1571. The attack on bookish culture reached the point—in Robert Boyle and others—of invective aimed at any and all tradition. It gave rise to a form of "scientific primitivism" that preferred the experiments taking place in craftsmen's workshops and foundries to what was in libraries, historical and literary studies and to theoretical research.

The ancients, Bacon wrote, had followed the wrong road:

> I profess to have something better to offer you than the ancients. If I
> did this while pursuing the same path as they, then by no verbal ingenuity
> could I avoid challenging them in intellect, excellence, or capacity. . . . In as
> much as a lame man on the road will outstrip an athlete who is off it, the
> case is altered. Remember that the question concerns the path to follow,
> not strength, and that we support the role of the guide, not that of the
> judges. (Farrington translation)

Bacon thought it necessary to "strip ourselves of our character of
learned men and try to become common men." Descartes stated that
those who had never studied could judge "with much greater solidity and
clarity" than those who had attended the schools in which traditional
knowledge was transmitted. Hobbes held that, given the culture of his
time, those who lacked learning, who "content themselves with daily experience," and who "reject . . . philosophy" were men "of sounder judgment" than those who practiced scholastic disputation.

The intellect needed to be cleansed of the false images that assaulted
it and were as if encrusted onto it, rendering opaque what had originally
been lucid and clean. Minds needed to be refurbished and remade in the
image of children's minds. A philosophy potentially present in all humankind needed to be made explicit, trusting the good sense that was
"the best distributed thing in the world" and that was "naturally equal
in all men." Things learned in the schools and the universities should be
forgotten, along with many centuries of history. These ideas were to give
rise to the image (which persisted for more than two hundred years) of a
medieval "dark ages" full of barbarity and superstition. There was a tradition and persons within that tradition that Bacon thought should be
consigned to oblivion.

> I do not conceal from you that we must find a way of clearing sham philoso-
> phers out of our path. Your philosophers are more fabulous than poets.
> They debauch our minds. They substitute a false coinage for the true. And
> worse still are the satellites and parasites of the great ones, the whole mob
> of professorial teachers. How shall truth be heard, if they maintain the din
> of their grovelling and inconsequent ratiocinations? Will not someone recite
> the formula by which I may devote them all to oblivion? (Farrington trans-
> lation)

The medieval image of dwarfs standing on the shoulders of giants
was ambiguous. Undeniably, "we moderns" have seen farther than Plato
or Aristotle, but we are nonetheless dwarfs, condemned to remain so in
comparison to those insuperable giants. The notion of the "superiority"
of the moderns took on a variety of tones and forms, but many texts

shared the idea that the first inhabitants of the earth were barbarian and rough creatures, incapable—like Vico's *bestioni*—of moving on the terrain of "reason unfurled." Bacon stated all these notions concisely, expressing a dimension that had become an essential trait of science and a part of its image as early as the start of the early modern age. Forgetting the past and going beyond all that had been said in the past are positive values for scientific knowledge. The light of nature lay ahead; behind there was the darkness of the past. Scholars' interests should be turned toward the future, not to the past; what remained to be done was more important than what had been done. In Bacon's words: "Scientia ex naturae lumine petenda, non ex antiquitatis obscuritate repetenda est. Nec refert quid factum fuerit. Illud videndum quid fieri possit."

THE PORTRAIT OF THE "SCIENTIST"

During the course of the seventeenth century not only an image of science but also a "portrait" of the natural philosopher took shape in Europe. This portrait differed both from that of the ancient philosopher or sage and from the image of the saint, the monk, the university professor, the courtier, the perfect prince, the craftsman, the humanist, or the magus. The ends theorized by the composite groups of intellectuals who contributed to the development of scientific knowledge were clearly different from the goals of individual sanctity or literary immortality and from the aims of the exceptional "demonic" personality.

A chaste patience, a natural modesty, grave and composed manners, a great capacity for understanding others and a smiling pity for them were the characteristics of the man of science in Bacon's portrait of him. Bacon wrote in the *Refutation of Philosophy*:

> There were some fifty men there, all of mature years, not a young man among them, all bearing the stamp of dignity and probity. . . . At his entry they were chatting easily among themselves but sitting in rows as if expecting somebody. Not long after there entered to them a man of peaceful and serene air, save that his face had become habituated to the expression of pity. . . . He took his seat, not on a platform or pulpit, but on a level with the rest and delivered the following address. (Farrington translation)

Bacon's portrait of the "new sage" doubtless resembles Galileo or Einstein more than it does the turbulent Paracelsus or the restless and adventurous Cornelius Agrippa. The titanic force of the Renaissance magus now seems supplanted by a classical tranquility and an atmosphere similar to that of the "conversations" of the earliest humanists.

Even the discussions that took place between the protagonists of Descartes's *Recherche de la vérité* have none of the initiate's fervor about them. Their style was "that of a conversation in which several friends, frankly and without ceremony, disclose the best of their thoughts to each other." Salviati and Sagredo use much the same "familiar" tone as they debate the new science in Galileo's *Dialogo sopra i due massimi sistemi*. Bacon's writings added two notes to that civil, well-mannered humanistic atmosphere: first, an awareness that by the use of technology and collaborative efforts among scholars humanity would be able to dispose of unlimited power; second, the realization that the theater of human initiative was no longer one city or one nation but the entire world.

SCIENCE AND POLITICS

Galileo invited the theologians of his age (in vain) to "consider the difference that there is between opinionable and demonstrative doctrines." Those whose vocation was the demonstrative sciences did not have the option of "changing their opinions at will," and there was a vast difference "between commanding a mathematician or a philosopher and disposing a merchant or a man of law." Furthermore, "demonstrative conclusions about the things of nature and heaven cannot be changed as easily as opinions about what is or is not licit in a contract, a census, or an exchange."

When political power exerted pressure on science—when, as Galileo wrote, "persons who know absolutely nothing about a science or art have occasion to judge the intelligent"—the effect was devastating for science. Political intervention into scientific matters was particularly devastating when—in our own century as in the seventeenth century—religions, ideologies, or philosophies came to be conceived as totalizing visions or touchstones for judging the truth or falsity of varied kinds of theories.

Both the visions of an infinite cosmos, derived from Copernicus and propagandized by Giordano Bruno, and "mechanical philosophy" seemed to challenge points of major importance in the Christian tradition—in the first case, man's central position in the universe and, in the second, the presence of ends or goals in the universe.

When the tension (which is of a structural nature) between political power and science becomes open conflict, men of science are faced with several ineluctable decisions. First, they may draw a firm distinction between politics and science or take care to separate religion and science; second, they can conceal or mask doctrines that are viewed as dangerous; third, they can put aside research projects and problems that might lead to solutions that had been "condemned" or might lead to taking a position opposed to ones that the power structure considered acceptable. All these solutions were adopted, in varying ways and measure, by the natural philosophers and the scientists of the seventeenth century.

The affirmation of distinct or separate realms operated differently in Catholic and in Protestant countries. Two widely publicized cases—Galileo's and Bacon's—can serve to exemplify the difference.

In 1613 Galileo wrote a famous letter to Benedetto Castelli in which he expressed a number of theses. First, where Scripture was concerned one could not stop at the simple meaning of the words, given that many propositions were expressed so as to "accommodate the incapacity of the common people." Second, in scientific discussions Scripture should be "reserved to the last place." God expresses himself through Scripture and through nature, and we must keep in mind that while Scripture was accommodated to the human understanding of men and women and its words embodied varying meanings, nature was instead "inexorable and immutable" and did not care "whether or not her recondite reasons and modes of operation are revealed to human understanding." Third, nature had within it a coherence and a rigor absent in Scripture: "Not every statement of the Scripture is bound to obligations as severely as each effect of nature." The "natural effects" that experience places before us or that seem proved by necessary demonstrations "should not in any way be called into question on account of Scriptural passages whose words appear to have a different meaning." Fourth, given that the truths of Scripture and Nature could not contradict one another meant that the task of the "wise interpreters" of Holy Writ was to work to "produce [the] true meanings" of scriptural propositions, which were in agreement with ascertained and demonstrated conclusions. Furthermore, given that many passages in Scripture "admit of interpretations far removed from the literal meaning" and that it was by no means sure that all interpreters were inspired by God, it would be prudent not to permit anyone to use passages from Scripture to support or declare as true conclusions regarding nature that might later be proved false. Fifth, Scripture tends to persuade people of the truths that are necessary for salvation, but it is not at all necessary to believe that the information gathered by the senses, by discourse, or by the intellect (with which we have been endowed by God) has been given us by Scripture.

When Galileo deliberately limited science to the level of natural things, recognized an indispensable moral significance in the truths of the faith, and expressed his respect for the supernatural dimension, it could not and did not prevent his statements from seeming dangerous and subversive. In the eyes of the defenders of acquired institutional power such notions threatened to break apart the bond between philosophy and theology that for centuries had seemed to guarantee the church's function as a guide not only to the individual conscience but to knowledge and culture. Clearly, the bravura of the final words of Galileo's letter, in which he attempted to divide his adversaries by stating that the Copernican theory could be made to accord with the text of the Bible much more easily than the Aristotelian and Ptolemaic theory could be made to do so, did little to smooth things over.

Galileo often alternated between excessive certainty and captiousness. He did not always have a clear view of the great question that had been opened up. In what sense had the traditional bond between philosophy and theology been broken? The moment the rigorous language of nature was compared to the metaphorical language of the Bible, did not natural philosophers become the only authoritative interpreters of the meaning of those metaphors as well? Was it not their duty to point out to the interpreters of Scripture which "meanings" were in agreement with the truths of nature? And if the Bible contained *only* propositions necessary to salvation, what sense was there in stating that the famous passage on God's holding back the sun for Joshua "shows clearly the *falsity and impossibility* of the Aristotelian and Ptolemaic world system [emphasis added]"?

Francis Bacon had also become aware, between 1608 and 1620, that the new type of knowledge involved a decisive break with all forms of theology that claimed to be systematic or universal. The fact that philosophers had the temerity "to incorporate the contentious and thorny philosophy of Aristotle with the body of religion" indicated that knowledge was in decline and showed proof of a morally culpable attitude. A "pact" or "marriage" between theology and philosophy would make the resulting union both "iniquitous" and "fallacious." In such a mixture of theology and philosophy, "only the received doctrines of philosophy are included: while new ones, albeit changes for the better, are all but expelled." The truths of science were not to be sought in Scripture, and it was neither proper nor possible to seek natural philosophy in Holy Writ. Anyone devoting himself to such a task would produce not only an "imaginary and fabulous philosophy" but a "heretical religion."

Theology, Bacon insisted, was concerned with knowing the book of the Word of God; natural philosophy regarded the book of God's works. Heaven and earth, which were temporal things, were not to be sought in the word of God, which is eternal. Citing Matthew 22.29, Bacon insisted at some length on the distinction between the will and the power of God. The book of Scripture revealed the will of God; the book of nature, his power. The study of nature offered no enlightenment on God's essence or his will. The end of the "contemplation of the creatures of God" was knowledge, "but, as to the nature of God, no knowledge, but wonder; which is nothing else but contemplation broken off, or losing itself." Modern scientific opinions could not be found in the Bible, therefore it made no sense to seek for meanings in it that might, now and then, be in agreement with the truths discovered by science. Science, on the other hand, could reinforce Christian truth, arousing marvel at the order and harmony of creation. This image of science was to find expression above all in the writings of Robert Boyle and John Ray. The notion continued to be central to English culture until the age of Darwin.

In the history of ideas and the history of science, 1633 was a decisive year. Only a few months after Galileo's condemnation, Descartes wrote to Mersenne to say that he had "almost taken the decision to burn all [his] papers, or at least not to let anyone see them." He chose to suppress his work rather than have it published in an altered version, stating that for nothing in the world would he want anyone to find in it "even a single word disapproved by the church." In a letter dated January 10, 1634, he returned to the topic. The theses contained in his treatise (among them, his opinion on the earth's motion) were so interdependent "that it is enough to discover that one of them is false to know that all the arguments I was using are unsound." This was a significant conclusion, and it returns us to the notion of "dissimulation":

> I desire to live in peace and to continue the life I have begun under the motto *to live well you must live unseen [bene vixit qui bene latuit]*. And so I am more happy to be delivered from the fear of my work's making unwanted acquaintances than I am unhappy at having lost the time and trouble which I spent on its composition.

The notion of "dissimulation" in seventeenth-century science deserves more thorough investigation than it has received to date. The text of Galileo's *Dialogo sopra i due massimi sistemi* leaves no doubt regarding the ontological aims of his theses or their reference to the real world. Nonetheless, Galileo opened his preface "Al discreto lettore" (To the Discerning Reader) with a reference to the "salutary edict" of 1616, noting that persons unknown "impudently asserted" that "this decree had its origin not in judicious inquiry but in passion none too well informed" and that "advisers who were totally unskilled in astronomical observations ought not to clip the wings of reflective intellects by means of rash prohibitions." Such complaints were dangerous, however. The aim of the *Dialogo*, Galileo stated, was to "show to foreign nations that as much is understood of this matter in Italy, and particularly in Rome, as transalpine diligence can ever have imagined." In his earlier writings Galileo had asserted that the Copernican system was a true description of reality. Here he insisted that Copernicus's ideas were totally hypothetical and that he himself was "proceeding as with a pure mathematical hypothesis." Thus he shifted the debate from the plane of the real to that of the possible; from the plane of astronomy as physics to that of astronomy as a purely mathematical construction. The theory of the tides, which for Galileo had been decisive proof of the Earth's motion, became an "ingenious speculation."

Before his condemnation in 1616, Galileo had formulated a very different program. Writing to Piero Dini in May 1615, he stated that there was only one "most expeditious and very sure" way of showing that the Copernican theory was not contrary to Scripture, which was to "show with a thousand proofs that it is true and that the contrary can in no way subsist." Given that two truths cannot contradict one another, it necessarily followed that the Copernican thesis and Scripture "were much in agreement."

Descartes, in a fragment datable to 1630, also asserted that he was able, on the basis of his "fantasies," to explain the first chapter of Genesis much better than other interpreters. He proposed to show clearly that his "description of the birth of the world" agreed "with the verities of the faith" much better than Aristotle's explanation. Like Galileo, Descartes did not continue on that path. He too later abandoned references to the real world for the world of the possible, presenting his cosmology as "an hypothesis which is perhaps very far from the truth." His reference was to an imaginary world; he disclaimed any intention to imitate other philosophers by explaining "the things actually found in the real world." Rather, he would "take the liberty to fashion this matter according to our fancy." He was presenting a fable, and the fable of the formation of an imaginary universe no longer had room—precisely because it was a fable and an imaginary world—for either God or Moses. As a good pupil of the Jesuits, however, Descartes hinted to his reader that his fable might say more about the real world than they could find in the philosophies that claimed to describe it.

Avoidance of the more dangerous notions has frequently been noted by historians of science. After John Milton visited a group of learned Italians he stated that they had envied him for living in England and complained of the state of servitude to which science had been reduced in their country. In more recent years, historians (particularly in Risorgimento Italy) exaggerated in their interpretations; it is fashionable to praise the science of the Jesuits. Their efforts were undeniably deserving of respect, but it is equally undeniable that, beyond all attempts at reevaluation, astronomy after the second condemnation of Galileo's writings in 1633 concentrated more on calculation and less on cosmology and that biology involved the analysis of organs and structures more and focused less and less on general theories concerning animate beings. The "science" of Francesco Lana Terzi and Daniello Bartoli and the monumental works of Athanasius Kircher attempted a sort of grandiose compromise

between the findings of the new science and the legacy of magical naturalism. In his *Mundus subterraneus* of 1644, Kircher examined fossils and
rocks and found in them geometric figures, letters of the Greek and Latin
alphabet, images of celestial bodies, the forms of trees, animals, and
people, and mysterious symbols linked to profound messages that provided a key to revealing the divine meanings pervading the world. Kircher
was seeking, once again, the "hidden sacraments of latent nature" (*ab-
scondita latentis naturae sacramenta*). Science returned to an examination
of the "marvelous"; once more it became a "pleasurable" activity important for its "utility." Scientific knowledge went back to being precisely
what Francis Bacon had said it should not be: "a couch whereupon to rest
a spirit, a terrace for a wandering and variable mind, a shop for profits or
sale."

Like no other philosopher of his time, Bacon had an extremely clear
sense of the scientific enterprise as a collective effort that invested all of
society and required institutions specific to it. He also raised the problem
of the relationship between science and politics. The solution he offered
in the *New Atlantis* was, once more, a clear, firm "separation." The scientists of the New Atlantis lived in solitude, away from the rest of the population. Their place of work reminds us of a university campus cut off from
the world, a peaceful but busy place for research not bothered by the
daily concerns of common mortals. But there was something else: the scientists of the New Atlantis held meetings to decide which of the discoveries that had been made should be communicated to the public at large
and which should not. When a decision was negative they vowed secrecy.
Some of the discoveries that they decided to keep secret were revealed to
the state; others were kept hidden from the political power structure.

Bacon, as we have seen, held that choices regarding values pertained
to ethics and religion. On the problem of the uses that might be made of
scientific and technological discoveries he was no optimist. The wise men
who decided to keep some of their "dangerous" discoveries to themselves
did not live in our own dissolute and corrupt world but within the imaginary civilization of the New Atlantis, an extremely peaceful and tolerant society.

In our contemporary world the figure of the scientist-craftsman who
relies on methods of his or her own to "seek what he wants"—a figure
once so prevalent—has almost totally disappeared. Everyone involved in
scientific research today needs a project, and that project has to be considered worth pursuing (for theoretical or practical reasons or both) and to
be approved by some committee of experts that represents a government,
a public or private institution, or an industry, public or private. Some
research projects find favor and are moved ahead; others are discouraged.
Often the costs and the advantages of competing projects are calculated

not in relation to generic "interests of science" but rather in relation to the interests of individual countries. Participation in scientific development has become everywhere a form of national investment.

Who evaluates and who decides on the utilization of the findings of scientific research? In the civilization that we have brought into being two opposed and contrasting tendencies share a difficult and complex existence, reflecting both the need to have competent persons (who are always few in number) make decisions and the need for the many to control the decisions of the few. During the three centuries that separate us from the seventeenth century, answers to problems of this nature have made less progress than science and technology.

BIBLIOGRAPHY

Altieri Biagi, Maria Luisa, et al., eds. *Scienziati italiani del Seicento*. Milan: Ricciardi, 1969.

Ben David, Joseph. *The Scientist's Role in Society: A Comparative Study*. Englewood Cliffs, N.J.: Prentice Hall, 1971.

Borselli, Lucilla, Chiaretta Poli, and Paolo Rossi. "Una liberacomunità di dilettanti nella Parigi del '600." Pages 11–65 in *Cultura popolare e cultura dotta nel Seicento*. Atti del Convegno di Studio, Genoa, November 23–25, 1982. Milan: Angeli, 1983.

Bühl, Walter Lugwig. *Einfürung in die Wissenschaftssoziologie*. Munich: Beck, 1974.

Butterfield, Sir Herbert. *The Origins of Modern Science, 1300–1800*. London: Bell, 1950; rev. ed. New York: Free Press, 1965.

Cohen, Bernard I. *The Birth of a New Physics*. Garden City, N.Y.: Anchor Books, 1960.

———. *Revolution in Science*. Cambridge, Mass.: Belknap Press of Harvard University Press, 1985.

Crosland, Maurice P., ed. *The Emergence of Science in Western Europe*. New York: Science History Publications, 1976.

Debus, Allen G. *The Chemical Philosophy: Paracelsian Science and Medicine in the Sixteenth and Seventeenth Centuries*. New York: Science History Publications, 1977.

Fleck, Ludwik. *Enstehung und Entwicklung einer wissenschaftlichen Tatsache*. Basel: B. Schwabe, 1935. Available in English as *Genesis and Development of a Scientific Fact*. Edited by Thaddeus J. Treun and Robert K. Merton; translated by Fred Bradley and Thaddeus J. Treun. Chicago: University of Chicago Press, 1979.

Galluzzi, Paolo. *Momento: Studi galileiani*. Rome: Edizioni dell'Ateneo/Bizzarri, 1979.

Garin, Eugenio. *L'educazione in Europa: 1400–1600*. Rome and Bari: Laterza, 1957, 1976.

————. *Medioevo e Rinascimento: Studi e ricerche*. Bari: Laterza, 1954; 2d ed., 1961.

————. *Rinascite e rivoluzioni: Movimenti culturali dal XIV al XVIII secolo*. Rome and Bari: Laterza, 1990.

————. *Lo zodiaco della vita: La polemica sull'astrologia dal Trecento al Cinquecento*. Rome and Bari: Laterza, 1976. Available in English as *Astrology in the Renaissance: The Zodiac of Life*. Translated by Carolyn Jackson and June Allen; translation revised by Clare Robertson and the author. London and Boston: Routledge & Kegan Paul, 1983.

Hall, A. Rupert. *The Revolution in Science, 1500–1750*. 3d ed. London and New York: Longman, 1983 (a revision of his *The Scientific Revolution, 1500–1800*, 2d ed. 1962).

Jones, Richard Foster. *Ancients and Moderns: A Study of the Rise of the Scientific Movement in Seventeenth-Century England*. 2d ed. reprinted Berkeley: University of California Press, 1965.

Koyré, Alexandre. *From the Closed World to the Infinite Universe*. New York: Harper, 1968.

Kuhn, Thomas. *The Essential Tension: Selected Studies in Scientific Tradition and Change*. Chicago: University of Chicago Press, 1977.

————. *The Structure of Scientific Revolutions*. Chicago: University of Chicago Press, 1962; 2d ed. enlarged, 1970.

Merton, Robert King. *Science, Technology, and Society in Seventeenth-Century England*. New York: Harper, 1970; Atlantic Highlands, N.J.: Humanities Press, 1978.

————. *The Sociology of Science: Theoretical and Empirical Investigations*. Edited and introduction by Norman W. Storer. Chicago: University of Chicago Press, 1973.

Pagel, Walter. *Paracelsus: An Introduction to Philosophical Medicine in the Era of the Renaissance*. Basel and New York: S. Karger, 1958; 2d rev. ed., 1982.

————. *William Harvey's Biological Ideas: Selected Aspects and Historical Background*. New York: Hafner Publishing Co., 1967.

Rossi, Paolo. *I filosofi e le macchine: 1400–1700*. Milan: Feltrinelli, 1984. Available in English as *Philosophy, Technology, and the Arts in the Early Modern Era*. Edited by Benjamin Nelson; translated by Salvator Attanasio. New York: Harper & Row, 1970.

————. *Francesco Bacone: Dalla magia alla scienza*. Turin: Einaudi, 1974. Available in English as *Francis Bacon: From Magic to Science*. Translated by Sacha Rabinovitch. Chicago: University of Chicago Press, 1968.

————. *Immagini della scienza*. Rome: Editori Riuniti, 1977.

————. *La scienza e la filosofia dei moderni*. Turin: Bollati Boringhieri, 1989.

Salomon, Jean Jacques. *Science et politique*. Paris: Editions du Seuil, 1970; new ed., Paris: Economica, 1989. Available in English as *Science and Politics*. Translated by Noël Lindsay. Cambridge, Mass.: MIT Press, 1973.

Singer, Charles Joseph, et al. *A History of Technology*. 8 vols. New York: Oxford University Press, 1954–84.

Walker, D. P. *Spiritual and Demonic Magic from Ficino to Campanella*. London, 1958; Notre Dame, Ind.: University of Notre Dame Press, 1975, reprint of

Nendeln, Liechtenstein: Kraus Reprint, 1969 (Studies of the Warburg Institute, 22).

Webster, Charles. *From Paracelsus to Newton: Magic and the Making of Modern Science*. Cambridge and New York: Cambridge University Press, 1982.

———. *The Great Instauration: Science, Medicine, and Reform, 1626–1660*. London: Duckworth, 1975.

Yates, Frances A. *Giordano Bruno and the Hermetic Tradition*. Chicago: University of Chicago Press, 1964.

Zambelli, Paola. *L'ambigua natura della magia*. Milan: Il Saggiatore, 1991.

———. "Platone, Ficino e la magia." *Studia Humanitatis* 1973.

The Artist

Giovanni Careri

T HE BAROQUE ARTIST had no idea that he was a Baroque artist, or, at least, he had no strong awareness of belonging to a new phase of the art and culture typical of the Renaissance artist. A feeling of continuity reached across the Mannerist parenthesis to link the Baroque artist to the great protagonists of the art of that rebirth. Only during the second half of the seventeenth century did the France of Colbert recast culture and art in a way comparable to the "invention" of the Renaissance.

The advent of French classicism, with its strictly national character, was an eloquent sign of the great changes that had occurred in more than two centuries of the history of European culture. The French initiative was a new—though certainly not the last—return to classical origins, one which provided compelling arguments for proclaiming a break with Baroque art. Perrault recounted in verse the fable of art as a pilgrim moving from Greece to Italy and finally to France. Little wonder that the term "Baroque" was first used in France, and used with pejorative overtones, in an operation similar to the one that led Italians of the Renaissance to apply the term "Gothic" to older styles in art. The negative connotations lent to the term prevented Baroque art from having the conceptual instruments it needed for self-definition and from being viewed as an autonomous style; Baroque art was condemned (until the nineteenth century) to playing a negative role—or, rather, to providing a negative contrast to the classical vision of the history of art.

This negative image was certainly not anything that Bernini, Rubens, and Pietro da Cortona felt, throughout their lives, might apply to their own highly sought-after works. And when we consider that until the late eighteenth century the French likened Bernini to Michelangelo and considered the works of Borromini a highly dangerous temptation for young architects, we can understand some of the reasons for the great confusion that the term "Baroque" produced as long as it communicated a negative evaluation of certain portions of seventeenth-century art.

When Heinrich Wölfflin constructed formal stylistic categories to oppose Baroque and Renaissance art he did much to create a positive image of seventeenth-century art, but it is nonetheless significant that "Baroque" was still seen as the contrary of something else. Writing at a time when impressionism was gaining acceptance, Wölfflin introduced the idea of a perpetual cycle of styles in which a classical phase is followed by a Baroque phase. Thus "Baroque" became an ahistorical term that defined the style that arose when the rules of art were broken and transformed, bringing dynamism to Renaissance forms. This was a notion coined in an enthusiasm for anti-academic impressionism that turned out to be extremely efficacious for the description of some seventeenth-century works, but it failed to grasp the transformation in content that necessarily accompanied changes in form.

Wölfflin's image of the Baroque was undeniably closer to the mark in his characterization of the aesthetic of some artists of the Baroque period, as manifested in their works and, much less frequently, as stated explicitly in their writings. One example of an explicit statement is a phrase of Bernini's on the Baroque unification of the visual arts, reported by Baldinucci:

> It is universally acknowledged that he [Bernini] was the first who attempted to unite architecture with sculpture and painting so as to make a fine mixture [*bel composto*] of all three; which he did by eliminating some odious uniformities of approach, *at times breaking the good rules without violating them,* but without subjecting himself to a rule: and it was his wont to say, in this connection, that anyone who does not sometimes stray from the rule will never surpass it. [Emphasis added]

In this statement the traditional problem of a unified rule for art is replaced by a new notion regarding the relationship between the "rules of the arts": it was the violation of commonly accepted rules that made possible the unification of the arts in one *bel composto*. But exactly what was meant by "rompendo talora senza violarle le buone regole"? Baldinucci may have been speaking of a minimal infraction of the rules, of something in any event less sweeping than the break set off by the "good heretic" Francesco Borromini.

Nonetheless, because Baldinucci was speaking not only of architecture but of all the arts in relation to one another, he may have been thinking of a sort of dynamic process in which the rules of each individual art, pushed to the limit, burgeoned into a new growth that would support the graft of a rule from another art. And that was just what happened, to pick one example, in the church of Sant'Andrea al Quirinale (fig. 1), where the sculpted figure of St. Andrew's soul soars upward, detached from the painted figure of the saint on the altarpiece, to break out of the pediment and give visual expression to the contrast between architectonic structure and figures moved by Grace that informs the architectonic plan of the entire church.

Bernini's *bel composto* is a very specific case of the operation of Baroque aesthetic, but, thanks precisely to the complexity of its internal articulation, it is one that furnishes a model for how a sizable portion of the religious art of the seventeenth century was received. There were two ways of perceiving that "mixture": from the point of view of the artist assembling his varied elements, and from the point of view of the devout spectator perceiving them. The way in which each particular "mixture" was realized induced in the spectator an equally particular operation of recomposition. Today we would without hesitation qualify that operation of reunification of a heterogeneous whole as an aesthetic process, but in the seventeenth century it was an exact parallel to the progress of religious contemplation.

The church of Sant'Andrea al Quirinale was used for the initiation of Jesuit novices, and the contrast it provided between the weight of the body and the flight of the soul echoed a first and fundamental moment in the candidate's meditation. When the novice had constructed an image of heroic sanctity within himself, he was ready to be admitted into the presbytery, where he would confront the martyrdom of St. Andrew face to face and the image of the martyr's soul in apotheosis would be hidden by the pediment and no longer visible.

Like St. Ignatius at Manresa, however, the novice had to give up the image of himself as a saint; only then, and only in an unquenchable desire to conform to the Christ of the Passion, would he experience authentic contact with God. Instead of the luminous spectacle of the martyrdom and the glory of St. Andrew, what the novice would see crowning the lantern above the presbytery was a fresco showing God the Father surrounded by angels, an image that was rendered equally difficult to see by the blinding light of day and by the shadows that invaded the church by night. This veil of light or shade gave the image of the fresco a quite different status from that of the altarpiece. It was semi-invisible, and by that token it strove to break out of the limits of its condition as an image by presenting the invisible as invisible and as impossible to represent. The *composto* exemplified in Sant'Andrea al Quirinale almost leads one to think of a purely instrumental religious art in which the sole purpose of the spectacle of the martyrdom and the apotheosis of the saint was to be expelled, at the proper moment, from the imagination of the novice/spectator.

Fig. 1. Gian Lorenzo Bernini, main altar, Sant'Andrea al Quirinale (ca. 1670).
Photo Denis Bernard.

Jesuit texts and devotional practices—first among them, the *Spiritual Exercises* of Ignatius of Loyola—functioned in precisely that manner: new images came to dislodge old ones until the viewer reached the ideal goal of an imageless contemplation. Still, it was not their ultimate objective that distinguished the contemplative practices of the Jesuits from those of other orders but rather the intense training of the senses, the imagination, the intellect, and the passions that went into preparing for that moment. And Bernini's Jesuitic *composti* were mechanisms designed for just that sensitivity training and that exercise of the faculties.

The fundamental mechanism at work in the reception of a Baroque work of this sort was "conformity." The spectator was called upon to become like the painted or sculpted figures in places of prayer and, in the last analysis, to conform to Christ. Obviously, the similarity achieved by contemplation arose not from corporeal imitation but rather from a spiritual conformity seated deep within the soul. That meant, on the one hand, that the artist's aim was to represent the stirrings of the soul by portraying attitudes of the body; on the other hand, it meant that the spectator had to exercise his own imagination and emotions in order to make his own soul as much as possible like that of the saint or martyr he was contemplating. Conformity resulted in a moment of contact with Christ that the viewer felt with varied intensity. It was a moment of the reception of Grace that the theologians of the age called "affective conformity" to emphasize its essentially emotive character. It is worth recalling that in the seventeenth century affect was opposed to action; being "impassioned" involved being acted upon by someone; in the case of conformity with Christ, it meant renouncing one's own will in order to be acted upon by him.

The ecstatic abandonment visible in the bodies of Baroque saints represented the abandonment of their souls to the action of Christ, which the mystics described as a luminous infusion or, on the eucharistic model, as the embodiment of Grace. Still, in both the texts and the works of art of this period in spiritual history, the soul and the body were never definitively separated. The body signified the soul and, at the same time, resisted it; the soul yearned to abandon the body, but it remained imaginary and anthropomorphized. That is how it was in the church of Sant'-Andrea al Quirinale, where Borgognone's painting in the monumental altarpiece depicted the moment in which a miracle paralyzes the jailers' arms, stopping them from freeing the martyr after his long suffering, permitting his return to life. As he is depicted, St. Andrew has already seen God the Father and is asking him to let the earth take his body, that "most heavy garment" that keeps the soul from flying upward toward the divine light. In this critical moment St. Andrew is still alive but has already "come out of" himself; his soul is still tied to his body but is being drawn out of it irresistibly. The figure of the martyr shows this duality in an opposition between the contracted lower half of Andrew's body and the abandonment of its upper half. The sudden passage from tension to relaxation produces an effect of intense pathos: the spectator wonders whether the saint is suffering or exulting; whether he is alive or on the point of death.

The stucco figure of St. Andrew's "soul in apotheosis" resembles the painted figure, but here the saint is "stretching out his arms in an expression of affection and divine love," to borrow a phrase coined by Bellori to describe Duquesnoy's statue of St. Andrew in Saint Peter's. Bernini's sculpture no longer shows the contrast we see in the painted figure, and it has taken on the univocal and harmonious guise of ecstatic joy. The soul in flight represents a moment in time that follows immediately after that of the painting, but it represents the same situation, freed of the conflict connected with the persistence of the martyr's corporeality.

That conflict became "translated" and reformulated in a clash between sculpture and architecture when the physical barrier of the pediment was challenged and overcome by the soul's ascent. In its upward flight toward the lantern of the church, the "body" of St. Andrew's soul, made of soft stucco, breaks out of the marble "body" of the tympanum to cross the last frontier between the terrestrial zone and the celestial zone of the church. The same principle of opposition between architectonic structure and figurations of divine Grace is exemplified by the imposing Corinthian columns on either side of the altar, which seem to swell all the more excessively for being cunningly infused with divine light falling from the lantern and from the painting. The columns, like the anthropomorphic figures, act and are acted upon: they support the pediment but they are permeated by a light that dapples them with stripes and clear veinings, weakening their solidity and blurring the geometric tracing of their channels. The surface of the columns recalls a freckled, reddish skin more than the rigid and impermeable covering of a sturdy support.

The "pathos" of the architecture of Sant'Andrea al Quirinale resides in the deep-set framing of the tympanum, in the enlarged columns, and in the colored marble—all elements that react to changes in the illumination of the church as the day advances and that construct a space dominated by phenomena of tension and release that "translate" the spiritual adventure of the saint and lend themselves to uses of a fundamentally emotional sort.

Bernini's *composto* broke the accepted rules (*le buone regole*) of architecture in the interest of touching the spectator's soul. He lent dynamism to Renaissance forms as a way to create a dynamic in contemplation. He made use of an aesthetic of the heterogeneous and of transference in which choice of materials played a determinant role: only stucco could give form to the instability of the soul in apotheosis; only Cottanello marble had mottling that could take on a luminous veining in such an effective manner. It was a regimen of representation in which sensibility and intellect were informed by the passions and had the human body as their model.

This type of Baroque aesthetic was not invented by Bernini alone; he shared it, at least in part, with Guido Reni, Rubens, Guercino, and even with the "classicist" Nicolas Poussin. The targeted audience of that aesthetic was lovingly and almost prophetically described by Torquato Tasso in his *Gerusalemme Liberata*.

What is more, Bernini's was not the only way of "breaking out of the rules." This is clear in the classical comparison between Bernini's work and that of Francesco Borromini, an artist who broke the rules of architecture, twisted them, and turned them upside-down in a much more radical and systematic fashion than Bernini. Borromini countered Bernini's intent to unify the arts with a richly ornamented but nonanthropomorphic architecture. In Borromini's churches painting and sculpture were solidly contained within their architectonic framework. Tension and release stood face to face as he curved his facades and stretched his arches in a dynamic and purely architectonic opposition.

Eugenio Battisti has shown how deeply rooted was Borromini's disinclination for the human figure, demonstrating Borromini's use of mottoes and emblems sacred and profane, attributes, heraldic devices, hieroglyphics, geometrical forms, numbers, and epigraphs, and his avoidance of personification in the depiction of virtues or conceits. When Bernini set the sacred emblem of the flaming heart into the altar containing the sarcophagus of the Blessed Lodovica Albertoni in the church of San Francesco a Ripa, he did so as a way of giving clear conceptual form to the ambiguous emotion that the sculpture embodied and, even more, as a way of producing a yet more violent change of regimen between the disembodied symbol of divine love and the concrete representation of emotion in the fold of the variegated pink marble drapery that linked the sculpture to the altar. In the church of Sant'Ivo alla Sapienza Borromini carried the upward thrust of the cupola still higher with a lantern in the form of a temple surrounded by twelve columns, in turn surmounted by a spiral reaching still higher and ending in a finial in the form of the holy emblems of Purity and Love of God (fig. 2). These symbols were strictly subordinated to the overall dynamic of the spire that determined their form, and they had no autonomous coloration to highlight them. They formed an emblematic whole that even contemporary viewers found difficult to interpret—a web of rigidly codified conceits that could only be read with the *Cannocchiale aristotelico* in hand.

Bernini's emblematic heart could be understood in terms of the rela-

Fig. 2. Francesco
Borromini, summit of
the cupola of Sant'Ivo
alla Sapienza (from the
Opus Architectonicum).

tionship that it set up with the human body; Borromini's emblems had the immediately architectonic sense of a thrust upward, but their meaning was concealed from the common herd. The conflict between architectonic structure and decoration that had functioned so successfully in Bernini's *composto* did not exist in Borromini's work, where architecture reigned unchallenged. Here tensions were not resolved with a swift transition of register, but remained dramatically and dynamically open. In Bernini the hidden face of the Baroque was a skeleton with a clepsydra; Borromini presented a spatial drama with no figures and with no resolution. His extreme form of Baroque spirituality was closer to the religiosity of Central Europe, where his most enthusiastic followers were Dientzenhofer, Neumann, and Santini.

The differences between the ways that Borromini and Bernini "broke out of the rules" tell us something about one component in Baroque representation that has prompted strong protests from neoclassical academic criticism, then and after. Still, as we have already seen, neither man was playing the provocateur, nor were they toying gratuitously with the traditional rules. Both were bending the rules constructively.

Bernini's and Borromini's aesthetics were antithetical historically and theoretically, but both were founded on a dialectic of tension and release. In fact, despite the lucid rationality that guided Bernini's "deviations," his architecture stretches and shrinks as the illumination changes through the day and as the spectator changes position. Thus the observer encounters a form of construction that demands the application of the intellect, but also a dynamic of tension and release that moves the soul and appeals to the emotions.

These two great architects differed just as much in their culture and their mode of life. Bernini, who had been trained in the court of the pro-French pope Maffeo Barberini (Urban VIII), worked almost exclusively for papal patrons. He was very well remunerated, he dressed elegantly, his conversation was pleasing and witty, and he was well versed in theology. He lived in princely fashion in a handsome patrician palace with his large family. Borromini always dressed in black, in the Spanish fashion. He was a difficult man, and he lived with a serving woman in a modest house near the church of San Giovanni dei Fiorentini. He owned a bust of Seneca and many works of philosophy and spent the greater part of his earnings on books. Most of his commissions came from such new Counter-Reformation religious orders as the Oratorians and the Jesuits.

Bernini died in his eighties, in his own house and with the pope and Princess Christina of Sweden at his bedside. His great rival Borromini died at the age of sixty-eight by throwing himself on his sword in a suicide in the classical style that was perfectly in keeping with his Stoic philosophical credo. Together, such details provide a clearer definition of the personality of the two artists and help us to understand something of the self-image that they constructed. Bernini, like many other great artists of the seventeenth century, adopted the noble, courtly model of Raphael; Borromini, the brusque and uncompromising manners of Michelangelo. Still, overemphasizing the relationship between an artist's life and his works risks repeating the vague psychological interpretations dear to so much bad writing on art. It is more important to ask what seventeenth-century society expected of its artists, investigating not only the level on which they were called upon to operate but also the new horizons of expectation that they may have helped to construct.

At first sight the social position of the seventeenth-century artist is undistinguishable from that of the artist in the immediately preceding centuries: he worked, for the most part, in direct connection with the centers of political power, and he received money and prestige in exchange for his art. The sovereign's glory was enhanced by the artist's work, but above all the princely patron obtained objects that gave form and figure to his own power. This does not mean that the artist was a passive servant of the powerful, nor that his work was only a sort of makeup to mask the unaesthetic brutality of power. Just as the courtier worked out a comportment to "civilize" power, cultivating an "honest dissimulation" of the violence of power in order to regulate its use and create a space for social life, so the artist elaborated ways to represent power, offering both society and the princely patron the thousands of images that gave tangible and rational support to an appearance that served as a base for the prince's power. Such images rooted the prince in a dynastic, urban, or national tradition; they testified to his religious faith and his own sacrality; they made explicit his function of public protection. They might also display his more menacing face. This model of the relationship between the artist and power, like most of the institutions in early modern Europe, had been elaborated in the courts of Renaissance Italy. There the architect, the painter, and the sculptor not only constructed the spaces in which power was exercised and the life of the court took place but also gave form, through their works, to the prince's special grace—a seeming gift for natural elegance that was in reality the hard-won result of an intense effort to civilize power.

Along with an etiquette whose demands were more and more minutely regulated, the seventeenth-century European court inherited a need to be represented in spectacle and in written works as well as in architecture, sculpture, and painting. When the character of government changed, the need for "representation" became even more imperious, eventually becoming as absolute as the power from which it emanated. For the administration of his state, the Baroque prince became increasingly skilled at replacing the actual use of violence with a government founded on the efficacy of a representation of force.

The first laboratory of that "absolutist" form of the power of representation was perhaps the long reign of the Barberini pope, Urban VIII (1623–44). His papacy displayed traits specific to both religious and secular government, and, for that very reason, it served as a model for Louis XIV's nearly theocratic exercise of power, with the important difference that the crown of the king of France was transmitted hereditarily whereas a papal election brought a new family to power. The congenital instability of papal rule was, paradoxically, favorable to increased papal commissions; every new pope brought with him kin and friends eager to establish their own positions and ready to invest money in the construction of a palace or a church. As Francis Haskell has demonstrated, Urban VIII inherited from Paul V (1605–21) and Gregory XV (1621–23) a full range of objectives worthy of a pope's artistic ambitions: the completion of St. Peter's, the construction and decoration of villas and palaces, the realization of a luxurious family chapel in a venerable Roman church, financial support to a variety of religious orders for their building projects or to a favorite nephew interested in building up a rich collection of paintings and sculptures.

Maffeo Barberini had been trained in the Rome of Sixtus V, a pope who had quelled the murmurs of the aristocracy of the *campagna Romana* and had returned the city to its role as the great capital of Christendom. Sixtus V had also acted to give visible form to his government by the redesign, ex novo, of the city's principal thoroughfares and the construction of bridges and fountains.

Urban VIII ruled with an even more iron hand and left an even more indelible mark on the city. He turned first to the burial place of St. Peter and St. Paul, the symbolic heart of the Church of Rome and the architectonic center of the new construction of St. Peter's. Less than a year after his election in 1624, he commissioned Bernini to construct a bronze baldachin over the relics of the two saints that was as high as the facade of the Palazzo Farnese. After the baldachin, Urban concentrated on the decoration of the four niches of the transept, commissioning large statues of Saints Andrew, Longinus, Veronica, and Helen, placed to correspond with the four most important Christian relics (the head of St. Andrew, the Holy Lance, Veronica's veil, and the True Cross). Next Urban commissioned his own funeral monument, which, placed in a niche at the far right of the transept, seems to give a somewhat threatening blessing.

These works, later completed by the Cathedra Petri, enhanced the role of the papacy and the Church of Rome and left a detailed record of the pope who had restored both of these to dignity and splendor. The pope's relationship with Bernini is admittedly an extreme example of complicity between artist and patron, but it reveals, better than any other example, the value that the culture of the time put on visible representation of both spiritual and temporal power. The success of Bernini's efforts in St. Peter's won him urgent requests for works from the king of England, Charles I, and Cardinal Richelieu, to cite only two persons to whom the pope granted that honor (in return for notable advantages). The powerful of Europe expected Bernini to give them effigies worthy of their rank and portraits in which their own physical traits were blended with those of their function. The cult of the royal person demanded that the heroic image of the king—his effigy as Alexander the Great—be fused with his own unique, unmistakable figure, "comparable only to himself."

Bernini rose to the challenge of that paradox in admirable fashion in the bust of Louis XIV that he made during a stay in Paris in 1665. The Sun King had managed to lure Bernini away from Pope Alexander VII to have him draw up plans for the royal residence of the Louvre, and Bernini was quick to demonstrate his idea of royalty with a portrait in which the king's traits were transfigured into a haughty and impassible face reigning over a tempest of pleats. Louis XIV truly seemed endowed with *misterium imperii* and to be beyond and above human passions, ever ready to strike out with a sudden, dazzling coup d'état.

The king liked the bust very much but ended up turning down the project for the Louvre. Bernini's defeat at the height of his glory had more to do with Colbert than with the cabal organized by local architects. The superintendent of the king's palaces had in fact understood the need to build a palace that unequivocally stated the uniqueness of French art. Perrault's Louvre, although not completely successful, should be viewed in light of Colbert's other enterprises as Louis XIV's great "minister of culture"—among them, the founding of the Académie des Beaux Arts and the French Academy in Rome. The latter institutionalized the tradition of a Roman sojourn for French artists, and the Academy became a sort of agency for artistic espionage and a center for the communication of information necessary to the full development of French art of the classical age.

Bernini's complicity with those who held power had another side to it. He circulated impertinent caricatures of popes and lords (with impunity), and he put on irreverent comedies in his house. These expressions of license, like Rome's famous "pasquinades," were not so much expressions of insubordination to papal power as daring manifestations of a courtly game of wit much appreciated at the time. The exceptional license that Bernini enjoyed was in fact one of the objectives of his caricatures, as it served to demonstrate his intimacy with the Roman aristocracy and to manifest his extraordinary skill as a courtier.

An interesting contrast to Bernini's heroic portraits and his caricatures is Velázquez's *Las Meninas* (1656), a work in which the artist transformed his relationship with the powerful into a form of the representation of power that has the force, the refinement, and the complexity of
some of Pascal's *Pensées* (fig. 3). Michel Foucault saw this painting as
emblematic of the form that representation took in the classical age. The
spectator's gaze parallels that of the royal couple, who are reflected in the
mirror in the middle of the room, but it also parallels the painter's gaze.
The three functions to which these three gazes correspond are reiterated
in the painting, in which a spectator appears in a doorway at the back of
the room and the painter in the picture is at work on a canvas whose back
is toward us. The concealment of the painting in the picture reinforces
the spectator's uncertainty concerning his position and his role in the representation before our eyes. The many interpretations of this painting
have failed to resolve that uncertainty, and the question in fact has to be
left open, inasmuch as it gives the work its entire force. With *Las Meninas,* Velázquez insinuates the idea that the person contemplating the
painting (primarily, the king) is a subject who exists only to the extent
that he finds a representation and manages to occupy one of the positions
that the painter has predisposed.

The Renaissance operation of turning mimesis of the real world into
the creation of a world reproduced by art gives way here, according to
Foucault, to a form of representation that is no longer based in imitation
but rather is given as pure representation. This representation has a value
because it produces effects that appeal to the senses, to pathos, or to the
intellect—effects that in turn produce acceptance—rather than because
it corresponds analogically to a stable, preexistent reality.

Bernini's heroic portraits and caricatures of courtiers demonstrated
his perfect grasp of the efficacy of Baroque representation; in *Las Meninas*
Velázquez used that efficacy as his theme and exhibited its mechanisms
in painting.

Velázquez nonetheless dedicated himself totally to the service of his
king. In return, he received the high honors that he yearned for, as demonstrated by the knight's cross of the Order of Santiago that was added to
the painting, probably in 1658, two years after the work had been completed. One interesting aspect of that enigmatic painting is precisely its
demand for due recognition of the role of the artist in the production of
the effects on which the efficacy of royal power was founded.

The Flemish artist who best corresponded to Bernini and Velázquez
was undoubtedly Rubens, who provided the grandiose paintings that decorated the Luxembourg Palace in which Queen Maria de'Medici was presented as a heroine of classical mythology. During her sojourn in Paris
in 1623, the infanta Isabella, governor of Flanders, asked the painter to

Fig. 3. Diego Velázquez, *Las Meninas* (1656). Madrid, Prado. Courtesy Alinari/ Art Resource, N.Y.

persuade the queen of France to grant a truce to Spain. In 1629 Count-Duke Olivares sent Rubens to King Charles I of England in an attempt to enroll the king as Spain's ally against France. This intense diplomatic activity bears witness to the high social status that Rubens had acquired. In Antwerp he built a patrician residence and filled it with a splendid collection of works of art that included paintings by Titian, Tintoretto, Holbein, and Ribera, among others.

304 / Chapter Eleven

Rubens also provides a figure representative of the Baroque artist for reasons more intrinsically tied to his painting and to his profession as a painter (above all for the nearly industrial organization of his studio), and for the care and attention that he paid to widespread diffusion of his works in print reproduction. Professional organization and engravings had already existed in the Roman *bottega* of Raphael, but with Rubens these acquired a new dimension that considerably transformed the works' channels of diffusion and that made possible a large-scale and extremely fruitful interpretation of paintings, thanks to transformations introduced into print copies of them and then into painted copies made in turn from the engravings.

For example, Borgognone's *Martyrdom of St. Andrew*, described above, borrows the idea of the paralysis afflicting the executioners' arms from a painting of Rubens that circulated in an engraving. We have seen how Bernini fully exploited the possibilities of "translation" and sculptural and architectonic development offered by that critical moment.

The transformation of Rubens's idea into Bernini's *bel composto* is emblematic of an artistic season typified by an extremely high level in the "translation" of artistic forms and ideas. The many different painted "illustrations" of Tasso's *Gerusalemme Liberata* provide one of the most interesting examples of the phenomenon of borrowing and "translation." The phenomenon occurred throughout Europe, and although it too had many precedents in the cultivated and literary painting of the Renaissance, during the seventeenth century it acquired new dimensions and characteristics.

In his *Gerusalemme Liberata* Tasso developed an extremely rich phenomenology of the passions, focused in the meeting point of the physical sign and the impulses of the soul. In a letter to Ferrante Gonzaga, Tasso defined his way of poetizing as a "disjointed way of speaking—that is, linking more by the union and dependence of the senses than by conjunctions or other joinings of words." The fluid continuity among the senses and their tendency to combine in a thousand different syntheses provided Tasso with material out of which to forge mobile and vibrant images. The dynamic realm of the senses had a counterpart in the realm of the emotions that had the same constant fluidity and was equally apt to produce unstable and dynamic images. It was precisely that encounter between pathos and the senses that interested seventeenth-century painters, and some of them went a good deal farther than simple representation of one or another episode of Tasso's poem toward a realization, in paint, of the temporal, sensual, and affective dynamic of Tasso's verse.

One of these was Nicolas Poussin. Although he has been considered an anti-Baroque artist, Poussin was one of the Baroque's most faithful and inventive painters of subjects from Tasso. Indeed, even though Poussin's

Fig. 4. Nicolas Poussin, *Rinaldo and Armida,* from Torquato Tasso's poem
"Gerusalemme Liberata." London, Dulwich Picture Gallery. Courtesy of Erich
Lessing/Art Resource, N.Y.

aesthetic was in no way focused on "breaking rules," much of his work
remains within the realm of fluid and metamorphic representation that
we have seen among the fundamental characteristics of a Baroque aesthetic interested in such rule-breaking. In practice, however, where in the
work of Rubens and Bernini the dynamics of that approach to representation led to a violation of norms, in the work of Poussin breaking rules
was kept within measure. Nonetheless, that fluidity remained a basic,
structuring principle for Poussin, as we can see in one of his works,
the *Rinaldo and Armida,* also called *Rinaldo Asleep,* painted in 1625 for
Cassiano Dal Pozzo and now in the Dulwich College Picture Gallery in
London (fig. 4).

The painting recalls two famous octaves (66, 67) in canto XIV of
Gerusalemme Liberata. In this passage Armida, who has set a trap for
Rinaldo by putting him to sleep with melodious song by the banks of the
Orontes river, throws herself upon his sleeping figure to kill him, but is
suddenly smitten with love for him. The only way in which we can grasp
how Poussin's treatment of Tasso's verse exemplifies a new relationship
between painting and poetry is by close analysis of both. Tasso's passage
reads:

Ma quando in lui fissò lo sguardo e vide
come placido in vista egli respira,
e ne' begli occhi un dolce atto che ride
ben che sian chiusi (or che fia s'ei li gira?),
pria s'arresta sospesa, e gli s'asside
poscia vicina, e placar sente ogn'ira
mentre il risguarda; e 'n su la vaga fronte
pende omai sì che par Narciso al fonte.

E quei ch'ivi sorgean vivi sudori
accoglie lievemente in un suo velo,
e con un dolce ventilar gli ardori
gli va temprando de l'estivo cielo
Così (chi 'l crederia?) sopiti ardori
d'occhi nascosi distemprar quel gelo
che s'indurava al cor più che diamante:
e di nemica ella divenne amante.

*(But when she fixed her gaze upon him and saw
how calm of countenance he breathes, and how
charming a manner laughs about his lovely eyes,
though they be closed [now what will it be if he
opens them?], first she stands still in suspense, and
then sits down beside him, and feels her every wrath
becalmed while she gazes upon him; and now she
bends so above his handsome face that she seems
Narcissus at the spring. And those trembling drops
of sweat that welled up there she softly takes off
into her veil and with a gentle fanning tempers for
him the heat of the summery sky. So [who would
believe it?] the slumbering warmth of hidden eyes
dissolved that frost that had hardened her heart
even more than adamant, and from his enemy she
became his lover; Nash translation)*

The sixteen hendecasyllables separate but also fuse together the initial and concluding instants of the change in Armida's high emotion. The poet of course does not say why the beautiful Muslim witch, after having carefully prepared her trap for Rinaldo, succumbs before the warrior's inert figure, although he hints that in reality the sleeping Rinaldo's eyelids conceal a formidable weapon. Tasso simply tells us that she "feels her every wrath becalmed while she gazes upon him" ("placar sente ogn'ira / mentre il risguarda"), and that she "bends so above his handsome face that she seems Narcissus at the spring" ("'n su la vaga fronte / pende omai sì che par Narciso al fonte"). By suspending and delaying the moment of

Armida's gaze, Tasso leaves in doubt the fatal instant of her falling in love. The "but" (*ma*) with which the octave begins is the first element that slows the witch's murderous assault. The next is "when" (*quando*); and it is within the suspension of time prompted by "*But when* she fixed her gaze upon him" ("*Ma quando* in lui fissò lo sguardo") that Tasso arrives at a new segmentation of time: first a second stopping point, "*first* she stands in suspense ("*pria* s'arresta sospesa"), then a pause, "*and then* sits down beside him" (e gli s'asside / *poscia* vicina"). He then returns to the first point when time was suspended, the moment of "But when": "and feels her every wrath becalmed *while* she gazes upon him" ("placar sente ogn'ira / *mentre* il risguarda"). Her gaze is no longer the same as before; it has been changed by the halt of "first" and the pause of "while." In fact, Armida is not looking at Rinaldo but looking at him again: "il *ri*sguarda."

"And *now* she bends so above his handsome face that she seems Narcissus at the spring" ("e 'n su la vaga fronte / pende *omai* sì che par Narciso al fonte"). After the two suspensions of time, "now" is a leap ahead: the witch falls in love in an instant hidden in the sudden move from "while" to "now." The adverb sequence stretches time and binds together the time progression that begins with the past definite of the verbs "fixed" (*fissò*) and "saw" (*vide*) and arrives in the subsequent lines at a series of verbs in the present tense: "breathes," "laughs," "stands still," "sits," "feels," "bends" (*respira, ride, s'arresta, s'asside, sente, pende*). The past definite returns only at the end of the second octave to complete the transformation of the love-smitten Armida.

During this time, the witch "*softly* takes off into her veil" ("accoglie *lievemente* in un suo velo") the sweat running from the sleeping Rinaldo's brow, "and with a *gentle* fanning *tempers* for him the heat of the summery sky" ("e con un *dolce* ventilar gli ardori / gli va *temprando* de l'estivo cielo"). The aggressive thrust has been transformed into a "soft" gesture and a "gentle" fanning. Armida is invaded by the languor of a "calm" (*placido*) and "charming" (*dolce*) Rinaldo. Her actions take on the softness of the "charming manner" (*dolce atto*) of the object of her love. But the full value of the gentle fanning—her "dolce ventilar gli ardori"—can be understood only when we read the last four lines. While Armida is busy cooling down the overheated young man, the "slumbering warmth" (*sopiti ardori*) of Rinaldo's "hidden eyes" (*occhi nascosi*) are working their magic, dissolving in her "that frost that had hardened her heart even more than adamant" ("quel gelo / che s'indurava al cor più che diamante."

Tasso's "gentle fanning" has an effect that is the analogic model of the inverse effect, the "dissolved that frost" (*distemprar quel gelo*). In the four final lines the witch's falling in love takes the form of a reversal of increased tension: hard frost dissolves, becoming warm and conforming with the "gentle fanning" and the "softly" (*lievemente*) of the earlier lines.

Rinaldo certainly had no idea that baring his forehead to refresh himself by the "soft breathing of the gentle breeze" ("soave spirar di placid' aura"; XIV, 59) would arm him with a power of fascination equal to that of Narcissus's spring. Abandoned to sleep, "quiet imaging of death" ("quieta imagine di morte"; XIV, 65) at the extreme limit of passivity, the young man's laughing but hidden eyes perform "un dolce atto che ride," a passive act all the more efficaciously seductive because it is involuntary and minimal. Thus, incredibly—"Così (chi 'l crederia?)"—the "slumbering warmth of hidden eyes" ("sopiti ardori d'occhi nascosi"), precisely because their force is attenuated, becomes irresistible to Armida in a new reversal, and she is instantly transformed from "his enemy" to "his lover" ("di nemica . . . divenne amante").

"Ma quando in lui fissò lo sguardo e vide . . . e di nemica ella divenne amante": Poussin takes the first and last moments of Tasso's two octaves and distributes them between the two hands of his figure of Armida. Her "enemy" right hand grips the homicidal dagger; her "lover" left hand rests softly on Rinaldo's hand. Poussin produces the same pauses, temporal leaps ahead, and reversals that marked the two poles of the emotional change in Armida and stretched out or speeded up the instant of her conversion in Tasso's poem, but Poussin uses means appropriate to painting.

A white cloth thrown over the witch's shoulders and knotted behind her back returns, with diminished energy, to its flowing course. This is how Poussin signals the stopping of Armida's homicidal thrust, its suspension, and its return on a more peaceful level. The agitated end of the cloth corresponds to the tension in her right arm, a tension amplified by the resistance of the little cupid who holds back her hand.

A second suspension is situated in the shadowed zone that interrupts the line of Armida's left arm. In this darker area the witch's arm meets that of the sleeping young man. When her arm emerges into the light, her hand is "now" (*omai*) resting languidly on Rinaldo's hand. Both the painter and the poet veil the fatal instant of Armida's emotional conversion. The shadowed area in the painting corresponds to the turning point hidden between the "while" (*mentre*) and the "now" (*omai*) of Tasso's text.

The joining of the two lovers is echoed in the background of the painting by the shift from the one isolated tree on the left to the two united trees on the right. The parabola formed by Armida's open arms is accompanied by a descending curve that begins at the rise in the background and ends at Rinaldo's right hand, limply posed on his shield.

As in the poem, the witch's gestures immediately take on the softness of Rinaldo's attitude; the passage from tension to abandon is accompanied, on the chromatic scale, by a shift from the cold colors of Armida's clothing to the warm colors of Rinaldo's gilded armor and orange trousers. Rigid cold, "that frost that had hardened her heart even more than adamant" ("che s'indurava al cor più che diamante") dissipates into soft warmth through the shaded spot where the lovers' arms touch.

The painting presents the "softening" of Rinaldo as well as Armida falling in love. Rinaldo's left hand is abandoned on his shield, carefully placed between his helmet and his sword. Where is the martial young man in whom God the Father had discerned "a warlike mind and spirits impatient of rest" ("animo guerriero e spirti di riposo impazienti"; I, 10)? Poussin's Rinaldo is already the knight of the sixteenth canto, the hero who has abandoned war, and the effeminate man whose sword, once a "fierce instrument of war" ("militar fero instrumento"), has become "a useless ornament" ("inutile ornamento"; XVI, 30).

In the poem, in fact, when Rinaldo awakes on the Island of Fortune, he becomes the witch's love slave, the lover who offers her a mirror in which she admires herself even more explicitly than she had before the sleeping warrior, "like Narcissus at the spring."

In Poussin's painting the witch is moving in the direction of languor, but her domination of Rinaldo is still virile as Rinaldo lies supine beneath her, his legs spread open before her knife and his hand inertly at rest among his weapons.

Armida in love is an unexpected plot development, but it respects all the rules of relations between the sexes. For the Christian warrior to abandon himself to a loved one and neglect warfare, on the other hand, was a worrisome and dangerous exchange of roles. Forgetful of his insatiable desire for honor, Rinaldo is momentarily attracted by an absolute subordination to Armida. The painting does not represent the intensity of his passion by any action but rather through the feminization of his figure as a whole. The "abnormality" of the relationship between the two already hints at strong passion and implies a negative judgment.

Passion takes form in violation of the norm as well as in a refined manipulation of the times and modes of action. Armida is dominant but seduced. Rinaldo, the passive and unconscious seducer, has taken in his sleep the feminine posture that becomes characteristic of him in the poem during his entire stay on the Island of Fortune. The spell is broken when another mirror, brought by his companions Carlo and Ubaldo, shows him what he has become:

> Egli al lucido scudo il guardo gira
> onde si specchia in lui qual siasi e quanto
> con delicato culto adorno spira
> tutto odori e lascivie il crine e il manto;

e il ferro, il ferro aver, non ch'altro, mira
del troppo lusso effeminato a canto:
guernito è sì ch'inutile ornamento
sembra, non militar fero instrumento.

Qual uom da cupo e grave sonno oppresso
dopo vaneggiar lungo in sé riviene,
tale ei tornò nel rimirar se stesso,
ma se stesso mirar già non sostiene:
giù cade il guardo, e timido e dimesso,
guardando a terra, la vergogna il tiene.
Si chiuderebbe e sotto il mare e dentro
il foco per celarsi, e giù nel centro.

*(He turns his gaze upon the shining shield, in which
is mirrored for him what manner of man he is become, and how much adorned with delicate elegance: he breathes forth all perfumed, his hair and
mantle wanton; and his sword, he sees his sword
(not to speak of other things) made effeminate at his
side by too much luxury; it is so trimmed that it
seems a useless ornament, not the fierce instrument
of war. As a man by deep and heavy sleep oppressed
returns to himself after long delirious raving, so he returned by gazing upon himself: but truly he cannot
bear to look at himself; his gaze sinks low; and de-
jected and abashed, staring at the ground, he is possessed by shame. He would have shut himself under
the sea and within the flame, be concealed, and deep
within earth's core; XVI, 30–31; Nash translation)*

Poussin's sleeping Rinaldo shows a close resemblance to that "uom da cupo e grave sonno oppresso," but we need not postulate that the painter "borrowed" images from the poet. It was enough for Poussin to show the sleeping Rinaldo as an effeminate warrior, thus implying his later subordination and shamed awakening.

De Sanctis wrote of Tasso's "lyrical, subjective, and musical world," a "sentimental" world that pervaded the literature, music, and painting of the seventeenth century. Poussin understood the sensual and affective dynamic of that world and faithfully "translated" it into painting. He responded to one client who had ventured a criticism concerning the composition of one of his paintings, "Read the story and [examine] the painting if you want to know whether everything is appropriate to the subject." Poussin had shown the same pride in a *painterly* fidelity to the literary texts in his younger years in Paris, when he had illustrated Giambattista Marino's *Adone.*

It was in fact Marino who brought Poussin to Rome and introduced him to his first protector, Marcello Sacchetti, a cultivated member of an extremely wealthy Florentine merchant family and a great friend of Urban VIII. Sacchetti's activities as a patron were highly important for the rise of Roman Baroque painting. He was a man of very decided tastes, who encouraged the young Pietro da Cortona to copy Raphael and Titian as a way of developing the "grand manner" that Giuliano Briganti considered the first authentically Baroque style in painting.

Before he was named treasurer to the pope and assumed a prominent role in papal artistic policies, Sacchetti had concentrated primarily on enriching his own private collection. Collections of the sort originated in the Renaissance, in particular in Venice, but, once again, they grew in scope in the seventeenth century, to the point of at least partially changing character. From the beginning of the century, in fact, with Marquess Giustiniani, Caravaggio's protector and patron, the private gallery became a place for defining an alternative to the taste of the great public or private patrons, the great lords and religious orders.

The greater part of Poussin's pictorial works were destined for the galleries of private clients—cultivated persons who were willing to put up with his slow rate of production. The situation involved a certain tension, but it permitted Poussin to carry on the extraordinary hermeneutic labor of studying the basic texts of both Christian culture and the Greek and Latin world.

Cassiano Dal Pozzo, who commissioned Poussin to "illustrate" Tasso's *Gerusalemme Liberata,* was the most cultivated of his patrons. In his house on via dei Chiavari, Dal Pozzo had gathered a collection of medals, prints, scientific instruments, and books that was unique in Europe, not so much for its size as for its novelty and its usefulness for serious study. Poussin contributed to one of Dal Pozzo's major intellectual enterprises, the *Museum Chartaceum,* a sizable collection of rubbings and drawings from Roman "antiquities." The young painter's relationship with this extraordinary personage not only influenced Poussin's artistic choices but gave him a deep-rooted need to have a patron capable of fully appreciating his work. None of his subsequent patrons satisfied that need as well as Dal Pozzo; indeed, Poussin's correspondence shows him doing his best to educate his clients' taste, an effort that was often thwarted but that is nonetheless significant. It was Poussin's desire for understanding that led him to produce a number of theoretical works and to collaborate with Giovanni Pietro Bellori in defining the classical approach of the latter's *Vite de' pittori scultori e architetti moderni.*

Poussin was a painter of the first rank who nearly always worked outside the circuits of religious and princely patronage. He was a somewhat exceptional case, even if Salvator Rosa went even farther than he by proclaiming his complete autonomy, refusing commissions, and demanding the right to paint only when he was inspired and to display his works for sale. Both Poussin and Rosa demonstrated a gradual broadening of the court artist's area of autonomy, a phenomenon that paralleled the artist's integration into the market. The movement of the artist as economic operator was fully deployed only in the nineteenth century, but its prototype went back to the entrepreneurial activities of Rubens and the even more radically modern economic activities of Rembrandt, as Svetlana Alpers has recently shown.

The seventeenth century was an epoch in which different models of the artist coexisted; a period that witnessed the consolidation of an improved social status for the artist (which had begun in the Renaissance) and a hint of a new type of relationship between the artist, society, and the market.

If, however, the role of artists as social agents was not transformed deeply enough to change their function, their works nonetheless testify to a moment of intense creativity. The arts were in an uncertain phase: they had lost the Renaissance baseline of permanence and similitude, and they were dominated by an anguished sentiment of mutability and change. Perhaps working in the arts responded best to men's expectations precisely because it managed to represent mutability and change efficaciously.

Baroque religious work, for example, offered the believer the cognitive, sense-related, and emotional instruments he needed for an inner metamorphosis and an affective conformation with Christ. This was exactly the opposite course from the one that led the seventeenth-century Christian to feel himself radically unlike his Lord—a "nullity"; just "skin, bones, dung, carrion," as the Bohemian Jesuit poet Bedrich Bridel wrote.

The agent in this chain of metamorphoses or possible corruptions had a penchant for strong emotions and was dominated by his senses and by an intellectual *habitus* not yet bent to the requirements of the scientific method. Both subject and object of change and metamorphosis, he was represented in Baroque art and poetry, but he was also in part formed by that same art and poetry. He was the novice entering the church of Sant'Andrea al Quirinale and becoming "another man"; he was the spectator of *Las Meninas* seeking a representation of himself in order to find his place within the painting and appear on the stage of the court. He was the viewer of *Rinaldo e Armida,* transformed, like the witch, from enemy to lover.

BIBLIOGRAPHY

Alpers, Svetlana. *Rembrandt's Enterprise: The Studio and the Market.* London: Thames & Hudson; Chicago: University of Chicago Press, 1988.

Briganti, Giuliano. *Pietro da Cortona, o, Della Pittura barocca.* Florence: Sansoni, 1962; 2d ed. enlarged, 1982.

Buzzoni, Andrea, ed. *Torquato Tasso tra letteratura, musica, teatro e arti figurative.* Bologna: Nuova Alfa Editoriale, 1985.

Careri, Giovanni. *Voli d'amore. Architettura, pittura e sculturanel "bel composto" di Bernini.* Rome and Bari: Laterza, 1991. To be published in English translation as *Bernini: Flights of Love, the Art of Devotion.* Chicago: University of Chicago Press, forthcoming.

Foucault, Michel. *Les mots et les choses.* Paris: Gallimard, 1966. Available in English as *The Order of Things: An Archaeology of the Human Sciences.* London: Tavistock, and New York: Pantheon, 1970.

Haskell, Francis. *Patrons and Painters: A Study in the Relations between Italian Art and Society in the Age of the Baroque.* New York: Harper & Row/Icon, 1971; 2d ed. rev. and enlarged, New Haven, Conn.: Yale University Press, 1980.

Lavin, Irving. *Bernin et l'art de la satire sociale.* Paris: Presses Universitaires de France, 1987.

———. *Bernini and the Unity of Visual Arts.* New York: The Pierpont Morgan Library by Oxford University Press, 1980.

Marin, Louis. *Le portrait du Roi.* Paris: Editions de Minuit, 1983.

Poussin, Nicolas. *Lettres et propos sur l'art.* Edited by Anthony Blunt. Paris: Hermann, 1964, 1989.

Studi sul Borromini. Atti del convegno promosso dall'Accademia nazionale di San Luca. Rome: Accademia nazionale di San Luca, 1967.

THE BOURGEOIS

James S. Amelang

W HO WAS THE BOURGEOIS of the Baroque? If one were to paint his portrait, what would he look like, what traits would his visage reveal? The most famous bourgeois of this era was of course Monsieur Jourdain, the foolish if sympathetic protagonist of Molière's *Le Bourgeois Gentilhomme,* whose attempt to rise above his station converted him into the dupe of both greedy servants below him and unscrupulous nobles above. Yet although one can be sure that there were Jourdains aplenty in the aristocrat-dominated, conformist societies of seventeenth-century Europe, we nevertheless would probably not choose him for our sitter; surely such extreme social pretense did not represent the experience of the vast majority of the members of the bourgeoisie. In fact, Molière (1622–73) himself provides a better example of the "typical" bourgeois, at least at first glance. Of respectable background (his father was a merchant turned officeholder), as a boy he attended a Jesuit school and then spent some years at a university studying law. His upbringing was impeccably middle class, until he took the very unbourgeois step of signing away his inheritance and joining an itinerant troupe of actors to tour the provinces. No, Molière is not our man either: his willingness to take risks, his immersion in the thoroughly unrespectable world of the theater, even his later social as well as literary success (Louis XIV himself stood godfather to his first child) mark him as too atypical for our portrait. Clearly we must look elsewhere to find our bourgeois.

One could start by asking what the word itself meant to contemporaries. To the inhabitants of the Baroque age, the term "bourgeois" evoked a broad range of meanings. Two in particular were linked to formal definitions of social rank. In northwestern Europe, a bourgeois (or *burgher, Bürger,* and the like) was, in the strict sense, a city-dweller endowed with certain rights and privileges. Membership in this status category, often denoted by registry in an official list, was based upon birthright or long years of residence within the city. It also rested on the ownership of a certain minimum of wealth, which usually included a house or other urban real estate. Thus as late as the eighteenth century, a *bourgeois de Paris* was "anyone who had lived in Paris for a year and a day, who was not employed as a domestic, who did not live in rented lodgings, and who shared in the common taxes." In some countries, to be a bourgeois was moreover to possess a legal title indicating a certain status and rank, one associated with rentier economic activity and a quasi-noble lifestyle. In this second sense, a bourgeois was a person of substantial means and respectability, either a member of, or not far removed from, the municipal elite.

The term also suggested a variety of status relations outside the sphere of legal titles and ranks. From below, the term meant a "boss," a wealthy person with property who usually related to his social inferiors as an employer. From above, however, "bourgeois" was a term of derision and contempt, indicating in aristocratic eyes a person made ridiculous by his bad manners, lack of proper taste, and general social impropriety. With time, however, a broader and less dismissive definition found increasing acceptance. Today most historians regard "bourgeois" as synonymous with "middle class," especially its higher and more visible reaches. To be sure, "middle class" is hardly a precise category. It refers generally to the residual middle of society, the crossroads between high and low that made up the comfortable part of the third estate before it began commonly to be called such.

Understood in this sense, the bourgeoisie or middle class occupied a broad berth within the social spectrum. Its members included the wealthier artisans and shopkeepers as well as merchants, professionals, bankers, and governmental officials (usually on the lower rungs of the state bureaucracy). As a class or estate the bourgeoisie was characterized by a high degree of internal inequality and even of inner tensions and inner conflicts. At times social relations within the middle class involved the direct subordination of its lesser members (especially the artisans) to the higher strata of merchants and financiers. This was certainly the case in seventeenth-century Nördlingen, where a small handful of merchant-capitalists who successfully dominated local cloth production found social expression in a similar preeminence within the urban *Mittelstand*. Still, in other cities the greater merchants might adopt a different tack and choose deliberately to protect the interests of the lesser members of the class, as in certain Flemish towns. In any event, at least one common denominator united the members of this class despite their often considerable differences in rank and wealth. This was the possession of property in one form or another. The respectability and, in particular, the relative security accruing from the ownership of capital (obtained in a variety of ways, not all of which were necessarily capitalistic) were the social and economic glue that held this diverse grouping together.

Our principal concern, however, is not so much with the middle class as a whole but rather with its upper strata—with the merchants, professionals, and officials who constituted the non-noble civic elite. These leading citizens were, in the eyes of contemporaries, the true bourgeois of the Baroque era; in fact, in certain parts of Europe they were literally referred to as "citizens." Such was the case of seventeenth-century Venice, where this intermediate stratum between patriciate and *popolo* constituted some 4 to 5 percent of the local population. Rich, educated, increasingly avid consumers of goods both material and intellectual, these were the most highly visible commoners within the variegated world of the seventeenth-century city. (There was of course a rural bourgeoisie, but it was much less significant, and certainly less visible, than its urban counterpart.) Thanks to their correspondence, diaries, and other writings, to the abundant documentation engendered by their commercial and other economic activities, and even to the preservation of their likenesses (if the portraits of anyone outside the nobility survive from this period, it is theirs), we may come to examine them at three levels: in public, in private, and from within.

HOMO OECONOMICUS

Like everyone else, the bourgeois divided his economic activities between production and consumption, only more so, as his wealth permitted him a broader range of choice in both spheres. As producers, members of the middle class engaged in a wide variety of activities. Commerce was especially important, not only because of the large numbers of urban inhabitants whose livelihood derived from wholesale and retail trade, but also because the greater merchants specializing in long-distance trade often proved the most distinguished members of the class, thanks largely to the ties to political power that their superior wealth created. Industry, which ranged from small-scale, petty craft production to the employment of large numbers of dependent workers, also contributed to the fortunes of the bourgeois. While capitalist forms of industrial organization were still rather atypical, master artisans in a wide assortment of trades could often accrue substantial riches, which would further facilitate their upward mobility as they left behind the socially denigrated sphere of manual labor from which they originally hailed. Finally, liberal professionals—judges and lawyers, physicians, educators, and other successful marketeers of the "business of knowledge"—also contributed a significant number of recruits to the bourgeoisie.

Yet in most European cities, and especially in the Mediterranean, the economic activity most sought after by the bourgeois was no activity at all. His economic ideal was a passive one, that of a rentier. Living off investments in government debt, in mortgages tied to real estate, both urban and rural, and even in stocks and bonds (a riskier, yet buoyant form of investment thanks largely to the expansion of the Atlantic economy) provided the wealthy commoner the best means of aping the lifestyle of the aristocracy. This was especially true in the larger cities, which saw a greater tendency on the part of their bourgeois to detach themselves from commerce and other productive activities. Closely allied to this trend was the bourgeois's penchant for the purchase of public office, especially in France and Castile, where the central state played an especially pronounced role in the conversion of the middle class from entrepreneurship to economic passivity. In short, the bourgeoisie was not necessarily capitalist, nor were capitalists necessarily bourgeois, since the long-term goal of many wealthy commoners was to abandon active economic roles altogether.

The same cannot be said for consumption, however. Our rich city-dweller was far from passive in his role as consumer of an expanding variety of goods. Economic historians have traditionally studied the seventeenth century in terms of the pronounced transformation in the organization and control over commodity production (the "rise of capitalism," which has fascinated Marxists and non-Marxists alike). More recently, however, they have begun to pay greater attention to the appearance and expansion of modern consumer society as well. Within this trend the bourgeois looms large in importance, for he had few rivals in his relentless self-gratification. He spent considerable sums of money throughout this period, first in improving his immediate physical surroundings, especially through better housing. This included employing not only more durable construction materials but also indulging in the added convenience of putting glass in his windows. His more secure and better-lit house would, moreover, contain more objects: more and better-quality furniture, clothing, decorative elements, books, paintings, and an endless stream of goods designed to surround him with comfort, whenever outright luxury could not be afforded. The colonial expansion of the period was both cause and consequence of the burgeoning market for goods formerly too expensive to be consumed by any but the very wealthiest members of urban society. As a result, luxury became an increasingly relative concept, thanks to the broader diffusion and commercialization of a growing variety of commodities. The trend toward the development of specifically middle-class markets for art and other fine articles of consumption was most evident in northern European countries like England and especially Holland, owing to the emergence and consolidation of a prosperous bourgeoisie based upon the widespread (though not equal) distribution of wealth. The city itself also changed as a consequence of the new buying habits of the bourgeois as well as the noble. As Daniel Defoe (1660–1731) noted, London's "gay and luxurious" citizenry "made a great trade in the city, especially in everything that belonged to fashion and finery." Even urban residential patterns altered as the wealthier members of urban society tended toward greater concentration—if not exclusive segregation—in certain areas of the city, especially in its center.

The economic functions of the bourgeois were thus as much to consume wealth as to acquire it. The contemporary adage "Le marchand acquère, l'officier conserve, le noble dissippe" ("The merchant acquires, the official conserves, the noble dissipates") captures well the generational cycle that underlay the changing fortunes over time of the more successful bourgeois families as they gradually made their way upward into the ranks of the aristocracy. Yet how much space was there for the socially ambitious members of this group? How many bourgeois were there, and how large was their collective niche within urban society?

According to a recent estimate, slightly over 10 percent of the people of Europe in 1600 lived in cities of five thousand or more inhabitants, and their number increased during the course of the seventeenth century. Yet in terms of wealth not that great a proportion of urban society qualified for membership in the middle class, much less in its higher reaches. For example, in the mercantile entrepôt of Antwerp during this period, fully two- thirds of the adult male population was classified as *arme ghemeynte,* or propertyless "poor commoners." And in late sixteenth-century Nördlingen around one-half of the citizens owned only 4 percent of the city's wealth, while the top 10 percent of city dwellers possessed some 60 percent of local resources. Thanks to this skewed distribution of wealth the vast gap separating the small handful of rich from the great mass of urban poor left precious little room (or resources) for the modest citizen living in the middle.

Similar conditions prevailed in other European cities, where perhaps one-half to two-thirds of urban inhabitants lived near or below the poverty line. Yet not all cities revealed the same pattern. In Rotterdam, for example, a 1674 tax assessment revealed that about half of its population lived in households assessed at a modest level of prosperity or better; though of the 4,300 households paying taxes, only 658 did so at the higher level, which shows that the truly well-off bourgeoisie still remained a distinct minority. To be sure, significant regional variations existed, not only between northern and southern but also between eastern and western Europe. Yet the fact remains that in some cities as much as one-third of the civic population fitted into the space of the "middle class," while the proportion belonging to the civic elite shrank to 1 or 2 percent. The bourgeoisie as a recognized social category may thus have constituted a fairly large group; in most cases, however, the truly wealthy bourgeois were few, and they lived within a numerically reduced and socially exclusive circle.

THE BOURGEOIS AND THE CITY

As the term suggests, the *bourg*, or city, formed the very center of middle-class existence. Not surprisingly, the Baroque era gave voice to a swelling discourse lauding the city as a privileged locus for that favorite bourgeois activity, consumption. Many contemporary descriptions of cities waxed lyrical about the material benefits of urban living. Thus a 1662 gazetteer disingenuously praised Holland's largest metropolis as a "city that overflows with milk and with cheese." The same text went on to list in meticulous detail all the different products that could be bought in Amsterdam's richly stocked shops, ranging from nautical goods, exotic medicines, and rich pastries to jewelry, porcelain, and all types of imported merchandise. Special praise was reserved for the most select residences in the city on the Herengracht, so "full of priceless ornaments that they seem more like royal palaces than the houses of merchants." And so on. This was consumption with a vengeance, and in the eyes of its practitioners the city was unquestionably the best place for it.

Yet not all this spending was on material objects. Far from it, for the Baroque age proved especially fruitful in the development and extension of new patterns of cultural consumption. It is true, as noted above, that some contemporary use of the term "bourgeois" associated it with crudity and lack of gallantry, grace, and politeness. This was indeed the case of the hapless Monsieur Jourdain, who felt obliged to undertake crash courses in fencing, music, dance, and philosophy in order to rise higher on the social scale. In reality the bourgeois was refining as well as expanding his role as a consumer of culture during this era, especially if one links culture to tangible products like books, works of art, and newspapers, along with attendance at performances of all kinds (music, opera, theater, and dance). Literacy and regular contact with the printed word had of course long been a crucial dimension of the life of the urban middle classes. It was precisely during the Baroque period, however, that newer and more sophisticated forms of cultural expression began to form part of the daily lives of the wealthier city-dwellers. "Culture" and class became linked in especially intimate ways as claims to social superiority found increasing validation through the bourgeois's adoption of a new pattern of leisure rooted in the visible display of distinct, even superior, cultural attainments. As a result a new model for social as well as moral comportment emerged in the learned man, whose pursuit of letters (amateur as well as professional) found warm recommendation in influential manuals such as *L'uomo di lettere,* published in 1645 by the Ferrarese Jesuit Daniello Bartoli (1608–85).

The new pattern of conspicuous consumption of culture was, not surprisingly, more easily adopted by the nobility and rentier elite than by the whole of the middle class. Many bourgeois found it hard to reconcile the desires of the nobler existence of the mind with the practical demands of business and everyday life. This certainly was the case of Jean Maillefer (1611–84), the son of a prosperous silk merchant of Reims, who recorded in his autobiography his perpetual struggle in favor of learning and against the drudgery of making a living. Maillefer, like many other bourgeois children, attended a local school, and he recalled with pride (fifty-six years later!) his having won as a boy a prize in Greek composition. Despite his marked inclination to study, however, the death of his father when he was fourteen forced him to leave school and to earn his living, first as an apprentice tailor and then in a string of odd jobs. Throughout the rest of his life he never was at ease in the business world; instead he yearned for the "pleasures of the mind," which he saw as "pure, agreeable, [and] eternal," especially when compared with shopkeeping. An assiduous reader of Montaigne, this bourgeois looked to the essayist as a model for the higher purpose of life, the "knowledge of self." A dreamer who would rather stay in the back of his store reading books than attend customers, Maillefer was obviously the prototype of a private (and highly frustrated) consumer of culture, forced by circumstances to take a lesser role in the new public life of the mind and spirit than he would have wished.

That the city was both the central space and instrument for the increased marketing of cultural commodities is beyond doubt. That this expanding urban culture involved its devotees in the sort of genuine participation in the life of the mind that the unfortunate Maillefer fantasized about is more questionable. Not surprisingly, the discourse that celebrated the seventeenth-century city as a privileged locus for consumption—that, indeed, placed this consumption at the very center of urban existence—engendered a counter-discourse criticizing the artificiality and superficiality of city life and its pretensions to cultural superiority. This is one of the dominant strands in the many-faceted work of Jean de La Bruyère (1645–96), one of the best known and most acute observers of urban life during the Baroque age. Despite his aristocratic-sounding name, La Bruyère was of solidly middle-class background; his father was in fact a public official of the city of Paris. After studying law (for which he evinced a hearty dislike), La Bruyère purchased an office and settled down to his lifelong task as a social and moral critic and educator. In his *Les Caractères* (first published in 1688), La Bruyère censured urban life for

its vanity, ostentation, and frivolous artificiality. In his penetrating witti-
cisms one glimpses another side of the bourgeois mind, one which established a critical distance not only from the social climbers attempting to
shed their lower-class origins through "excessive expenditure and absurd
ostentation" but also from their model, the nobility itself, revealed to be
vain, wastrel, and a charge upon society. La Bruyère exposes the brave
new world of urban consumerism to be nothing but artifice and public
pretense as he transposes the traditional metaphor of the world as a stage
to city life: "Where women gather together to show off fine materials and
to reap the fruit of their toilette, they walk in pairs not for the sake of
conversation but to seek mutual support on the stage, to acquire familiarity with their audience and strength to resist their critics." Not surprisingly, urban culture rests upon superficial personal contacts. The very size
of a city like Paris causes its inhabitants to judge each other (usually dis-
approvingly) exclusively by external show, a habit that favors the crass
display of wealth and the fawning imitation of court manners. The result
is a society composed of "faithless copies of worthless originals," condemned to an artificial existence within a world of deceitful appearances
and deliberate trickery.

As moral criticism there is little that is innovative here. As social discourse, however, a new path is being explored in that attention is focused
not upon the undifferentiated world of human behavior in general but
upon the specific qualities of urban life in particular. La Bruyère's was
hardly a voice in the wilderness; throughout Europe a rich chorus of criticism connected the emerging identification of the city with the ostentatious display of wealth and leisure habits by both middle and upper
classes. Urban living was seen at best as a mixed blessing, with its opportunities extolled and its excesses deplored. Yet on the whole the bourgeois
found far more to celebrate than to condemn in his city, and naturally
so—was he not its owner? In fact, it would not be out of place to speak
of a distinctive bourgeois style within urban culture, one that (at least at
first glance) exalted abundance while depicting everyday life and its material objects and surroundings in a highly realistic style. This trend was
most apparent in those parts of Europe such as Holland, where the political and cultural influence of the rural aristocracy was most limited. It is
hardly a coincidence that in the sort of republican, civic atmosphere that
prevailed in the Low Countries and (more exceptionally) in Venice, there
developed in the Baroque period a specific genre of painting that exalted
urban life while rendering it in minute, affectionate detail. The cityscape
soon became the expressive emblem of a specifically urban culture firmly
perched upon the twin foundations of ostentatious wealth and prideful
civic independence.

The notion of civic pride serves as a reminder that there is another and equally important dimension to the relationship between the respectable citizen and his urban surroundings. The city constituted the essential horizon of the bourgeois's world, and this was nowhere more true than in the sphere of politics. Despite his growing interest in national affairs, local matters marked the fundamental boundaries of his most vital interests and commitments. To begin with, civic obligations of all sorts occupied a substantial portion of his time. Service in the city militia was one significant form of participation in urban politics, even when such traditional forms of defense were slowly giving way to expanding professional armies. The massive turnout in arms of the bourgeoisie of Paris in January 1649 doubtless came as more of a surprise to Mazarin and the commanders of the royalist army besieging the city than to its Frondeur citizens. Traditionally seen as the swan song of urban militias in France—from this point onward they would be called out exclusively to quell internal disorders—the scale of mobilization of the Paris middle class was merely an exceptional instance of a more normal reality, that of a widespread sense of civic duty and participation among the bourgeoisie.

The middle classes regarded participation in the daily workings of the city as both a right and an obligation. A strong sense of civic consciousness can be detected at various levels within the bourgeoisie. Note, for example, the numerous urban chronicles written by people from the urban middle class, even by master artisans. These include John Stow's survey of London, the contemporary histories of Barcelona by the master tanner Miquel Parets and the shopkeeper Pere Serra i Postius, and the chronicles of Lille during the sixteenth and seventeenth centuries written by the textile workers Mahieu Manteau and Pierre Ignace Chavatte. In these and other documents the bourgeois revealed himself to be not just a commentator on the urban scene, like La Bruyère, but also an author of independent civic discourse, empowered by the citizenship and local knowledge that were his birthright to help shape public understanding of the polity shared in common by all "respectable" urban inhabitants.

Naturally, even more direct forms of participation in municipal life were open to the bourgeois. Local government was, without question, usually reserved to the higher reaches of the middle class or to a separate urban nobility, as in the case of Venice and Toulouse. In many cities the greater merchants and bankers held a firm grip on civic administration, as was certainly true in Rouen, Lille, Nuremberg, London, Geneva, Marseilles, and Genoa, to cite but a few examples. There were not many cities that did not reserve at least some form of participation in public life—usually in the form of minor offices—to the lesser members of the bourgeoisie. And in some instances (especially in the Empire, the Low Countries, and Switzerland), master craftsmen could hold quite significant posts in municipal government. In virtually all cases, the middle class played an active, and more often than not the most active, role in civic affairs.

But politics did not stop at the city walls. The bourgeoisie also claimed an increasingly important role within public matters on a regional and national level. This trend is observed most clearly in the case of England. While traditional arguments in favor of regarding the English Civil War and Interregnum of 1640–60 as a "bourgeois revolution" have long been discarded—among other reasons, the wealthy merchants of London and other major cities tended to be supporters of the king rather than of Parliament—there can be little doubt of the expanding involvement of members of the middle class in national politics as a whole. Not surprisingly, it has recently been argued that the overall consequences of the two constitutional crises in seventeenth-century England—the Civil War and the "Glorious Revolution" of 1688—included the removal of restraints to free enterprise along with the triumph of the "possessive individualism" so dear to the bourgeois and his ideologues. As the wealthier members of the middle classes began to achieve a place as protagonists in high politics matching their prominence in the economy, the merchants and financiers in charge of the larger cities became ever more closely linked to the influential landowning class—not only through a common interest in political stability but also through more direct and personal ties, including intermarriage.

England, along with the Dutch Republic, was to a certain degree an exception. Within the absolute monarchies of the Continent different patterns prevailed, more restrictive of the access of commoners to a voice in national (if not local) politics. All the same, one finds the bourgeois asserting his rights throughout the Baroque era, both directly—note the urban middle classes' participation in tax revolts in France during the 1630s and in the Fronde a decade later—and indirectly. In the latter case, many bourgeois militias refused to quell popular riots directed against tax collectors and detested representatives of the central government, especially during the first half of the seventeenth century. (Such forbearance was more the exception than the rule, to be sure, given the property owners' abiding fear of the dangerous classes beneath them.) Altogether, throughout Europe a crucial part of the public behavior, and even the very identity, of the bourgeois was his entitlement to a voice in local affairs. Whether his role was large or small usually depended on the extent of his wealth. Yet in most cases the bourgeois not only saw (and enjoyed) himself as a city-dweller but also took quite seriously his rights and responsibilities as a citizen.

PRIVATE VALUES

It is easier to study the behavior and public pronouncements of the bourgeois than to penetrate the inner world of his thoughts and sentiments. Nevertheless, any portrait of a person that does not attempt to reveal something of his more intimate self would provide a woefully inadequate likeness. We have already seen that contemporary literary depictions of the bourgeois, especially the famous caricature of Monsieur Jourdain, tended to portray him as a gullible social climber whose pretension and pathetic eagerness for advancement left him open to exploitation by those more clever than he. In the figure of Georges Dandin Molière castigated yet another bourgeois whose reputation suffered for his attempt to enter the nobility. Both portraits drew upon, and to a certain extent continued, a rich vein of criticism of the middle class (and of merchants in particular), who, in addition to being traditionally seen as greedy, were also depicted as pretentious social climbers whose grasping ambition finally led to their undoing.

It is hard to believe that the bourgeois viewed himself in the same light. One should in fact keep in mind the existence of an equally rich counter-discourse, one that emphasizes and even extols the positive contribution of the solid, wealthy burgher to the society surrounding him. This portrait rests firmly on the rhetoric of what has been dubbed the "Protestant Ethic," which posits a uniquely intense relationship between the bourgeoisie and the social virtues of devotion to work, sobriety, austerity, cleanliness, and deferred personal gratification. As we have seen, parts of this congeries of virtues hold up with only the greatest of difficulties. Even the most Protestant of Protestant middle classes, the English and the Dutch, gave way in time to the temptations of modern consumerism. Yet the other components of this ideology—especially its emphasis on the positive, productive contribution of the middle class to society as a whole, along with its insistence on the virtues of honesty, sobriety, and the redeeming value of labor—strike a more resonant chord. They not only found their way into the many influential panegyrics of bourgeois economic behavior such as Jacques Savary's *Le parfait négociant* of 1675, which enjoyed a wide readership, in part because of the seventeenth-century state's support of the diffusion of the tenets of mercantilism. They also can be found to an impressive degree within the private writings of merchants and other bourgeois themselves. Pride in work, a firm belief in *honnêteté*, devotion less to a rigid ideal of austerity than to a more flexible notion of economy that permitted consumption as long as it could be supported by production—these were the words that made up the private vocabulary of the bourgeois as he described (and justified) himself, his activities, and his place in the scheme of things.

This scheme pertained both to this world and the one thereafter, for religious belief stood firmly at the crossroads of the external and internal values and the comportment of the bourgeois. Any inquiry into his mentality must thus take into account not only his view of self and society but also his notions of faith, holiness, and sin. During the Baroque era bourgeois of all religious persuasions—Catholics, Protestants, Jews— conceived of and related to their world through the idiom of religion. As a result, social constructs of proper and improper behavior joined individual hopes and ambitions in taking shape within the contours of a religious world view often quite intensely held. What most distinguished the spiritual life of the urban bourgeois from that of other social classes, however, was its highly personal character. In every religious camp the bourgeois tended to develop an actively intellectual and, to a certain degree, individualistic approach to the divine, which centered around the instruments of literacy, especially through private meditation aided by personal reading of scripture and devotional works. Predictably, this personalization of piety did much to set the bourgeois off from the world of popular religion, which was much more given to public rituals and to the corporate organization of religious identity.

Between the external world in which much daily activity took place and the secluded inner sanctum of individual faith, beliefs, and emotions lay an intermediate zone, the private world of the middle-class citizen and his immediate family. This intimate realm was both the cause and the consequence of what has come to be known as "bourgeois individualism," the most significant dimension of which was a perceptible retreat toward privatism. It has recently been argued that the early modern era, and the seventeenth and eighteenth centuries in particular, presided over the consolidation of a new pattern of sociability based upon the growing division of existence into two separate spheres, public and private. It was moreover the middle class that participated most intensely in this development as it increasingly sought refuge in the atomized world of the self and its immediate surroundings. It would not do to exaggerate this trend: society was far from the point where, in the words of Alexis de Tocqueville (1805–59), "each person, withdrawn into himself, behaves as though he is a stranger to the destiny of all the others." And while there is no mistaking the gradual drift toward the construction of a class ethos of controlled egoism, the notion that a "rise in individualism" characterized this period merits at least one important qualification.

This new individualism was more than anything else remarkably family-centered. The inner world to which the bourgeois retreated when weary of the outdoor stage of city life was one cast firmly in the terms of solid virtue achieved through familial existence. "Family," of course, was understood in a new sense: the bourgeois family stood opposed to the aristocracy with its traditional obsession with the honor and interests of lineage (usually patrilineage) to refer more specifically to the nuclear unit of the two generations of parents and children. It was in this reduced, home-centered unit that the new and highly domestic middle-class approach to the family took hold. In the words of Philippe Ariès:

> Ultimately the family became the focus of private life. Its significance changed. No longer was it merely an economic unit for the sake of whose reproduction everything had to be sacrificed. No longer was it a restraint on individual freedom, a place in which power was wielded by women. It became something it had never been: a refuge to which people fled in order to escape the scrutiny of outsiders; an emotional center and a place where, for better or worse, children were the focus of attention. (Goldhammer translation)

Thus the rise of the nuclear family to a central position within the new patterns of social contact and exchange was perhaps the most significant change in value and behavior that the bourgeoisie experienced during the Baroque century.

A central, guiding ideal linked these parallel trends toward the personalization of religion, increased privatism, and the growing resort to domesticity: moral virtue. As distinct from the heroic virtue of the aristocratic past, the bourgeois mentality celebrated piety, sobriety, and the willing assumption of responsibility. In so doing it created an effective formula for reconciling the conflicting demands of public good versus the pursuit of private interest. The ideal of virtue lay behind the avid acceptance among middle-class readers of moralizing treatises like François de Fénelon's *Télémaque* (first published in 1699), the runaway best-seller of the final decades of the Baroque. It also explains the firm assertiveness of the bourgeois in devising formulas of social discipline for other members of society as well. Morality soon came to reside at the very center of the bourgeois's identity, especially since it provided a uniquely effective means of distinguishing his activities, his values, and even his self from the dissolute aristocracy above and the promiscuous popular classes below. If one is justified in linking the bourgeois to a sort of "Protestant ethic," this value system pertains less strictly to the realm of theology than to that of morality. Responsibility, accountability, economy: these were the demands the bourgeois made upon himself and upon others.

THE BOURGEOIS FROM WITHIN: SAMUEL PEPYS

No portrait of a bourgeois would be complete without some depiction of the final level beyond his public and domestic circles: his intimate self.

Fortunately, there exists a splendid means to this end in the lengthy diaries written from 1660 to 1669 by the Londoner Samuel Pepys (1633–1703). It would be hard to imagine a more revealing self-portrait than that offered by this hardworking and socially ambitious public official, who not only took considerable pains to provide a detailed catalogue of his experiences and emotions but also did his best to ensure their confidential nature (he wrote in shorthand, and he confided the secret of his diary's existence to only one person, a lapse that he later regretted). Like most accurate portraits, his is a study in contradictions. It exposes with admirable candor the conflicts between his aspirations and attainments, and between expectations toward himself and others and the realities of city life in an era of pleasure and peril.

To begin with, Pepys's social background was a mixed one. His parents lived and worked in humble circumstances—his father was a tailor and his mother a washerwoman—although his father's family could boast some genteel connections. Pepys's childhood was certainly one of preparation for better things: he studied in the distinguished St. Paul's School, and he later took a degree at Cambridge. He began to write his journal in coincidence with what was perhaps the central historical event he was to experience in person, the restoration in 1660 of the monarchy through the return to England of Charles II following the brief but intense period of the Cromwellian republic. Much to his later embarrassment, the youthful Pepys had been a Roundhead, or supporter of Parliament; his reaction to the execution of Charles I (which he himself attended as a boy) was to quote the biblical verse, "The memory of the wicked shall rot." Later, as he began to scale the ladder of social success and play an ever more important role within the royal administration, he did his best to put his past behind him, although from time to time he let slip in his diary an unguarded remark that betrayed traces of his older, more republican sympathies (including a lifelong admiration for Oliver Cromwell). Yet, overall, Pepys had no reason to fear the new regime; he proved a skillful adapter in politics as in many other things.

The record of Pepys's decade of achievement—he rose from being an obscure minor civil servant to the front ranks of officialdom, gaining increasing power and prestige within the administration of the Royal Navy—is that of a dedicated social climber. His self-proclaimed aim was to "increase my good name and esteem in the world and get money." He moreover saw diligence as the key to success. While Pepys was aware that chance played a greater role in promoting men's fortunes than merit, he nevertheless believed sincerely in his professional ethic, and he applied his energies to his work in no halfhearted fashion. Increasing wealth and rising social status rewarded his efforts: the modest official who owned twenty-five pounds when he began his diary in 1660 could boast over ten thousand pounds a decade later, and this without having been too corrupt a functionary.

Riches and public recognition brought Pepys firmly into the world of urban sociability and consumerism. Literally hundreds of entries in his diary reveal his childish delight in his newly bought objects, in his learning to dance (à la Monsieur Jourdain!), in his being able to afford to purchase a wig, silver plate, even a coach and horses, and in his employing a growing number of servants. He matched the acquisition of these visible tokens of social success with an increasingly deep plunge into the social scene of London. Pepys eagerly took to its active stage life (now restored, following the suppression of the theaters by the Puritans), musical offerings (both professional and amateur, since Pepys himself greatly enjoyed singing and playing instruments with friends at home), numerous court processions and rituals, along with London's many taverns and coffeehouses (he dutifully recorded drinking his first cup of tea in 1660). Nor did Pepys lack for more elevated gatherings: in 1665 he was admitted to the Royal Society, and he served in it as an active member, although he confessed to his diary that "I do lack philosophy enough to understand the very fine discourses and experiments" that he attended. With philosophy or not, Pepys delighted in reading, and he recorded many of his frequent visits to London's busy booksellers. Without question, Pepys did not spend all his time scribbling in his daybook; instead he was an active, even enthusiastic, participant in the many leisure opportunities to be found in the metropolis.

Yet Pepys's attachment to both his possessions and his active social life did not come without personal cost. His religious background, like that of many Roundheads, was Puritan in sympathy, and while he expressed a thorough distrust of the more fanatic of the religious Nonconformists, on the whole his world view retained significant legacies from his Puritan past. Hence many of the contradictions in his personality and the sudden shifts of mood recorded in moving frankness in his diary. Pepys professed a sincere attachment to the "Protestant" values of modesty and frugality, which at times led him to develop rather tortured justifications of his material acquisitions. The resolution of this conflict between austerity and consumerist self-indulgence found expression in a 1662 entry containing a reflection on what to do with his money: "Though I am much against too much spending, yet I do think it best to enjoy some degree of pleasure now that we have wealth, money and opportunities, rather than to leave pleasures to old age or poverty, when we cannot have them so properly." At a later date (1668) he confirmed this sentiment: "I do really enjoy myself, and understand that if I do not do it now, I shall not hereafter, it may be, be able to pay for it or have health to take pleasure in it, and so fool myself with vain expectation of pleasure and go without it." This, surely, is the true voice of a Puritan pleasantly embarrassed by worldly success.

Pepys's sexual life provides an even more thorough portrait in contradiction. While not torn by a burning consciousness of sin and guilt, Pepys nevertheless often expressed (subsequent) regret over his frequent dallying—he had sexual contact of one sort or another with no fewer than fifty women during the decade treated in his diary—and constantly made resolutions to live a more chaste life. And while he recorded news of sexual laxity at the court with open distaste and was liable to frequent attacks of jealousy thanks to his fears (groundless, it turns out) about his wife's fidelity, he nevertheless proved incapable of correcting the same habits in himself. A philanderer with a conscience, a moderate Puritan given to the flesh, Pepys surely did not lack for company among his middle-class peers. What was unique about his experience was less his mixture of sermonizing and sinning than his willingness to record it so frankly on paper.

Many other journals written by bourgeois have survived from the Baroque era. We have access to the intimate reflections of middle-class citizens from all levels ranging from lawyers, clergymen, and greater merchants to more humble artisans and shopkeepers. Yet none of these documents turns out to be as revealing of the inner life of the bourgeois as the journal of this singularly engaging Englishman. Therein we can chart the doubts that match his success and the hesitations that accompany his ambitions. In its pages we can also relive the domestic life of the middle class, its purchases, clothes, and cooking; its day trips out of the capital to nearby tourist attractions; its lavish and frequent entertainments (how Pepys loved "good dinner and feasting"!) alternating with quiet soirées and late night reading at home. Here is urban middle-class life in all its dimensions, great and small. One could not ask for a finer portrait or a more willing sitter.

It is time to try to summarize these findings and to give a brief assessment of the historical significance of our protean city-dweller of the Baroque century. To begin with the obvious: the middle class was literally that, the stratum that occupied the middle or center of the social order. As a result, and despite some individual exceptions, it was a class impregnated with a strong sense of distance from both the nobility above and the "plebs" below. The latter sentiment was rooted in a fear of poverty and possible *déclassement*—always a real threat in the uncertain times of the early modern period—and in the threat to property and order posed by the "dangerous" classes. The former sentiment, the awareness of the multiple boundaries separating even the wealthiest of bourgeois from the aristocracy, was omnipresent as well, for even those commoners with the best chance of entering into the nobility proved acutely conscious of the social limitations of their non-noble status. This *mediocrity*, the sense of belonging to the middle, was perhaps the dominant characteristic of the bourgeois. Molière certainly emphasized its importance by having the message expressed not by the foolish Jourdain but instead by his commonsensical wife, who with considerably dignity defends "plain decent folk" against the deceivers and wastrels of both gentle and humble rank who preyed upon them.

Closely allied to this mediocrity—indeed, holding it in place—was the bourgeois's attachment to the notion of order. Order, and the fear of disorder, presided over the center of his universe. To be sure, faith in order, the order of all bodies and persons consigned to their proper spheres and performing their proper tasks therein, did not preclude a sense of motion. Social mobility, especially upward through advancement and promotion, was perfectly acceptable as long as the rules of the game were recognized and respected. Closely allied to this adherence to order and regulation was the bourgeois's marked rationality, a confidence in reason and logical procedure that well predated its deification by the Enlightenment. Hence also his innate conservatism and conformity, his vested interest in stability, and his distrust of risk and innovation.

His clearly is not a portrait in heroism. The average bourgeois was not a dynamic capitalist entrepreneur, a gambler with fortune, a harbinger of modernity, although those relatively few inhabitants of the Baroque era who did assume these roles more often than not did belong to the bourgeoisie. Instead, he prized security over willingness to risk, and he preferred to travel familiar paths rather than to explore new ones. Recently this caution and distaste for adventure have earned him the harsh judgment of historians. He has even been accused of "treason," and he has been written off in dramatic language as a member of a "bankrupt class" that was "on the verge of disappearing" during the seventeenth century, especially in the Mediterranean countries. This is surely an exaggeration, one that has placed too much emphasis upon the collective escape through ennoblement of a visible but tiny minority of bourgeois. Even the much vaunted shift in middle-class investment patterns away from trade and toward land did not necessarily mean that the class was turning its back upon its business origins. Rural properties were often obtained for quite practical reasons such as—to cite one example—to enhance one's possibilities of obtaining mortgages and other sorts of credits. Nor can one escape the fact that a recourse to forms of investment that lowered risks while enhancing security of return constituted highly rational behavior. This was especially true for periods like the seventeenth century, when increasing economic difficulties rendered traditional patterns of trade and production less profitable, especially within the mature urban economies of southern Europe.

Clearly it is anachronistic to charge the bourgeois with treason. Only a rigidly teleological view, one that high-handedly assigns to historical actors specific and predetermined parts to play in the human comedy, would fail to note the considerable rationality, and even predictability, of the bourgeois's persistent drive for security. Conformity to the expectations of the dominant class—and the aristocracy continued to dominate virtually all European societies throughout the Baroque era—was the hallmark of the bourgeois's strategy for survival and (with luck) social advancement within an unpredictable and threatening environment. From the vantage point of a later period, and given the multiple similarities between middle-class existence in the past and the present, one can hardly be surprised that the bourgeois did not play a more heroic role. That would be to expect too much from the members of a class then as now all too conscious that, unlike most others, it had something to lose.

BIBLIOGRAPHIC NOTE

The bourgeois has been more talked about than studied in detail. Apart from Werner Sombart's *Der Bourgeois* of 1913, a classic essay in historical sociology, few monographic works have been devoted to the early modern bourgeoisie. As a result, basic information about this class has to be gleaned from a wide variety of general studies. Among the best of these are: Robert Mandrou, *Introduction à la France moderne* (Paris: A. Michel, 1961), available in English as *Introduction to Modern France, 1500–1640: An Essay in Historical Psychology*, trans. R. E. Hallmark (New York: Holmes & Meier, 1976); Pierre Goubert, *L'Ancien Régime* (Paris: Armand Colin, 1969), chap. 10, available in English as *The Ancien Régime: French Society, 1600–1750*, trans. Steve Cox (New York: Harper Torchbooks, 1974); Henry Kamen, *The Iron Century: Social Change in Europe, 1550–1660* (New York: Praeger, 1972), chap. 5; Roland Mousnier, *Les institutions de France sous la monarchie absolue, 1598–1789*, 2 vols. (Paris: Presses Universitaires de France, 1974–80), vol. 1, chap. 6, available in English as *The Institutions of France under the Absolute Monarchy 1598–1789*, 2 vols. (Chicago: University of Chicago Press, 1979–84); J. L. Price, *Culture and Society in the Dutch Republic during the Seventeenth Century* (New York: Scribner; London: Batsford, 1974); Peter Clark and Paul Slack, *English Towns in Transition 1500–1700* (London and New York: Oxford University Press, 1976).

Studies of specific cities with attention focused on their middle classes include: Pierre Deyon, *Amiens, capital provinciale: Etude sur la société urbaine au XVIIe siècle* (Paris and The Hague: Mouton, 1967); Christopher R. Friedrichs, *Urban Society in an Age of War: Nördlingen, 1580–1720* (Princeton: Princeton University Press, 1979); Mack Walker, *German Home Towns: Community, State, and General Estate, 1648–1871* (Ithaca, N.Y.: Cornell University Press, 1971); Philip Benedict, *Rouen during the Wars of Religion* (Cambridge and New York: Cambridge University Press, 1981); and James S. Amelang, *Honored Citizens of Barcelona: Patrician Culture and Class Relations, 1490–1714* (Princeton: Princeton University Press, 1986).

The economic activities and aspirations of the bourgeoisie are dealt with in: Michel Vovelle and Daniel Roche, "Bourgeois, rentiers, propriétaires," *Actes 84e Congrès national des Sociétés Savantes, Section d'Histoire moderne et contemporaine* (Paris: Imprimerie Nationale, 1960), 419–52; George V. Taylor, "Noncapitalist Wealth and the Origins of the French Revolution," *American Historical Review* 72 (1967): 469–96; Jan De Vries, *The Economy of Europe in an Age of Crisis, 1600–1750* (Cambridge and New York: Cambridge University Press, 1976), chap. 7; Régine Pernoud, *Histoire de la bourgeoisie en France*, 2 vols. (Paris: Editions du Seuil, 1981), vol. 2, *Les temps modernes;* Robert S. DuPlessis and Martha C. Howell, "Reconsidering the Early Modern Urban Economy: The Cases of Leiden and Lille," *Past and Present* 94 (1982): 49–84; Henry Horwitz, "The 'Mess of the Middle Class' Revisited," *Continuity and Change* 2 (1987): 263–96. On artisans as members of the middle class, see James Richard Farr, *Hands of Honor: Artisans and Their World in Dijon, 1550–1650* (Ithaca: Cornell University Press, 1988). George Huppert, *Les bourgeois gentilshommes: An Essay on the Definition of Elites in Renaissance France* (Chicago: University of Chicago Press, 1977), treats the issue of middle-class upward social mobility. Fernand Braudel leveled the charge of treason against the bourgeoisie in his influential *La Méditerranée et le monde méditerranéen à l'époque de Philippe II*, 2d ed. rev., 2 vols. (Paris: A. Colin, 1966), pt. II, vol. 2 (available in English as *The Mediterranean and the Mediterranean World in the Age of Philip II*, trans. Siân Reynolds, 2 vols. [New York: Harper & Row, 1972–73]). For the best response to Braudel, see Hugo Soly, "The 'Betrayal' of the Sixteenth-Century Bourgeoisie: A Myth?" *Acta Historiae Neerlandicae* 8 (1975): 31–49.

For the bourgeois in politics, see Jack H. Hexter's influential "The Myth of the Middle Class," in Hexter, *Reappraisals in History* (London: Longman, 1961; 2d ed., Chicago: Phoenix, University of Chicago Press, 1979), along with K. G. Davies's critical comments, "The Mess of the Middle Class," *Past and Present* 22 (1962): 77–83. Other studies include: Brian Stuart Manning, *The English People and the English Revolution* (London: Heinemann, 1976); Lawrence Stone, "The Bourgeois Revolution of Seventeenth-Century England Revisited," *Past and Present* 109 (1985): 44–54, and the reply by Christopher Hill, "Sex, Marriage and Parish Registers," now in Hill, *Collected Essays*, 3 vols. (Amherst, Mass.: University of Massachusetts Press, 1985–86), vol. 3, pp. 188–209. Note also Joseph di Corcia's careful "*Bourg, Bourgeois, Bourgeois de Paris* from the Eleventh to the Eighteenth Century," *Journal of Modern History* 50 (1978): 207–33.

Studies of bourgeois culture, family life, and the retreat to privatism include: Lawrence Stone, *The Family, Sex, and Marriage in England, 1500–1800* (London: Weidenfeld & Nicolson; abridged ed. New York: Harper & Row, 1977); Philippe Ariès and Georges Duby, gen. eds., *Histoire de la vie privée*, 4 vols. (Paris: Editions du Seuil, 1985–87), vol. 3, *De la Renaissance aux Lumières*, ed. Roger Chartier, available in English as *A History of Private Life* (Cambridge, Mass.: Belknap Press of Harvard University Press, 1987–89), vol. 3, *Passions of the Renaissance*. Laura Caroline Stevenson's *Praise and Paradox: Merchants and Crafts-*

men in Elizabethan Popular Literature (Cambridge and New York: Cambridge University Press, 1984) discusses literary depictions of the middle class, while Simon Schama, *The Embarrassment of Riches: An Interpretation of Dutch Culture in the Golden Age* (New York: Knopf, distr. Random House, 1987; Berkeley: University of California Press, distr. Random House, 1988) provides a stimulating perspective on both the bourgeoisie's cultural consumption and the hangovers (more moral than physical) that it suffered afterward. On this question, see also the essay by Peter Burke, "Conspicuous Consumption in Seventeenth-Century Italy" in his *The Historical Anthropology of Early Modern Italy: Essays on Perception and Communication* (Cambridge and New York: Cambridge University Press, 1987), chap. 10.

I have cited from the magnificent eleven-volume edition of Samuel Pepys's *Diary* by Robert Latham and William Matthews (Berkeley: University of California Press, 1970–83). Readers looking for a more abridged version may wish to consult the same editors' *The Illustrated Pepys* or *The Shorter Pepys* (Berkeley: University of California Press, 1983 and 1985, respectively). Also of interest is Christopher Driver and Michelle Berriedale-Johnson, *Pepys at Table: Seventeenth-Century Recipes for the Modern Cook* (Berkeley and Los Angeles: University of California Press, 1984), a collection of modern recipes for the many dishes referred to by the gourmand diarist. Finally, see the short but suggestive portrait of Pepys in vol. 2 of Christopher Hill, *Collected Essays* and Lawrence Stone's succinct reflections on Pepys's sexual life in Stone, *The Family, Sex, and Marriage*, chap. 11.

Studies of the bourgeoisie in other historical periods and contexts that have proved useful to the writing of this essay include: Elinor G. Barber, *The Bourgeoisie in 18th-Century France* (Princeton: Princeton University Press, 1955); Richard Sennett, *The Fall of Public Man* (New York: Knopf; Vintage Books, 1977); Peter N. Stearns, "The Middle Class: Toward a Precise Definition," *Comparative Studies in Society and History* 21 (1979): 369–88; Gary W. McDonogh, *Good Families of Barcelona: A Social History of Power in the Industrial Era* (Princeton: Princeton University Press, 1986); Immanuel Wallerstein, "The Bourgeois(ie) as Concept and Reality," *New Left Review* 167 (1988): 91–106; and Stuart M. Blumin, *The Emergence of the Middle Class: Social Experience in the American City, 1760–1900* (Cambridge and New York: Cambridge University Press, 1989).

INDEX